Non-Inclusive Education in Central and Eastern Europe

Also available from Bloomsbury

Gender Diversity and Sexuality in English Language Education,
edited by Darío Luis Banegas and Navan Govender
Disabled Children and Digital Technologies, Sue Cranmer
Teaching for Peace and Social Justice in Myanmar, edited by
Mary Shepard Wong
Education for Social Change, Douglas Bourn
Transnational Feminist Politics, Education, and Social Justice,
edited by Silvia Edling and Sheila Macrine
The Roma in European Higher Education, edited by Louise Morley,
Andrzej Mirga and Nadir Redzepi
Identities and Education, edited by Eleftherios Klerides and
Stephen Carney

Non-Inclusive Education in Central and Eastern Europe

Comparative Studies of Teaching Ethnicity, Religion and Gender

Edited by
Katarzyna Górak-Sosnowska and
Urszula Markowska-Manista

BLOOMSBURY ACADEMIC
LONDON • NEW YORK • OXFORD • NEW DELHI • SYDNEY

BLOOMSBURY ACADEMIC
Bloomsbury Publishing Plc
50 Bedford Square, London, WC1B 3DP, UK
1385 Broadway, New York, NY 10018, USA
29 Earlsfort Terrace, Dublin 2, Ireland

BLOOMSBURY, BLOOMSBURY ACADEMIC and the Diana logo are
trademarks of Bloomsbury Publishing Plc

First published in Great Britain 2023
Paperback edition published 2024

Copyright © Katarzyna Górak-Sosnowska and
Urszula Markowska-Manista and contributors, 2023

Katarzyna Górak-Sosnowska and Urszula Markowska-Manista and
contributors have asserted their right under the Copyright, Designs and
Patents Act, 1988, to be identified as Author of this work.

Cover image © Ana Maria Serrano / EyeEm/ Getty Images

All rights reserved. No part of this publication may be reproduced or transmitted in
any form or by any means, electronic or mechanical, including photocopying,
recording, or any information storage or retrieval system, without prior
permission in writing from the publishers.

Bloomsbury Publishing Plc does not have any control over, or responsibility for, any
third-party websites referred to or in this book. All internet addresses given in this
book were correct at the time of going to press. The author and publisher regret any
inconvenience caused if addresses have changed or sites have ceased to exist, but
can accept no responsibility for any such changes.

A catalogue record for this book is available from the British Library.

Library of Congress Cataloging-in-Publication Data

Names: Górak-Sosnowska, Katarzyna, editor. | Markowska-Manista, Urszula, editor.
Title: Non-inclusive education in Central and Eastern Europe : comparative
studies of teaching ethnicity, religion and gender / edited by Katarzyna
Górak-Sosnowska and Urszula Markowska-Manista.
Description: New York, NY : Bloomsbury Academic, 2023. |
Includes bibliographical references and index.
Identifiers: LCCN 2022036563 (print) | LCCN 2022036564 (ebook) |
ISBN 9781350325265 (hardback) | ISBN 9781350325302 (paperback) |
ISBN 9781350325272 (pdf) | ISBN 9781350325289 (epub)
Subjects: LCSH: Educational equalization–Europe, Central. | Educational
equalization–Europe, Eastern. | Inclusive education–Europe, Central. |
Inclusive education–Europe, Eastern. | Ethnicity–Study and teaching–Europe, Central. |
Ethnicity–Study and teaching–Europe, Eastern. | Religion–Study and teaching–Europe, Central. |
Religion–Study and teaching–Europe, Eastern.
Classification: LCC LC213.3.E85 N66 2023 (print) | LCC LC213.3.E85 (ebook) |
DDC 379.2/60943–dc23/eng/20220818
LC record available at https://lccn.loc.gov/2022036563
LC ebook record available at https://lccn.loc.gov/2022036564

ISBN: HB: 978-1-3503-2526-5
PB: 978-1-3503-2530-2
ePDF: 978-1-3503-2527-2
eBook: 978-1-3503-2528-9

Typeset by Newgen KnowledgeWorks Pvt. Ltd., Chennai, India

To find out more about our authors and books visit www.bloomsbury.com
and sign up for our newsletters.

Contents

List of Illustrations	vii
List of Contributors	viii
Foreword	xi
Jacqueline Bhabha	
Introduction	1
Katarzyna Górak-Sosnowska and Urszula Markowska-Manista	
1 Intercultural Teaching in a 'Monocultural' Country: Why Do We Need a Decolonial Approach to Teaching about Diversity?	11
Urszula Markowska-Manista	
2 A Cultural History of the Other in Curriculum Design Transformation and Practice	27
Rafael Filiberto Forteza Fernández	
3 The Pluralist Paradigm in the Czech Educational Process: Teaching about Collective Identities and Democracy in the Constructivist Educational Project	41
Jan Květina	
4 Preparedness of Estonian Teachers to Tackle Extremism in a Classroom: A Systematic Review of Empirical Studies Published in *Estonian Journal of Education* (2013–21)	63
Alar Kilp and Heidi Maiberg	
5 Are Muslims Scared of Pork?: Teaching about Islam in Polish Schools	83
Katarzyna Górak-Sosnowska	
6 Representations of Islam in the Romanian History Textbooks in the Post-1990 Period	101
Adriana Cupcea	
7 Othering through Textbooks: Teaching about Roma in Contemporary Hungarian Schools	115
Jekatyerina Dunajeva	
8 Social Exclusion and the Construction of the Other at a Czech Basic School: An Anthropological Perspective	133
Radek Vorlíček	

9	Present but Absent: Education about the Roma and Sinti Genocide in Poland	155
	Joanna Talewicz-Kwiatkowska and Dominika Zakrzewska-Olędzka	
10	Polish-Jewish Rivalry for Memory	175
	Lech M. Nijakowski	
11	Teaching Queer Post-Soviet Perspectives: Intersectional Pedagogy and Global Knowledge Inequalities	189
	Masha Beketova	
12	Teaching Gender and Queer Studies at Polish Universities: Challenges, Limitations, Perspectives	205
	Magdalena Stoch	

Index 229

Illustrations

Figures

5.1	Stages of intercultural education for monocultural groups	91
7.1	Drawing of a fifth-grade student	125
7.2	Drawing of a fourth-grade student (2020)	126

Tables

2.1	Overview of Historical Topics	33
4.1	Categories Relevant for the Study of Teaching Extremism Related to Content and Codes Used in the Analysis	68
4A.1	Systematically Reviewed Research Articles, *Eesti Haridusteaduste Ajakiri* (Estonian Journal of Education)	78
7.1	'Gypsy Folk Tales' and Any Literature about Roma in Children's Readers and Literature Books for Grades 1–8 from the Online Textbook Database of the Education Authority for 2019–20 Academic Year	123
8.1	Wishes for Christmas Presents	141

Contributors

Masha Beketova, MA, studied gender studies/Slavonic studies in Berlin and Moscow. Masha is currently working on a PhD thesis in Slavonic cultural studies at Humboldt University in Berlin. Masha's research focuses on queer migration and asylum, migrant literature, queer Ukrainian and Russian literature as well as intersectionality.

Adriana Cupcea is a researcher at the Romanian Institute for Research on National Minorities in Cluj-Napoca, Romania. She holds a PhD in history (2009) from the 'Babeș-Bolyai' University of Cluj-Napoca. Her research interests focus on Muslim community in Romania and the construction of modern identities. She is co-author of the book *The Image of the Ottoman in the History Textbooks from Romania and Bosnia and Herzegovina in the Post-Communist Period* (2015).

Jekatyerina Dunajeva holds a PhD in political science from the University of Oregon. Currently she is a research fellow at the Hungarian Academy of Sciences, Centre for Social Sciences, Institute for Political Science; Assistant Professor of Political Science at Pázmány Péter Catholic University; and a Researcher at Central European University's Center for Teaching and Learning. She is the author of the book *Constructing Identities over Time* (2021), and her research has been published in multiple book chapters and peer-reviewed journals, exploring topics such as Roma identity, discrimination, youth politics, nationalism, state- and nation-building, education, fieldwork as research methodology as well as contemporary Russian and Hungarian politics.

Rafael Filiberto Forteza Fernández is a Cuban-Russian Associate Professor with a PhD in pedagogical sciences teaching academic English and country studies at the Ural Federal University, Russia. His research interests focus on multimodal critical literacy, critical discourse analysis, the portrayal of culture and history in language textbooks, neoliberalism in language teaching and neoliberalism in higher education. His most research papers are 'Content Edulcoration as Ideology Visualization in an English Language Coursebook' (2021), 'Miseducating about the Other in Foreign Language Textbooks' (2021) and 'Critical Literacy in Russia' (2022).

Katarzyna Górak-Sosnowska is an Associate Professor at the Institute of International Studies and head of the Middle East and Central Asia Unit at SGH Warsaw School of Economics, Poland. Her research interests focus on Muslim minorities in Poland and wider Europe. She has published five monographs, including *Deconstructing Islamophobia in Poland* (2014) and *Muslims in Poland and Eastern Europe* (editor,

2011) as well as articles in journals such as *Sociology of Religion* and *Journal of Muslims in Europe* and book chapters. In 2021, she was awarded with a grant by the European Commission (CERV-2021-EQUAL) to challenge the negative discourse about Islam in Poland.

Alar Kilp is Lecturer in Comparative Politics at the University of Tartu, Estonia. His research specializes in religion and politics, scholarship of teaching and learning in political science. He has published on religious nationalism, European normative power, religious authority, threshold concepts in political science and legal regulation of same-sex relations. His most recent paper is titled 'The Influence of the European Union's Liberal Secularist Policy on Religion upon Religious Authority in Estonia Since 2004' (2021).

Jan Květina is a researcher at the Institute of History of the Czech Academy of Sciences in Prague, Czech Republic, and Assistant Professor at the University of Hradec Králové, Czech Republic. His main research interests focus especially on Central European political thought and identity, discourse analysis, republicanism, nationalism and theory of education. He has published several papers or chapters on Central European history of ideas in English, German and Polish journals and books. His most significant and recent monograph in Czech entitled 'Myth of the Republic. Identity and Political Discourse of the Early Modern Polish Nobility' was published in 2020.

Heidi Maiberg is a PhD student of sociology and criminology at Royal Holloway, University of London, UK. In her dissertation, she studies how the impact of voluntary-based deradicalization and disengagement programmes is assessed. She also researches developments in the Estonian and Baltic right-wing milieu and educational initiatives aiming to prevent and tackle extremism. She has published about disengagement and deradicalization methods, processes and models.

Urszula Markowska-Manista is Assistant Professor in the Faculty of Education at the University of Warsaw, Poland, and a field researcher in education in culturally diversified environments and indigenous childhood concerning children's rights. She was the director (2016, FU Berlin) and co-director (2017–21, F.H. Potsdam) of the MA Childhood Studies and Children's Rights programme. She has conducted extensive field research in Central and the Horn of Africa, the South Caucasus and Europe. She is the author of numerous books, articles, chapters in monographs published by Sage, Springer, Routledge. Her most recent book is *Childhood Studies and Children's Rights between Research and Activism* (2020).

Lech M. Nijakowski is Associate Professor in the Faculty of Sociology at the University of Warsaw, Poland. He is also permanent adviser to the National and Ethnic Minorities Committee of the Polish Sejm (since 2001), member of the editorial teams at *Przegląd Humanistyczny* (Humanities Review), *Studia Socjologiczno-Polityczne. Seria Nowa* (Sociological and Political Studies. New Series) and *Zdanie* (Opinion). His areas of academic interest include genocide studies, sociology of ethnicity, sociology of conflict, historical sociology, memory studies, discourse analysis and contemporary sociological theory.

Magdalena Stoch, PhD, is Assistant Professor in the Department of Media and Cultural Studies at the Pedagogical University of Krakow, Poland. Her research interests focus on the reception of literature, gender studies and emancipatory pedagogy. In addition, she has collaborated with non-governmental organizations in implementing anti-discrimination solutions at universities. She is a scholarship holder in US Department of State programme titled '21st Century Changemakers: Trend Leaders Promote Social Media Discernment among Youth'. Her most recent book is *Jak czytamy książki? Recepcja literatury w krakowskich i wielickich grupach czytelniczych* (How Do We Read Books? Reception of Literature in Reading Groups of Cracow and Wieliczka) (2021).

Joanna Talewicz-Kwiatkowska holds a PhD in anthropology and works as Assistant Professor at the Institute of Ethnology and Cultural Anthropology at the University of Warsaw, Poland. In addition, she collaborates with the Institute of Intercultural Studies at the Faculty of International and Political Studies of the Jagiellonian University and the Polish University Abroad in London. Her research interests include Roma communities in Europe and the United States, focusing on the Roma Holocaust.

Radek Vorlíček is a researcher in the Institute of Social Work at the University of Hradec Králové, Czech Republic. His specialization is anthropology of education. His research interests focus on inclusive education, peer relations and ethnicity. He has been doing ethnographic fieldwork for several years in educational settings in the Czech Republic and the Slovak Republic. His most recent book titled *Jak se daří inkluzi u nás a na Slovensku?: Pohled do konkrétních základních škol* (How Inclusive Education Succeeds and Fails in the Czech Republic and Slovakia: Comparison of Specific Primary Schools) was published in 2019.

Dominika Zakrzewska-Olędzka is a social psychologist and an educator, holding PhD in social sciences. She works as Assistant Professor at the Psychology Institute at the Maria Grzegorzewska University in Warsaw, Poland. Her research interests focus on the intergroup relations, identity building and cultural diversity in education, with a special focus on Polish-Jewish and Polish-Israeli relations. She was a grantee of the Fulbright Slavic Award (2020–1) and scholar in residence at the Oxford Summer Institute for the Development of Curriculum in Critical Contemporary Antisemitism Studies (2019).

Foreword

It is something of a paradox that a book advancing a powerful case for inclusive education in a region where this approach is novel and radical should advertise itself, through its title, as being about 'non-inclusive education'. But this is only one of the surprises lurking in this highly original and timely volume. In the decade of Black Lives Matter and attacks on the teaching of 'critical race theory', at a time of concerted efforts to mainstream refugee education into majority settings in the face of growing government pushbacks against asylum seekers, and in a period of intense debate about fairness and natural justice as neglected priorities in the way educational institutions investigate allegations of sexual and gender-based violence, it is fascinating to learn of a vibrant but largely neglected arena where the battle for pedagogical decolonization and post-'dependent' educational exploration is being advanced from previously uncharted territory, Central and Eastern Europe.

In the context of this rich volume, adopting a postcolonial stance means something more than what many of us have simplistically come to assume. It is not only about addressing the enduring legacy on Black and brown populations of enslavement, and of imperial and colonial appropriation in the Global South; nor is it only about engaging with the persistent impact of settler genocide and colonization on indigenous populations the world over, critical and vast as these topics are. Rather, this remarkable volume targets the imperative of liberating oneself from the ubiquitous, one might say hegemonic, dominance of a Cold War defined, West European perspective. It criticizes the dominant, liberal notion of 'inclusivity' for being a stand-in for a highly partial and incomplete transatlantic, Euro-American perspective. It offers a useful opportunity to consider how to reconfigure one's approach to inclusive education, whether history, political science, cultural/gender studies, anthropology or education is one's primary disciplinary home.

We learn from the contributors to this volume that, from the perspective of teachers, students and other residents of Central and Eastern Europe, mainstream 'inclusive pedagogy' represents a different form of colonization: an often patronizing, belittling or obscuring appropriation of a very different historical experience. From the vantage point of Central and Eastern Europe, it is Prussian, Austrian and Russian colonization and their enduring legacies that are centre stage and missing from the curriculum; it is the rivalry for wartime memories between Jews and Poles that needs addressing as histories are re-examined; it is the unrepaired enslavement of Roma that demands scholarly and pedagogical attention; it is the ongoing experience of virulent extremism that targets Muslims, Jews, Roma and LGBTQ individuals as despised 'Others' that calls for urgent inquiry and inclusion in educational theory and practice. Many participants in the global field of inclusive pedagogy have missed or neglected these urgent issues altogether. And yet they are crucial for half the European continent.

It is therefore a great pleasure to learn from this powerful and multifaceted volume. Thought-provoking chapters on general issues such as curriculum design, tackling extremism in the classroom and decolonizing 'diversity' are complemented by more narrowly focused, fascinating case studies, including pieces on the representation of Islam in Romanian textbooks, teaching about Roma in Hungarian schools, social exclusion in Czech schools, and gender and queer studies at Polish universities. They encourage readers to question their own orthodoxies as they accompany the authors on an intriguing investigation into fast-changing demographic and social structures. As one of the co-editors insightfully put it in an email to me, 'Central and Eastern Europe is like a third eye – you have to open it slowly and you will be surprised.'[1] She is absolutely right.

Jacqueline Bhabha
Harvard University

Note

1. Personal communication from Urszula Markowska-Manista, 29 January 2022. On file with the author.

Introduction

Katarzyna Górak-Sosnowska and Urszula Markowska-Manista

Inclusive education is intended to lead to changes in attitudes towards Others and to lay the foundation for a just and non-discriminatory society (UNESCO 2009). This means that, to be effective, it should be adapted to the local historical and cultural contexts. It should not be a carbon copy of solutions used elsewhere but a lens through which to look at one's own prejudices. Inclusive education is, to date, a well-established interdisciplinary area of theoretical and empirical inquiry and a global field of educational research and practice embedded in policy areas of universal education for all. It has become both an educational goal and a methodology (Slee 2018) leading to changes in the inclusion process of diverse minority and majority groups. However, researchers and practitioners of inclusive education in different parts of the world still witness many challenges and gaps between the philosophy and principles of inclusive education and systemic practice (Boyle et al. 2020).

In this book we focus on comparative studies of teaching ethnicity, religion, and gender fitting into broadly understood education that is intended to be inclusive, but due to the range of social, political, historical and cultural conditions of the subjects it addresses, it becomes education with sensitive topics. Until recently, inclusive education about sensitive topics was implemented in Central and Eastern European (CEE) countries based on the Western model of understanding diversity, which was not fully adequate in CEE context. In the book, we refer to the concept of 'leveraged pedagogy' developed by Kulpa (2014) in which the West taking care of CEE is perceived as a form of cultural hegemony, ignoring their past experiences and contemporary social structure, as well as educational context.

Context, Scope and Nature of the Book

This book is about teaching sensitive topics in CEE countries presented through the narratives of local researchers. The authors address conflicts, tensions and inequalities present in education that are rarely discussed or acknowledged. Teaching such topics in educational and academic settings has been a challenge in all multicultural societies, illustrated in various studies and education guides at national and international levels. Most of these publications have been developed for intercultural or culturally diverse settings within a relatively inclusive and open framework of democratic/liberal and multicultural Western societies. While Western Europe definitely belongs to the West – and it is not only through its name – the position of CEE is much more ambiguous.

This ambiguity is less about geography, and more about the meaning attributed to the West and to the East, and how these two regions differ. From a territorial and historical perspective, the nature of the classical division of Europe into East and West had been problematic. According to Halecki (1950), such a division suggests that what is geographically 'Eastern' is perceived as foreign and alien to 'Western' European civilization, with the latter perceived as the core of Europe. Thus, the geographical location of countries influenced the development of the idea of freedom, around which European civilization formed and evolved. According to him, it was paradoxical to overlook and disregard the existing similarities and cultural and political ties between certain Eastern and Western European countries. Thus, European identity (also in relation to Eastern and Western Europe) has been constructed over the centuries on the basis of opposition to what is different, distinct and alien (Delanty 1995). Since 1989 when many East European countries started their political transition with the ultimate goal to become a part of the West, they seem to be in a permanent state of transition (Kulpa 2014).

Our publication provides a framework for understanding why teaching about 'invisible' Others is a challenge in CEE and why specific educational tools from the multicultural and often liberal West do not necessarily work in the CEE context. CEE countries may seem close to the West in many ways, but this is not the case with the core issues addressed in this book. Unlike many Western societies, these countries are often much less culturally diverse, with different and fragile historical and political processes, which puts tackling sensitive topics in a different context. Three factors contribute to this environment.

The first one is the marginal number of third-country nationals and ethnic homogeneity of CEE countries (except for the borderline type of multiculturality, which is from neighbouring countries). Most of the foreign-born population consists of the citizens of neighbouring countries, often embedded in local cultures as national minorities. Moreover, indigenous and ethnic groups have lived there for centuries and became familiar to mainstream society. The 'distant' Others – newcomers originating from countries with significant cultural distance – started arriving only recently, and their numbers are still marginal, as most of CEE countries are economically unattractive compared to Western Europe.

The second one is the lack of colonial past and colonial connections, typical for Western Europe (and relevant reflection after the subsequent process of decolonialization). Consequently, studies on gender or race have been neglected for many years across CEE, and the idea that the region is free from the challenges of Western multicultural society related to race or Islamophobia has been attractive (Polynczuk-Alenius 2021). While postcolonial theories have naturally emerged in ex-colonial powers and countries that have been colonialized, they have been absent from intellectual reflection in CEE countries for a long time. Until the early 1990s, many of these countries were behind the Iron Curtain. They were dominated by another superpower – the USSR – though this type of domination was never perceived through a colonial lens as it resulted directly from the political division of Europe after the Second World War. That is why, despite growing (mostly Western) scholarship on CEE colonialism (e.g. Mick 2014), the term is hardly understood in the local context. If CEE every had anything to do with colonialism, it was being a victim of colonializing policies of their more powerful neighbours (usually the superpowers Russia, Germany/ Prussia, Austria, but also in the case of Ukraine, Poland).

The third factor refers to the centuries of political struggles, territorial losses and acquisitions, and around five decades under USSR umbrella that created a narrative of threat and victimization which have fuelled the sense of national unity. The decades following the political shift and breaking of the USSR dominance brought new social and economic turbulences which impacted the fragile CEE collective identities often built around ethnic lines. The fear of Other that occurred during the post-communist transformation derived from the crisis of collective identity and unexpected changes, and it was often directed towards different 'Others' (Graff 2008).

All these factors make the CEE context unique while presenting challenges in teaching about Others who are invisible in the public sphere. This brings about the non-contextual teaching (Markowska-Manista 2021), teaching 'by dry run', that is, without the established presence of Others, and often in classrooms lacking inclusiveness and diversity. We wish to fill this gap with the present book, written by authors who understand local peculiarities of CEE and can identify and explain these contexts and challenges to an international reader. Thus, we hope to add our academic perspectives and contextual research to the general discussions on global, intercultural and inclusive education in schools.

Distancing oneself from Others, putting them in opposition to the majority and reproducing narratives about them without them seems to be another burning topic in CEE education. Interestingly, CEE societies that have embraced their newly acquired 'Europeanness' by entering the EU seem to compensate for their long experience of being 'post-Soviet Other' migrants from Eastern Europe in Western Europe by instrumentalizing and Orientalizing 'Others' coming to their part of the continent. At the same time, by strengthening the borders in the migration crisis of 2015–16, 2020+ and by pursuing a policy of cultural closure, they forget the migration paths of their ancestors during the First and Second World Wars and during the Cold War. We introduce this context to address the complexity of these issues.

The dominant ideas in contemporary publications on sensitive topics in the globalized world are Eurocentric ideas: strictly connected with the division into the Global North (formerly the First World) and the Global South (formerly the Third World), which completely ignores the so-called Second World that included CEE countries along with their input, approaches, research and methodology. This omission, or rather the peripheral placement of CEE, has led researchers representing those countries to use clichéd methodologies based on Western models, frequently ignoring the local methodological contributions and the theoretical legacy of 'domestic' researchers. We want to fill this gap through a publication that allows a group of silent researchers from CEE to speak (Spivak 2013) as representatives of their contexts, who are familiar with the local languages and cultural codes, discourses as well as mentality (Mach 1998). Our book fits into post-dependence discourses and is situated at the crossroads of interdisciplinary approaches to global education in teaching about ethnicity, religion and gender in the CEE context.

Bearing in mind the global, capitalist dependencies and post-dependence and postcolonial studies on education in CEE, we would like to present research 'in context' from below. By doing so, we wish to reverse the victimizing, one-sided perspective of looking at global education in CEE through the Western perspective. We aim to decolonize the dominant perspective of a unifying account of sensitive topics concerning Others and Otherness in CEE and build a sustainable, equitable educational experience for all. Following Moncrieffe (2020, 2022), we believe that it is important in teaching to build critical awareness of diversity and to recognize opportunities for transformation and empowerment through knowledge.

The authors of the chapters are seen as key actors who can influence, shape and therefore also modify and decolonize established patterns and unilateral approaches to sensitive topics in education of different societies and cultures. This also applies to the development of new knowledge and insights into what we call the integration of new perspectives and approaches in the educational process. The historicity of Europe, including the impact of the First and Second World Wars, with Yalta order keeping CEE behind the Iron Curtain, means that the history of twentieth century still has consequences for the societies of the old continent including influence on the ways of thinking of people in its different parts. Europe is simultaneously postcolonial (the West) and post-dependent (the East) in the dual sense that the former follow the colonial era and the latter the communist era. These divisions and processes connected with them have left a strong mark on the shape of education and the teaching process, and they dominate thinking.

In this sense, we draw attention to the need to decolonize Western thinking and narratives on teaching about sensitive topics in CEE, which seems to have been ignored for a long time or perceived in a very one-sided light due to existing stereotypes, oppositions and the lack of voices of CEE researchers on this topic. At the same time, we recognize the need to decolonize teaching in inclusive education itself, which we understand as a process that is important for critiquing existing asymmetrical post-dependency and postcolonial dependencies and disenchanting the Other and its context. The more explicit application of a decolonial approach directed towards themes and contents that can be sensitive in CEE allows for a shift from a narrow to a broader understanding of the diverse near and distant worlds, phenomena and processes within them.

The topics covered in this book thus allow for the inclusion of the voice of minority people. By including them, we draw attention to the fact that the dominant understanding of the Other in the context of CEE is closely intertwined with the process of its centuries-long dependency or longstanding colonialization (in various configurations of power relations) and needs to be decolonized through the deconstruction of knowledge and its sources (Mignolo 2009). In the context of how the sensitive topics collected in this book are presented, we seek to bring about a questioning of schematic, established assumptions and a verification of preconceptions regarding perceptions and attitudes towards underrepresented groups.

In this book, the reader will find what is lacking in teaching (what is excluded from it) in CEE and what is available but needs to be deconstructed (because it cannot be representative of the past) due to changing sociocultural realities in the twenty-first century.

Main Themes and Structure of the Book

Most of the chapters are based on empirical research that is predominantly qualitative. In some cases, the authors themselves represent the minority groups they write about. In other cases, their experience – though coming from the majority group – can be positioned in between. Due to the lack of visible 'Others' in the public sphere, many of the authors take the roles of the 'allies' of the minority groups. Taking into account the political atmosphere around some of these minorities (e.g. LGBT+ in Poland, Muslims in Romania), it is easier for the authors to act as an ally, rather than put representatives of the minorities in jeopardy or in a vulnerable position.

The need for decolonizing the educational approach has been raised in several chapters. Decolonization is about noticing and appreciating the world of both groups by ensuring that the views and voices of a marginalized group are heard, recognized and appreciated (Migliarini and Elder 2019). This approach benefits all groups. Yet, in the CEE it is often hard to apply it, as the voices of 'Others' exist only on the margins. Moreover, as in the case of Muslims, they are not even in charge of the narratives about Islam, as the discourse builds predominantly on what is happening in the West or Middle East (Górak-Sosnowska 2014). This leads in a way to the paradox of Schrödinger's cat: on the one hand, we should include the minority groups in the educational practices, and on the other, exposing them might hurt them and turn them into 'living cultural laboratories' – a 'duty Muslim' or a 'duty lesbian' who is supposed to become the only known example of the minority.

A similar situation applies to national and ethnic minorities, who are usually seen as a problem rather than a potential for the development of societies (Markowska-Manista 2019). These groups are often spoken about and written about from a position of superiority, without taking into account their perspectives and counter-histories, which are so important in the dominant majority discourse about minorities. There is a dearth of research and publications based on the multiple voices of researchers from both majority and minority societies.

The book consists of twelve chapters that have been thematically arranged and offers case studies that are country-based. The first four chapters address the challenge of applying knowledge and concepts from global and inclusive education developed in the West to local CEE realities and contexts. These are followed by case studies of teaching ethnicity, religion and gender in CEE. We selected relevant and appealing cases that illustrate these challenges. The final selection seems in our opinion to cover the most significant social categories, that is minorities, who are often strongly stigmatized and who serve in a way as a litmus test for inclusive education. These are Jews and Roma – as representatives of communities with a long presence in CEE, and Muslims and LGBT+ – as communities who have been recently strongly politicized, which has impacted the way they are approached in the educational setting. These case studies are by no means representative of the whole region. Teaching gender in Poland is far more challenging than in Latvia for political reasons. Including Roma voices in the Czech educational framework is much more needed than in Estonia due to the size of local Roma community. Yet, all these case studies contribute to a coherent picture of how local educational frameworks respond to educational paradigms developed and applied in the West.

The first chapter, 'Intercultural Teaching in a "Monocultural" Country: Why Do We Need a Decolonial Approach to Teaching about Diversity?' by Urszula Markowska-Manista, presents the challenge of performing intercultural education without context, namely, in a monocultural Polish school where the natural channels of exposure to other cultures through peers, local community or recent history are missing. Markowska-Manista calls for rethinking decolonial approaches to become adaptable to the CEE context.

In the second chapter, 'A Cultural History of the Other in Curriculum Design Transformation', Rafael Filiberto Forteza Fernández addresses learning English as a way of being exposed to the history and culture of the Western countries. According to him, the content of the teaching materials is loaded with Western discourses and concepts that are presented in a lecture-style and therefore do not fit students' needs. Through his action research conducted in a Russian university, Forteza Fernández advocates for a radical transformation of curriculum design.

Jan Květina addresses the process of adapting the liberal pluralist educational paradigm in Czech educational setting, in the third chapter titled 'The Pluralist Paradigm in the Czech Educational Process: Teaching about Collective Identities and Democracy in the Constructivist Educational Project'. Despite significant political changes from post-totalitarian to democratic rule, some key concepts of the latter are still considered as controversial. In fact, combination of traditional language with liberal educational paradigm might have serious consequences for Czech students.

The last chapter in this section, 'Preparedness of Estonian Teachers to Tackle Extremism in a Classroom: A Systematic Review of Empirical Studies Published in *Estonian Journal of Education* (2013–21)' by Alar Kilp and Heidi Maiberg shows the absence of extremism-related materials that could support teachers pedagogically in tackling this topic in Estonian classrooms. The identified gap results from the local context as Estonia has not been affected by radical extremism. Still, the topic is key to understanding global and European challenges and affairs.

The chapters engage with the Western concepts or paradigms in different manners. Markowska-Manista, Kilp and Maiberg point at the actual lack of relevant context to tackle and meaningfully implement concepts such as intercultural education or tackling extremism. Forteza Fernández and Květina point at existing gaps that limit the application of these paradigms in the CEE educational context. Moreover, Forteza Fernández and Markowska-Manista address the need to transform these concepts and paradigms to better fit CEE realities.

The chapters that follow address the three concepts listed in the title – ethnicity, religion and gender. Groups and communities covered in the case studies include those that are rooted in the collective memory of CEE societies, and their relationship with the mainstream society have been uneasy – that is, Jews and Roma as well as those who are more recently acknowledged Others, who had been securitized and (mis)used in political agenda – namely Muslims and LGBT+. Teaching about those groups and communities brings in difficult knowledge, often loaded with stereotypes as some of these groups are hardly visible in the public space, or marginalized.

In the chapter 'Are Muslims Scared of Pork?: Teaching about Islam in Polish Schools' Katarzyna Górak-Sosnowska analyses the challenges related to teaching about Islam and Muslims in Polish monocultural schools. Not only is the number of Muslims in Poland marginal, but they also provoke strong negative feelings based on stereotypes, which makes the learning process even more challenging. She discusses possible strategies to introduce topics related to Islam and Muslims in the classroom. For instance, using a 'duty Muslim' to visit the class might be the students' only encounter with a Muslim person, but at the same time it might strengthen some stereotypes and turn him or her into a 'living cultural laboratory'.

Adriana Cupcea looks at the other side of teaching about Islam and Muslims – namely in the Romanian curriculum and textbooks. Her chapter 'Representations of Islam in the Romanian History Textbooks in the Post-1990 Period' systematically analyses the main categories, (mis)representations and narratives related to Islam and Muslims in Romanian textbooks. While the Romanian educational system has been undergoing transformation and the textbooks have become differentiated, compared to the Socialist era, the representation of Islam and Muslims seems to reveal and strengthen the same core stereotypes that exist in Romanian society. Moreover, the textbooks omit the existence of local Muslim communities in Romania. Thus, Islam and Muslims are related and discussed only as concepts external and alien to the local society.

The next two chapters raise the topic of teaching Roma students and teaching about Roma in CEE countries. Two countries with significant Roma communities – the Czech Republic and Hungary – are presented as case studies. Jekatyerina Dunajeva investigates the curricula and textbooks in the chapter 'Othering through Textbooks: Teaching about Roma in Contemporary Hungarian Schools'. She points at the ways Roma are presented by Othering them from mainstream society (often through folklore) and marginalizing them. Dunajeva advocates for decolonizing knowledge and engaging the Roma in the process of changing the content of education. Yet, she considers it to be a challenge in the current nationalist political setting in Hungary.

Radek Vorlíček approaches the topic of teaching Roma students from a classroom perspective. In his chapter 'Social Exclusion and the Construction of the Other at a Czech Basic School: An Anthropological Perspective', the Other are Roma students. Through extensive fieldwork study in one of the Czech basic schools, he analyses the group dynamics and relations between Czech and Roma students, where ethnicity and socioeconomic status set the main boundaries between students. Also, the teacher's role in setting and maintaining the boundaries has been critically assessed.

The next two chapters that follow engage in teaching and exploring the subject of the Holocaust in Poland. Joanna Talewicz-Kwiatkowska and Dominika Zakrzewska-Olędzka look at the other side of teaching about the Holocaust – one that is often omitted. In their chapter 'Present but Absent: Education about the Roma and Sinti

Genocide in Poland', they explore Roma and Sinti Genocide as suffering that has been overlooked in school curricula in Poland and in other CEE countries. They reflect that this omission should be interpreted in the light of contemporary anti-Gypsyism.

Lech Nijakowski frames Polish discursive strategies about Jews as an example of 'Polish-Jewish Rivalry for Memory' – as the title of his chapter indicates. While the Jewish community in Poland is marginal, it has been strongly represented in the public discourse. One of the main reasons behind that rivalry for memory is the troubled history of Poland in the Second World War and a competition for the status of the main victim of these tragic events. The author offers recommendations on how to tackle this issue at school, taking into account the emotional load of this difficult knowledge.

The final two chapters bring in the issues of gender and LGBT+ in two opposite contexts. Masha Beketova presents their experiences of teaching queer studies at a university in Germany in the chapter 'Teaching Queer Post-Soviet Perspectives: Intersectional Pedagogy and Global Knowledge Inequalities'. They critically address the Western knowledge hegemonies in how post-Soviet queer studies are approached and reflected, pointing at the absence of perspectives from the post-Soviet area in shaping global queer and gender studies.

The context of Magdalena Stoch's chapter on 'Teaching Gender and Queer Studies at Polish Universities: Challenges, Limitations, Perspectives' is completely different from that of Beketova, as the author presents the struggles and concerns of gender studies lecturers at Polish universities who teach their subject despite the negative political climate around gender in Poland, labelled 'gender ideology'. By applying the concept of emancipatory pedagogy, Stoch presents how these lecturers use the tools of emancipatory education and try to overcome the challenges related to teaching gender and queer studies in Poland.

To summarize, this is a monograph that advances perspectives from the CEE and explains why CEE countries (located peripherally and therefore 'in-between' the West and the East) seem to be unable to catch up with the West in embracing multiculturalism or liberalism. The rise of populism and the renaissance of traditionalism, understood in narrow ethnic terms, might be perceived as paradoxical. Having joined the EU club and benefiting from becoming EU members, CEE states should welcome EU values. The book identifies and discloses the shortcomings and inabilities to transfer Western-style pedagogy to the CEE context. Using case studies to teach about ethnicity, religion and gender exposes the clash between concepts that became universal in the Western context and demonstrates that they do not fit into local CEE realities. Moreover, they seem invisible to Western scholars, as they are marked by the stigma of decades of Soviet, post-Soviet, post-dependent pedagogy and Eurocentric pedagogy. The main topic we selected has been considered important for understanding the complicated present day educational realities of CEE countries.

Finally, to reinforce the reflexive approach to the topics presented in our book, we pose the following questions to our readers:

- What are the non-contextual teaching characteristics of education in countries with little cultural diversity in the population?
- How to decolonize knowledge and education about CEE, to avoid colonizing it?

- How to teach multiculturalism 'by dry run' in an effective way?
- How to integrate 'sensitive topics' from CEE into inclusive education in other contexts to avoid the danger of single narration?

We hope this edited volume will inspire readers and becomes a guidebook for those wishing to understand the conditions of inclusive education and teaching about 'Invisible Others' in CEE contexts.

Acknowledgements

This book came as a result of a collaborative project: 'Sensiclass: Tacking Sensitive Topics in a Classroom' (funded by the European Commission, Erasmus+ Strategic Partnerships for Higher Education. Project number 2019-1-EE01-KA203-051690) led by the University of Tartu (Estonia) with partners from Central European University (Hungary/Austria), SGH Warsaw School of Economics (Poland) and University of Hradec Králové (Czech Republic). The consortium was set by partners from four CEE countries. In the three-year course of the project, we were struggling on how to accommodate the knowledge on inclusive and global education to local CEE realities.

Our position of being an 'in-between' of Western and CEE pedagogies (thanks to the EU enlargement we have been able to pursue our academic interests abroad) and experiences empowered us to tell our story – one of teaching global and inclusive education 'by dry run' – that is, without the presence of 'cultural Others', and one of trying to adapt teaching concepts and paradigms developed in the West to our local realities. We would like to thank the authors for accepting this quest and their willingness to share their research and personal experiences of making the 'classrooms' and spaces for the transfer of knowledge more diverse and inclusive. It was a privilege to cooperate with all the scholars contributing to this book, and we are proud of the final edited collection.

We also extend our thanks to the 'Sensiclass' partners with whom we shared our approaches and solutions on how to teach sensitive topics in CEE. Last but not least, we thank the reviewers of the proposal who helped us to make the book concept more approachable for the international reader, who otherwise might have got lost in the complicated sociohistorical burdens of CEE countries. Finally, we would like to thank Bloomsbury Publishing for their support in bringing our contribution to publication and actually making our voices heard and making the invisible – visible.

References

Boyle, C., J. Anderson, A. Page and S. Mavropoulou (2020), *Inclusive Education: Global Issues and Controversies*, Leiden: Brill.

Delanty, G. (1995), *Inventing Europe. Idea, Identity, Reality*, London: Palgrave Macmillan.

Górak-Sosnowska, K. (2014), *Deconstructing Islamophobia in Poland. Story of an Internet Group*, Warsaw: University of Warsaw.

Graff, A. (2008), *Rykoszetem. Rzecz o płci, seksualności i narodzie*, Warszawa: WAB.

Halecki, O. (1950), *The Limits and Divisions of European History*, London: York, Sheed & Ward.

Kulpa, R. (2014), 'Western Leveraged Pedagogy of Central and Eastern Europe: Discourses of Homophobia, Tolerance, and Nationhood', *Gender, Place & Culture: A Journal of Feminist Geography*, 21 (4): 431–48.

Mach, B. (1998), *Transformacja ustrojowa a mentalne dziedzictwo socjalizmu*, Warszawa: ISP PAN.

Markowska-Manista, U. (2019), 'Migrant and Refugee Children in Polish Schools in the Face of Social Transformation', in C. Maier-Höfer (ed.), *Die Vielfalt der Kindheit(en) und die Rechte der Kinder in der Gegenwart. Praxisfragen und Forschung im Kontext gesellschaftlicher Herausforderungen*, 79–100, Wiesbanden: Springer.

Markowska-Manista, U. (2021), 'Non-Contextual Teaching of Sensitive Topics Focusing on Cultural Diversity in Polish Schools', *Rocznik Lubuski*, 47 (1): 143–58.

Mick, C. (2014), 'Colonialism in the Polish Eastern Borderlands 1919–1939', in R. Healy and E. Dal Lago (eds), *The Shadow of Colonialism on Europe's Modern Past*, 126–41, New York: Palgrave Macmillan.

Migliarini, V., and B. Elder (2019), 'Decolonizing Inclusive Education: A Collection of Practical Inclusive CDS- and DisCrit-Informed Teaching Practices Implemented in the Global South', *Disability and the Global South*, 7 (1): 1852–72.

Mignolo, W. D. (2009), 'Epistemic Disobedience, Independent Thought and Decolonial Freedom', *Theory, Culture & Society*, 26 (7–8): 159–81.

Moncrieffe, M. L. (2020), *Decolonising the History Curriculum: Euro-Centrism and Primary Schooling*, London: Palgrave Macmillan.

Moncrieffe, M. L., ed. (2022), *Decolonising Curriculum Knowledge: International Perspectives, Interdisciplinary Approaches*, London: Palgrave Macmillan (in print).

Polynczuk-Alenius, K. (2021), 'At the Intersection of Racism and Nationalism. Theorizing and Contextualizing the "Anti-Immigration Discourse in Poland"', *Nation and Nationalism*, 27 (3), 766–81.

Slee, R. (2018), 'Defining the Scope of Inclusive Education'. Available online: http://repositorio.minedu.gob.pe/bitstream/handle/20.500.12799/5977/Defining%20the%20scope%20of%20inclusive%20education.pdf?sequence=1&isAllowed=y (accessed 9 January 2022).

Spivak, G. (2013), 'Can the Subaltern Speak?', in P. Williams and L. Chrisman (eds), *Colonial Discourse and Post-Colonial Theory. The Reader*, 66–111, New York: Routledge.

UNESCO (2009), 'Policy Guidelines on Inclusive Education'. Available online: http://unesdoc.unesco.org/images/0017/001778/177849e.pdf (accessed 2 January 2022).

1

Intercultural Teaching in a 'Monocultural' Country: Why Do We Need a Decolonial Approach to Teaching about Diversity?

Urszula Markowska-Manista

Introduction

The history of the Polish state, as well as the turbulent history of other countries in Central and Eastern Europe (CEE), is one of tolerance intertwined with nationalism and xenophobia towards others. It is also a history of being between the periphery and the core in the colonial world order (Puchalski 2022), as well as partitions, dependency and struggle for independence. On the one hand, there was a move towards unity and integration, towards familiarity with otherness, a search for common paths and themes, an expansion of contacts in order to build links and understanding on the Eastern borderline of European cultures. On the other hand, there were walls, fear of the unknown, divisions between the in-group and out-group. In this atmosphere, for centuries 'there was a clear articulation of national, ethnic, religious and regional needs' (Nikitorowicz 1995: 105). This dual reality sought to preserve and perpetuate the existing state and order of things, and at the same time to change it. The increasingly complex process of layering and differentiation of the needs of the national majority as well as the ethnic and national minorities resulting from the coexistence of different nations and groups with different cultural heritage has created new educational challenges and a new perspective on education in terms of respect for diversity and interculturality (Lewowicki 2017).

The historical memory (Theiss 1999) of the fate and heritage of minorities, of otherness, 'strangeness' and of the events that took place during the Second World War in the borderlands are important elements in creating a peaceful world of multicultural diversity. Before the war, ethnic minorities, including a large number of Jews, constituted 30 per cent of the population (Davies 1981). However, from the onset of the war until the breakthrough year 1989, Poland was officially presented as a homogenous country, in which national minorities did not actually exist, while 'Polish history was perceived as belonging completely to Poles' (Mach 2010: 149). The reality so created was reflected in the attitude of Polish society towards representatives of other nationalities living within the borders of the Polish state. It was either hatred and hostility, nurtured by prejudice and skilfully fuelled by stereotypes of the Other, or complete indifference, anaesthesia or lack of interest in linguistic or religious diversity. Currently, Poland is a country where autochthonous minorities constitute a small percentage (3.3 per cent according to the 2011 Census) and new cultural groups a slightly larger portion of the total population. According to the 2019 estimates of Główny Urząd Statystyczny (GUS) (Central Statistical Office), foreigners in Poland constituted about 5.2 per cent of the population. The majority of them were Ukrainians (64 per cent), followed by Belarussians, Germans, Moldavians and citizens of the Russian Federation. Moreover, due to its geographical location, the scarcity and poor quality of integration programmes, the politicization of refugeeism, a low number of positively processed applications for refugee status and a lack of foreign diasporas, Poland is treated by refugees and economic migrants as a transit country on their way to Scandinavia and Western Europe. In addition, Poland does not participate in European Union (EU) relocation projects (Narkowicz 2018). At the same time, multiculturalism in Poland – as a country inhabited by many nations and nationalities – is a centuries-old phenomenon. However, the researcher Pasieka implies that there is a different overtone to this term in Poland: 'the Polish-centric narrative of the communist era has been replaced by another Polish-centric narrative, which ... has today taken the name of multiculturalism' (2013: 130). The researcher concludes that 'using the category of multiculturalism is a mechanism which, instead of making the society aware of the real diversity, strengthens Polish, and at the same time Polish-Catholic, domination' (Pasieka 2013). The Polish understanding of multiculturalism, based primarily on historical memory and sentiments, differs from the way it is understood in other European countries (Buchowski and Chlewińska 2010). In the super homogenous Polish society (Buchowski 2016), multiculturalism is not recognized as a normative-axiological category, that is, as the affirmation of the multiplicity and equality of cultures, since the mere coexistence of various nations and communities does not constitute multiculturalism.

Nevertheless, we have to bear in mind that in Poland (Polish mentality) two traditions have been fighting against each other for many, many years, which are reflected in political practice and the polarization of society. The first of these is the Jagiellonian tradition – showing the face of an open, multi-ethnic Poland (Jasienica 1963; Tazbir 1997). The second is the tradition of Piast Poland – closed and hermetic. These two strong currents played a significant role in the formation of further attitudes and approaches to the multiculturalism of Poland and the Poles' view of cultural diversity in society.

Due to its geographical location in the European Union, Poland appears to be a borderland country, where two traditions clash: the Western tradition, dominated by strong state organisms based on nations that emerged in the seventeenth century, and the tradition of Eastern influences (Janion 2014) where borders were fluid and poorly defined. This borderlessness also created a hybrid identity, borderland identity and so bonding identity and cross-border identity (Nikitorowicz 2019; Melosik 2021), as well as a cultural mindset that allowed people to survive in this kind of world (Nikitorowicz 2020). The past and memory are very important elements characterizing borderland countries, especially if we consider that until the time of transformation in 1989, the discourse in Poland was silent about resettlement, displacement and marginalization of the rights of national and ethnic minorities, showing their heritage through the prism of folklore.

As a nation afflicted by these historical processes, Poles have become accustomed to living in a practically homogenous national state. They have also become used to being migrants themselves, with around twenty million people claiming to be Polish or to have Polish ancestry living abroad (Pavliuk 2018: 184). Meanwhile, Polish society is becoming increasingly more intercultural. An increasing number of migrants, re-emigrants and refugees always challenges education with the task of embracing diversity and so is the case today. On the educational level, there is a new task of learning to live in an ethnically, nationally and culturally diverse society, to recognize 'the rights of national minorities and ethnic groups to cultivate their language, culture, preserve their national identity, … to introduce into the educational system of the dominant group the content devoted to national minority cultures and to show their values' (Lewowicki 2001: 12). This task is also connected with an attempt to deconstruct education and decolonize educational content included in Polish school textbooks and literature, necessary for creating inclusive, interculturally open learning environments. The need for decolonization in the Polish context draws attention to the complexity of factors forming the school as an environment for transmitting and acquiring knowledge and learning to live in peace. Decolonization in this aspect therefore requires at least two approaches:

- overcoming the monocultural, selective view of the world in and through education and thus looking at school as a place for diverse groups of children and adults with diverse needs and diverse sociocultural experiences and with access to diverse sources of knowledge about the world;
- overcoming the dominance of a monocultural (nationally centred) pattern of education as a measure of 'right' or 'good' education by recognizing inclusive and open education for others and their cultural worlds, enabling intercultural exchange in the sense of 'critical interculturality' (Walsh 2012) and mutual learning on an equal footing.

Hence, the aim of this chapter is to outline the specificity of the implementation of intercultural education in Polish monocultural schools. Bearing in mind the historical context, the author first outlines how intercultural education is understood and practiced in Poland (essentially, positioned between regional, European and global education). This is followed by an analysis of the aberration of intercultural education as 'teaching without context' as well as dilemmas connected with teaching about cultural diversity in schools, which were culturally homogenous for a long time but are becoming increasingly culturally diverse as a result of the growing migration processes.

The text is based on a review of interdisciplinary academic literature crucial for understanding the formation of intercultural education in Poland in the past three decades. The author refers to the first researchers of this subject in Poland and presents interdisciplinary contexts of the research, which shed light on the borderline multiculturalism of Polish society and challenges that this multiculturalism poses to school, education, teachers and the society.

Intercultural Education 'by Dry Run'

Intercultural education is 'an educational process aimed at understanding cultural differences and preparation for dialogical interaction with representatives of other cultures' (Markowska 1990: 111). Despite the fact that, since the 1990s, intercultural education has been present in the academic, educational and social discourse in Poland (Nikitorowicz 1995) – it has been written about, discussed and researched – cultural isolationism and homogeneity make it difficult to achieve its aims. Intercultural education seems to be incomplete in school curricula and the practice of Polish schools. This state of affairs is mainly related to non-educational factors, which include low cultural and national diversity among Polish society, polarization of social and political life as well as populist, nationalist movements and the linguistic legitimization of Polish anti-immigrant policy in media discourse (Cap 2018). It sanctions the conviction that there is no need to undertake activities oriented at shaping attitudes of openness and cooperation, intercultural and interreligious dialogue, joint problem-solving and reaching agreements, all of which is not without significance for the school environment. It is worth noting, however, that despite the monocultural orientation in the school environment, activities in the field of education for diversity and intercultural education are undertaken on the initiative of those employed in educational institutions and non-governmental organizations (Młynarczuk-Sokołowska and Szostak-Król 2019). They constitute a certain element of the education programme both in culturally homogenous schools and those with students from different cultural, national and ethnic backgrounds. However, it must be stressed that these activities are neither compulsory nor integrated nor planned in the long term. They are rarely part of the overall concept of school work and cooperation with the local environment. Hence, questions concerning the preparedness of Polish school and, above all, those who create it to build an intercultural pluralistic society – involved and responsible, enabling students to acquire intercultural competencies based on the theory of intercultural contact (Dąbrowa and Markowska-Manista 2014) – are justified. Research conducted so far on the readiness of Polish schools to work in a multicultural environment is incomplete, which makes it impossible to reliably describe the existing state of affairs. Conclusions concerning the preparation of schools in the intercultural field may be drawn from incidents of discriminatory and violent nature on cultural grounds (Chustecka et al. 2016) recorded in the school environment (and outside it) – whose number is increasing, mirroring the intensity of migration movements in Europe – moral panic as well as anti-migrant and nationalist rhetoric (Zielińska and Pasamonik 2021).

The regulations on education in force in the EU indicate that education for diversity, and in particular intercultural education, occupies an important place in preparing the younger generation to live in today's diverse world (Huber and Reynolds 2014). The reality seems to fall short of the interpretation and vision of the European community, as intercultural education has been only marginally implemented in Polish schools and, on top of that, education is being delivered 'by dry run' (Górak-Sosnowska 2011–12) about Others, without Others and without knowledge about their context (Markowska-Manista 2021). As such, it has little impact on shaping attitudes and skills of dialogue, cooperation, openness, respect, that is, those attitudes which condition the development of a multicultural society. Undoubtedly, the first of the essential conditions for the existence and effective implementation of intercultural education in the formal education system is political consent for this type of education and for the intercultural opening of schools (Januszewska and Markowska-Manista 2017) in the national educational policy. Second, teachers and educators carrying out didactic and educational work in a multicultural classroom should develop an open attitude towards people with different cultural and national origins. It primarily means thinking about students with migration experience not in terms of 'problem' but in terms of 'potential' (Markowska-Manista and Niedzwiedzka-Wardak 2014) and awareness of the relevance of an inclusive approach in a culturally diverse classroom. This multidimensional approach should be oriented not only towards equipping teachers with knowledge relating to current information about the world and the processes occurring in it, but also towards building social sensitivity and developing intercultural competences (Risager 2000).

According to this perspective, it is necessary to look for new solutions and educational strategies, and to develop forms of education based on teachers who are competently prepared to carry out professional tasks, which – in their assumptions – would take into account the fact that societies are diverse and the fact that diversification is growing in terms of ethnicity, culture, language, religion and values (Ogrodzka-Mazur 2018). If possible, in this perspective, these solutions would also consider the challenges that are part of the concept of mixing, interpenetration and hybridization in the process of communication between cultures and thus 'living in culturally different contexts' (Romanowska 2013: 150).

From Teaching in Monoculturalism to Teaching in Diversity

Since Poland joined the EU in 2004, the number of foreigners and Poles involved in migration processes, including return migration from abroad, has been on the rise (Anczyk et al. 2019). There is also an increase in the number of children born to mixed families and families with a migrant background who have been granted Polish citizenship and whose children were born in Poland. Thus, the profile of the student and parent is changing and becoming more intercultural, and with it, the circumstances of teaching in Polish schools. An awareness of the growing diversity implying diverse intercultural educational relations forces shift in the educational paradigm and a deconstruction of accepted patterns strictly connected with a monocultural view of the world. However, it is important to note the selective admission of Others and the strong selection processes, as clearly shown by the crisis on the Polish-Belarussian border and the political reluctance to admit and relocate refugees from Arab countries gripped by war or internal and humanitarian crises. By virtue of the Regulation of the Polish Minister of Interior and Administration of 13 March 2020, border traffic in Poland was suspended or restricted at selected border-crossing points. The list of foreigners authorized to cross the state border does not include persons seeking international protection (it includes, inter alia, foreigners holding Pole's Cards, foreign workers or spouses of Polish citizens).

Teaching about people from other countries and their cultures in a monocultural school attended until recently only by Polish students differs significantly from teaching about diversity in a culturally diverse school (both in terms of students and teachers). This applies both to the context of the interpenetration of multiple cultural worlds and the teaching atmosphere, the possibility of confronting the facts taught, and the use of diverse teaching methods and strategies. Importantly, it also refers to the awareness of the teaching staff of the importance of maintaining a didactic balance in the presence of students from different cultures and nationalities in the classroom. In the face of increasing migration, all these issues point to the need for reflection and rethinking of teaching in an increasingly culturally diverse school. It is important that education and school do not become a space for illusory actions (Dudzikowa 2013), as they equally harm all students (both Polish and foreign). This, in turn, affects the atmosphere, that is, relations and contact between school staff, students and parents, as well as the students' sense (or lack thereof) of connection with the school.

It should be mentioned that for many years the Polish education system functioned without the need to confront the so-called distant multiculturalism and intercultural relations from outside the CEE context (as was the case in Western Europe as a result of the process of increasing migration from non-European countries, especially former colonies).

Poland's post-Second World War 'homogeneity' is, as Zubrzycki (2001) points out, a product of the recent several decades of historical and political processes and events. However, those decades of teaching in monocultural schools, anchored in the construction of national identity, have built a pattern in which fragmentary, incomplete knowledge of different Others – the out-group – is still contrasted with its in-group. Parts of the world other than Europe and the United States are either barely or very stereotypically mentioned in school textbooks, reinforcing the Eurocentric narrative. The transmission of this knowledge is repeatedly based *on the written word and images* in textbooks and fiction (Zamojska 2013), which are full of colonial stories about the world and which fail to connect history with an understanding of the present. They often lack reliable educational commentary (Liebel 2022). In addition, they are not embedded in the current context and refer to colonial content in a way that reinforces the colonial perspective and does not allow the students to understand various points of view. As a result, they reproduce stereotypical images of the Other, Orientalist clichés; narratives about the Other as alien and distant; and affect the perception of migrants and refugees arriving in Poland.

Kuleta-Hulboj (2020) also points out that the dominant political discourse in Poland has a strong influence on curricula as it emphasizes national culture and values and stresses Polish martyrdom and heroism, which implies a turn towards historical sentiments and may result in a limited view of national identity and citizenship. In addition, the pupils' school experience resulting from the hidden school curriculum, which interweaves teaching content with words and images of subjective opinions of teachers, may affect relations and atmosphere in the school classroom. Teachers in a culturally diverse classroom – by virtue of the functions they perform, the influence they exert on students and the strength of the educational message in the explicit and implicit school curriculum – are key elements in the process of building sociocultural capital and effecting social change (Markowska-Manista and Niedźwiedzka-Wardak 2014). Their role and influence is also related to perpetuating stereotypes or breaking them down and counteracting social and cultural inequalities. This makes us think of education in a changing school as a process in which we recognize not only the transformations and challenges, but also the presence and needs of diverse groups of students and teachers related to the need to decolonize educational content.

Every school in Poland, which until recently was 'monocultural' in its own way, tries, often 'in the dark', to implement intercultural education related to the presence of children from different cultures and nationalities. It does this as much as it can, as much as it wants to (the populist, nationalist or neoliberal discourse should be taken into account here), using both colonial and postcolonial lenses to communicate, describe and explain similarities and differences in relation to the increasingly diverse Polish reality. An important element in the implementation of intercultural education and transmission of non-stereotypical knowledge at school is the preparation of teachers for such activities and the teaching methods and approaches they use (Markowska-Manista 2019). The work of each teacher takes place in the specific conditions of particular schools that are situated in particular contexts. It is influenced by many interrelated factors and by the teachers themselves with their cultural scripts, their experience and their approach to teaching and their world views.

On the Need for Change: Deconstruction and Decolonization in Education

Migrants and refugees living in Poland constitute only a small percentage of the country's thirty-eight million population. The low ethnic and national diversity and years of Eastern cultural isolation have meant that Poles' knowledge of foreigners living in Poland and foreigners who have chosen Polish citizenship and migrated to Poland is selective. Compared to the old EU countries, Poland has a low percentage of students with migration and refugee experience in schools (albeit the number of foreign students enrolled in education in the Polish educational system increased from 9,610 in 2009 to 51,363 in 2019 [Jaśkowiak 2021]). Until recently, due to the distribution of foreigners in refugee centres located far from urban centres, the presence of foreign children in Polish schools has been largely limited (Pędziwiatr et al. 2019).

There is an even smaller percentage of foreign teachers working in Polish schools (dominated by linguists and, in a small number, so-called intercultural assistants).

With the exception of national and ethnic minorities, whose educational rights are guaranteed by the Act on National and Ethnic Minorities of 2005, people with migration experience (except for the Polish community abroad and repatriates from the East) have been historically absent from Polish society.

Moreover, in recent years there has been no strategy for intercultural openness towards migrants and refugees related to the so-called global migration crisis. The humanitarian crisis on the Polish-Belarussian border at the end of 2021 exposed the polarization of Polish society on the issue of migrants and refugees. Moreover, this lack of strategy reveals the helplessness of teachers with regard to communication and interaction with students in both mono- and multicultural classrooms about the real and close – happening 'just around the corner' – tragic situation of children and adults stuck in the border strip. It revealed the problems of confusion about who are migrants and who are refugees, of being lost in a jungle of information, of fake news and of not being able to recognize what is true and what is false in borderline situations when human life is at stake, regardless of nationality. The conditions for intercultural education are becoming more complicated, especially since the Polish education system has for many years functioned without the need to confront multiculturalism (Lewowicki 2021) and the problems related to the construction of intercultural relations, solving conflicts with cultural background and cooperation at the meeting point of cultures from outside the CEE cultural circle. These situations indicate the need for a deconstruction of existing education, including with regard to perpetuated stereotypes and the absence of curricula promoting cultural diversity in schools. The increasing number of students with migration experience (mainly children of economic migrants) requires a revision of school curricula to include subjects and educational activities oriented towards embracing diversity and developing intercultural communication to promote the right of non-discrimination for all students and teachers.

Polish monocultural schools transforming into multicultural ones also lack strategies for teaching cultural competences which are necessary for successful coexistence of the younger generation in a multicultural world (Pająk-Ważna 2013). There is also insufficient current research on identifying the situations and needs of teachers working in culturally diverse schools with students from diverse cultural contexts. Undoubtedly, this is related to the fact that the majority of transit migrants and refugees crossing the Polish border did not consider Poland as a destination. Hence, teachers' knowledge, their intercultural needs and their competences in this field were treated marginally and reinforced the belief that these 'yesterday's' teachers, in the 'day before yesterday's' schools will be able to teach 'today's' students to solve tomorrow's problems (This sentence appears on many websites in relation to the state of the Polish school, burning educational problems and the lack of preparedness of teachers to work in schools in the twenty-first century).

Undoubtedly, the most important thing is creating an awareness among the teaching staff – as well as schools as institutions raising and educating young generations – about the need and importance of conducting anti-discriminatory intercultural education especially in the field of civic education – an education resulting from the need to produce students who base their actions on democratic and humanistic values.

From the perspective of inclusive pedagogy, the school, appearing as an epicentre of constructing new knowledge, assumes participation, emancipation and subjectivity of all students. Thus, it is supposed to be a place for shaping multidimensional dialogical relations between the more- and less-privileged individuals and groups, as well as for defining meanings, which – as an assumption – allow for the reduction of stereotypes and prejudices related to multiple otherness – both in the perspective of internal educational practices and external integration activities.

Challenges and Opportunities of Teaching about Diversity

Intercultural education, which Nikitorowicz pointed out as crucial for differentiating border societies (in the context of Eastern Europe) as early as 1995, today requires a decolonial approach in order to be able to teach responsibly about diversity in conditions of multidimensional cultural processes of differentiation. After almost three decades, intercultural education in the Polish European borderland is still a void, a taboo subject in school curricula and in the academic training of teachers. Polish schools have stopped at implementing the postulate of regional education, cultivating the heritage of national and ethnic minorities and theoretical understanding of multiculturalism without a deeper reflective look at the need for internationalization of education and preparation of prospective and professionally active teachers. Moreover, we lack spaces and places open to intercultural integration in local communities, which is evidenced by the location of centres for asylum seekers in remote territories in the Republic of Poland. Nation-centred education is currently taking over the place of intercultural education in the space of educational institutions by educating citizens of the nation and relegating the education of citizens of the world to a secondary role. This is demonstrated by school projects whose unilateral aim is to build a lasting emotional bond with the mother country and to strengthen civic awareness and patriotism. Among examples of this approach are actions militarizing the education of students, initiated by schools during the 2021–2 migration crisis ('A card for border defenders', 'Standing behind Polish soldiers', 'Children drawing for the defenders of our borders'), based on stereotypes, reinforcing divisions (in-group and out-group) and representing people in crisis on the Polish-Belarussian border as a threat.

Intercultural education and education supporting the process of intercultural integration enter Polish schools 'through the back door' or are smuggled into the school reality by pedagogues – enthusiasts. And yet, a Polish school has enough autonomy to decide on its own about the most important values and ways of conducting didactic and educational activities. Each school has the right to create its own mission, defining in it the values most important for the school community. Schools create their own preventive and educational programmes, which must be accepted by the parents' representation or be created with their participation, and which are the basis for everyday practical activities. The Education Act, which sets the legal framework for the system, has an important preamble since 1991, referring to the values that are fundamental to the whole system. The preamble has remained unchanged after the amendment and renaming of the act in December 2016. It reads:

> Education in the Republic of Poland is common good of the whole society; it is guided by the principles contained in the Constitution of the Republic of Poland, as well as by the indications contained in the Universal Declaration of Human Rights, the International Covenant on Civil and Political Rights and the Convention on the Rights of the Child. Education and upbringing – while respecting the Christian system of values – is based on universal principles of ethics. Education and upbringing serve to develop in young people a sense of responsibility, love for the country and respect for the Polish cultural heritage, while opening to the values of European and world cultures. The school shall provide each pupil with the conditions necessary for his/her development, prepare him/her to fulfil family and civic duties based on the principles of solidarity, democracy, tolerance, justice and freedom. (Act of 14 December 2016 on Educational Law, in force since 1 September 2017)

The above quotation clearly indicates the possibility of implementing intercultural education which appears as a holistic approach to teaching (Ogrodzka-Mazur 2018), based on the awareness that good teaching always takes place in relation to the students we teach, the community in which we teach, the culture of the school and the classroom, and the context in which the lessons are taught, created and co-created by the students. So it is important that the school is prepared for cultural diversity and operates on the basis of nurtured intercultural relationships. Of course, there are no ready-made solutions in school practice; the multiculturality of a school class as well as its monoculturalism can both contribute to integration and become a ground for conflicts and problems, far beyond the educational dimension.

Deconstructing patterns in education and decolonizing education is a long-term process of change embedded in reflective curricula and reflective teachers. Taking this approach, while not overstepping one's cultural heritage, makes it possible to overcome stereotypical ways of seeing and viewing the world and to fill in the gaps to access to recognized sources of knowledge. At the same time, it means providing an educational space for those whose stories and voices have not been taken into account (narratives of migrants, refugees). Decolonizing school curricula usually involves a fundamental revision of who teaches, how they teach, what the subject is and how teaching takes place within it (Moncrieffe et al. 2019). In this approach, any good curriculum should take into account the diversity of students taught by reflective teachers and relate to the multi-textual background of the classroom, school and community in which the teaching process takes place (Janus-Sitarz 2020).

This fact is important given the growing cultural diversity in Polish schools both in the local context – growing economic and educational migration from neighbouring countries (Ukraine, Belarus) – and in the global context related to the mobility of Poles and international migration flows.

Conclusion

The twentieth century was one of displacement (Borodziej et al. 2014), temporary or permanent, voluntary or forced migration. Millions of people were expelled or displaced, forced to flee to escape war, persecution, repression, oppression and starvation, facing threats to their lives because of their nationality, religion, culture and origin. The twenty-first century seems to be a continuation of these processes. From historical experience, we know how fluid the boundary between agreement, tolerance and manifestations of fanaticism is. Fanaticism which generates cultural, linguistic and territorial xenophobia (Kossak-Główczewski 1999) leads to acts of aggression, stigmatization or a latent form of adaptation of the Other. Communication and interaction among representatives of different religions, cultures and traditions may result in closing or opening to the world, breaking or strengthening prejudice and stereotypes. However, lack of intercultural education linking minorities and majorities can also lead to new antagonisms, neocolonial domination, aggravated hate speech and escalation of ethnic, religious and cultural conflicts (Grant 1994; Mikiewicz 2003). Golka writes that 'there is no single recipe for safe multiculturalism. When it seems that all its conditions have been met, something dangerous may emerge from the depths of human nature and demands food, unleashing hell. We have only one answer to this that we have to nurture: treating multiculturalism as a value' (1997: 60).

In the context of CEE, transnational movements will grow stronger, and the process of sociocultural differentiation will intensify. The key challenge for the countries of the European Union, including Poland, is to achieve a state in which the civic integration of people from different social and cultural contexts can be reconciled with disintegration, or cultural differentiation, understood as the preservation of its own canons (Krzysztofek 2003). Civic integration together with respecting the 'right to difference' is a postulate of almost all models of desired multiculturalism constructed today. In this form, it is also present in the documents of international organizations: the Council of Europe, the UN, UNESCO and the European Union. The directives contained therein are the determinants of standards of limited democracy, giving the statute of equality to minorities and majorities at the civic level, without interfering in the changes of cultural identity of the inhabitants, thus 'without making them culturally similar' (Krzysztofek 2003: 90). The above-mentioned international standards on how to treat the rights and freedoms of individuals from culturally different groups are a condition for being part of a democratic world.

Today, the apotheosis of multicultural diversity under the influence of social, cultural and political changes is intensifying. The concept of multiculturalism as defined by the authors of the book *U progu wielokulturowości* (At the Threshold of Multiculturalism) means 'the existence of differences in the discursive order, depending on its occurrence in a particular geographical, political or even philosophical context' (Kempny et al. 1997: 8). The world is becoming more and more multicultural, and in its multifaceted dimensions, global societies strive for integration across divisions, while local communities try to protect their group cultural distinctiveness. The planes of multiculturalism overlap, intermingle, interact, coexist with each other and alongside each other. Multiculturalism is an important attribute, a constitutive feature specific to the shape of European and non-European societies (Chromiec 2004).

Analysing the situation in Polish schools, several important regularities can be identified which are key to understanding why the decolonization of the teaching of cultural diversity seems to be a necessary tool here for building an intercultural opening of the educational institution (school) for diverse groups of pupils and a place where everyone, regardless of nationality, will feel safe. On the one hand, due to the increasing migration and re-immigration, the Polish school is becoming more and more multicultural. On the other hand, the national education policy tends to reinforce its monocultural, patriotically oriented character. This is done through the strong centralization and nationalization of the educational system, the enculturative slant in the curricula and the strengthening of the control apparatus over teachers' work. Control and lack of autonomy in turn reinforces the mechanisms of symbolic violence and deprives teachers of the right to raise and educate students who are open to diversity, are critical and are aware of the challenges of protecting the rights and freedoms of all. What and how we teach at school is the result of actions planned (top-down) by educational institutions. Today it is not enough to teach about Others and their cultures 'by dry run', and thus to implement the postulates of intercultural education understood as the transmission of knowledge about traditions, customs or works of culture, which highlight differences in lifestyles in different countries and on different continents.

Years of pushing the policy of a culturally homogenous country have contributed to changes in knowledge and attitudes, resulting in a long-term underestimation of minorities and foreigners in Polish society and the baseless fear of strangers (Goździak 2021). Instead of educating for the present and the future, creating a supportive, diverse, anti-discriminatory space, the school, trapped in the past and based on resentment, seems to rely on asymmetries, to exert pressure through cultural patterns, to form and indoctrinate through the transmission and dissemination of a uniform cultural canon. These aspects imply the need to question the unequal postcolonial constellation of the transmission of knowledge about the world and to revise the dominant educational standards that claim the only access to the 'right' knowledge about reality and truth. This is because they exclude many other ways of thinking and knowing based on the exchange of cross-cultural knowledge and mutual learning on equal terms. Hence, intercultural teaching in the Polish context needs an emancipatory and critical approach which, while recognizing the value of the multiplicity of diverse forms of knowledge, performs a transformative task aiming at decolonization (Walsh 2018).

The school is only one place (among educational environments) in which the process of forming attitudes towards one's own culture and the cultures of Others is carried out through the curriculum and within the framework of intercultural relations (or the lack thereof). There will always be different groups and individuals in every society. The presence of pupils with migration experience in Polish schools enriches the educational process, makes intercultural education a real process of intercultural communication and constitutes a value for the school, the pupils, the teachers and the majority society.

References

Act of 14 December 2016 on Educational Law, in force since 1 September 2017. Available online: https://www.ilo.org/dyn/natlex/natlex4.detail?p_isn=105967&p_lang=en (accessed 10 December 2021).

Anczyk, A., H. Grzymała-Moszczyńska, A. Krzysztof-Świderska and J. Prusak (2019), 'Wielokulturowość nowym wyzwaniem etycznym w pracy polskich psychologów szkolnych i akademickich', *Psychologia Wychowawcza*, 57: 126–38.

Borodziej, W., S. Holubec and J. von Puttkamer (2014), *Mastery and Lost Illusions: Space and Time in the Modernization of Eastern and Central Europe*. München: De Gruyter Oldenbourg, https://doi.org/10.1524/9783110364316.

Buchowski, M., and K. Chlewińska (2010), 'Tolerance and Cultural Diversity Discourses in Poland, Accept-Pluralism Project Report 2010/09'. Available online: https://ec.europa.eu/migrant-integration/library-document/tolerance-and-cultural-diversity-discourses-poland_en (accessed 10 December 2021).

Buchowski, M. (2016), 'Making Anthropology Matter in the Heyday of Islamophobia and the Refugee Crisis: The Case of Poland', *Český Lid*, 103: 51–67.

Cap, P. (2018), ' "We Don't Want Any Immigrants or Terrorists Here": The Linguistic Manufacturing of Xenophobia in the Post-2015 Poland', *Discourse & Society*, 29 (4): 380–98.

Chromiec, E. (2004), *Dziecko wobec obcości kulturowej*, Gdańsk: Gdańskie Wydawnictwo Psychologiczne.

Chustecka, M., E. Kielak and M. Rawłuszko (2016), *Edukacja antydyskryminacyjna. Ostatni dzwonek! O deficytach systemu edukacji formalnej w obszarze przeciwdziałania dyskryminacji i przemocy motywowanej uprzedzeniami. Raport z badań*, Warszawa: Towarzystwo Edukacji Antydyskryminacyjnej.

Dąbrowa, E., and U. Markowska-Manista (2014), 'Contact Theory in Multicultural School Praxis', *International Forum for Education School Quality and Culture*, 1 (7): 80–100.

Davies, N. (1981), *God's Playground. A History of Poland, Vol. 1: The Origins to 1795, Vol. 2: 1795 to the Present*, Oxford: Oxford University Press.

Dudzikowa M. (2013), 'Wprowadzenie', in M. Dudzikowa and K. Knasiecka-Falbierska (eds), *Sprawcy i/lub ofiary działań pozornych w edukacji szkolnej*, 14–24, Kraków: 'Impuls'.

Główny Urząd Statystyczny (GUS) (2019), 'Populacja cudzoziemców w Polsce w czasie COVID-19'. Available online: https://stat.gov.pl/statystyki-eksperymentalne/kapital-ludzki/populacja-cudzoziemcow-w-polsce-w-czasie-covid-19,12,1.html (accessed 26 December 2021).

Golka, M. (1997), 'Oblicza wielokulturowości', in M. Kempny, A. Kapciak and S. Łodziński (eds), *U progu wielokulturowości*, 51–63, Warszawa: Oficyna Naukowa.

Górak-Sosnowska, K. (2011–12), 'Edukacja międzykulturowa a postawy wobec "Innych" ', *Kwartalnik Kolegium Ekonomiczno-Społecznego Studia i Prace*, 4 (8): 51–66.

Goździak, E. M. (2021), 'Fortress Europe', in *Human Trafficking as a New (In)Security Threat*, 71–90, Cham: Palgrave Macmillan, https://doi.org/10.1007/978-3-030-62873-4_5.

Grant, N. (1994), *Ilustrowana historia konfliktów XX wieku*, Warszawa: Elipsa.

Huber, J., and C. Reynolds (2014), 'Developing Intercultural Competence through Education', Pestalozzi series No. 3, Council of Europe Publishing. Available online: https://rm.coe.int/developing-intercultural-enfr/16808ce258 (accessed 19 May 2022).

Janion, M. (2014), 'Poland between the West and East', *Teksty Drugie*, 1: 11–33.

Janus-Sitarz, A. (2020), 'Kali czy Nabu? Jaka literatura i jaki nauczyciel będą uczyć rozumienia drugiego człowieka?', *Polonistyka. Innowacje*, 11: 175–82.

Januszewska, E., and U. Markowska-Manista (2017), *Dziecko 'inne' kulturowo w Polsce. Z badań nad edukacją szkolną*, Warszawa: Akademia Pedagogiki Specjalnej.

Jasienica, P. (1963), *Polska Jagiellonów*, Warszawa: PIW.

Jaśkowiak, J. (2021), 'Interpelacja nr 26779 do ministra edukacji i nauki w sprawie nauki dzieci imigrantów'. Available online: https://www.sejm.gov.pl/sejm9.nsf/InterpelacjaTresc.xsp?key=C6UH87 (accessed 30 December 2021).

Kempny, M., A. Kapciak and S. Łodziński, eds (1997), *U progu wielokulturowości*, Warszawa: Oficyna Naukowa.

Kossak-Główczewski, K., ed. (1999), *Edukacja regionalna mniejszości narodowych i etnicznych*, Gdańsk: Uniwersytet Gdański.

Krzysztofek, K. (2003), 'Pogranicza i multikulturalizm w rozszerzonej Unii', *Studia Europejskie/Centrum Europejskie UW*, 1: 77–94.

Kuleta-Hulboj, M. (2020), 'The Critical and Postcolonial Perspectives on Global Education: The Case of Poland', *JSSE-Journal of Social Science Education*, 19 (4): 8–22.

Lewowicki, T. (2001), 'Wstęp', in Z. Jasiński and T. Lewowicki (eds), *Oświata etniczna w Europie Środkowej*, 11–16, Opole: Uniwersytet Opolski.

Lewowicki, T. (2017), 'Edukacja międzykulturowa – kilka lat później. Zmiana uwarunkowań, pytania o kondycję, wyzwania', *Edukacja międzykulturowa*, 2 (7): 19–36.

Lewowicki, T. (2021), 'Multiculturalism/Multinationalism and Multi- and Intercultural Education – An Essay on a Meandering Tradition and the Uneasy Modern Times (The Case of Poland)', *Edukacja Międzykulturowa*, 1 (14): 16–66.

Liebel, M. (2022), 'Kinder ohne Kindheit? Plädoyer für die Dekolonisierung der Kindheitsforschung und Kinderrechtspraxis', in P. D. Th. Knobloch and J. Drerup (eds), *Bildung in postkolonialen Konstellationen. Erziehungswissenschaftliche Analysen und pädagogische Perspektiven*, 139–76, Bielefeld: Transcript.

Mach, Z. (2010), 'Polskie tożsamości', in W. Kozub-Ciembroniewicz and B. Szlachta (eds), *Polska XX wieku*, 139–56, Kraków: Wydawnictwo Uniwersytetu Jagiellońskiego.

Markowska, D. (1990), 'Teoretyczne podstawy edukacji międzykulturowej', *Kwartalnik Pedagogiczny*, 4: 109–17.

Markowska-Manista, U. (2019), 'Migrant and Refugee Children in Polish Schools in the Face of Social Transformation', in C. Maier-Höfer (eds), *Die Vielfalt der Kindheit(en) und die Rechte der Kinder in der Gegenwart. Praxisfragen und Forschung im Kontext gesellschaftlicher Herausforderungen*, 79–100, Wiesbaden: Springer GmbH.

Markowska-Manista, U. (2021), 'Non-Contextual Teaching of Sensitive topics Focusing on Cultural Diversity in Polish Schools', *Rocznik Lubuski*, 47 (1): 143–58.

Markowska-Manista, U., and A. Niedźwiedzka-Wardak (2014), 'Mniejszości wzbogacające większość. O potencjale uczniów z odmiennym kontekstem kulturowym i możliwościach jego wykorzystania w warunkach wielokulturowości w polskiej szkole', in A. Wilczyńska (ed.), *Młodzież na biegunach życia społecznego*, 120–49, Warszawa: PWN.

Melosik, Z. (2021), 'Izolacjonizm mniejszości, hybrydyzacja tożsamości i dylematy edukacji międzykulturowej', *Edukacja Międzykulturowa*, 2 (15): 37–55.

Mikiewicz, P. (2003), 'Zagrożenia, konflikty i mnogie oblicza globalizacji', in E. Stadtmuller (ed.), *Wkraczając w XXI wiek – między globalizacją a zróżnicowaniem*, 13–28, Wrocław: Arboretum.

Młynarczuk-Sokołowska, A., and K. Szostak-Król (2019), 'Różnorodność i inkluzja w edukacji-wybrane aspekty wspierania uczniów z doświadczeniem migracji', in E. Śmiechowska-Petrovskij (ed.), *Różnorodność i inkluzja w edukacji-wybrane aspekty wspierania uczniów z doświadczeniem migracji*, 278–87, Warszawa: Fundacja Rozwoju Systemu Edukacji.

Moncrieffe, M., Y. Asare, R. Dunford and H. Youssef (2019), *Decolonising the Curriculum: Teaching and Learning about Race Equality*, Brighton: University of Brighton.

Narkowicz, K. (2018), '"Refugees Not Welcome Here": State, Church and Civil Society Responses to the Refugee Crisis in Poland', *International Journal of Politics, Culture, and Society*, 31 (4): 357–73.

Nikitorowicz, J. (1995), *Pogranicze. Tożsamość. Edukacja międzykulturowa*, Białystok: Trans Humana.

Nikitorowicz, J. (2019), 'Hybrydowa tożsamość na kulturowym pograniczu – potencjał i problem osobisty i grupowy?', *Annales Universitatis Mariae Curie-Skłodowska. Paedagogia-Psychologia*, 2 (32): 11–22.

Nikitorowicz, J. (2020), *Edukacja międzykulturowa w perspektywie paradygmatu współistnienia kultur*, Białystok: Uniwersytet w Białymstoku.

Ogrodzka-Mazur, E. (2018), 'Intercultural Education in Poland: Current Problems and Research Orientations', *Kultura i Edukacja*, 2: 65–82.

Pająk-Ważna, E. (2013), 'Teachers' Intercultural Competence and Teacher Education – A Case of Poland', *European Scientific Journal*, 9 (19): 318–22.

Pasieka, A. (2013), Wielokulturowość po polsku. O polityce wielokulturowości jako mechanizmie umacniania polskości, *Kultura i społeczeństwo*, 3: 129–55.

Pavliuk, O. (2018), 'Spojrzenie na termin Polonia – rozważania o tożsamości', in J. Malejka (eds), *Języki i kultury w kontakcie*, 184–97, Katowice: Wydawnictwo Uniwersytetu Śląskiego.

Pędziwiatr, K., M. Stonawski and J. Brzozowski (2019), *Imigranci w Krakowie w świetle danych rejestrowych*, Kraków: Centrum Zaawansowanych Badań Ludnościowych i Religijnych, Uniwersytet Ekonomiczny w Krakowie.

Puchalski, P. (2022), *Poland in a Colonial World Order. Adjustments and Aspirations, 1918–1939*, London: Routledge.

Risager, K. (2000), 'The Teachers' Intercultural Competence', *Sprogforum*, 18 (6): 14–20.

Romanowska, J. (2013), 'Transkulturowość czy trankulturacja? O perypetiach pewnego bardzo modnego terminu', *Zeszyty Naukowe Towarzystwa Doktorantów UJ Nauki Humanistyczne*, 6 (1): 143–53.

Tazbir, J. (1997), *Polska na zakrętach dziejów*, Warszawa: Wydawnictwo Sic!

Theiss, W. (1999), 'Pamięć społeczna i edukacja. Polsko-żydowska przeszłość w perspektywie międzykulturowej', *Wychowanie na co dzień*, 6: 3–7.

Walsh, C. E. (2012), *Interculturalidad, crítica y (de)colonialidad: ensayos desde Abya Yala*, Quito: Instituto Científico de Culturas Indígenas.

Walsh, C. E. (2018), 'Decoloniality in/as praxis', in W. D. Mignolo and C. E. Walsh (eds), On *Decoloniality: Concepts, Analytics, Praxis*, 13–102, Durham, NC: Duke University Press.

Zamojska E. (2013), 'Inny jako obcy. Imigranci w polskim dyskursie publicznym i edukacyjnym', *Studia Edukacyjne*, 28: 191–207.

Zielińska, I., and B. Pasamonik (2021), 'Polarizing Moral Panics: A Theory and Its Application to the Refugee Crisis in Poland', *Deviant Behavior*, doi: 10.1080/01639625.2021.2002672.

Zubrzycki, G. (2001), ' "We, the Polish Nation": Ethnic and Civic Visions of Nationhood in Post-Communist Constitutional Debates', *Theory and Society*, 30: 629–68.

2

A Cultural History of the Other in Curriculum Design Transformation and Practice

Rafael Filiberto Forteza Fernández

Introduction

Education is not repeating what textbooks say nor is it asking the students to regurgitate them. Education is an ideological enterprise enabling the students to resist oppression and build a better future. However, talking about ideology in education in Central and Eastern Europe after the demise of socialism seems, for many, a taboo, an eyebrow-raising topic, to the extent that the present and future generations are easy preys of the new wave of exploitation where historical domestic and Western elites reproduce their sociopolitical and -economic status, now under a new umbrella: neoliberalism in the age of globalization.

Russian public education for very many is of low quality and should be subject to changes to the extent that those who can afford it send their children to study abroad. The school, in the minds of not very few, is a place to obtain knowledge and skills to deal with the changes in technology, economy and the job market rather than prepare for life; in other words, this path suggested for the Russian school today is mostly 'technocratic' (Kirylo 2020: 17) while higher education seems to be driving towards the exacerbation of social problems (Lozovkaya et al. 2020). The narrow focus of this educational conception is an example of the dehumanization of pedagogy (Geduld et al. 2020) in close alignment with the ideology and policies of neoliberalism in its quest to create the homo economicus. This individual is 'an intelligent, single-minded, … and automated creature who, being fully aware of economic conditions, acts rationally solely on the basis of his or her personal interest' (Papadogiannis 2014: 51) to consistently make self-profiting individual choices regardless of the consequences to his social environment.

Contrary to the above neoliberal economically envisioned role of the Russian educational system, schools are to be conceived as institutions whose main role is to serve and improve society. Twenty years into the twenty-first century, a highly stratified and complex society such as the Russian as well as those of many others in the post-Soviet space are still begging for an education that addresses historical inequality and the many vices inherited from the turbulent twentieth-century local histories. Utopian though it may seem, empowering through education is approaching inequality from below, and thus contesting the hypocrisy of words enshrined in constitutions and the always poorly funded public policies addressing the manifestations and not the causes produced by social class divisions.

This chapter divorces itself from the traditional conception of the discipline *Lingvostranovedenie* (heretofore Language and Country Studies) by adopting a critical literacy approach to teacher formation and development. Its significance resides precisely in updating the components of the curriculum to effectively deal with the past and present historical and cultural representations in foreign language coursebooks as well as by giving voice to the students in glocalizing their dystopian present. In other words, it is a contribution to help decolonize the highly ideologized practices of foreign language teaching in neoliberal times (see Macedo 2019). In addition, this conception also paves the way for a practical course in foreign language teaching critical literacy.

Research in neoliberal ideology, its policies and its connection with foreign language teaching and discourse language teaching (Pennycook 2001, 2007, 2013; Kramsch 2010, 2013, 2017; Rigaser 2018; Gray 2000, 2010a, b, 2012; Blommaert 2005, 2010; Lakoff 1987; Lakoff and Johnson 1980, 1999; Block 2006, 2014, 2017, 2018; Block et al. 2012; Bori 2018) confirms the connection between English Language Teaching (ELT), the project of globalization and the neoliberal empire (Kumaravadivelu 2006) where English acts as the 'beachhead of globalization' (Block 2014: 115). In Russia, researchers on ELT (Forteza Fernandez 2019; Forteza Fernandez et al. 2020) and on Spanish as a foreign language (Forteza Fernandez and Rubtsova 2020) pin the denial or edulcoration of colonial atrocities and dirty episodes of Western history on the same agenda of world domination at a time where markets and technology are globalized. However, despite the unarguable ideological essence underlying language materials (dialogs, passages, exercises, visual support), teacher education in Russia is still focused on language teaching categories such as teacher language awareness (e.g. Thornbury 1997; Andrews 2007) and outdated structural definitions of discourse, discourse analysis and competence as well as communicative competence (e.g. Richards et al. 1985; Brown and Yule 1983; Hymes 1972; Canale and Swain 1980).

These conceptualizations deprive pre-service and in-service English language teachers of understanding textbooks as tools exercising power relations, much more when they no longer focus on native speaker culture but have become vehicles at the service of a neoliberal global culture (Hadley 2014), mostly communicated in English, by reproducing and legitimizing its discourse (Bori 2020). Moreover, the Language and Country Studies programme in Russia is conceived only as the UK and US cultural background necessary to teach English – a Western-centric epistemological construction – that ignores key areas of knowledge essential in the cultural history of the West (e.g. colonialism, slavery, the Age of Enlightenment) predating neoliberal globalization processes and the origin of political and socioeconomic issues such as inequality and discrimination in all its forms which are either silenced or distorted in ELT textbook discourse. In sum, the curricular articulation of Language and Country Studies with the contemporary developments in ELT plus the narrow vision of teacher formation are educational shortcomings, thus limiting the teacher's knowledge and skills to understand ELT textbook discourse and address the connection between the past and the present in the language classroom. This, in turn, makes teachers unwittingly complicit with promoting agendas of world domination (see Macedo 2019; Ricento 2000).

This chapter reports on the first pedagogical experience in curriculum design and implementation in the discipline Language and Country Studies, seen as a Cultural History of the Other (CHO, which is seen from the perspective of the colonized oppressed) in the third semester of a master's degree programme. This pedagogical experience carried out at the Foreign Languages and Translation Department at the Ural Federal University in Yekaterinburg, Russian Federation, during the academic year 2018–19, involved an international class of fourteen students from Russia, China, Vietnam, Syria and Ukraine working as language teachers or intending to specialize in other language-related professions.

The rationale behind the changes in Language and Country Studies towards a CHO perspective is, first, that ELT textbook themes and topics tend to erase or distort history (see Risager 2018) or edulcorate the present (see Forteza Fernandez et al. 2020), and second that teacher education must overtly be a political, ideological tool to understand the past-present connection and resist neoliberal globalization in the classroom, thus contesting the reproduction of the historical social division of classes which empower the rich in their quest to continue exploiting the disposed (Popkewitz 1991; Gentili 2004; Alexander and Potter 2005; Sayer 2005; Kumaravadivelu 2012; Paris and Alim 2017; Gudova et al. 2022).

Teaching about social class is teaching about the living heart of inequality for in its production and reproduction cycle it determines the individual's agency and affordances since the very moment of conception. That is, social class dictates the foetus's future position in a society (race, sex, ethnic origin or nationality, family, potential friends, habitus), and these, in turn, the entire life cycle from birth to adulthood and ultimately death in terms of access to health care, education, housing, work, income, food, among others, including life events such as who, when and where to marry and start a family, and social ones such as voice and representation. Besides, social class determines child and infant mortality rates, life expectancy and many other health indicators, including the likelihood to suffer certain diseases resulting from lifestyle or die from transmissible diseases. When the above is conceptualized within the North-South and East-West perspective, social class and thus inequality can be taught from a historical and socioeconomic perspective configurating the differences between world regions, countries and their regions on the basis not only of income but also of other constructs: citizenship-immigrant, white-Black, rich-poor, developed-developing (underdeveloped) which are at the core of the individual's historicity and subjectivity (see Milanovic 2010).

A Critique of Language and Culture Studies

The module 'World Culture and Professional Communication' of this master's degree programme conceptualization of the discipline Language and Cultural

Studies is still anchored in the past and in no way prepares the students to deal with the teaching of English in the twenty-first century. The objectives are stated in the form of *know* the periods of development, general and specific vocabulary, ethical and moral norms, humanistic values and their roles in the preservation of society. With that *knowledge*, it is supposed the student will be able to characterize historical periods in their socioeconomic, political and cultural processes guided by the principles of cultural relativism; however, conceiving characterization as an ability does not allow to see the essence of phenomena as a prerequisite to critique and transformation. From this perspective, the programme does not integrate with the students' future profession. In terms of content, more than 80 per cent of the discipline is devoted to Great Britain, and the rest to the United States; it dilutes in dynasties such as the Plantagenets, Lancasters, Tudors, and Stuarts with little or no impact on today's configuration of the world. Topics such as imperial wars during the British Empire and Victorian England precede the Second World War disregarding First World War and the pre-war colonial period and its relationship with the Enlightenment. In addition, though the content is to some extent pertinent, the four hours devoted to US history and culture ignore the role of this country in world affairs in the past two hundred years. In other words, the discipline's objectives and content lack continuity as the British-focused scope ignores the dynamics and interconnections of domestic events and their relationship with geopolitics in historical processes as well as phenomena such as inequality, racism, discrimination, also common to other countries in Western Europe and the United States in their interaction with the rest of the world and which are essential to understand the global village and glocalize events. In sum, this curricular construct helps anchor English only as a soft skill, disempowers teachers as social agents of change and limits not only their agencies and affordances, but also their students' potentials for empowerment.

Educating for Reading the Word and the World

Based on the critique of the discipline Language and Country Studies, this section of the chapter outlines the educational basis upon which the changes were introduced as well as the components of the programme in terms of its unique objective, course content – organized around historical periods – methods, material aids and evaluation.

Language and Country Studies as Education in the CHO

The teaching learning process of Language and Country Studies as a CHO is conceived as three distinct processes: *instruction*, comprised by the content and skills in the syllabus; *development* of intellectual skills, that is, finding, discriminating, organizing, processing and communicating information – all of which also imply taking sides for the formation of disciplinary cognitive paradigms. Both processes facilitate a qualitatively higher one: *education*, based on the development of convictions (Álvarez de Zayas 2000) premised on ethical and moral principles for a 'critical consciousness' (Freire 2005). The above envisions a teaching learning process where the student is led to recognize 'that History is time filled with possibility and not inexorably determined – that the future is problematic and not already decided, fatalistically' (Freire 2000: 26). This conception is 'situated within a theory of cultural production and viewed as an integral part of the way in which people produce, transform, and reproduce meaning, some of economic origin, such as inequality, rich and poor; and others socially constructed such as race, native speaker, and cast that are the bases of discrimination'. Therefore, Language and Country Studies is 'seen as a medium that constitutes and affirms the historical and existential moments of lived experience that produce a subordinate or a lived culture. The discipline is "eminently political" …, [and as such] … is taught "within the context of a theory of power relations and an understanding of social and cultural reproduction and production"' (Freire and Macedo 1987: 98) of historically unequal relations within and between social systems.

Language and Country Studies focuses, therefore, on *inequality*; that is, 'the conditions that allow certain groups to dominate over others [in the form of] a power relationship' (Mohanty 2018: 6 cited by Webster 2020: 221) as a 'result of history (colonialism), the skewed nature of international relations (neo-colonialism) or policy (structural adjustment, neo-liberalism)' (Menon 2020: 23). This focus on inequality seeks to foster opposition to all forms of discrimination from an ethical and moral perspective.

From an ethical perspective, the discipline is aimed at planting the seeds of social resistance against any form disempowering the Other because of, for instance, race, sex, sexual orientation, disability or ascribed social status. The moral perspective, on the other hand, sides with Chomsky (2017: 16) on the future graduates' responsibility as intellectuals 'to speak the truth and to expose lies' about political, economic and social injustice.

Language and Country Studies as a CHO

This conception of Language and Country Studies as a CHO draws from curricular theory and practice (Drake and Burns 2004; Nation and Macalister 2010) and its localization (Demarest 2015). The discipline's curriculum and its development entirely adopted Kalantzis and Cope's view (2012) that pedagogy is 'consciously designed to promote learning', 'the creation of knowledge' and further the capacity to create it (273) and the reflexive curriculum to 'allow [the formation and development of] alternative knowledge pathways to achieve social goals (276). As a result, based on a Critical Literacy (CL) conception (Freire and Macedo 1987; Freire 2000, 2005; Macedo 2019), the objective of Language and Country Studies as a CHO is to raise the students' critical consciousness, thus facilitating the adoption of ethical and moral positions in 'read[ing] the word and the world' (Freire and Macedo 1987) from a social class perspective in a world where global and local capitalist rules continually interact in the creation of inequality.

This discipline focuses on the historical roots of political and socioeconomic inequality that as an objective category manifests itself in structural exclusion and allows for the production and reproduction of socially constructed forms of discrimination such as race, colour, gender and sexuality, nationality, religion, disability and education among other aspects of identity (see Francis et al. 2020).

Content: The choice was based on three premises: (1) the study of in-the-market ELT textbook multimodal contents; (2) needs analysis based on the students' deficiencies noted in previous academic years; (3) the students' own suggestions. The programme, in its new version, in no way eliminates what is officially sanctioned. The CHO approach of the subject meant the addition, reorganization and a CL focus of contents. That is, the subject is organized in general themes subdivided into topics that offer a general view of historical development in interconnected cycles and their global and regional manifestations rather than the specificities of events chronologically organized but disconnected from the environment in which they occur. Mostly based on Hobsbawm's historical narrative style (see Hobsbawm 1975, 1989 1996), this approach offers a better perspective to understand the creation of inequality since the beginning of globalization processes in 1492 and promote the de-Westernization of academic thought.

Methods: The teaching learning process methodology in lectures and seminars facilitate formation and development of multi-literacies (Cope and Kalantzis 2015) in the form of an inverted or flipped classroom (see Ozdamli and Aşiksoy 2016; Brown 2016; Reidsema et al. 2017; Santos Green et al. 2017) where, based on previous knowledge in groups or individually, the students become active participants in lectures that prepare the field for the expansion of knowledge and development of critical thinking skills through independent research in seminars, rather than repeating the learning materials. In all cases, the students are encouraged to reflect and argue how the course contents were seen from the perspective of their native cultural history. This move should promote debate and allow the students to adopt informed ethical and moral positions.

The extra-class work is aimed at reinforcing independent work skills. The students organized in the form of a learning community must write a multimodal paper on a socioeconomic and political topic of interest and its local manifestations.

Material Aids: Multimodal means of knowledge communication that include, besides the written word, film, sound, pictures, graphics, statistics, artwork, alternative history websites, blogs and social media among others.

Evaluation: As this subject has no final exam, the results include only two levels: passed or failed which are based on the formative assessment of the student's engagement in all the learning activities along the course: participation in lectures, seminars and the extra-class work.

Table 2.1 Overview of Historical Topics

Theme	Topics
The Feudal Society in the European Middle Ages	• Feudalism as an Economic System. Serfdom. The Catholic Church and Women in the Middle Ages. The Inquisition. The Fate of Jews. The Discourse of Anthropology and Its Uses in the Medieval Period. The Portuguese in Africa: Black Slaves in Europe before 1492.
Empire Building	• The Spanish and Portuguese Colonial Empires in America. The Columbian Exchange. Evangelization and Slavery. Spanish America Riches and European Modernity. The End of the Spanish Golden Century. • The British Thirteen Colonies: Slavery and Indentured Servants. Women's Rights. Native Americans and Colonization. Colonial Slave Trade and Rivalry. Anglo-French Connections against 'Islamic' Resistance. Britain, India and the French. Imperial Interdependence in Indochina.
Revolution as Change of Master	• England (1640–60), American Independence from Britain (1775–83), Haiti (1797), France (1789–99), Latin American Independence (1808–26), the American Civil War (1861–5), Cuban Wars of Independence (1868–98): Spanish Concentration Camps in the Island and American Intervention. • The Industrial Revolution in Britain, Europe and the US (1760–1840). • The Hypocrisy of European Enlightenment. Islamic Roots. Philosophy and Reality in Europe (the Working Class, Women, Child Labour), The Colonies and Independent Countries. Russian Religious Philosophy. Framing the US Constitution, the Slaves and Native Americans. Independent Latin America and the Indigenous and Slave Population. The Scramble of Africa (1881–1914): Concentration Camps. First World War. The Birth of Soviet Russia and Western Intervention in the Civil War. Communism and World Revolution. • Development before and after Colonization. Views of the Colonized Other through Case Studies and Literature (China, India, Haiti, Amerindians, Palestine and Congo). The English-Speaking First Circle (Canada, New Zealand and Australia). Different Way of Development.
Industrial Capitalism	• The Working Class during the Great Depression. US Interventions in Latin America before and after Second World War. Spain in the 1920s and 1930s: The Civil War. The International Brigades. The Spanish Civil War as a Rehearsal of Fascism in Europe and the Politics of Appeasement. World Industry and Finances in the Building of Fascism. Nazi Ideology, the Jews and Slavs. The Munich Agreement and the Ribbentrop-Molotov Pact. The Pre-War Literature and the Arts. • Second World War • The Munich Agreement and the Molotov-Ribbentrop Pact. The Onset of the War. The German Blitzkrieg. The West-East Fronts. The Japanese Occupation of Manchuria. Japanese Colonialism in Asia. Pearl Harbor and the War in the Pacific. D-Day and the Soviet Support. Tehran and Yalta. The German Defeat and the Division of the Country. The Potsdam Conference Agreements. The Japanese Defeat: Hiroshima and Nagasaki. Two Systems in Europe. The Paris Agreements. The Bretton Woods Conference. The Foundation of the UN: Objectives. The General Assembly and the Security Council. Membership in 1945.

(continued)

Table 2.1 Overview of Historical Topics (continued)

Theme	Topics
The Cold War	• The Cold War: From Alliance to Antagonism. Ideological Confrontation. NATO and the Warsaw Pact. A Bipolar World. The Truman Doctrine (1947) and the Soviet Blockade of Berlin (1948). The Iron Curtain. The Soviet Nuclear Bomb. Independence and Partition of India and the Creation of Israel. • The War in Korea (1950–3). The Marshal Plan and the Economic Boom in the 1950s. The Left in Europe. Unequal Development in the West and the Soviet Union. The Situation of the Working Class. Hungary (1956) and Prague (1968). The Civil Rights Movement in the US. Unrest in Europe. The Cuban Missile Crisis and the Bay of Pigs Invasion. The Vietnam War and Extension to the Rest of Indochina. • Decolonization and National Liberation Movements in Africa. Fascism in Latin America. The Cold War Manifestations. Economic Issues in the West and in the Socialist Countries. Afghanistan and the Demise of the Soviet Union.
Financial Capitalism	• Globalization and Neoliberalism. World and National Financial Institutions. A Unipolar World. Global and Regional Organizations. The UN Today: The Security Council and the General Assembly, BRICS, the EU, SCO. Neoliberalism as a Policy Package, a Mode of Governance and an Ideology. The Application of Neoliberalism in Chile and Russia in the 1990s. Neoliberalism in Education and Healthcare. Knowledge Economies. • The Post-Truth Era in Politics, Economics and Society. Global Warming. The Digital Divide. Islam and Terrorism. Immigration. Proxy Wars. Social Class. Overt and Covert Discrimination. Sanctions as an Imperial Policy. Towards a Multipolar World. The Ethical and Moral Responsibility of Intellectuals and Educators. Trumpism. The Post-Covid-19 Future?

Source: Own elaboration.

Results and Conclusions

The implementation revealed weaknesses in undergraduate formation at the cognitive level in the processing of information and production of multimodal texts as well as in the development of social skills. Noticeably, the student showed poor social skills such as responsibility, cooperation and constructive criticism in teamwork.

At the cognitive levels, and partly attributable to undergraduate formation, the students' lack of an extensive English specialist vocabulary coupled with background knowledge on the course topics significantly affected the quality of learning and much more when their understanding of the bibliographical sources was considerably limited by the complexities posed by the grammar of written academic English. To tackle this situation, many recurred to machine translation into Russian, Chinese or Arabic followed by retranslation of their seminar answers into English. The same was perceived during lectures. Many of the Chinese students recorded the lectures and later used voice translation into their L1. These types of classroom behaviour reveal shortcomings in undergraduate formation caused by the teaching of content subjects in the students' mother tongue (MT). In addition, and owing also to the same problem, some students used sources written in their MT that lacked the postcolonial focus of the subject, thus affecting the full learning process within the scope of the subject. These background knowledge problems were partially solved first with the provision of more such information on each topic, the assignment of extra reading and visual materials in addition to detailed instructions referring to their preparation for lectures and seminars. These included discriminating among sources, choosing and organizing relevant information for the seminar, preparing the answer in multimodal format, and learning to effectively deliver it to the rest of the group. Nevertheless, some of these problems persisted well into the course mid-term.

The problems in lexico-grammar were approached from a different perspective. First, changes were made to the Practical English Language Course that runs parallel to the CHO. These included dictionary activities with the *Webster's Dictionary*, word choices (Latinate versus phrasal verbs), pronunciation, register and the use of synonyms. Second, several topics dealing with the densely information-packed grammar of academic English, for example, noun phrase structures, clause combinations and embedding among others as well as the different layers of meaning in a clause and hedging also became part of this course.

Another difficulty detected during the course implementation was the students' belief – and most probably out of habit – that the answers to a seminar question was to regurgitate book content without previously discriminating, analysing and processing information is a major limitation in learning how to read the word and world in CL terms. Because the bibliographical collection at the students' disposal was vast and varied,[1] often offering different viewpoints on the same topic, the very methodology of the flipped classroom implying discussion, exchange of knowledge that means, to a great extent, teaching their peers and be subject of their appraisal, the preparation instructions were scaffolded from the second to the fourth seminar. This process implied increasing the level of independence by decreasing the amount of help lent to students and putting more responsibility on their academic *ethos* (credibility). This approach improved, to some extent, academic exchange in the classroom. In other words, seminar answers, *logos,* had to be worthy enough to elicit positive learning responses from the audience, *pathos.* As a result, the students, rather than giving an oral response, started preparing short presentations with illustrations, cited their sources –most often not more than two or three – and seemed to be more convincing. Nevertheless, when dealing with contradictory viewpoints, it was evident that the students' were not ready to derive conclusive arguments based of their own analysis and assume an informed ethical position. This undoubtedly affected glocalization of similar events in their own countries as was the case of revolutions, civil wars, the outcomes of Second World War and neoliberal policies.

Organized in four small multinational groups, the extra classwork on the production and reproduction of inequality in Latin America, Africa, the Middle East and Asia on the *Scholar* platform revealed that the students could accomplish the objectives. Though individual in terms of evaluation, this work was to a great extent the product of peer collaboration. Developed on the learning platform *Scholar*[2] from the University of Illinois in Urbana-Champaign, Unite States, each of the fourteen student's production was automatically assessed on focus on the task, knowledge displayed while doing the task and help to other community members while doing the task by means of 228 metric values derived from 70.050 total data points collected across all the members of the learning community (see Kalantzis and Cope 2012 for more information on the pedagogical underpinnings of the *Scholar* platform).

In general, the students' work sometimes lacked coherence and had problems in flow of ideas and language accuracy as a result of poor revision and editing. These shortcomings in the *knowledge* and *focus* learning dimensions, however, were not so serious if appraised as a product because the overall text quality score was almost 83 per cent, and 75 per cent of the requests for publishing were accepted after serious revision; however, if judged by what the *Scholar* assessment system calculated in the *help* dimension, the development of social skills such as responsibility, cooperation and constructive criticism in teamwork was poor. This means the above scores would have been much higher had the team members helped each other. In other words, once the group agreed on the distribution of tasks, each student was left on their own to complete it and only summoned again to put all the parts together regardless of their quality. Cultural traits such as the hesitation to ask for/offer help and the avoidance of giving/receiving constructive criticism seem also to have considerably influenced the final results. At the end of the semester, though all passed, only 20 per cent obtained an excellent mark and 40 per cent, a good one. Rather than the academic result, what is worrisome is the total lack of camaraderie to reach out to those needing help and cooperation, especially in a project focused on inequality. Nevertheless, the anonymous feedback survey[3] responses were overwhelmingly positive, except for one student who gave a negative feedback for the entire course.

The experience posed a unique challenge to both the teacher, he himself a foreigner in the eyes of the students, and the class as whole, not only in the content area which is by itself vast and complex where many different historic perspectives conflate and conflict, but also on how to deliver a balanced programme to an international group where the Self and the Other are sometimes sitting next to each other and, probably, working together on the same project. In this case, only respect for and solidarity with the others' concerns and opinions as a human being can produce a comfortable learning atmosphere. In addition, whether the course will impact the group's future work prospects and make of each student a critical teacher remain to be seen.

Without doubt, most of the class understood how social class regardless of the socioeconomic formation have historically created inequality as an expression of sociopolitical and economic power of some groups upon others. The class also recognized how power expressed by historically otherizing discourses has stressed the differences and thus oppression of whole nations, social groups and individuals because of their race, sex, nationality, religious beliefs and political ideas, among many others, thus effectively limiting their agency and affordances, and in many cases served as the 'moral' justification for abominable actions such as war, ethnic cleansing, lynching, imprisonment and terrorism in all its forms including those justified by the state, dissent and religious reasons. In all cases and despite the different inherent perspectives of the students, an ethical response and consensus seemed to have been reached and judged as a need for the well-being of humanity.

Finally, because 2020 has brought with it an unprecedented pandemic accelerating the potential crumbling of the world exacerbated by the then US presidency, the very dynamics of curriculum updating demanded that Trumpism as well as the uncertainties of a post-Covid-19 world be included in the programme. This also implies that the discipline cannot be static in terms of contents and approach but in constant development and refinement.

Acknowledgements

This research was financially supported by the Russian Foundation for Basic Research (Grant No. 17-29-09136\20 'Multilingualism in the Era of Post-literacy: Philosophical and Cultural Studies and Methodological and Pedagogical Development of a Multilingual Education Model').

Notes

1. Available for consultation and download on request at: https://yadi.sk/d/5wZCLuA 42xDy3Q?w=1.
2. See https://newlearningonline.com/cgscholar.
3. https://docs.google.com/forms/d/1VUXDCzLsuJkfNQbmA1CrJq7rgSJXD-t1YZ gjV-dwze4/edit#responses.

References

Alexander, T., and J. Potter (2005), *Education for a Change. Transforming the Way We Teach Our Children*, London: Routledge Falmer.
Álvarez de Zayas, C. (2000), *La Escuela en la Vida*, Habana: Pueblo y Educación.
Andrews, S. (2007), *Teacher Language Awareness*, Cambridge: Cambridge University Press.
Block, D. (2006), *Multilingual Identities in a Global City. London Stories*, London: Palgrave Macmillan.
Block, D. (2014), *Social Class in Applied Linguistics*, Oxon: Routledge.
Block, D. (2017), 'Neoliberalism, the Neoliberal Citizen and English Language Teaching Materials: A Critical Analysis', *Ruta Maestra*, 21: 4–15.
Block, D. (2018), *Political Economy in Sociolinguistics: Neoliberalism, Inequality and Social Class*, London: Bloomsbury.
Block, D., J. Gray and M. Holborow (2012), *Neoliberalism and Applied Linguistics*, London: Routledge.
Blommaert, J. (2005), *Discourse. A Critical Introduction*, Cambridge: Cambridge University Press.
Blommaert, J. (2010), *The Sociolinguistics of Globalization*, Cambridge: Cambridge University Press.
Bori, P. (2018), *Language Textbooks in the Era of Neoliberalism*, London: Routledge.

Bori, P. (2020), 'Neoliberal Governmentality in Global English Textbooks', *Classroom Discourse*, 11 (2): 149–63.

Brown, B. A. (2016), 'Understanding the Flipped Classroom: Types, Uses and Reactions to a Modern and Evolving Pedagogy', *Culminating Projects in Teacher Development*, 12. Available online: https://repository.stcloudstate.edu/ed_etds/12 (accessed 8 August 2020).

Brown, G., and G. Yule (1983), *Discourse Analysis*, Cambridge: Cambridge University Press.

Canale M., and M. Swain (1980, 1 March), 'Theoretical Bases of Communicative Approaches to Second Language Teaching and Testing', *Applied Linguistics*, 1: 1–47.

Chomsky, N. (2017), *The Responsibility of Intellectuals*, New York: New Press.

Cope, B., and M. Kalantzis, eds (2015), *A Pedagogy of Multiliteracies. Learning by Design*, Illinois: Palgrave Macmillan.

Demarest, A. B. (2015), *Exceeding Standards through Local Investigations*, New York: Routledge.

Drake, S. M., and R. C. Burns (2004), *Meeting Standards through Integrated Curriculum*, Virginia: ASCD.

Forteza Fernandez, R. (2019), 'Historical Lies and Distortions in ELT: A Case Study'. Keynote Speech at the International Conference on Multilingualism, Multiculturalism and Literacy, Ural Federal University, Ekaterinburg, Russia.

Forteza Fernandez, R., and E. V. Rubtsova (2020), 'Cultural Representations of Spain and Latin America in Spanish as Foreign Language: A Critique', in M. Yu Goodova (ed.), *Communication Trends in the Post-Literacy Era: Polylingualism, Multimodality, and Multiculturalism as Preconditions for New Creativity*, 302–16, Ekaterinburg: Ural University Press.

Forteza Fernandez, R., E. V. Rubtsova and S. Forteza Rojas (2020), 'Content Edulcoration as Ideology Visualization in an English Language Coursebook', *Praxema. Problems of Visual Semiotics*, 4 (26): 172–93.

Francis, D., I. Valodia and E. Webster (2020), *Inequality Studies from the Global South*, Oxon: Routledge.

Freire, P. (2000), *Pedagogy of Freedom. Ethics, Democracy, and Civil Courage*, London: Rowan & Littlefield.

Freire, P. (2005), *Education for Critical Consciousness*, London: Continuum.

Freire, P., and D. Macedo (1987), *Literacy: Reading the Word and the World*, Westport: Bergin and Garvey.

Geduld, D., I. Baatjes and H. Sathorar (2020), 'Preparing Foundational Phase Educators: Reading the Word and World through Transect Walks', in J. D. Kirylo (eds), *Reinventing Pedagogy of the Oppressed: Contemporary Critical Perspectives*, 15–25, London: Bloomsbury.

Gentili, P. (2004), *Pedagogía de la Exclusión. Critica al Neoliberalismo en Educación*, Mexico City: UACM.

Gray, J. (2000), 'The ELT Coursebook as Cultural Artifact: How Teachers Censor and Adapt', *ELT Journal*, 54 (3): 274–83.

Gray, J. (2010a), *The Construction of English: Culture, Consumerism and Promotion in the ELT Global Coursebook*, Basingstoke: Palgrave Macmillan.

Gray, J. (2010b), 'The Branding of English and the Culture of the New Capitalism: Representations of the World of Work in English Language Textbooks', *Applied Linguistics*, 31 (5): 714–33.

Gray, J. (2012), 'English the Industry', in A. Hewings and C. Tagg (eds), *The Politics of English: Conflict, Competition, and Co-Existence*, 137–63, The Open University: Routledge.
Gudova, M., M. Guzikova and R. F. Forteza Fernández (2022), 'Critical Literacy in Russia', in J. Z. Pandya, R. A. Mora, J. Alford, N. Golden and R. de Roock (eds), *The Handbook of Critical Literacies*, 211–17, London: Routledge.
Hadley, G. (2014), 'Global Textbooks in Local Contexts: An Empirical Investigation of Effectiveness', in N. Harwood (ed.), *English Language Teaching Textbooks. Content, Consumption,* Production, 205–40, Basingstoke: Palgrave Macmillan.
Hobsbawm, E. (1975), *The Age of Capital 1848–1875*, London: Abacus.
Hobsbawm, E. (1989), *The Age of Empire 1875–1914*, New York: Vintage Books.
Hobsbawm, E. (1996), *The Age of Revolution 1789–1848*, New York: Vintage Books.
Hymes, D. (1972), 'On Communicative Competence', in J. B. Pride and A. Holmes (eds), *Sociolinguistics: Selected Readings*, 269–93, Harmondsworth: Penguin.
Kalantzis, M., and B. Cope (2012), *New Learning. Elements of a Science of Education*, Cambridge: Cambridge University Press.
Kirylo, J. D. (2020), *Reinventing Pedagogy of the Oppressed: Contemporary Critical Perspectives*, London: Bloomsbury.
Kramsch, C. (2010), 'The Symbolic Dimensions of the Intercultural. Revised Version of a Plenary Paper Presented on 29 January 2010 at the Second International Conference on the Development and Assessment of Intercultural Competence at the University of Arizona, Tucson, Arizona', *Language Teaching*, 44 (3): 354–67.
Kramsch, C. (2013), 'Culture in Foreign Language Teaching', *Iranian Journal of Language Teaching Research*, 1 (1): 57–78.
Kramsch, C. (2017, October), *The Challenge of Education in the Era of Globalization*. CARLA Presentation & Open House, University of Minnesota: Minnesota. Available online: https://www.youtube.com/watch?v=ye7oj4ETuF4 (accessed 8 August 2020).
Kumaravadivelu, B. (2006), 'Dangerous Liaison: Globalization, Empire and TESOL', in J. Edge (ed.), *(Re-)Locating TESOL in an Age of Empire. Language and Globalization*, London: Palgrave Macmillan.
Kumaravadivelu, B. (2012), *Language Teacher Education for a Global Society. A Modular Model for Knowing, Analysing, Recognizing, Doing, and Seeing*, New York: Routledge.
Lakoff, G. (1987), *Women, Fire, and Dangerous Things. What Categories Reveal about Mind*, Chicago: University of Chicago Press.
Lakoff, G., and M. Johnson (1980), *Metaphors We Live By*, Chicago: University of Chicago Press.
Lakoff, G., and M. Johnson (1999), *Philosophy in Flesh. The Embodied Mind and Its Challenge to Western Thought*, New York: Basic Books.
Lozovskaya, K. B., A. B. Menshikov and E. S. Purgina (2020), 'Horizons of the Future': Realities and Aspirations of Top-Ranking BRICS Universities (Analysis of Mission Statements). *Vestnik Tomskogo gosudarstvennogo universiteta. Filosofiya. Sociologia. Politologia* [Tomsk State University Journal of Philosophy, Sociology and Political Science], 55): 163–74. https:/doi: 10.17223/1998863X/55/17.
Macedo, D. (2019), *Decolonizing Foreign Language Education. The Misteaching of English and Other Colonial Languages*, New York: Routledge.
Menon, D. (2020), 'Is Hierarchy the Same as Inequality', in D. Francis, I. Valodia and E. Webster (eds), *Inequality Studies from the Global South*, 22–31, Oxon: Routledge.

Milanovic, B. (2010), *The Haves and the Have-Nots. A Brief and Idiosyncratic History of Inequality*, New York: Basic Books.

Nation, I. S. P., and J. Macalister (2010), *Language Curriculum Design*, New York: Routledge.

Ozdamli, F., and G. Aşiksoy (2016), 'Flipped Classroom Approach', *World Journal on Educational Technology Current Issues*, 8 (2): 98–105.

Papadogiannis, Y. (2014), *The Rise and Fall of Homo Economicus. The Myth of the Rational Human and Chaotic Reality*, South Carolina: CreateSpace Independent Platform.

Paris, D., and H. Alim (2017), *Culturally Sustaining Pedagogies. Teaching and Learning for Justice in a Changing World*, New York: Teachers College Press.

Pennycook, A. (2001), *Critical Applied Linguistics. A Critical Introduction*, Oxford: Oxford University Press.

Pennycook, A. (2007), *Global Englishes and Transcultural Flows*, London: Routledge.

Pennycook, A. (2013), 'Language and Mobility: Unexpected Places', *ELT Journal*, 67 (4): 491–4.

Popkewitz, T. S. (1991), *A Political Sociology of Educational Reform. Power/Knowledge in Teaching, Teacher Education, and Research*, New York: Teachers College Press.

Reidsema, C., L. Kavanagh, G. Hadgraft and N. Smith, eds (2017), *The Flipped Classroom. Practice and Practices in Higher Education*, New York: Springer.

Ricento, T. (2000), *Ideologies, Politics and Language Policies. Focus on English*, Philadelphia: John Benjamins.

Richards, J., J. Platt and H. Weber (1985), *Longman Dictionary of Applied Linguistics*, Harlow: Longman.

Rigaser, K. (2018), *Representations of the World in Language Textbooks*, Bristol: Multilingual Matters.

Santos Green, L., J. R. Banas and R. A. Perkins, eds (2017), *The Flipped College Classroom. Conceptualized and Re-Conceptualized*, New York: Springer.

Sayer, A. (2005), *The Moral Significance of Class*, Cambridge: Cambridge University Press.

Thornbury, S. (1997), *About Language*, Cambridge: Cambridge University Press.

Webster, E. (2020), 'Building Counter Power in the Workplace. South Africa's Inequality Paradox', in D. Francis, I. Valodia and E. Webster (eds), *Inequality Studies from the Global South*, 221–39, Oxon: Routledge.

The Pluralist Paradigm in the Czech Educational Process: Teaching about Collective Identities and Democracy in the Constructivist Educational Project

Jan Květina

Introduction

This chapter aims to analyse and present three correlated urgent issues whose impact might be considered as a crucial factor regarding the implementation of democratic values as well as pluralist world view into the process of Czech schooling. First, the study identifies the traditional and still prevailing narrative of modern Czech history and national identity as a serious challenge for the enhancement of democratic and pluralist patterns in civic education in the twenty-first century. Second, the discourse analysis of the current Czech educational curriculum is made to point out its main incoherencies, dilemmatic issues and verbal problems concerning the link between the setting of the expected pluralist outcomes of the educational process on one hand and unembedded usage of ideologically determined language on the other. In the last part of the study, the chapter presents and analyses the recent particular Czech educational programme that respects the current trends of constructivism, symbolic interactionism and Popper's anti-essentialism. In this regard, the it offers inspiring methodological materials for teaching controversial topics such as liberal freedom, universalism of democracy, collective identities or ideological narrativization of history and suggests the possible way from the pitfalls of traditional 'objective' categories in teaching to the more pluralist concept of civic education.

The Czech Narrative and Postmodern Identities: A Challenge for Schooling?

The transition of Czechoslovakian and later Czech society towards democracy after 1989 brought several significant challenges that did not only affect political and economic dimensions (Evans and Whitefield 1998), but also impacted the discursive level and symbolic sphere of desirable social behaviour. Of course, such changes did not occur only in the Czech environment, but they were part of a much broader transformation of the whole Central and Eastern European space (Wiatr 2020). However, in the process of the construction of a new post-communist narrative of national identity, there are distinctive attributes of Czech development stemming from particular local traditions as well as from ancient national traumas (Chlup 2020).

The question of discursive changes in the evaluation of national history after 1989 can be traced in a very wide spectrum of research agendas in sociology, history, philosophy and political science (Černý et al. 2004; Hlaváček 2018; Rupnik 2018; Hvížďala and Přibáň 2018). However, the specific aim of this study is to attempt to identify corresponding patterns of such a transformation in the particular discourse of the Czech education system. Its analysis is required to better assess the extent to which Czech educational language has managed to reflect the important transition from a universal, monolithic and content-based orientation to more pluralist, constructivist and interpretative approaches that are able to sensitively apprehend the postmodern reality of Czech social values in the twenty-first century. Moreover, due to these approaches, one can also recognize that relevant language terms and concepts in the educational process are the alpha and omega of the necessary skills that students need to internalize. This internalization is necessary for a better understanding of the meaning of words in a highly digitalized, medialized and politically biased world as well as for a proper orientation in symbolic labels concerning collective identification as a fundamental part of forming one's own personality and its reflected position in society (Ashmore et al. 2004).

To study the discursive forms of contemporary Czech educational language, several steps – both theoretical and empirical – must be taken. First, it is necessary to consider the main auto-stereotypes concerning Czech national identity that started to be both politically and socially relevant in the era of the modern Czech national revival in the second half of the nineteenth century. The framing of these stereotypes in the net of theories of nationalism enables an analysis of the extent to which the typical concept of Czechhood – deeply rooted in the past – is compatible with postmodern educational trends (Kritt 2018; Beck and Kosnik 2006; Richardson 1997) which struggle to instil a fragile harmony between the individualist and socially embedded self and thus form a stable, non-destructive and civic concept of collective identity. Only if one is able to engage with the traditional narrative of Czech national history, which remained dominant for the whole of the twentieth century, it is possible to see which patterns played an indispensable role in the self-perception of Czech society as well as to identify the changes that appeared in this self-identification during the transformation after 1989.

Nonetheless, to capture the trends of the pluralist paradigm in the contemporary Czech educational process, a general description of the principal values and identitary changes does not suffice, and therefore a discourse analysis of the so-called RVP, the official education curricular documents stemming from the term 'Rámcový vzdělávací program' (Framework Educational Programme) – approved by the Czech Ministry of Education as universal instructions obligatory for all levels of schooling – will be made in the second part of this study. Such an analysis will enable the identification of the extent to which the national education curriculum reflects the desirable post-communist shift from a traditional authoritative pedagogical approach to a more pluralist one (Aronowitz and Giroux 2003), where the former represents the tendency to provide students with clear-cut pieces of information rooted in a particular – though universally presented – world view, whereas the latter approach, stemming from the constructivist paradigm (Kritt 2018; Beck and Kosnik 2006), is capable of presenting social facts, roles and behaviour as an ongoing process of language interpretations and reinterpretations (Hanan 2015; Burtonwood 2006). In this regard, the classic model of the open society by K. R. Popper (2020) should prove useful, since it clearly demonstrates that democratic citizenship requires grasping values as possible interpretations that enable their own refutability. With the help of this theoretical prism, the discourse analysis of the curricular documents will try to demonstrate that the successful implementation of a constructivist approach to values and to a more open understanding of social identities in the education process requires not only a systemic re-evaluation of the discursive language that the curricula use, but also more coherent employment of corresponding teaching materials and worksheets.

Such materials should apply the concept of critical thinking about human values in schooling, not just in a formal way, and thus put the principle of discourse-based instead of fact-based or bias-based understanding of collective (self)-identification into practice (Petit 1999: 72). For this reason, the third and the last part of this chapter consists of a presentation and critical assessment of a particular contemporary Czech educational project whose essential traits are expected to meet the aforementioned criteria, pointing out the need to establish patterns of schooling about social values and distinctive kinds of identity on radical, pluralist and constructivist notions of social reality. In this regard, both the analysis of Czech educational discourse and the presentation of possibly inspiring solutions are supposed to reflect the key indicated questions: Which concept of national identity does the current Czech narrative incline towards: to the traditional ethnic or to the postmodern civic one?; What is the impact of postmodern – mostly constructivist and radical pluralist – patterns of thought on the structure of the contemporary Czech education curriculum in terms of presenting human identity and desirable social values?; And which methods, as well as specific activities, should be applied in the education process to enhance the student's orientation in the complicated world of overlapping and multilayered collective identifications?

The Traditional Heritage of Czech National Identity in the Twenty-First Century

Although the failure of the communist regimes in Central and Eastern Europe was frequently read as a triumph of universalism (Fukuyama 2006), the trends in the whole European region at the turn of the twentieth and the twenty-first centuries clearly indicated that the world of nationalist ideas and tribal connections had not vanished. Facing the rising popularity of populist radical right parties, building their main political images on 'time-proven' patterns of ethnic nationalism (Pirro 2015), it is necessary to abandon the influential neoliberal doctrine – so popular in the 1990s – which claimed that postmodern societies are able to base the affiliation of their members only on the concept of self-interest. Ethnic clashes linked to the very serious issue of Central European minorities and the recent dilemma of maintaining so-called homogenous societies within the refugee crisis (Bauerová 2018), as well as the discursive revival of the rhetoric of national interest in the narratives of certain political parties in this territory (Toomey 2018) clearly demonstrate the urgent social need for non-economic and holistic forms of collective self-identification.

It is therefore clear that one of the problems of the post-communist transformation lay in a too narrow and prejudiced understanding of national feelings, which were frequently presented as being an anachronist part of the fading world that was supposed to be replaced by the more universal values of the neoliberal doctrine. This severe black-and-white dichotomy, depicting liberal values and nationalism as two contradictory interpretations of a desirable social existence, created a very clear-cut, though dangerous, quandary in the ordinary perception of individual identity: if one accepts the progressive values of human rights, individual freedom, pluralism and tolerance, one has to resign from one's affiliation to traditions and national pride, or one can adhere to the essence of national identity, but then it means one prefers backward, irrational and atavistic illusions to the desirable trends of progressive and universal rationalism.

This danger of ideological simplification and the denouncing of attitudes touching on anything nationalist is especially typical of modern Czech liberals who started to develop older patterns of differentiation between true social elites and ordinary 'common Czech people' (*Čecháčci*) (Slačálek 2016). Bearing this difference in mind, it is possible to consider this elite and intellectual aversion of the mostly better-educated citizens to the majority of their fellow citizens precisely as a deeper expression of neoliberal inability to treat social reality in a discursive way, where social values are not rooted in universal principles without any cultural context, but reflect significant shifts in linguistic reality and thus vary according to pluralist social interpretations. In such cases, it is not possible to assume the existence of a binary world of two rival classes arguing whether nationalism is something inherited, sacrosanct and unquestionable or, on the contrary, something obsolete, reactionary and pernicious. Instead, one strongly needs an approach that would neither adore nor ignore the presence of nationalist feelings and thus also accept their contradictions and tensions in the postmodern reality of the twenty-first century.

Moreover, the aforementioned redoubtable trends of populism, xenophobia and illiberalism in the past two decades in Central Europe (Ágh 2015; Zakaria 1997) apparently suggest that the dominant interpretations of collective – and especially national – identity still represent one of the most serious challenges to social stability and also to the question of the optimal implementation of nationalism and national discourse in the paradigm of contemporary schooling. Hence, the acceptance of the fact that there must be some space for national discourse in politics, society and culture as well as in educational documents and study materials should also be related to a correlated assumption that different ways of reading and defining national identity must be found. However, in this regard, it is not the invention of completely new approaches, but a consideration of fruitful constructivist theoretical notions about nationalism in the educational process that is necessary.

With regard to the above-mentioned problem of modern Czech nationalist discourse, there has always been a deeply rooted concept of 'Czechoslovakianism' during the whole of the twentieth century; a concept that was based not only on the universal, humanist and democratic philosophy of the first Czechoslovakian president, T. G. Masaryk, but also on ethno-nationalist beliefs in the cultural supremacy of the Czech element (Heimann 2009). When the intellectual fathers of the modern Czech nation based the idea of the Czech community and its right to its own sovereign existence on the principle of the cultural clash between aggressive German and peaceful Slavonic forces, they influenced the prevalent identitary discourse of Czech society until the twenty-first century, because even if they did not belong to the camp of radical nationalists, they helped establish the image of the Czech national community as a 'purified' and homogenous society that should distinguish itself from non-Czechs on the basis of their language and ethnic bonds of presupposed affinity.

When the famous Hungarian philosopher István Bibó proclaimed his prophecy about the post-war expulsion of German minorities from the Central European countries, which he considered harmful to the majoritarian societies of Czechs, Poles and Hungarians as it caused the loss of their ability to live in an atmosphere of otherness (Bibó 2015), he had anticipated a threat to Central European identities many years before it occurred. The evolution of these identities – with the Czech one at the forefront – might be seen as a permanent shift towards the 'ideal' of the hermetically sealed community that must care about its own purity and thus has to expel everything which might be assessed as foreign and alien. Since the second half of the nineteenth century, when the fatal dispute between Czech-speaking and German-speaking inhabitants of the Bohemian kingdom was disseminated (King 2018), the 'spectre' of a closed concept of collective identity started to haunt Central Europe and the heritage of a heterogenous identity of patriotism, not based on language or ethnicity but on belonging to a political community, had been lost (Snyder 2003).

However, which role should these former alternative and non-primordial patterns of collective togetherness play right now? And how should this thesis be applied in current educational processes and techniques? As I tried to suggest already in the introductory part, the reformulation of fundamental social values and the re-understanding of one's individual identity is crucial, since the knowledge that Czech national identity used to be based on completely different patterns is able to contribute to a significant shift in the identification of the relation between language and reality. Nonetheless, the ability and willingness to perceive national identity as something different from the primordial categories require not only critical reflection on shifts in language meanings (highlighting the fact that the same term might have stood for something different in the discourse of the past), but also need the implementation of the aforementioned constructivist approaches to the research into and the popular image of nationalism.

Current and very influential Czech scientists keep warning that there are long-term problems concerning the typical auto-stereotypization of Czech national identity

(Hlaváček 2019; Rupnik 2018; Hvížďala and Přibáň 2018) including the 'eternal' perception of Czech history as a series of foreign betrayals (Tesař 2014) or a permanent doubting of the meaning of one's collective existence because of the quandary of the so-called small 'uncertain nations'. It is apparent that these momentous traits of self-identification play a decisive role in the prevailing position of ethnic nationalism, and the lack of a pluralist respect towards other nations and minorities is one of the main threats to democratic stability in the Czech Republic in the twenty-first century (Hejnal 2012; Burjanek 2001).

Hence, to avoid the traditional depiction of the Czech nation as a perpetual victim of other bigger nations and to weaken its popular aversion to neighbours, foreigners, incomers and minorities, the implementation of non-primordial approaches such as Renan's concept of a 'daily plebiscite' (Renan 1939), Anderson's thesis about imagined communities (Anderson 1983) and a discursive understanding of collective identities (Wodak 1999) should be employed in the public discourse as well as in education curricula much more significantly. Although the traditional dichotomy between the old, 'dangerous', backward and Eastern understanding of ethnic nationalism and the progressive, civilized, democratic and Western concept of civic nationalism has already been overcome (Jaskulowski 2010), it is clear that any strengthening of pluralist and liberal values in contemporary Czech society requires the promotion of the thesis that nations are not predestined communities based on their 'blood' origins, as many proponents of ethnic purity in Central Europe still claim (Kamusella 2012).

Collective Identity and Social Values in the Czech Education Curriculum: Discourse Analysis

The question of the optimal implementation of constructivist approaches, along with the adjustment of pedagogical methods and techniques in the educational process, requires the following analysis of the current Czech education curriculum. In this regard, the discourse analysis below aims primarily to ascertain the extent to which one can consider the language as well as content of the current RVP as an apt and sufficient platform for building the concepts of social values and collective self-identification in the above-mentioned way.

The framework educational programmes have already been studied recently from the perspective of discourse analysis (Havlíček 2018; Květina 2016; Kaščák and Pupala 2011). Nonetheless, all these analyses were either presented as considerations of the impact of neoliberalism on the educational process in general, or concentrated on particular issues which differ from our dominant focus on democratic pluralist values and the depiction of national identity. For this reason, one should not understand the description below as a thorough and multilevelled discourse analysis of the sort that has been performed previously (Květina 2016), but as a specific and focused study which tries to capture the main problems in the assumed correlation between democratic and pluralist settings of the main framework educational programme as a whole. Furthermore, it also endeavours to grasp several language expressions which might be considered as highly controversial and counterproductive when speaking about the expected process of forming a tolerant and open-minded interpretation of social values in the school environment.

Regarding this kind of analysis, the most necessary focus is on the Czech state educational programme for grammar schools since the questions of national identity and their linkage to the values of liberal democracy are most significantly presented and discussed in the framework of adolescent education. Of course, the principles of collective self-identification and a pluralist world view are supposed to have been learnt in the previous phases of children's social development, but concerning a constructivist approach based on the ability to reinterpret language, the adolescent age of the focus group is optimal. The education curriculum called 'The Framework Educational Programme for Grammar Schools' (RVP 2007) outlines the basic strategies for the upper level of secondary education with a special emphasis on schools that are supposed to prepare students for university education. The RVP programme therefore contains two distinctive dimensions of schooling which are both obligatory for the level of education: the first dimension is represented by key competencies (i.e. skills that are divided into five different categories – learning, problem solving, communication, social and personal orientation, civic skills and enterprise), whereas the second dimension is the expected knowledge that a student is supposed to acquire in different fields, such as biology, history, mathematics and the like.

If one therefore identifies the main problems concerning the language interpretation of social reality with a special emphasis on the correlation between the concept of collective identity (i.e. the dimension of schooling about nationalism) and the constructivist notion of social terms as being never-ending interpretations (i.e. the dimension of schooling about the pluralist and non-definite essence of world views), four main drawbacks in the Czech national curriculum should be highlighted: the dominance of a possessive, individualist world view, a false universalism of ideological values, an unclarified concept of collective identities and non-reflected understanding of democracy.

In the first case, the excessive use of possessive language forms in the context of human values (MacPherson 2010; Thayer-Bacon 2006) should be mentioned as the crucial aspect of too atomist an understanding of human beings in the process of providing students with the promoted key competencies. The domination of a possessive evaluation of collective identity, which is able to present society only as a sum of individuals striving for private interests and convergent goods (Taylor 2003), can be found all through the national curriculum; for instance, in the passages where the RVP claims that a student in the learning process must be led to 'take their own needs into account ... to develop their own potential and capacities as well as use opportunities to their own favour' (RVP 2007: 11). A similar attitude can be traced in the question of human rights, which are explicitly defined as a matter of individualist perspective, since each student has their own right to 'widen their own understanding of cultural values and protect their own rights' (RVP 2007: 10) with a particular stress on the protection of human rights which are, however, again presented as individualist demands without their social embeddedness in the variable collective context (RVP 2007: 41).

This pre-social approach towards human society is furthermore to be found in the statement that all past social reality should serve as a sum of model patterns of universal human behaviour (RVP 2007: 39). This means that there is in fact no space for the possible admission that human nature might vary depending on different historical and cultural contexts and their distinctive understandings of language, as post-structuralism suggests (Foucault 2002). This traditional approach unfortunately intensifies the main problem of the student's understanding of social values in schooling, since the objectivist perception of terms like freedom, democracy or nation determines a biased world view, leading students to treat their ancestors, as well as members of various past and contemporary societies, as representatives of the same sum of finite and a priori given attributes. This consideration of the world as a complex of already finished truths and absolute meanings can be moreover observed in the way the RVP depicts the leading benefits of promoting discussion in the educational process, which are, for instance, described as the exchange of pre-adopted stances between individuals, without stressing the importance of constructing attitudes and shared meanings in the actual process of the language exchange as such.

A related problem of false universalism of the expected values should also be mentioned, since when one considers the key competencies in the RVP as obligatory outcomes, a discrepancy can be identified between the proclaimed pluralist paradigm (KK 2008: 94) and the presentation of key competencies as particularly promoted attitudes and values (RVP 2007: 8). The promotion of vague 'attitudes and values' without their specification and framing within a definite and declared paradigm is therefore both ideological, with the most neoliberal principles being presented as apolitical and universal and also confusing, since social situations that should be treated as indispensable parts of the public debate might be veiled by the language to appear as natural and indisputable facts. When the concept of the RVP assumes that the education process should guarantee the 'protection of the traditional values of our civilization' or ensure that students will be able to 'distinguish between what is real and what is not', it is not obvious which social authority in the schooling framework should be allowed to decide which values might be assessed as the 'right tradition' and to what extent they correspond to the scope of our civilization (RVP 2007: 38-9).

The tension between a presupposed universalism and a declared affiliation to the distinguished tradition of a particular civilization can also be identified in the third mentioned ambiguity of the Czech RVP. This unclarified concept of collective identities is especially apparent when this national material expects that students will 'develop and cultivate a consciousness of a personal, local, national, European and global identity' (RVP 2007: 39). Similarly as in the previous cases, such a formulation assumes that all forms and levels of collective identities can be peacefully and harmoniously reconciled without taking possible tensions in the founding of one's identity on dichotomous contradictions into account (Schmitt 2000: 15). Hence, the national framework programmes contain neither general nor specific analyses of possible situations that might occur when the different understandings, levels and interests of particular identities stand against each other, since it is not clear how collective identities should be interpreted in terms of learning. For instance, is national identity something that is expected to be highlighted as a principle of inherited loyalty and considered superior to any other affiliations? Or are students supposed to read collective identities as a question of their own individual choice irrespective of historical determination and development? Is the discourse of education supposed to treat the Czech nation as something tangible or as a shared collective consciousness?

Unfortunately, there is no single indication of possible responses to the above questions in the Czech national curriculum. When the national framework programmes state that students must be tolerant of minorities and require equal respect for different systems of values at the same time (RVP 2007: 39), one is confused about which concept of identity is prevalent: one that reasons in terms of passive toleration on the side of the universal majority, or one that does not differentiate between 'majorities' and 'minorities' and interprets social reality as a multilayered complex of various self-reflections where everyone can be a part of distinctive majorities and minorities at the same time?

The Enhancement of Constructivist and Interpretative Approaches in Czech Schools: The Project on Identity and Values in Context

Having demonstrated that the reading of collective identities according to the national framework programme is not coherent enough and having suggested the importance of a more pluralist promotion of social values and collective affiliations in the Czech environment due to the still prevalent impact of the traditional narrative of ethnic nationalism, it is the right time to indicate possible ways of employing the above-mentioned desirable trends in practice. In this regard, a specific current educational project that aims to boost a pluralist understanding of democratic values and their relation to personal identity will be presented and analysed. The main aim of this project is to demonstrate in which way the postmodern educational process at grammar school level should be routed to reflect the main aforementioned weaknesses of the Czech national curriculum in terms of questions of identity. Furthermore, it also endeavours to find a safe path from the 'snares' of the Czech historical heritage of ethnic nationalism without ignoring the need for national feelings entirely.

This educational programme is designed as a coherent complex of three specific blocks which reflect the main civic skills that the programme endeavours to enforce, that is, Cooperation – Conflict – Compromise. The first part of the project contains activities and methods which support the idea that students, as members of the public community, should take part in behaviour that limits individual selfish interests in favour of a discursively constructed and negotiated 'common good'. In contrast to this, the second block presents conflict situations as an irremovable part of human life that students have to accept and learn how to tackle; that is especially why questions of the contextual determination of human values, ideological reinterpretations and the historical background of collective memory and identity are treated here. The last part of the project is then focused on the optimal methods of compromise-solution training as an indispensable skill of democratic reasoning in a pluralist society.

Taking these three parts into account, it is reasonable to mainly analyse selected activities from the second block in this paper, since this part is primarily the one which works with the discursive notion of social values and collective identity in the broadest extent. One can highlight that the second part of the project endeavours to:

- replace the traditional conception of language as a universal depiction of social reality and sum of absolutes with a discursive understanding of terms as merely floating signifiers (Mehlman 1972) that need to be permanently discussed and re-interpreted;
- emphasize the historical and cultural determination of the understanding of social values such as 'nation', 'democracy' or 'freedom';
- present a more holistic challenge to the dominance of a possessive interpretation of liberal individualism as a possible solution to tensions in the current setting of the Czech RVP.

With these aims in mind, this analysis points particularly at four materials that should be considered to enhance a constructivist application of socially and culturally determined understanding of values with a theoretical and philosophical justification of their conceptual framing.

Manipulation as an Inherent Part of Human Life

The first activity focuses on the consideration of manipulative behaviour as an inherent though unfavourable part of social life that every human being is capable of and needs to understand. In this regard, the material called 'Famous Heroes as Manipulators' endeavours to suggest that there is neither a universal nor clear-cut definition of acceptable ways to persuade or, on the contrary, inappropriate manipulative techniques, since the delimitation of suitable and unsuitable acts is dependent on the variable contexts of their use. To demonstrate this quandary, students are provided with several extracts from famous movies that most students are expected to know and whose main characters they may identify with. The selection of the movies might, of course, vary depending on the particular context and on the peculiar purpose of each teacher, but in the initial setting, excerpts from these movies have been selected:

1. 'The roof scene' from the movie *The Shawshank Redemption*, in which the main character, Andy Dufresne, manages to persuade the chief warder to carry out a mutually beneficial though illegal transaction (Darabont 1994);
2. 'The removal of the chancellor scene' from the first episode of *Star Wars*, in which Queen Amidala initiates the process of removing the current chancellor and thus unwittingly brings the dark side to power (Lucas 1999);
3. 'The restarting of the reactor scene' from the series *Chernobyl*, in which the shift manager blackmails his subordinates (Renck 2019);

4. 'The trial scene' from the movie *Harry Potter and the Order of the Phoenix*, in which Albus Dumbledore convinces the wizard jury not to sentence Harry for his law-breaking (Yates 2007);
5. 'The meeting of the board scene' from the Czech comedy *My Sweet Little Village*, in which the chief of the collective farm pleads for the transfer of the mentally ill employee to another company (Menzel 1985).

The students are then told to distinguish good and bad characters in each of the excerpts and to support their decisions with reasonable argumentation; moreover, they are also supposed to think about the possible connection between all the excerpts with regard to the presented social behaviour. After the presentation, students comment on all the characters in the particular excerpts one by one and observe whether they are able to reach a consensus or not, which is complicated by the fact that some of them might be very well aware of the entire plots of the chosen movies whereas some of them might not. After having seen all the excerpts, the students are invited to formulate what the link between all the situations is, and they are expected to focus on the fact that in all cases some kind of successful process of convincing takes place. On the basis of this revelation, students should identify the particular examples of this persuasion and also decide whether they assess them as acceptable or as inappropriate ways of manipulation. Of course, individual observations will probably differ, because possible reasons, such as various interpretations of good and bad characters, the level of knowledge of the plots or willingness to accept the principle of 'the ends justify the means' and so on, might be dissimilarly significant for each student. On the basis of such reasoning, students should realize that the evaluation of nearly the same behaviour might vary completely depending on the particular context and on the personal affiliation to particular characters, groups or identities. To sum up, the complexity of such activities therefore enhances a desirable understanding of social values and deeds as something which cannot be judged once and for all and which also requires the taking of historical, cultural as well as minority points of view into account.

What if Great Figures of History Used Online Social Networks?

As the second activity developing the thesis about language manipulation and the ideologically determined character of public speech, the specific educational application 'History Social Network' (socialnetwork.envio.cz)[1] should be mentioned. The application's online software enables teachers to set up their own online classroom in which selected historical characters (famous people from both the Czech and the world's past) are assigned to individual students or student groups. These groups then become teams of 'image makers' that are expected to make up and administer profiles of these historical characters on this fictional 'social network'. The student groups thus create the profiles of people such as Otto von Bismarck, Napoleon Bonaparte, Maria Theresa, Queen Victoria or Tomáš Garrigue Masaryk by presenting their basic biographical information, posting photos or pictures from their lives that the students can make on their own, sharing online statuses which would vividly describe the famous moments from their public lives, and writing comments on the posts of other historical characters administered by the competing teams. In the end, the online classroom as the fictional social network represents a complex of made-up historical conversations, pictures and statements which students and their teams are expected to present and advocate together.

By presenting their team strategies, the students are able to delve deep into the main principles and techniques of ideological promotion as well as to understand the difference between the effort to capture the national past through the objectivist paradigm of science and the attempt to adjust the interpretation of particular historical narratives to specific political purposes. In this regard, the above-mentioned activity might be divided into two different stages: in the first, which is mostly inspiring and stimulating, students should be intrigued by the process of looking for the relevant information, having fun and experiencing the flow phenomenon (Seligman and Csikszentmihalyi 2000) by creating the most fitting and convincing profile of the assigned character. In the second stage, when the teams have already got familiar with the basic information and style of their 'hero of the past', a more sophisticated aim is to be achieved, since they are supposed to put themselves in their character's place and identify both with his or her language and with the corresponding way of thinking. During this stage, the teacher is ready to establish a common and controversial topic from the national past such as the fall of the Habsburg Empire or the expulsion of Germans after Second World War in the Czech case, which all the participating student teams are obliged to reflect and comment on through the eyes of their assigned historical characters. Of course, since this second stage might be very difficult for some students who do not want to identify themselves with a particular historical figure that they do not like, a teacher is expected to be very perceptive both in the case of the selection of controversial topics as well as in the assignment of students to each team. Students must be therefore informed that they are assumed to play the roles they want to and not to perform the role of 'devil's advocate' at any cost, because the effective activity presupposes that the teams of 'image makers' will not rebel against their own characters, even though, of course, the whole activity as such is based on a very jocular concept of learning and any efforts of students to implement irony, sarcasm or even revolt should be didactically reflected in a relaxed way and atmosphere.

However, taking the cultural, historical and ideological differences of the selected characters into account, it is apparent that the resulting outcome is frequently full of contradictory interpretations as well as misinterpretations, since, for instance, the debate between the fictional social network profiles of Winston Churchill, Tomáš Garrigue Masaryk, Joseph Stalin and Wenzel Jaksch regarding the question of Germans in Czechoslovakia after 1945 will represent both historical dilemmas as well as space for gaining public popularity.

After the common presentation of such conversational threads, the mutual analysis of all the differences between the selected characters and intentional misinterpretations must be made. This analysis should reveal how the student teams used the depiction of a very concrete historical topic for the required impression and thus demonstrate that our understanding of past events cannot be fully universal since it first requires an understanding of the corresponding national narrative. Having a constructivist approach in mind, the whole of this activity is able to combine three distinctive dimensions of teaching about social values and identity: first, it clearly shows how these phenomena are culturally and historically formed and thus dependent on variable contexts; second, it demonstrates the pros and cons of promoting public behaviour on social networks in a safe fictional environment of characters from the past, where the danger of the politicization of current ideological clashes between real political agents is minimized; and third, it uses amusing and relaxed approaches towards knowledge with a focus on finding and sorting relevant information.

What Does It Mean to Be Free?

As the contextual framing of the most desirable social values represents the crucial principle of the whole project, the third presented activity concerns the question of students' own freedom and its dependence on permanently changing circumstances. Due to the fact that freedom represents possibly the most significant value in liberal democratic society, the state of being free can be assessed as the most valuable for most young people educated in the postmodern period. However, the anachronistic implementation of the concept of freedom as a universal value of all individual human beings in every phase of human history might be dangerous because it underestimates the importance of the different values of distinctive historical periods and also overlooks the possible other interpretations of the phrase 'being free' that might bear completely different meanings according to different conditions, contexts and situations. Hence, one of the main aims of this activity lies in the demonstration of liberty as multilayered value that should not be interpreted only in the over-individualist framework as a right to do anything one wants, but as historically determined balance between total arbitrariness and oppression. Besides other things, this activity is therefore supposed to facilitate the very urgent and ongoing dilemma of how to teach about freedom of speech and behaviour of each individual as indispensable human values without losing the limits of such freedom due to its dependence on social and cultural background from one's own perspective at the same time. When students are actually confronted with the quandaries below and expected to decide whether they would assess the particular cases and everyday situations as the ones which support or rather limit freedom, they are supposed to realize that instead of the typical understanding of freedom as 'my right to do something', the additional consideration 'what defines one's freedom, for whom and under which circumstances' should always be taken into account.

In this respect, the activity analysed below demonstrates that the question of whether a particular human being feels free is impacted by many variables including ideology, culture, and the historical past or personal preferences. The worksheet simulates several social situations that students are expected to assess and decide if they consider that the behaviour presented in the various examples is free. For a better understanding of the tensions in modern interpretations of freedom, the conceptual scheme of Berlin's dichotomy between the negative and positive notions of liberty is introduced and applied (Berlin 1969). Even though this dichotomous scheme has been frequently criticized and might be assessed as already outmoded in current political theory (Skinner 1998; Pettit 1999), the suggested binary model of freedom prevents students from thinking about freedom as something undoubted and problem-free.

The interpretative activity therefore starts with a few questions on which the students are supposed to reflect, which should indicate the significant though controversial character of liberty in our modern society. These questions such as 'Is a society which allows all its members to steal and kill more free than one that restricts them?'; 'How is it possible that French revolutionaries pleaded for freedom and used the guillotine for mass executions at the same time?'; or 'Would we be free if we voluntarily let computers to control our brains?' are thus destined to bring the traditional understanding of freedom as arbitrary behaviour into question and show that the question 'What kind of liberty, and whose, should be saved or sacrificed?' might be a very serious riddle.

After this initial ice-breaking and incentivizing discussion, teams of students are confronted with several quandaries in the worksheet – described in written form and symbolically depicted in pictures as well – that all refer to the 'everyday situations' in which people face grave dilemmas regarding their decisions. These simulated examples (A–H) combine a variety of cases from different historical periods and cultural backgrounds to demonstrate that although the question of liberty is omnipresent and crosses distinct times and places, its interpretation is precisely dependent on the particular context. Hence, student teams discuss and interpret these situations one by one:

A. What if a slave got permission from his slave master to do whatever they wanted for one day – would they be free?;
B. What if I am a drug addict and decide to take another dose – am I free?;
C. Am I still free if a policeman forces me to pay a fine for speeding?;
D. What if parents do not let their child to go to a party – is the child free?;
E. Am I free if my employer makes me redundant?;
F. What if the government ordered the Jewish population to leave their homes – would the Jews be free?;
G. What if a girl broke off her university studies and left to take care of her married lover's needs – would she decide freely?;
H. What if I were to be executed for reading a banned pornographic book – would I die as a free person?;
I. If I am a loving woman suffering from the violence of my husband who I do not want to leave – am I free?

After the student groups make their decisions, they are expected to present their solutions and to explain any disputes that arose when particular members differed in their responses. On the basis of their reasoning as well as the subsequent discussion, it is obvious that contradictory interpretations of liberty will occur. As it has been suggested, the teaching material enables the framing of all presented answers with the help of Berlin's dichotomy, but one should recognize that the main message of this activity is not a demonstration of the theory of negative and positive freedom as such, but the development of the students' ability to think about the most frequently used social values in an interpretative way.

It is necessary to point out that the practical application of the worksheet in the Czech educational process proved the anticipated goals to be achievable, since the student teams at various grammar schools concluded very dissimilar outcomes regarding the question of under which circumstances one is (not) free. Taking the examples one by one, important tensions between a more individualist and arbitrary concept on the one hand, and a more collectivist and reasonable understanding of freedom on the other hand, can be identified in the students' answers. From this perspective, the situation of the slave (A) is often read as being both free and unfree at the same time, because they are able to do anything they want but this possibility is dependent on the sudden kindness of the slave master and the freedom is thus not in their own hands. The students are therefore able to deduce a significant conclusion from this finding: that the question of freedom might be strongly dependent on the political constitution, because if slavery is legal – which it used to be in the past – even slaves can be considered to behave freely when they are out of their master´s control. Another observation was made by students in the case of the drug addict (B) who is not forced to take the dose and in that respect remains free, but many students were troubled by the fact that it is not 'the real him', but his physical addiction that decides.

The situations of the punished driver (C) and the controlled child (D) refer again to the political determination of any kind of liberty, and students thus have to think about the consensual basis of the symbolic border between legal/illegal and legitimate/illegitimate behaviour: what determines whether the authority of the police and parents is an unacceptable violation of personal freedom? Similar questions are also raised in the cases of a discriminated minority (F) and a reader who has been executed (H), because both cases conceptualize the dilemma of the extent to which freedom is inherently linked to personal inviolability and what the relation is between liberty and democratic government. In both situations, students argue using the majority principle whose application in the theory of democracy enables the claim that one can remain free even if the majority of citizens decides on expulsion or even execution for breaking the rules. As far as one is allowed to take part in the decision making and is aware of the consequences of one's behaviour, the final decision – no matter how cruel – can be assessed as democratic and free, especially when one brings the ancient practice of ostracism or Rousseau's famous concept of democracy as 'forced freedom' (Rousseau 1999: 58) into the argument.

The desirable 'paradigm shift' (Kivunja 2014) that students are supposed to experience regarding their present understanding of social values can even be extended through the examples of the girl (G) and the woman (I) that reflect a fundamental dimension of freedom as an act of rational agency. If the cases (G) and (I) are used, significant dependence of the concept of liberty on the culturally and ideologically determined notion of rationality might be tracked. Both the girl in love (G) or the abused woman (I) can be treated as free agents who decided on their own – no matter if correctly or wrongly – or, on the contrary, as the victims of the prevalent symbolic culture that traditionally assigns very definite kinds of behaviour to certain genders. Hence, using a wide range of situations, the essential aim of this educational material can be achieved in the required way, because only when students experience a deliberative interpretation of fundamental social values on their own, can a pluralist understanding of social relations and identities become something more than just a formal setting.

News Writing in a Time Machine: Our Narratives of the Past

In the last part of the presented educational project, I would like to focus on the specific activity called 'The Time Machine', which is designed to develop all the soft skills mentioned already in the previous three parts with a special stress laid on various historical narratives and language games as necessary tools for grasping our identities.

The central idea of this activity is the fictional concept of a time machine, and students are invited to imagine that humankind is endowed with the possibility of time travelling and thus teams of adventurers, scientists and journalists are setting out on their journeys to the past. Their task is to get to famous moments in history, observe the deeds of our ancestors and then to tell us what 'really happened'. The students' activity as such starts when they are told to find the lost testimonies of four expeditions that travelled in time before but did not come back, so the task is to save at least the news that they wrote to depict several significant historical moments.

The material contains several packages of historical narratives concerning particular historical events that have been selected according to the traditional Czech paradigm; hence, moments such as the death of the reformer John Huss in 1415, the discovery of America in 1492, the outbreak of First World War in 1914, or the accession of East European countries to the EU in 2004 are employed. However, all the packages are made in a similar way, which means that not only can each teacher choose their own version to work with, but new packages regarding other moments from both national and general history can also be made. The important aspect is that four expeditions that travelled together to a definite historical period (for instance to the year 1415) differed in their world views and so, even though they had the same opportunity to see the same historical event with their own eyes, their reflections about these events might be completely dissimilar.

And this is the moment where the effort of the student teams begins, because each team has to compose all the news from each expedition in the best possible complete form. The teams are also informed that each expedition wrote its message in the form of a journal article but due to an unknown tragedy, all their messages were unfortunately torn to pieces and mixed together. All student teams have therefore a limited amount of time to find all the pieces of all the articles in the classroom – which is supposed to be treated like the time machine of the previous expeditions – and put them together to get four coherent testimonies about what happened in the past.

It should be pointed out that all four articles – created and 'torn up' by the authors of the materials as a prepared set of worksheets – were written in different language styles and narratives corresponding to four current world views, that is (1) a liberal human rights discourse (i.e. a politically correct one), (2) a nationalist and xenophobic discourse (i.e. a chauvinist one), (3) a left socialist discourse (i.e. a Marxist one) and (4) a populist discourse (i.e. a tabloid one). Before the articles relating to each historical event were created, the authors of the concept prepared a list of fifty key words and phrases that had been identified as typical collocations of each of the above-mentioned types of discourse and were selected on the basis of academic research as well as on current journal languages (Cvrček et al. 2010; Fidelius 2016). The writing of articles from four different perspectives was therefore based not only on interpretative distinctions; for example, the discovery of America is presented as an enrichment of humanity by the liberal discourse, as a danger for ethnic 'purity' of European nations by the chauvinist discourse, as the opportunity to fight for social justice all over the world by the Marxist discourse and as a civilizational shock and conspiracy by the populist tabloid discourse. Of course, the differences in ideological explanations are supposed to be the first clue that the teams should follow to 'find the truth', that is, to sort lots of snippets into four consistent articles. However, as it is quite hard to put all the pieces together with the help of content analysis alone, all the teams can be equipped with the 'discourse dictionaries' that are a part of the worksheet as well. Students are able to find there all the typical collocations that together represent the coherent discourses mentioned above and thus they can, for instance, easily recognize that the snippet including phrases such as 'dangerous refugees' or 'state sovereignty' might match another snippet with statements about 'treasonous European elites' and 'national pride'.

In this regard, it is necessary to emphasize that the students need not be completely aware of the existence of all four discourses before the activity starts, since they are supposed to sort out the articles mostly on the basis of their language intuition. Only after this part of the activity is finished and the teams can present their suggested solutions, is the discussion opened and students present their modus operandi, that is, explain how they proceeded in their assembling and which attributes were decisive for the recognition of significant nuances in each of the articles. Thanks to these presentations, all the teams can then try to delimit and name four different styles of 'history writing' as well as define their typical traits, phrases, interpretative tools and so on. The extent and application of the worksheet might, of course, vary depending on the size of the groups, age of students and the main aim that each teacher wants to achieve, because all the 'packages' contain different levels of difficulty, differing, for instance, in the number of snippets or the intricacy of the language used. Furthermore, the activity is not planned as a single-use one, because identical groups of students can start with level 1 (the easiest) and carry on to the more demanding levels. This also includes the final level where student teams become the members of a new expedition and are charged with writing their own interpretation of an assigned historical event from one of the above-mentioned perspectives with the use of the vocabulary that they have already learnt.

No matter which level of difficulty is chosen, the essential meaning of this complex educational programme should remain the same: to present both historical events and social values not as absolutes and final facts that must be just accepted, but as a space for various interpretations. Students should also find out that even though these interpretations might be dangerous when they are misused for ideological purposes, we should still understand them if we do not want to get lost in the contemporary world of narratives, in which the ability to work with words and symbols is crucial.

Conclusion

As was already indicated in the introductory part, this study endeavours to identify the most urgent challenges in the current situation of the Czech education system regarding learning about desirable social values – which are indispensable for the stability of the liberal democratic paradigm – as well as the optimal consideration of collective identities in the schooling process. For this purpose, the chapter focuses on three particular though interlinked dimensions: first, the specific traits of the contemporary Czech national discourse were described to demonstrate how the dominant depiction of the Czech collective identity still uses traditional ethno-nationalist patterns of thought and thus is not able to accept more open concepts of identity based on civic and constructivist – instead of primordial – notions of behaviour. If the complicated historical narrative as well as mythical self-perception of Czechhood as victimhood have been revealed as one of the main causes of the above-mentioned dominance of ethnic patterns, the study also tries to suggest possible ways to promote dissimilar attributes in thinking about social cohesion in the Czech case.

Both the other parts of this chapter therefore reflect the question of identity and social values in the process of education, which must be considered as the fundamental platform for shaping the public image of our self-perception, including the narratives of the past. As the discourse analysis of the framework educational programme (RVP) proved, the contemporary official setting of the Czech national curriculum is full of vague and unclear formulations especially in the case of treating phenomena such as freedom, democracy and national or global identities, which unfortunately consolidate a traditional and thus uncritical understanding of collective values as a priori absolutes. Hence, the last section of the study presents and analyses crucial parts of the new educational project that is being applied in Czech schools and that predominantly endeavours to form the student's perception of collective identity while promoting the liberal canon of values, not through a traditional descriptive, but with the help of constructivist and interpretative approaches. By foregrounding questions of social manipulation, ideological interpretations of the national past, and the link between individual and collective levels of freedom as the crucial points of educational reflection and debate, the presented project – as well as this chapter – clearly supports the thesis that the development of critical and interpretative non-biased skills within the sphere of social reality is necessary if one wants to adhere to pluralist and open-minded attitudes towards fellow citizens in the twenty-first century.

Note

1. This online platform was developed by didacticians, historians and teachers at the University of Hradec Králové in 2018–20 in collaboration with Masaryk University in Brno and Palacký University in Olomouc in the framework of the common project focused on the enhancement of civic education and civic skills of Czech grammar school students.

References

Ágh, A. (2015), 'De-Europeanization and De-democratization Trends in ECE: From the Potemkin Democracy to the Elected Autocracy in Hungary', *Journal of Comparative Politics*, 2 (8): 4–26.
Anderson, B. (1983), *Imagined Communities: Reflections on the Origin and Spread of Nationalism*, London: Verso.
Aronowitz, S., and H. A. Giroux (2003), *Education Under Siege: The Conservative, Liberal and Radical Debate Over Schooling*, London: Routledge & Kegan Paul.
Ashmore, R. D., K. Deaux and T. McLaughlin-Volpe (2004), 'An Organizing Framework for Collective Identity: Articulation and Significance of Multidimensionality', *Psychological Bulletin*, 130 (1): 80–114.
Bauerová, H. (2018), 'Migration Policy of the V4 in the Context of Migration Crisis', *Politics in Central Europe*, 14 (2): 99–119.
Beck, C., and C. Kosnik (2006), *Innovations in Teacher Education. A Social Constructivist Approach*, New York: State University Press.
Berlin, I. (1969), 'Two Concepts of Liberty', in I. Berlin (ed.), *Four Essays on Liberty*, 118–72, London: Oxford University Press.
Bibó. I. (2015), 'The Miseries of East European Small States', in I. Bibó and I. Z. Dénes (eds), *The Art of Peacemaking: Political Essays by István Bibó*, 130–80, London: Yale University Press.
Burjanek, A. (2001), 'Xenofobie po česku: jak si stojíme mezi Evropany?', *Sborník prací Fakulty sociálních studií*, 6: 73–89.
Burtonwood, N. (2006), *Cultural Diversity, Liberal Pluralism and Schools: Isaiah Berlin and Education*, New York: Routledge.
Černý, J., M. Sedláčková and M. Tuček (2004), *Zdroje utváření skupinových mentalit v České republice po roce 1989*, Praha: Sociologický ústav AV ČR.
Chlup, R. (2020), 'Competing Myths of Czech Identity', *New Perspectives. Interdisciplinary Journal of Central & East European Politics and International Relations*, 28 (2): 179–204.
Cvrček, V., F. Čermák and V. Schmiedtová (eds) (2010), *Slovník komunistické moci*, Praha: NLN.
Darabont, F., et al. (1994), [Movie] *The Shawshank Redemption*, Burbank, CA: Warner Bros. Pictures.
Evans, G., and S. Whitefield (1998), 'The Structuring of Political Cleavages in Post-Communist Societies: The Case of the Czech Republic and Slovakia', *Political Studies*, 46 (1): 115–39.
Fidelius, P. (2016), *Řeč komunistické moci*, Praha: Triáda.
Foucault, M. (2002), *The Order of Things: An Archaeology of the Human Sciences*, London: Routledge.
Fukuyama, F. (2006), *The End of History and the Last Man*, New York: Free Press.
Hanan, A. (2015), *Reimagining Liberal Education: Affiliation and Inquiry in Democratic Schooling*, New York: Bloomsbury.
Havlíček, J. (2018), 'Rámcové vzdělávací programy a paradigma světových náboženství', *Orbis Scholae*, 12 (1): 51–67.
Heimann, M. (2009), *Czechoslovakia: The State That Failed*, London: Yale University Press.
Hejnal, O. (2012), 'Nacionalismus, multikulturalismus, sociální vyloučení a "sociálně nepřizpůsobiví": Analýza dominantního politického diskurzu v České republice (2006–2011)', *Antropowebzin*, 2: 47–66.

Hlaváček, P. (2019), *Nesamozřejmý národ?*, Praha: Academia.
Hvížďala, K., and J. Přibáň (2018), *Hledání dějin. O české státnosti a identitě*, Praha: Karolinum.
Jaskulowski, K. (2010), 'Western (civic) versus Eastern (ethnic) Nationalism. The Origins and Critique of the Dichotomy', *Polish Sociological Review*, 171 (3): 289–303.
Kamusella, T. (2012), *The Politics of Language and Nationalism in Modern Central Europe*, New York: Palgrave Macmillan.
Kaščák, O., and B. Pupala (2011), 'Governmentality – Neoliberalism – Education: The Risk Perspective', *Pedagogický časopis*, 2 (2): 145–60.
King, J. (2018), *Budweisers into Czechs and Germans: A Local History of Bohemian Politics, 1848–1948*, Princeton: Princeton University Press.
Kivunja, Ch. (2014), 'Do You Want Your Students to Be Job-Ready with 21st Century Skills? Change Pedagogies: A Pedagogical Paradigm Shift from Vygotskyian Social Constructivism to Critical Thinking, Problem Solving and Siemens' Digital Connectivism', *International Journal of Higher Education*, 3 (3): 81–91.
KK (2008), *Klíčové competence na gymnáziu*, Praha: VÚP.
Kritt, D. W., ed. (2018), *Constructivist Education in an Age of Accountability*, New York: Palgrave.
Květina, J., ed. (2016), 'Koncepce liberalismu a demokracie v edukačním procesu: dekonstrukce neoliberální dominance v RVP', *Pedagogika*, 66 (3): 312–29.
Lucas, G. (1999), [Movie] *Star Wars*, Episode I: The Phantom Menace, New York: Ballantine.
MacPherson, C. B. (2010), *The Political Theory of Possessive Individualism: Hobbes to Locke*, Oxford: Clarendon Press.
Mehlman, J. (1972), 'The "Floating Signifier": From Lévi-Strauss to Lacan', *Yale French Studies*, 48: 10–37.
Menzel, J. (1985), [Movie] *Vesničko má středisková* (My Sweet Little Village), Prague: Filmové studio Barrandov.
Pettit, P. (1999), *Republicanism: A Theory of Freedom and Government*, Oxford: Oxford University Press.
Pirro, A. L. P. (2015), 'The Populist Radical Right in the Political Process: Assessing Party Impact in Central and Eastern Europe', in M. Minkenberg (ed.), *Transforming the Transformation?: The East European Radical Right in the Political Process*, 80–104, New York: Routledge.
Popper, K. R. (2020), *The Open Society and Its Enemies*, Princeton: Princeton University Press.
Renan E. (1939), 'What Is a Nation?', in A. Zimmern (ed.), *Modern Political Doctrines*, 186–205, London: Oxford University Press.
Renck J. (2019), [TV series] 'Vichnaya Pamyat', *Chernobyl*, Episode 5, Episode aired 3May 2019, HBO, Warner Bros. Television Distribution.
Richardson, V., ed. (1997), *Constructivist Teacher Education: Building New Understandings*, London: Falmer Press.
Rousseau, J. J. (1999), *Discourse on Political Economy and the Social Contract*, Oxford: Oxford University Press.
Rupnik, J. (2018), *Střední Evropa je jako pták s očima vzadu*, Praha: Novela bohemica.
RVP (2007), *Rámcový vzdělávací program pro gymnázia*, Praha: VÚP.
Schmitt, C. (2000), *The Crisis of Parliamentary Democracy*, Cambridge: MIT Press.
Seligman, M. E. P., and M. Csikszentmihalyi (2000), 'Positive Psychology. An Introduction', *American Psychologist*, 55 (1): 5–14.

Skinner Q. (1998), 'The Idea of Negative Liberty: Philosophical and Historical Perspectives', in R. Rorty, J. B. Schneewind and Q. Skinner (eds), *Philosophy in History: Essays in the Historiography of Philosophy*, 193–222, Cambridge: Cambridge University Press.

Slačálek, O. (2016), 'Čechofobie', *Revue Prostor. Anatomie Nenávisti*, 106. Available online: https://revueprostor.cz/ondrej-slacalek-cechofobie (accessed 7 July 2020).

Snyder, T. (2003), *The Reconstruction of Nations: Poland, Ukraine, Lithuania, Belarus, 1569–1999*, London: Yale University Press.

Taylor, Ch. (2003), 'Cross-Purposes: The Liberal-Communitarian Debate', in D. Matravers and J. E. Pike (eds), *Debates in Contemporary Political Philosophy: An Anthology*, 195–212, London: Routledge.

Tesař, J. (2014), *Mnichovský komplex: Jeho příčiny a důsledky*, Praha: Prostor.

Thayer-Bacon, B. (2006), 'Beyond Liberal Democracy: Dewey's Renascent Liberalism', *Education and Culture*, 22 (2): 19–30.

Toomey, M. (2018), 'History, Nationalism and Democracy: Myth and Narrative in Viktor Orbán's "Illiberal Hungary"', *New Perspectives*, 26 (1): 87–108.

Wiatr, J. J. (2020), 'The Crisis of Democracy: An East-Central European Perspective', *Politics in Central Europe*, 16 (2): 353–65.

Wodak, R. (1999), 'The Discursive Construction of National Identity', in R. Wodak, R. de Cillia, M. Reisigl and K. Liebhart (eds), *The Discursive Construction of National Identity*, Edinburgh: Edinburgh University Press.

Yates, D. (2007), [Movie] *Harry Potter and the Order of the Phoenix*, Burbank, CA: Warner Bros. Pictures.

Zakaria, F. (1997), 'The Rise of Illiberal Democracy', *Foreign Affairs*, 76 (6): 22–43.

4

Preparedness of Estonian Teachers to Tackle Extremism in a Classroom: A Systematic Review of Empirical Studies Published in *Estonian Journal of Education* (2013–21)

Alar Kilp and Heidi Maiberg

Introduction

The chapter consists of five parts. It starts with the introduction focusing on extremism and education as well as the present situation of teaching of (violent) extremism in Estonia. Introduction is followed by methodology, research results, discussion and conclusion.

Extremism and Education

Extremism is mainly discussed in the context of schools in terms of preventing and tackling radicalization. Literature brings out several reasons why schools are a suitable place for discussing topics related to extremism and conducting preventative activities. Radicalization Awareness Network (2015) sees that among the other aims and duties, schools have the objective to provide a safe and respectful learning environment for their students. Therefore, in cases of possible danger to the safe and suitable learning environment, schools must protect their students and react to the changes. At the same time, schools are a good platform for discussing such topics due to their structure. Through the education system, it is possible to reach many youths simultaneously, whether they are at risk of radicalization or recruitment or not (Wallner 2020).

An additional advantage on behalf of the schools to be a place where extremism is discussed is their ability to form a community. They are the connection point between homes, parents, local government and other services. Therefore, in case some changes occur, it is possible to react fast. Research supports school's role as the leading reactor. For instance, former extremists in Sweden claim that young people's situation at school and pupils' relationships with their teachers clearly impact the processes that lead to their radicalization (Mattsson and Johansson 2018, 2020).

Practice in those countries where the education sector is allocated as a place for prevention shows that educators can have a leading role in the fight against (violent) extremism with necessary training and teaching materials. For instance, in the UK, pedagogues are in a key position to protect children and young people from the dangers of extremist narratives. They have to protect students from radicalizing influences, build resilience to extremist narratives, identify any vulnerabilities or worry about changes in students' behaviour, and be aware of the next steps when a student causes further concern (Educate against Hate), Their lack of knowledge may cause schools inability to take responsibility. Studies show that first, teachers feel uncomfortable and concerned about pupils and therefore prevent them from discussing the named topics (Higton et al. 2018). Second, although educators often are aware of ongoing radicalization processes, they either underestimate their seriousness or simply do not know what to do (van San et al. 2013).

In summary, schools are suitable places for preventing and tackling (violent) extremism. They have a key role in the communities; educators have long-lasting relations with the students and according to studies, they notice changes in students' behaviour and world view. The problem is that if educators do see signs of radicalization, it might be unclear how to react to the issues. Although radicalization is a very individual process, the unsolved identity, domestic, socioeconomic or other problems might make students vulnerable to extreme ideologies and/or movements. For the named reasons, the school's and educators' role in preventing and tackling (violent) extremism is essential.

(Violent) Extremism in Estonia

In terms of violent extremism, Estonia is a safe country in CEE. According to Global Terrorism Index, Estonia is ranked 126th in the countries impacted by terrorism with zero attacks (Institute for Economics & Peace 2020). Nevertheless, there are cases known to the general public that have caught the attention of law enforcement agencies. For example, regarding extremism inspired by violent Islamism, around twenty people with ties to Estonia have been or remain in the Syrian-Iraqi conflict zone (Estonian Internal Security Service 2021). Also, it is known that individuals who have engaged in active combat in the mentioned region have moved through and to Estonia.

There is a growing interest in right-wing ideas in society mainly due to increased electoral support of right-wing populist party named Estonian Conservative People's Party (Petsinis 2019; Kasekamp et al. 2019). However, despite the (currently) non-violent paradigm of populists, there are cases of individuals sharing materials online supporting violent right-wing extremism. Therefore, in 2020, the Estonian Internal Security Service had to intervene repeatedly to prevent the implementation of possible threats in the so-called offline space (Estonian Internal Security Service 2021). Also, in 2021, the government of Estonia decided to establish an anti-Semitism working group, which aims to create a common information field to combat anti-Semitism (Ringvee 2021).

In Estonia, the connections and places of cooperation between education and extremism have been little studied and include, above all, the prevention of violent extremism. Recently, within the framework of the RITA-Migration project, two guides were published which are 'Extreme Violence and Radicalization at School – 10 Answers That a Teacher Needs to Know' (Maasing and Salvet 2018) and a similarly comprehensive document 'Prevention of Ethnic Conflict and Radicalization: Recommendations for Schools' (Nahkur and Maasing 2020). In both materials, the authors discussed the role of schools and teachers in preventing and tackling radicalization and extremism, and provided recommendations. Lack of studies and the small number of materials covering the above-mentioned topic is linked to the high level of security in Estonia – there has not been a need for materials or training that provide information about preventing or tackling extremism in a classroom or school environment. Due to the societal changes, however, the need for such supportive materials might increase. For instance, in their 2020–1 yearbook, the Estonian Internal Security Service (2021) emphasized the role of the school. They highlighted the importance of the teachers as well as parents in the prevention of violent extremism (Estonian Internal Security Service 2021).

Methodology

This study conducted a systematic review (Čablová et al. 2017: 177), following a step-by-step approach suggested by several previous studies (Petticrew 2001; Umscheid 2013; Verbeek et al. 2012). We started with identifying a topic of interest and formulated a research question that guides the whole study.

Research Question

The study aims to determine teachers' preparedness (Ingvarson et al. 2007; Udegbe 2016) to deal with extremism-related content in the classroom irrespective of whether they have formally taught extremism-related classes or passed extremism-related training in their teacher education training. We selected this research question to guide our study because we find it too naïve (and un-academic) to assume that teachers who have not passed any extremism-related teacher training are totally unprepared for tackling extremism-related content in the classroom and will not discuss above-mentioned topic with students.

For this reason, the research question is divided into three segments. Preparedness of Estonian teachers to deal with extremism-related themes is studied in three dimensions: (1) content knowledge, (2) social, organizational and interpersonal pedagogical skills that are necessary in the teaching profession in general as well as in the cases where teaching involves extremism-related content; (3) sensitive, 'hidden' and 'invisible' aspects and themes related to both dimensions mentioned above.

For starters, teaching of extremism-related content overlaps partly with teaching of history, where tackling of some historic as well as current examples of extremism is unavoidable. Teaching of history involves controversial and sensitive issues (Tribukait

2021), wherefore all teachers of history will sooner or later encounter issues that are met with feelings of discomfort, protest or disbelief by the students (Savenije and Brauch 2019). Therefore, it is reasonable to expect that at least some teachers in Estonia are capable of handling extremism-related content in their classrooms also in cases where their professional preparation and teaching courses have not focused explicitly on extremism.

Like any other subject matter, teaching extremism involves – besides 'content knowledge' and 'pedagogical content knowledge' (Shulman 1987) – also general pedagogical expertise.

In order to be 'prepared' to teach extremism-related themes, teachers need to have several general pedagogic skills, which are learnt and enhanced in the teacher education of all subject domains. They also need to *believe* in their pedagogical skills (Udegbe 2016) and to have a positive perception of 'self-efficacy' (Bandura 1977), which is defined as an intuitive understanding of one's capabilities to bring about the desired student outcomes in teaching (Brown et al. 2015). All teachers need to be able to guide classroom discussions and to manage the emotional atmosphere in class. They need to be able to 'read' adequately what goes on in each and every learner. Like any other teacher, the sense of preparedness of a teacher of extremism-related content is dependent on professional experience in an organization (school, university) (Ingvarson et al. 2007 and on how confident and professional one feels in a teaching profession.

However, not every subject domain involves controversies and sensitive issues which are similar to those that emerge in extremism-related themes. Some degree of emotional discomfort (e.g. 'pedagogy of discomfort', Zembylas 2015) is unavoidable in children's school experience irrespective of the subject domain, because the emotional 'comfort zone' is not an environment most appropriate for learning. However, topics related to extremism – discussing actual terror attacks that have taken place, online recruiting mechanisms and the like – can be emotionally extraordinarily difficult to understand. In addition, interpretation of content knowledge and pedagogical content knowledge (and also teachers' skill to present content in ways that build on students' existing understanding) that teachers of extremism-related themes are expected to master overlaps most with content knowledge and pedagogical content knowledge they need in classes of history, religion and social education. In these subject domains, the examples and phenomena discussed in classroom are often related to the identities, interests and status of those present in the classroom and society, wherefore the related knowledge also becomes sensitive and 'difficult knowledge' (An 2021). Teaching of the latter subject areas involves (political, religious, ethnic, moral etc.) controversies, which teachers have a choice to avoid or embrace (Girard et al. 2021: 237).

Selection of Main Source

Our choice of topic and the related research question deals with a question that has not been sufficiently taught or studied in an Estonian context. In many other countries – such as France or Finland – extremism has been recognized as a subject matter requiring its place in teacher education programmes and national educational programmes.

Sensitivity to specific controversial issues differs significantly from country to country (Tribukait 2021), Estonian society has been divided over the experience, meaning and memory related to the Second World War (Raudsepp and Zadora 2019). Correspondingly, what issues become 'hidden' (recognized in the experience of at least some actors, but not included in the public debate and/or decision-making process) and 'invisible (not recognized as an issue to be raised) (Gaventa 2021) or 'silenced' in order to protect group identity (Savenije and Goldberg 2019) are contextual and specific to a given society.

As the study focuses on Estonia, we selected *Eesti Haridusteaduste Ajakiri* (Estonian Journal of Education, https://eha.ut.ee/en/), which is a bi-annual, peer-reviewed journal publishing high-quality original research in all areas of education. It publishes predominantly empirical research with samples (including teachers and teaching) from Estonia. It is the only open-access academic journal focusing on pedagogy in Estonian that has published in a sufficient amount of high quality empirical research about Estonian education at all levels.

Rationale for Inclusion and Exclusion of Articles

We screened all articles published from the first issue of this journal (2013) until the summer of 2021. During this period, the journal published 124 research articles (we did not include editorials and book reviews) in sixteen issues (only one issue was published in 2013, and we included only one issue for 2021, because the second issue of 2021 was not published by summer of 2021).

We focused on articles that studied teachers and/or teaching empirically in Estonia and selected 34 articles out of 124 (27.5 per cent), We excluded: translated articles, research articles with samples outside of Estonia, studies that did not involve the empirical study of teachers and pre-school level of education. Our selection was limited to basic, secondary and higher levels of education.

Among these thirty-four, five articles studied teachers and teaching *indirectly*. Their empirical sample did not include teachers, but they examined either how students perceived teacher and teacher's teaching style, how teachers contribute to value education, school microclimate or bullying free school programme according to students or school management. We excluded one article, which studied didactical choices of four Estonian language teachers because it discussed too narrowly curricular decisions of a specific subject matter.

Data Analysis

We used eight categories that we identified inductively to be relevant to our review question (Cremin and Chappell 2021) and seventeen codes (Table 4.1) when we screened the selected articles' content. Were *reviewed* selected articles and *synthesized* the relevant focuses and findings for each category (analysed in the Results section).

We carefully collected data regarding the level of education, subject matter, methods used and gender (of teachers and students), but did not review systematically along these dimensions.

Table 4.1 Categories Relevant for the Study of Teaching Extremism Related to Content and Codes Used in the Analysis

Category	Code
1 Extremism-related (pedagogical) content knowledge	Pedagogical content knowledge
	Content knowledge
2 Tackling emotions and sensitive issues	Sensitive for the teacher
	Sensitive for students
	Socially sensitive
3 Bullying	Teachers as victims of bullying
	Students as victims of bullying
4 Teacher's self-reflective attitudes and practice	Perception of professional competence
	Perception of self-efficacy
5 Teacher-learner interaction in social media	Professionalism
6 Teacher-learner interaction in classroom	Learners' perceptions of the teacher
	Teachers' perceptions of learners
	Influence of teachers' choices on students' learning
7 Teachers' professional experience	Novice teacher
	Experienced teacher
8 Context of teaching	Organizational context
	Social context

Source: Own elaboration.

However, we did not systematically review the *methods* dimension because the methods used varied significantly. Studies often relied on semi-structured or structured interviews or questionnaires, photo interviews, autoethnographic material and the like. Therefore, a more systematic and comprehensive analysis of the methods used would not have added value to our present study.

Also, *gender* of teachers was identified in the samples of most studies, but as it was not an explicit research question and theme in any article, we did not review this dimension systematically. As a rule, studies presented demographic data regarding the proportions of men and women, girls and boys in the sample, but studied teachers and students as aggregate phenomena without explicit research focuses on gender differences. Nevertheless, we do recognize gender of teachers to be a significant aspect that would require further research. For example, the sample of teachers in several articles (by numbers of articles listed in Appendix, Table 4A.1: **4, 12, 13, 25**) consisted only of women, or the proportion of men was below 10 per cent (articles **1, 9, 16, 30**).

We could have focused on the *subject domain*, as there was one article directly focusing on history teaching, but because in several other studies the sample of teachers included, among others, teachers of history or teachers studied were not grouped according to their subject domain, we had to drop this aspect from systematic review.

We faced similar problem with the *level of education*, which was not identified in all studies and would have extended this study beyond the present scope. Four studies involved teachers without specifying at what level of education they were working on, while several studies involved teachers from both basic and secondary level of education. Although we did have a general overview of the level of education (half of articles were limited to basic education, grades 1–9 and about one in six dealt with higher education, secondary school or primary school, grades 1–3, respectively), comparative study of findings according to level of education was beyond the scope of this study.

Results

Results section is structured according to eight categories listed in Table 4.1.

Category 1: Extremism-Related (Pedagogical) Content Knowledge

'Extremism' was not mentioned in the titles or keywords of any of the articles. The content related to 'extremism' was dealt with by one article out of thirty-four. Article **22** dealt with sensitive issues in Estonian history teacher's ($n=37$) experiences in two ways – by content and by practical teaching experience. Examples of extremism-related content were terrorism, nationalism, the Second World War, violence against women, violence in war, refugees, religion, genocide of Armenians and Islamic State. Most history teachers felt most confident in tackling controversial themes when they felt having sufficient amount of knowledge and arguments about the theme involved.

Category 2: Dealing with Emotions and Sensitive Issues

Three articles dealt with teacher-related emotional challenges and sensitive issues. Article **6** studied the influence of teacher parenting style and school-related adverse experiences on school satisfaction of students. Although the study found higher level of negative affect among pupils to be concurring with low school satisfaction in grades 4 and 5, a high level of encouragement and affection reflected in teachers' classroom management practices appeared together with more frequent school satisfaction. As a result, the study concluded that supportive teachers' parenting style is one of the mechanisms which helps pupils to cope with negative affects at school that to some extent unavoidably accompany learning experiences.

Article **22** deals with sensitive issues in history classes as they were self-reported by teachers. Issues become sensitive mainly in two ways – they are sensitive to individual(s) in the classroom (for teacher or student) or controversial and heatedly debated in society. Sensitive topics include current sociopolitical issues such as the refugee crisis, ongoing wars (e.g. Ukraine, Syria) and geopolitical relations with Russia and historical themes like Second World War (including war crimes, Holocaust), events in 1939–40 and 1944 (Soviet occupation) in Estonia. They become sensitive because students, their families or communities take them personally. Therefore, collective memories and general world views as well as direct personal involvement are at play when sensitive issues are tackled in the classroom.

Article **32** studies a theme – student cyberbullying of teachers – which is highly sensitive because all teachers in the sample ($n=14$) had experienced some form of student cyberbullying. Still, only some of them were ready to talk about it in public. This is because the teacher, who has experienced student cyberbullying, is concerned about the relationship with students and may feel insecure and vulnerable also in relations with colleagues and school management. Hence, cyberbullying is a sensitive and 'hidden' topic. Results show that teachers prefer not to talk about being bullied in cyberspace. Some teachers do not inform school management about it for fear of shame. Others abstained from making the issue public because they felt that school management did not support them sufficiently on a previous occasion.

Category 3: Bullying

Two of three articles (**23** and **32**) which addressed bullying in school deal with teachers as victims. While school bullying is not a new phenomenon or a new research theme, focusing on teachers is new and controversial.

Articles reviewed yield highly different results on how many Estonian teachers have experienced bullying by students. Some form of cyberbullying (such as degrading visuals, flaming, denigration, harassment, impersonation or cyberstalking) had been experienced by all teachers of the sample ($n=14$) of article **32**, while 'only' 35 per cent of teachers ($n=564$) self-reported having been victims of student bullying and 25 per cent of adult (including parents, colleagues, school leadership, other school staff) in article **23**. Furthermore, besides vastly different sizes of samples, these studies also followed different methods (online questionnaire versus semi-structured interviews) and conducted the empirical study at different years (2016 in article **23** and 2019 in article **32**).

It is likely that from 2016 until 2019, the theme of bullying in schools had become more of a legitimate theme for public discussion. To the extent that bullying remains a 'hidden' and 'invisible' (unrecognized) aspect of teachers' practical experience (article **32**), its presence is unlikely to decrease. Degrees of victimization and bullying decline when both students, teachers and school managements are committed to anti-bullying programmes in schools. The study of two-year anti-bullying pilot programme in twenty Estonian schools (article **20**) discovered that the average prevalence of victims in schools taking anti-bullying programme dropped by 17 per cent. The anti-bullying programme works better in classrooms where students feel that the teacher strongly condemns bullying, is involved and supports measures to eliminate bullying in the school context.

Category 4: Teacher's Self-Reflective Attitudes and Practice

In their teaching practice, novice teachers focus more on the subject matter (articles **1**, **2**), whereas experienced teachers recognize better and focus more on student learning and understanding (article **1**), The main exceptions are teacher-practitioners in applied higher education (article **8**) and science teachers in primary and secondary schools (article **21**) who use more lectures and teacher-centred practices, probably due to particularities of their subject domains.

In one way or other, several articles deal with the way (confident, empowered, efficient) the teacher feels at work. Article **21** used survey data (Teaching and Learning International Survey, OECD, years 2008 and 2013) covering 22 per cent of primary and secondary school teachers in Estonia, focused on teachers' self-efficacy and found the level of self-efficacy of Estonian teachers to be low in international comparison. Article **26** focused on teachers' attitudes, the identity of self and 'inner discourse' regarding competitive or collaborative organizational culture and classified about one-third of teachers ($n=45$) to a 'non-empowered' group, because these teachers do not express confidence in the impact and value of their work. Remaining teachers expressed discourses of collaboration and competition. In the discourse of competition, teachers see themselves as resources and perceive colleagues and/or leadership as obstacles. Collaboration discourse aims at self-realization, meaningful work, learning and experimenting together, school development as well as teachers' responsibility towards school development. The non-empowered discourse is articulated through no-messages (do not see, do not know, have not heard, did not do, do not know how, have not understood).

Teachers ($n=101$) can boost self-confidence by a guided reflection procedure (article **30**), which has the potential to increase their sense of responsibility and empowerment. The guided reflection procedure enabled teachers with varying degrees of experience, expectations and needs to utilize the different supportive aspects integrated into the design to enhance reflection. As a result, teachers who passed the guided reflection procedure felt empowered, more responsible for their teaching, better able to connect theory with practice and engage in deeper thinking about their teaching practice.

Two articles dealt with additional challenges that accompany the teaching profession. Article **31** found out that teachers in primary schools ($n=47$) have too little autonomy over the choice of teaching materials. Article **27**, which studied just two university teachers – one novice teacher and the other assistant – highlighted different roles and statuses that may in contradicting ways shape the practice of teachers, who need to take full responsibility, feel the need for guidance and have to navigate different, often contradictory, roles (colleague, mentor, mentee).

One of the articles (**33**) analysed self-analysis reports of Estonian schools ($n=39$) and highlighted that teachers contribute to values (and character) education at schools by discussing values, managing the classroom environment in a value-oriented way, and setting personal examples.

Category 5: Informal Teacher-Learner Interaction – Social Media

All three articles devoted to teacher-learner relations in social media recognized that teachers and learners use social media differently and identified several dilemmas faced by teachers as professionals: when and how it is proper for them to intervene in cases where children are facing risks (articles **9**, **10**), how much of privacy and status differences is it appropriate to abandon in social media settings (article **9**), what will students do with the content that teacher has made available on social media (article **32**), and whether to leave children/learners in social media alone (article **10**).

Category 6: Formal Teacher-Learner Interaction – Classroom

Formal teacher-learner interaction was a theme covered by the largest number of articles (thirteen). Dependent on the direction of influence and on the variation of agency, the section is divided into three sub-themes: learners' perceptions of the teacher, teachers' perceptions of learners, influence of teachers' choices on students' learning.

Learners' Perceptions of the Teacher

How are teachers' behaviour, relations to students and course organization being perceived by students? What in students' view hinders their learning most and least? Three articles dealt with these questions. The answers are ordered from most negative to least negative:

- too ambiguous expectations and instructions upset students most (article **29**),
- imbalance (too little or too much, too easy or too difficult) in the extent of guidance, feedback, learning challenge and workload (article **29**),
- teachers' 'perceived care' (article **34**) and supportive behaviour (article **10**) have a contradictory impact. Certainly, for a segment of students, such teacher behaviours are beneficial for learning (and for developing other-oriented and conservation values in adolescents), but perceived care of teachers is not beneficial to those who are committed to values such as self-enhancement and openness to change (article **34**), and lack of supportive teacher behaviour does not hinder learning for others (article **10**),
- least hindering is the extent to which the teacher uses different teaching methods and styles (article **29**). It can be said that learners 'do not mind' any teaching technique or approach when they understand clearly how this method works and what teacher expects from them.

Teachers Perceptions of Learners

'Pygmalion effect' (Chang 2011) – that is that teachers' expectations and beliefs in the student have an influence on student motivation and achievement – seems to work at all levels of education. Both in primary (article **3**) and higher education (article **15**), the teachers' ($n=15$ and $n=20$, respectively) expressed beliefs in the abilities of students have an influence on student performance. 'Pygmalion effect' works best when teachers believe in both students *and* themselves. According to article **15**, this causal chain presupposes a degree of inner confidence in a teacher: students in experienced teachers' classes feel more confident and satisfied, and vice versa, namely, experienced teachers are more confident than novice teachers in what they do.

Two articles (**4, 17**) emphasize that a positive learning environment requires the teacher to support 'autonomy' (freedom of learner) and 'structuring' (clear rules and instructions) and to avoid 'control' and 'chaos'. Teachers tend to be biased or misled in their assessments about the character and individual challenges of learners. For example, they ($n=118$) tend to expect that students with good grades and introverts have less self-regulatory problems than extroverts and low-performing students (article **7**), A similar misled expectation was also found regarding 'outcome-based education', which was expected to be a means of 'student-centred learning where students take an active role and responsibility for their learning experiences' (article **24**), but the study did not find such a correlation.

Lastly, two articles (**18, 19**) dealt with special needs from different perspectives – one focused on special education (inclusive education for the disabled) and the other on 'giftedness as a special educational need'. Despite focuses on different groups of students, they arrived at four overlapping conclusions. First, a novel understanding of learning in Estonian educational system is committed to supporting both disability and giftedness as special educational needs. Second, both kinds of special needs require teachers to put in extra work. Third, from teachers' perspective, both disability and giftedness need to be observed, recognized and supported on an individual basis. Fourth, the individual work (with both) contradicts the general organization and logic of the educational system, which expects learners to study and progress as a group.

Influence of Teachers' Choices on Students' Learning

Articles which relied on quantitative data and test/examination results found correlation between teachers' choice of study methods and student performance, while studies that relied on learners' perceptions (analysed above) did not. Articles **5** and **16** emphasize that variation in teaching methods is likely to enhance student performance, but the given subject matter still conditions it. As a rule, students whose teachers ($n=48$) used a larger variety of teaching practices achieved better results (in text comprehension and verbal abilities) than students in classes where teachers did not vary or adapt teaching in accordance with the student's cognitive development (article **5**). However, students of Estonian language classes of teachers ($n=46$) using verbal communication means more diversely and flexibly did not achieve higher level of language proficiency than students of teachers who did not use different communicative components that frequently (article **16**).

Category 7: Novice and Experienced Teacher

General findings from six articles studying the experience and challenges of novice teachers are as follows: the main challenge for a (really) novice teacher is the management of classroom conduct (article **15**); novice teachers focus more on subject matter than on learner or learner's understanding (articles **1, 15**); they gain self-confidence with experience (all six articles); they are more likely to remain in the teaching profession when they identify positively with a subject field (article **2**) and teaching (and are not primarily oriented to a scientific career in a university) (article

11); they adapt to the workings of school/educational institution (article **11**); they have amicable relations with colleagues (article **12**); and learn how to navigate efficiently through multiple, often contradictory, roles in teaching profession (article **27**).

In particular, novice teachers ($n=20$) tend to focus their teaching more on the memorization of subject matter (article **1**); their ($n=13$) identification with the professional identity (identification with the subject field) is a work in progress (article **2**); they are less likely to drop out of teaching profession if their ($n=13$) value orientations do not contradict the attitudes of their colleagues, while they experience supportive attitude from their colleagues (article **12**); and they (n=20) are more likely to express uncertainties related to the adaptation to the school environment than experienced teachers do (article **15**).

Category 8: Teacher's Organizational and Social Context

Lastly, ten articles analysed teacher's work in the contexts of an organization (school, university) and society.

Organizational Context

Seven articles analysed the impact of an organizational context on the work experience of teachers. Teachers ($n=47$), particularly novice teachers, do not identify much with organizational aims (article **14**) or communicate much with school management, and the little interaction that they ($n=13$) have, however, may influence their adaptation to the school environment (article **12**). Teachers' identification with teaching is influenced by the value attributed to teaching in a given organizational culture (article **2**) and enhanced when they ($n=54$) feel to be fully fledged members of the organization (article **11**). Teachers' ($n=45$) relations with colleagues involve both collaboration and competition, and their relations with colleagues are shaped by a given organizational culture which may cherish cooperation over competition, or vice versa (article **26**). Students learn better in an organization that supports students and learning (article **10**) – correspondingly, organizational microclimate that does not support student learning is also inhibiting the self-efficacy of an individual teacher. In cases of interaction problems (such as being a victim of bullying), teachers ($n =14$) may feel vulnerable also vis-à-vis colleagues and organizational management, and they expect more support and protection, particularly from the side of management (article **32**).

Social Context

The social context was a relevant aspect in the studies of three articles. Discussion of issues which are 'societally sensitive' (article **22**) may not always be sensitive to individuals present in the classroom. In the Estonian case, current and historic themes closely related to Russian and Estonian identities are usually sensitive both for social groups and for individuals.

Neoliberal changes in the organization and management of education in Estonia have brought along several positive trends – overall levels of economic welfare have risen steadily over the decades, while educational policy has become committed to principles that have shifted focus from teachers to learners and from subject matter to human learning. However, neoliberal changes of educational system have also brought some new tensions and challenges that increase demands and expectations for teachers' professional practice. At present, teachers face several contradictory expectations: they ($n=33$) need to assess learners' performance both based on learner's individuality and uniform standards of student performance (article **25**); their ($n=13$) students are simultaneously learners in an educational institution and clients in an educational market (article **28**); and teachers' performance has to deliver both understandings in learners and to be efficient (in time expenditure) (article **28**).

Discussion

In this section, we discuss themes which, during the process of conducting this study, we recognized as highly relevant, but were not explicitly reviewed by us in this chapter or were not dealt with in the journal.

Surprisingly, we did not find any article that would have been devoted to *media literacy* and critical media reading and interpreting skills, that is, to skills which should mostly be developed in schools and also skills without which it would be almost impossible to efficiently prevent violent terrorism, radicalization or the spread of extremism in and through schools (Vallinkoski et al. 2021), Surely, if there would have been any such study, we would have added 'communicative skills' to our list of themes.

'Age of the teacher' was documented in most studies (typically they identified the youngest, oldest and average age of the teacher) and was indirectly also studied under the theme 'novice and experienced teacher'; however that theme requires more focus study. For example, the age difference between teacher and learner may be highly relevant for the pattern of interaction in social media, where the strategy of interaction which works well with students who are 'about teacher's age' may not be an efficient one for those teachers who are several generations older than their students.

We feel that there is also something important to be discovered about 'level of education'. It is expected that teachers will have different 'good practices' regarding adjusting teaching of 'difficult issues' (like war and violence) to different age groups. We were unable to study this thoroughly formally because not all studies presented sufficient information about the level of education and due to lack of studies that directly dealt with extremism, sensitive issues or 'difficult knowledge' in general.

Conclusion

The sample of our study consisted of pedagogical research published in an educational journal. As we found, no article was directly devoted to extremism-related content knowledge, and it is fair to conclude that as far as pedagogical research is concerned, extremism as a subject domain is still largely 'invisible' (neither recognized nor analysed as a relevant research field) in Estonian educational research.

Our study was not about teacher education, however, and our findings indicate a need for more formal training in the subject matter because its teaching requires, besides general pedagogic competence, content expertise and pedagogical content expertise. The results indicate that content-related skills are most present among teachers of disciplines (such as history) where the cases and examples studied often overlap with teaching of extremism-related themes. In the introduction, we cited some online resources available that certainly some Estonian teachers have consulted, and in many cases, teachers have also taken some courses that deal – in some way or another – with the teaching of extremism-related content.

In addition, the studies reviewed presented quite a list of themes related to teaching extremism in one way or another – for example, bullying, values education, sensitive issues, feelings and perceptions of self and others in teacher-learner interaction. Therefore, it can be concluded that educational research in Estonia has addressed quite substantially a broader set of skills and competencies relevant for the pedagogy of extremism-related content.

In particular, our findings are most positive regarding the large scope of studies that dealt with teachers' social, emotional and interpersonal pedagogic skills; teachers' experience in organizational and social settings; and formal and informal teacher-learner interaction. With this finding, we know that at least Estonian educational research is highly committed to developing general skills necessary for tackling efficiently extremism-related content in the classroom, although explicitly extremism as a subject matter has remained either hidden or invisible subject domain so far.

An ideal teacher would master both content knowledge and pedagogical skills. However, not in every subject area (e.g. mathematics) exists a duty to tackle extremism-related topics, but the latter can pop up in any classroom, wherefore some preparedness to tackle such topics is a need for any teacher. Conversely, also those who are competent in content related to extremism need, in addition to competence in the subject domain, efficient perceptions of preparedness and self-efficacy as a teacher.

References

An, S. (2021), 'Engaging with Difficult Knowledge of U.S. Wars in Elementary Social Studies Methods Course', *Social Studies*, 113 (1): 17–29, doi:10.1080/00377996.2021.1945995.

Bandura, A. (1977), 'Self-Efficacy: Toward a Unifying Theory of Behavioral Change', *Psychological Review*, 84 (2): 191–215.

Brown, A. L., J. Lee and D. Collins (2015), 'Does Student Teaching Matter? Investigating Pre-Service Teachers' Sense of Efficacy and Preparedness', *Teaching Education*, 26 (1): 77–93.

Čablová, L., R. Pates, M. Miovský and J. Noel (2017), 'How to Write a Systematic Review Article and Meta-Analysis', in T. F. Babor, K. Stenius, R. Pates, M. Miovský, J. O'Reilly and P. Candon (eds), *Publishing Addiction Science: A Guide for the Per-Plexed*, 173–89, London: Ubiquity Press.

Chang, J. (2011), 'A Case Study of the "Pygmalion Effect": Teacher Expectations and Student Achievement', *International Education Studies*, 4 (1): 198–201.

Cremin, T., and K. Chappell (2021), 'Creative Pedagogies: A Systematic Review', *Research Papers in Education*, 36 (3): 299–331.
Educate Against Hate (n.d.), 'Top Tips to Help Teachers Discuss Radicalisation with Pupils'. Available online: https://educateagainsthate.com/wp-content/uploads/2020/04/EAH_Teachers_Top-Tips_English_AW_V5_interactive.pdf (accessed 30 July 2021).
Estonian Internal Security Service (2021), 'Kaitsepolitsei Aastaraamat 2020–2021'. Available online: https://kapo.ee/sites/default/files/public/content_page/Aastaraamat-2020-2021.pdf (accessed 30 July 2021).
Gaventa, J. (2021), 'Linking the Prepositions: Using Power Analysis to Inform Strategies for Social Action', *Journal of Political Power*, 14 (1): 109–30.
Girard, B., L. M. Harris, L. K. Mayger, T. M. Kessner and S. Reid (2021), '"There's No Way We Can Teach All of This": Factors That Influence Secondary History Teachers' Content Choices', *Theory & Research in Social Education*, 49 (2): 227–61.
Higton, J., R. Patel, I. Mulla, N. Francis, A. Choudhoury and A. van Rij (2018), *Prevent and Counter Extremism in General Further Education Colleges*, London: King's College London, Department for Education.
Ingvarson, L., A. Beavis and E. Kleinhenz (2007), 'Factors Affecting the Impact of Teacher Education Programmes on Teacher Preparedness: Implications for Accreditation Policy', *European Journal of Teacher Education*, 30 (4): 351–81.
Institute for Economics & Peace (2020), 'Global Terrorism Index 2020: Measuring the Impact of Terrorism'. Available online: http://visionofhumanity.org/reports (accessed 30 July 2021).
Kasekamp, A., M. L. Madisson and L. Wierenga (2019), 'Discursive Opportunities for the Estonian Populist Radical Right in a Digital Society', *Problems of Post-Communism*, 66 (1): 47–58.
Maasing, H., and S. Salvet (2018), *Äärmuslik vägivald ja radikaliseerumine koolis – 10 vastust, mida õpetaja peab teadma. RITA-ränne projekt 2018*. Available online: https://sisu.ut.ee/sites/default/files/ranne/files/maasing_ja_salvet_2020_aarmuslik_vagivald_ja_radikaliseerumine_koolis_juhend_opetajatele.pdf (accessed 30 July 2021).
Mattson, C., and T. Johansson (2018), 'Becoming, Belonging and Leaving – Exit Processes among Young Neo-Nazis in Sweden', *Journal for Deradicalization*, (16): 34–69.
Mattsson, C., and T. Johansson (2020), 'The Hateful Other: Neo-Nazis in School and Teachers' Strategies for Handling Racism', *British Journal of Sociology of Education*, 41 (8): 1149–63.
Nahkur, O., and H. Maasing (2020), 'Etniliste konfliktide ja radikaliseerumise ennetamise soovitusi koolidele', RITA-ränne projekt 2020. Available online: https://sisu.ut.ee/sites/default/files/ranne/files/konfliktide_ja_radikaliseerumise_ennetamise_soovitused_koolidele.pdf (accessed 30 July 2021).
Petsinis, V. (2019), 'Identity Politics and Right-Wing Populism in Estonia: The Case of EKRE', *Nationalism and Ethnic Politics*, 25 (2): 211–30.
Petticrew, M. (2001), 'Systematic Reviews from Astronomy To Zoology: Myths and Misconceptions', *BMJ: British Medical Journal*, 322 (7278): 98–101.
Radicalisation Awareness Network. (2015), *Manifesto for Education – Empowering Educators and Schools*. Available online: https://ec.europa.eu/home-affairs/sites/homeaffairs/files/what-we-do/networks/radicalisation_awareness_network/docs/manifesto-for-education-empowering-educators-and-schools_en.pdf (accessed 30 July 2021).
Raudsepp, M., and A. Zadora (2019), 'The Sensitive Scars of the Second World War in Teaching European History', *Pedagogy, Culture & Society*, 27 (1): 87–110.

Ringvee, R. (2021, May 28), Euroopas tõstab antisemitism üha enam pead, *ERR*. Available online: https://www.err.ee/1608228510/ringvee-euroopas-tostab-antisemitism-uha-enam-pead (accessed 30 July 2021).

Savenije, G. M., and T. Goldberg (2019), 'Silences in a Climate of Voicing: Teachers' Perceptions of Societal and Self-Silencing Regarding Sensitive Historical Issues', *Pedagogy, Culture & Society*, 27 (1): 39–64.

Savenije, G. M., N. Brauch and W. Wagner (2019), 'Sensitivities in History Teaching across Europe and Israel', *Pedagogy, Culture & Society*, 27 (1): 1–6.

Shulman, L. S. (1987), 'Knowledge and Teaching: Foundations of the New Reform', *Harvard Educational Review*, 57 (1): 1–22.

Tribukait, M. (2021), 'Students' Prejudice as a Teaching Challenge: How European History Educators Deal with Controversial and Sensitive issues in a Climate of Political Polarization', *Theory & Research in Social Education*, doi:10.1080/00933104.2021.1947426.

Udegbe, B. (2016), 'Preparedness to Teach: Experiences of the University of Ibadan Early Career Academics', *Studies in Higher Education*, 41 (10): 1786–802.

Umscheid, C. A. (2013), 'A Primer on Performing Systematic Reviews and Meta-Analyses', *Clinical Infectious Diseases*, 57 (5): 725–34.

Vallinkoski, K., P. M. Koirikivi and L. Malkki (2021), ' "What Is This ISIS All About?" Addressing Violent Extremism with Students: Finnish Educators' Perspectives', *European Educational Research Journal*, doi: 14749041211010074.

van San, M., S. Sieckelinck and M. de Winter (2013), 'Ideals Adrift: An Educational Approach to Radicalization', *Ethics and Education*, 8 (3): 276–89.

Verbeek, J., J. Ruotsalainen and J. L. Hoving (2012), 'Synthesizing Study Results in a Systematic Review', *Scandinavian Journal of Work, Environment & Health*, 38 (3): 282–90.

Wallner, C. (2020), *Preventing and Countering Violent Extremism through Education Initiatives Assessing the Evidence Base*, London: RUSI.

Zembylas, M. (2015), ' "Pedagogy of Discomfort" and Its Ethical Implications: The Tensions of Ethical Violence in Social Justice Education', *Ethics and Education*, 10 (2): 163–74.

Appendix

Table 4A.1 Systematically Reviewed Research Articles, *Eesti Haridusteaduste Ajakiri* (Estonian Journal of Education)

Study number	Title in English	Original full reference
1	Teachers' practical knowledge in novice and experienced teachers' comments on classroom interactions.	A. Okas, M. van der Schaaf, E. Krull (2013), Algajate ja kogenud õpetajate praktilise teadmise avaldumine tunnisündmuste kommenteerimisel stimuleeritud meenutuse meetodil. *Eesti Haridusteaduste Ajakiri*, 1(1): 24–45.

Table 4A.1 Systematically Reviewed Research Articles, *Eesti Haridusteaduste Ajakiri* (Estonian Journal of Education) (continued)

Study number	Title in English	Original full reference
2	Novice university teachers' teaching conceptions based on photo interviews.	M. Karm, M. Remmik (2013), Algajate õppejõudude õpetamisarusaamad fotointervjuude põhjal. *Eesti Haridusteaduste Ajakiri*, 1(1): 124–55.
3	Associations between first-graders' maths knowledge and their class-teachers' profiles of ability beliefs and outcome expectations.	A.-L. Jõgi, K. Aus, E. Kikas (2014), Esimese klassi õpilaste matemaatikateadmiste arengu seosed klassiõpetajate võimekususkumuste ja tulemusootuste profiiliga. *Eesti Haridusteaduste Ajakiri*, 2(1): 50–66.
4	Relations of reading skills and motivation with teaching styles in first grade.	P. Soodla, E. Kikas (2014), Lugemisoskuse ja -motivatsiooni seosed õpetajate kasvatusstiilidega esimeses klassis. *Eesti Haridusteaduste Ajakiri*, 2(1): 67–95.
5	Teaching practices and text comprehension in students during the transition from the first to second stage of school.	K. Uibu, M. Männamaa (2014), Õpetamistegevused ja õpilaste tekstimõistmine üleminekul esimesest kooliastmest teise astmesse. *Eesti Haridusteaduste Ajakiri*, 2(1): 96–131.
6	Pupil well-being and the development of word meaning structure: Differences in school satisfaction resilience in the context of class teacher parenting style and school-related adverse experiences.	A. Ots (2014), Õpilaste heaolu resilientsus ja mõistestruktuuri areng: erinevused kooliga rahulolu säilitamisel ebameeldivate koolikogemuste ja klassiõpetaja kasvatusstiili taustal. *Eesti Haridusteaduste Ajakiri*, 2(1): 132–61.
7	No deed goes unnoticed? Associations between teachers' noticing academic procrastination and individual differences in students.	K. Aus, G. Arro, A.-L. Jõgi, E. Malleus (2014), Kus tegijaid, seal nägijaid? Akadeemilise prokrastineerimise õpetajapoolse märkamise seosed õpilaste individuaalsete erinevustega. *Eesti Haridusteaduste Ajakiri*, 2(1): 217–40.
8	Teaching conceptions of practitioner-lecturers in applied higher education institutions.	E. Reva, M. Karm, L. Lepp, M. Remmik (2014), Praktikute-õppejõudude õpetamisarusaamad rakenduskõrgkoolis. *Eesti Haridusteaduste Ajakiri*, 2(2): 116–47.
9	Teacher-student interaction on social networking sites: teachers' perceptions and experiences.	S. Raim, A. Siibak (2014), Õpetajate-õpilaste interaktsioon ja sisuloome suhtlusportaalides: õpetajate arvamused ja kogemused. *Eesti Haridusteaduste Ajakiri*, 2(2) 176–99.
10	School microclimate: Teachers' supportive behaviour and student performance.	M. Kitsing, K. Täht, H. Kukemelk (2015), Kooli mikrokliima: õpetajate toetav käitumine ja õpilaste tulemuslikkus. *Eesti Haridusteaduste Ajakiri*, 3(1), 127–47.
11	Novice teachers' perception of senior management support and its connection with involvement in school development and collegial cooperation.	E. Eisenschmidt, E. Reiska, T. Oder (2015), Algajate õpetajate tajutud juhtkonna tugi ning selle seosed kooliarendusse kaasatuse ja õpetajate koostööga. *Eesti Haridusteaduste Ajakiri*, 3(1): 148–72.

(*continued*)

Table 4A.1 Systematically Reviewed Research Articles, *Eesti Haridusteaduste Ajakiri* (Estonian Journal of Education) (continued)

Study number	Title in English	Original full reference
12	Novice teachers' workplace experiences of collegiate support.	M. Remmik, L. Lepp, I. Koni (2015), Algajad õpetajad koolijuhi ja kolleegide toetusest esimestel tööaastatel. *Eesti Haridusteaduste Ajakiri*, 3(1): 173–201.
13	The role of Estonian teachers in the social mediation of children's internet use.	K. Soo, V. Kalmus, M. Ainsaar (2015), Eesti õpetajate roll laste internetikasutuse sotsiaalses vahendamises. *Eesti Haridusteaduste Ajakiri*, 3(2): 156–85.
14	Perceptions of primary school teachers on the disciplines related to the learning of organization leadership.	K. Uibu, M. Kaseorg, T. Kink (2016), Klassiõpetajate arusaamad õppiva organisatsiooni juhtimise distsipliinidest. *Eesti Haridusteaduste Ajakiri*, 4(1): 58–91.
15	Students' perception of their teachers' behaviour in the classroom and its coherence with teachers' own understandings.	A. Okas, M. van der Schaaf, E. Krull (2016), Õpetaja tegevus tunnis: õpilaste hinnangud ja nende kooskõla õpetajate arusaamadega. *Eesti Haridusteaduste Ajakiri*, 4(1): 195–225.
16	Evaluation of primary school teachers' exemplar-based linguistic communication based on structured observation.	K. Uibu, M. Padrik, S. Tenjes (2016), Klassiõpetajate keele- ja suhtluseeskuju hindamine emakeeletunnis struktureeritud vaatluse teel. *Eesti Haridusteaduste Ajakiri*, 4(1): 226–57.
17	Associations between teachers' instructional practices and student engagement in the second- and seventh-grade classrooms.	K. Poom-Valickis, A.-L. Jõgi, I. Timoštšuk, A. Oja (2016), Õpetajate juhendamispraktika seosed õpilaste kaasatusega õppimisse I ja III kooliastme tundides. *Eesti Haridusteaduste Ajakiri*, 4(1): 258–78.
18	The notion of inclusive education and challenges for the teacher in kindergartens and the first stage of school.	P. Häidkind, K. Oras (2016), Kaasava hariduse mõiste ning õpetaja ees seisvad ülesanded lasteaedades ja esimeses kooliastmes. *Eesti Haridusteaduste Ajakiri*, 4(2): 60–88.
19	Construction of the meaning of giftedness as a special educational need in the context of the changed learning approach in Estonia.	H. Põlda, K. Aava (2016), Andekuse kui haridusliku erivajaduse tähenduse konstrueerimine Eesti muutunud õpikäsituse kontekstis. *Eesti Haridusteaduste Ajakiri*, 4(2): 89–117.
20	KiVa anti-bullying programme in Estonia – the results from a two year cluster-randomized pilot trial.	K. Treial (2016), KiVa kiusamisvastase programmi prooviuuring Eestis: kaheaastase klaster-randomiseeritud kontrollkatse tulemused. *Eesti Haridusteaduste Ajakiri*, 4(2): 191–222.
21	Estonian science teachers' pedagogical beliefs, teaching practices and self-efficacy based on the results of the TALIS 2008 and 2013 reports.	I. Henno, L. Kollo, R. Mikser (2017), Eesti loodusainete õpetajate uskumused, õpetamispraktika ja enesetõhusus TALIS 2008 ja 2013 uuringu alusel. *Eesti Haridusteaduste Ajakiri*, 5(1): 268–96.

Table 4A.1 Systematically Reviewed Research Articles, *Eesti Haridusteaduste Ajakiri* (Estonian Journal of Education) (continued)

Study number	Title in English	Original full reference
22	If that's the goal, any topic can be sensitive? Estonian teachers' experiences with sensitive issues in history.	K. Kello, M. Raudsepp (2017), Kas kui hästi tahta, võib iga teema tundlikuks muuta? Eesti õpetajate kogemused tundlike teemadega ajalootunnis. *Eesti Haridusteaduste Ajakiri*, 5(2): 106–32.
23	Teachers and social pedagogues as victims of bullying.	K. Kõiv (2017), Õpetaja ja sotsiaalpedagoog kui kiusamise ohvrid. *Eesti Haridusteaduste Ajakiri*, 5(2): 133–54.
24	Learning in outcome based education – does it lead to student engagement?	K. Kumpas-Lenk, E. Eisenschmidt, K. Rumma (2017), Väljundipõhine õpe – kas õppimisse panustava ja kaasatud üliõpilase kujundaja? *Eesti Haridusteaduste Ajakiri*, 5(2): 206–28.
25	Teachers' learning experiences in the context of neoliberal educational change.	I. Timoštšuk, A. Ugaste, K. Mets-Alunurm (2018), Õpetajate õppimiskogemused neoliberaalsete haridusmuutuste taustal. *Eesti Haridusteaduste Ajakiri*, 6(1): 77–101.
26	Teachers' experiences of collaborative learning culture based on examples from Estonian general education schools.	P. Slabina, K. Aava (2019), Õpetajate koostöise õpikultuuri kogemused Eesti üldhariduskoolide näitel. *Eesti Haridusteaduste Ajakiri*, 7(1): 76–100.
27	Lecturers' and assistants' views on collaborative teaching at the university.	E. Lõhmus, H. Narits, K. Ugur (2019), Koostöine õpetamine ülikoolis: õppejou ja assistendi vaade. *Eesti Haridusteaduste Ajakiri*, 7(2): 209–33.
28	Investigating refractions – the impact of neoliberal education reforms on the teachers working life in Estonia.	M. Tinn (2020), Murrangute uurimine – neoliberaalsete haridusreformide mõju õpetajate tööelule Eestis. *Eesti Haridusteaduste Ajakiri*, 8(1): 156–82.
29	Relations between teachers' approaches to teaching and students' perceptions of enhancing and hindering elements of the teaching-learning environment.	K. Uiboleht, M. Karm (2020), Seosed õppejõu õpetamisviisi ja üliõpilase õppimist toetavate ning takistavate tegurite vahel õppeaines. *Eesti Haridusteaduste Ajakiri*, 8(2): 57–84.
30	The main benefits and challenges of implementing a guided reflection procedure as perceived by student teachers and teachers.	R. Allas, Ä. Leijen, A. Toom (2020), Suunatud refleksiooni protseduuri rakendamise peamised kasutegurid ja kitsaskohad õpetajakoolituse üliõpilaste ja õpetajate hinnangul. *Eesti Haridusteaduste Ajakiri*, 8(2): 85–110.

(continued)

Table 4A.1 Systematically Reviewed Research Articles, *Eesti Haridusteaduste Ajakiri* (Estonian Journal of Education) (continued)

Study number	Title in English	Original full reference
31	Principles and goals that determine the choice of Estonian language and mathematics learning materials as reported by pre-school and primary school teachers.	M. Taimalu, K. Uibu, H. Leola (2020), Eesti keele ja matemaatika õppevara valiku põhimõtted ja eesmärgid lasteaia- ja klassiõpetajate hinnangul. *Eesti Haridusteaduste Ajakiri*, 8(2): 164–91.
32	Teacher cyberbullying and possible interventions at school: a view of teachers experiencing student cyberbullying.	K. Jürisaar, A. Siibak (2020), Õpetajate küberkiusamine ja võimalikud sekkumised koolis: õpilastepoolset küberkiusamist kogenud õpetajate vaade. *Eesti Haridusteaduste Ajakiri*, 8(2): 192–218.
33	Practices supporting value education and its assessment in Estonian schools.	M.-L. Parder, H. Hirsnik (2020), Väärtuskasvatust toetavad tegevused ja nende enesehinnanguline tulemuslikkus Eesti üldhariduskoolide näitel. *Eesti Haridusteaduste Ajakiri*, 8(2): 245–71.
34	Estonian late adolescents' values: links with perceived care, school location and family socioeconomic status.	A. Tamm (2021), Väärtuskasvatust toetavad tegevused ja nende enesehinnanguline tulemuslikkus Eesti üldhariduskoolide näitel. *Eesti Haridusteaduste Ajakiri*, 9(1): 117–37.

Source: Own elaboration.

5

Are Muslims Scared of Pork?: Teaching about Islam in Polish Schools

Katarzyna Górak-Sosnowska

Introduction

This chapter's title is based on a story that a friend of mine, a female convert to Islam and an active member of the local Islamic community in Warsaw, has recently told me. A couple of years ago, a young man was regularly coming to the mosque carrying pork sausages in a plastic bag. He was sitting among Muslim men and looking around, hoping to get some attention. As nothing has happened, after some time, he changed the bag into a transparent plastic one so that everyone could see that he was carrying pork sausages inside. Again, there was no reaction. The sausages smelled like it was summer, but the Muslim hosts were hospitable and decided not to point out to the man. After some time, the man stopped visiting the mosque.

This story illustrates several critical points when it comes to teaching about Islam. First, it is a clear example of a blatant Islamophobia that aims to demonize Muslims by considering them as subhuman monsters that can be fought off with charms. Just as vampires are afraid of garlic, Muslims should react to pork similarly (Chambers and Chaplin 2013). Second, this kind of pork-related Islamophobia has been visible in other countries inhabited by Muslim minorities, most of Western Europe. It might not be a coincidence that such a way of getting rid of Muslims or maybe just offending them has been used in Poland, as the bulk of Islamophobic actions and narratives have been transplanted from the West (Górak-Sosnowska 2011). Third, the local Muslim community has decided not to react to the pork sausages, even if they had known that the man was trying to offend them. The friend who told me this story was quite amused by the man's attempts to provoke them with pork sausages. Despite that, Polish Muslims seem to have only marginal control over Islam's Polish discourse. Whatever they do and act, it seems not to influence the dominant narrative, according to which Islam and Muslims are narrated as the key threat to the Polish nation (Pędziwiatr 2019). Muslims in Poland constitute less than 0.5 per cent of the whole population (for thirty-eight million inhabitants), and there has never been a single terrorist attack carried out by Islamists (Górak-Sosnowska and Pachocka 2019).

This chapter aims to analyse the challenges of teaching about Islam and Muslims at Polish schools, which means teaching 'by a dry run' – that is teaching about Others who are not even there and teaching about Others who activate strong negative sentiments and stereotypes. In the first section, I will analyse the state of the art, namely the body of knowledge that students (and their teachers) have about Islam and Muslims. I will elaborate on the kind of information about Islam in the current school curricula. Then I will analyse briefly how Islam has been (mis)used in the political and national discourse since the conservative Law and Justice Party (Prawo i Sprawiedliwość) had won the parliamentary (and later presidential) elections in 2015. The last part of this section will be dedicated to the marginal size of the Muslim community in Poland and its impact on the body of knowledge. In the second section, I will discuss three possible strategies to teach about Islam and Muslims in a hostile and monocultural school context analysing their strengths, weaknesses, opportunities and threats. Thus I will start with the concept of (exotic) 'distant Other' (Górak-Sosnowska and Markowska-Manista 2010) and the limits of Orientalization of the Other to turn him into a close Other. I will then turn to another strategy of having a 'duty Muslim' (i.e. a Muslim who will serve as an exemplary Muslim for the homogenous class) or everyday explainers in the classroom (Harris and Hussein 2018). In the final part, I will elaborate on alternative methods of introducing content related to Islam and Muslims in a homogenous classroom.

I will build my analysis by combining desk research (analysis of primary sources – curricula, quantitative and qualitative studies, and the body of literature about Islam in Poland and intercultural education) and my own over fifteen-year experience in providing workshops and training about Islam and Muslims for primary and secondary school pupils as well as teachers of general education (over 400 hours of training) and lectures about Islam, Muslims in Europe and the Middle East at my home university. I have also co-authored several textbooks in the area of intercultural and global education that include teaching about Islam and Muslims. While I will refer to other textbooks, if relevant, I decided not to pick any negative examples of essentialized images of Muslims, biased information or factual mistakes, which unfortunately are not seldom in a Polish school setting to avoid stigmatization and public shaming (Oravec 2019). While some of these sources might provide only anecdotal evidence, together with vast international literature and research on narratives about Islam and Islamophobia as well as much more scanty data on these phenomena in Poland, they will shed some light on why teaching about Islam in a Polish school setting is challenging, yet needed.

Not Even a Vacuum: Teaching about Islam in Polish Schools

There is not much space left to teach about other cultures or religions in the official educational programme of the Polish school. According to the core curriculum, pupils can learn about different cultures, mainly in Polish, minorities and foreign languages classes, geography classes and knowledge about society classes, while history classes are very Poland-oriented. There is also religious instruction, which focuses only on the Catholic religion.

It seems that geography is the course that provides pupils with the most knowledge about the whole world. Parts of the curricula in primary and secondary school are dedicated to Islamic cultures. One of the eighteen topics of the core curriculum for primary school pupils is dedicated to Asia (and one of the regions is the Middle East), while another one to Africa – both of which are huge and very diverse continents. In the case of the Middle East, pupils learn about the region through 'cultural features and oil assets, as well as the level of economic development'. They should also identify the main conflicts in the region (Geografia, Szkoła podstawowa IV-VIII). In secondary school, there are twenty-three problem-oriented topics about different parts of the world. One of them includes 'Causes and Consequences of Terrorism, Relations between Western and Islamic Civilization' (Geografia, Liceum/technikum).

In history, the focus is much more oriented towards Polish history; only those historical events that have affected Poland are presented. The world of Islam occupies only a tiny part of the curricula, consisting of forty-two topics. In the case of primary school, the pupils learn about Byzantium and the Islamic world (the focus is on Arab territorial expansion and the influence of Islamic civilization on Europe), and later on, they learn about the Middle Eastern conflict and war in Afghanistan as a part of the topic 'World after the Second World War' (Historia, Szkoła podstawowa IV-VIII), In secondary school, among fifty-nine subjects, the pupil learns again about Byzantium and the Islamic world and this time, he or she also gets to learn about 'the genesis of Islam and main rules of this religion'. Later on, there is one general topic titled 'Decolonialization, Integration and New Conflicts' which presents decolonization of Asia and Africa (only politically – as becoming independent from colonial powers, and thus without any further critical reflection), as well as Middle Eastern conflicts, with a focus on the Arab-Israeli conflict (Historia, Liceum/technikum). There are also several other instances when one can learn about the Islamic world, but they are not explicitly mentioned in the curriculum. However, one can assume that the Islamic world is mentioned within the topics of crusades, the Mongol invasion of Eastern Europe, the Polish-Ottoman war (including the siege of Vienna in 1683) and terrorism in Europe. In other words, what a pupil learns about Islam is that it was established in the seventh century, that later Arabs expanded to Europe, and then – after thirteen centuries of hardly any information – that there are many conflicts in the Middle East.

One crucial point ought to be made to provide a broader picture, namely, that the Polish school system does not pay a lot of attention to other cultures or religions. According to a study carried out in 2008–9, teachers in the Mazovian district (including the capital city of Warsaw) declared an intermediate (47 per cent) or low (27 per cent) level of preparation to teach about other cultures (Dąbrowa and Markowska-Manista 2018: 176). According to another study, every fourth teacher believes that intercultural education is included in the school curriculum, and that means tolerance for other nations (18 per cent indications) predominantly and learning other cultures (19 per cent); only 5 per cent of teachers believed that the Polish school teaches how to live together with people of different nationalities (Kitlińska-Król 2013: 284). There is not much about Islamic cultures, just as there is not much about African, Asian or Latin American cultures in Polish schools. However, there is one significant difference: Islam and Muslims are strongly stereotyped against, unlike other distant cultures. The reasons behind this stereotypization will be presented in the subsequent sections.

Islam as a Monotheistic Religion: The Case of Religious Instruction

The Polish name of the subject can be translated as 'religious instruction'; however, it is only Catholic religious instruction in practice. According to the Concordat signed in 1993 between the Polish government and the Holy See, public preschools, primary and secondary schools provide religious instruction according to an official educational programme for which the church authorities design both the programme and class content. Since the Catholic Church has the sole power to create religious instruction, the content focuses only on one religion. Available textbooks on religious instruction teach religious belief and practice rather than knowledge about different faiths. Moreover, the core curriculum of religious instruction for all education levels issued by the Episcopal Conference of Poland has hardly any space for religious traditions other than the Catholic one. It is grounded in the Catechism of the Catholic Church.

The few times that Islam was mentioned offer a minimal picture of this religion. Islam is enumerated with other non-Christian religions and sects in the core curriculum. This point is under 'Introduction to the Mission', while the role of the teacher is to 'present the novelty of Christianity and warning against cults' activity' (Komisja Wychowania Katolickiego Konferencji Episkopatu Polski 2010: 58). Pupils (or their parents) who do not want to participate in religious instructions may attend ethics classes (or neither) one hour weekly. During these ethics courses, students have an opportunity to learn about Islam, namely its moral foundations, in primary school. Interestingly, there has never been any other alternative to religious instruction (teaching particular religion – usually Catholic, occasionally minority religion) than ethics in the Polish school system (neither philosophy nor religious studies; Zwierżdżyński 2017: 154).

Current religious instruction in Polish schools produces young people who are highly focused on their religion, without learning about other religious traditions. In this respect, they seem to fit perfectly into religious illiteracy – being ignorant about other religious traditions. As Diane Moore indicates (2007), religious illiteracy can efficiently fuel culture wars and religious bigotry. This is crucial especially in Islam and Muslims whose image is shaped predominantly by 'transplanted discourse' from Western media while literal, one-fits-all interpretations are taken for granted without any further reflection. Moreover, it is possible that religious instruction does produce or strengthen negative stereotypes against Islam.

According to a study carried out among future Polish priests, they hold negative attitudes towards Islam as does the general Polish population. Eight out of ten believed that Islam encouraged violence more than other religions, and many claimed that Muslims are more aggressive and less tolerant than others (Pędziwiatr 2018: 472). What is more, almost half of them sympathizes partially or fully with the idea of banning Islam (Pędziwiatr 2018: 475). Some of these beliefs seem to be implemented during religious instruction classes. Among young participants of a focus group organized by the Polish Migration Forum, it was noted that both secular teachers and priests often lack the knowledge and willingness to discuss Islam. One pupil was afraid of going to a mosque while on vacation because she was not supposed to learn any other religion than 'our' (i.e. Catholic) religion, Another pupil was told that Muslims and Christians believe in two different Gods, and that he is not Catholic if he thinks differently. Yet another pupil learnt that all religions but Catholicism are false by default, and reading the Qur'an is a sin (PFM 2020). Lack of knowledge combined with negative sentiments against Islam make teaching about this religion particularly difficult in a school setting.

Learning by Living Together

Traditionally, intergroup contact has been one of the best ways to decrease mutual prejudices (Allport 1954), even if many factors should be taken into account to make this process meaningful. However, in Poland's case, this can hardly be the case. Regardless of the source of estimation, the proportion of Muslims in Poland does not exceed 0.1 per cent of the total population, meaning that there are around 30,000 to 40,000 Muslims in a country of thirty-eight million inhabitants. Again these numbers have to be put in a broader context: generally, Poland is one of the most homogenous countries in the world, both ethnically and religiously, with only 1.5 per cent of inhabitants with non-Polish ethnicity or nationality, and over 95 per cent of Catholics (out of those who answered the question about their religious belief (GUS 2013: 89–99).

Several factors have contributed to this monolith. The first one relates to border shifts and related relocation of different ethnic and national groups and minorities after the Second World War and ethnolinguistic homogenization that was its direct consequence (Kamusella 2009: 644). Second, unlike many Western European countries, Poland never had had any colonial past. Postcolonial studies are marginal, while postcolonial reflection is hard to understand as Poland has been dependent on European superpowers while its territory was divided between three different countries. The lack of this reflection and experience is very much visible in the way Others are presented in the school curriculum in or without context. However, coming back to the religious and ethnic monolith, the lack of a colonial past means that there has been no interest in immigration to Poland after decolonization. Third, moreover Poland was behind the Iron Curtain as one of the Central European umbrella states of the USSR, which significantly impacted transnational flows of goods, services and people. There used to be some immigrants from Muslim majority countries that belonged to the USSR bloc, but the scope was minimal. Moreover, one could say that the USSR has colonized Poland after the Second World War. Fourth, even nowadays, Poland is still a labour exporting country; migrants from third countries are more interested in Western Europe. Comparatively, Poland has a low economic standing and is culturally homogenous, which does not enhance others' acculturation.

The small Muslim population in Poland can be divided into several groups. The Tatars – autochthonous Polish Muslims – have been present for over 600 years and have assimilated into mainstream society. They kept their faith, but it is often called folk Islam (e.g. Dziekan 2011). The Tatars are the old established Muslims in Poland, often juxtaposed against the newcomers – Muslims of immigrant origin (Pędziwiatr 2011) – although the ancient Muslim diaspora is also found; they arrived in Poland in the socialist era, primarily as students, and have mastered Polish language, settled down and started their families – often with Polish spouses. A significant group in between are the New Muslims – they are native Polish citizens but religiously closer to the immigrant population, not only by mixed marriages, but also because the Tatar type of Islam is linked to Tatar ethnicity.

Despite the marginal number of Muslims in Poland, Islam and Muslims have been promoted to one of the most potent enemies alien to Polish culture and tradition. According to the IPSOS study which illustrates this (2016: 4–6), Poles have overestimated the number of Muslims in their country; 70 per cent higher than the actual proportion. What is more, they have been attributed behaviours and ideas so abstract that one can hardly rationalize them. There was a rosary organized all across Poland's borders to protect the country from Islamization (Pędziwiatr 2019). There were self-proclaimed patrols in discos that ensured Polish girls did not flirt with Muslim-looking (whatever that meant) men. An old lady stopped the train because a Moroccan man started to pray, and she got scared (Górak-Sosnowska 2014).

These examples show that many Poles have never had any contact with a Muslim person. Only 12 per cent of Poles declared to have met a Muslim (Stefaniak 2015). As the body of more in-depth knowledge was missing, just as real Muslims to provide a counter-narrative, this literal, essentialized understanding of Islam and Muslims became dominant in media and started to be used in political agendas.

Inventing the Muslim Other in the Public Discourse

Until the European refugee crisis of 2015, or rather the crisis of refugees, which coincided with the rise of the conservative and right-wing Law and Justice Party, Islam and Muslims have occupied the Polish public only minimally. It was not more than some Orientalist clichés with literal representations of 'exotic' Muslims from far away. Even the 9/11 terrorist attacks and later attacks carried out by Islamist terrorist did not strengthen the narrative about Islam much; they only added some new elements as the notion of a clash of civilizations, Islamist terrorism or challenges related to the integration of Muslims in Europe. There was a potential for Islamophobia, but it was latent (Górak-Sosnowska 2014).

In 2015, Poland took the nationalist path. Polish national identity has shifted from a more Europe-oriented to an ethnic concept, with the Catholic religion becoming one of the primary identity markers. Almost two-thirds of Poles believe that religion is a critical component of national identity, while over half claims that Polish culture is superior to that of the others (Pew Research Center 2018: 8–26). Islam and Muslims became the best enemy that one could have invented, for they can be related to both elements of the newly constructed Polish identity. The shift in the national orientation from European Union to Poland stemmed from the European Union's (EU) ineffective and gullible handling of the refugee crisis which ultimately resulted in the rise of terrorism and violence. With respect to religious orientation, Muslims are the inherent enemy and a means of the Islamization of Europe. Poland has significantly shifted away from the EU on the political level in recent years. Inventing the Muslim enemy serves as a good excuse and is presented as not yielding to the EU 'dictate' (Górak-Sosnowska and Pachocka. 2019). Polish national identity is juxtaposed against the European one, and Islamophobia is one way to do it.

Unlike their Western counterparts, young Poles are more Eurosceptic and express stronger anti-Muslim sentiments. According to an IPSOS survey from 2016, 27 per cent of the youngest respondents (aged eighteen to twenty-nine) would like Poland to leave the EU (comparing to the 16 per cent average; Pacewicz 2016). In 2018, only 36 per cent of the youngest respondents favoured integration, while 42 per cent opted for limiting cooperation to economic affairs only and 18 per cent wanted to leave the EU (Pacewicz 2018). Young Poles are also more inclined to believe that Islam causes danger (59 per cent of people aged eighteen to twenty-four supports that claim compared to 37 per cent of people over the age of sixty-five; CBOS 2015: 9). They also hold more anti-Islamic prejudices and are more prone to accept Islamophobic hate speech (Stefaniak 2015: 32). These factors make teaching about Islam in schools even more difficult. Islam and Muslims serve as the enemy of Polish national identity, but these negative sentiments are powerful among young people. Looking at the social media content and scanty analyses of this particular kind of hate speech, one can assume that many of them are not fully aware of what are they posting (Szymanik 2015).

The Challenge for Intercultural Education: Teaching about Islam

While most EU societies are multicultural, this has clearly not been the case for Central and Eastern European (CEE) countries, including Poland. According to Markowska-Manista (2019: 83), 'until recently, the Polish system of education operated without the confrontation with multiculturalism (unlike Western European countries)'. Intercultural education should prepare individuals to live in a world where coexisting in a diversified cultural environment is natural. In Poland's case, intercultural education has been understood chiefly in terms of borderland, that is, a territory in which neighbouring cultures (local, ethnic, national minorities and majority) interpenetrate (Nikitorowicz 1995).[1]

Becoming a member of the EU in 2004 and consequently opening borders rendered the existing framework of intercultural education in Poland as too narrow. While Poland is still not an immigration country, many Poles travel abroad and work in a multicultural environment that often comprises people of different nationalities and from diverse migration background. As economic migrants, Poles often compete with labour migrants from third countries in Western EU countries' local labour markets (Goździak and Márton 2018). This makes intercultural competence a very much needed asset. Even at home in Poland, having intercultural competencies can be helpful. Thanks to global media and social media, Poles have access to information about international events that need intercultural competencies and critical thinking to interpret them.

In the case of competencies related to Islam and Muslims, the need is even more urgent due to the solid negative anti-Muslim discourse that is often in tune with a broader range of negative attitudes to core European values such as equality, tolerance and the rule of law. The threat of Islamization often comes together with the demonization of LGBT (which is claimed to be an ideology in the dominant political narrative) and goes with an exhaustive and extensive list of different EU's moral decay indicators. This might come as a paradox, as Poles still belong to the top EU enthusiasts. However, they cherish the EU for economic benefits. It seems that by focusing on economic convergence, Poland has lost sight of the political and social ones. The emergence of semi-authoritarian regimes in some CEE countries, including in Poland, is vital proof (Kelemen 2017).

As Izabela Czerniejewska notices (2008: 109), Polish teachers introduce intercultural education content in their classes. Moreover, a part of the pedagogical curriculum for future teachers is dedicated to intercultural education. However, the way in which this is implemented raises some objections. The way non-Western cultures are presented often bears the hallmarks of cultural determinism (or culture bias) and Orientalism. The first concept refers to the dominating role of culture in explaining social realities, behaviours or attitudes of individuals belonging to that particular culture. The second concept relates to Edward Said's work, in which he criticized the Western approach to the Orient, which was perceived in an instrumentalized and exotic way.

In terms of a school class, both concepts mean that different cultures are presented through their folklore and traditions, without a link to social realities and the everyday lives of people belonging to these cultures. In other words, the most exotic, visible and different elements are picked and presented as the way these cultures are. This way a cultural composite ,deemed as exotic as possible, is created and offers a very simplified and superficial knowledge about the other culture. If the teacher has insufficient knowledge, this composite might contain factual errors or oversimplifications. During several events titled 'Days of Arabic Culture', there were Polish female pupils who had their hair visible but faces covered and children who were praying in the Catholic way (by having both hands folded); on the 'Day of Afghan Culture', for example, students got to know Arab customs.

Leaving the potential errors aside, the challenge related to teaching about Islam involves creating the right balance between the 'exotic' and the non-exotic. My argument is that some elements of the 'exotic' (e.g. clothes, food, customs) are necessary at this stage – provided that they are presented adequately. Since the vast majority of Polish classes are culturally homogenous, the Other (regardless of the culture) is not a neighbour or a classmate but a distant Other from a faraway culture. What makes the Other different is what might interest the pupils. In other words, the colonial, exotic Oriental Other – whom Edward Said (1978) wanted to deorientalize so much – is the key. This makes the teaching about the Muslim Other particularly tough: to move from

Are Muslims Scared of Pork? 91

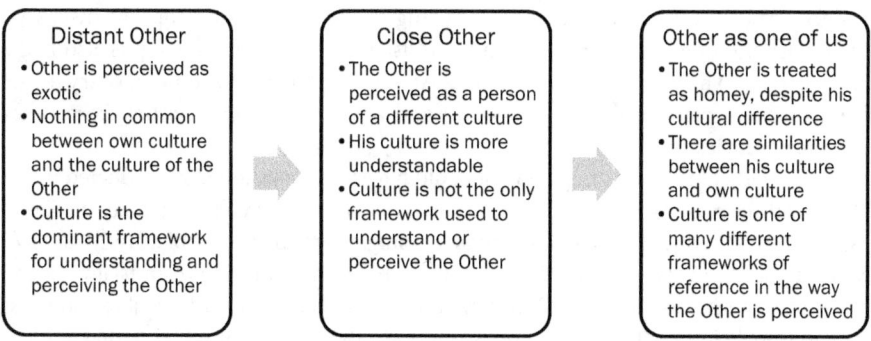

Figure 5.1 Stages of intercultural education for monocultural groups.

Source: Own elaboration.

the distant Other to the close Other, one has to make at least some use of Orientalist clichés, as presented below.

In monocultural societies, it seems crucial to move from the distant Other to the close Other before reaching the ultimate level of making the Other one of us. While neighbouring cultures can easily fit the close Other (unless there are long-lasting intergroup conflicts), non-Westerners are often perceived as distant Others. The alien Other is often perceived through folklore and essentialized culture. He or she differs from the close Other, who is not perceived as exotic but homier while he or she is still a bearer of a different culture. Simultaneously, as the Polish educational system pays a lot of attention to acquiring new knowledge (i.e. to theory), this can be used (and in fact is used) to provide information about different cultures.

Regardless of their ethnic origin, Muslims are framed as exotic, distant Others (Górak-Sosnowska and Markowska-Manista 2010). It corresponds to the cultural racism which focuses on a deterministic culture that defines and regulates the lives, deeds and thoughts of individuals naturalized into this culture (Jackson 2018: 149). At the same time, it goes further by claiming that all Muslims are religious by default and exotic. The crucial difference between Western Europe and Poland (as a country located in Eastern Europe) is the marginal number of Muslims who make learning the Other 'by dry run' – that is, without any direct contact.

From a Distant Other to a Close Other?

In 2005, I co-designed a workshop project, 'In the World of Islam', for school pupils.[2] Back then, careful consideration was not given to Islam or Muslims in mainstream society, nor was Islam used in political discourse. At the same time, Poles had even more limited contact with non-European cultures than nowadays, and so the bulk of knowledge about the Muslim Other was limited to some Orientalist clichés flavoured by the notion of the clash of civilization. The workshop aimed to challenge existing stereotypes about Islam and Muslims by providing knowledge and some 'dry run' experience of the Islamic world. Thus during the six-hour workshop, we discussed the pillars and dogmas, women in Islam and Islamist terrorism. The pupils also had a chance to learn how to write their name in Arabic script, listen to contemporary music from different parts of the Islamic world and try on traditional clothes from other Islamic countries.

Some parts of the workshop content could have been questioned if conducted in the West for three reasons. The first one is the Orientalizing gaze which reproduces monolith essentialism to reduce Islam and Muslims to a single core (Bevir and Blakely 2018: 119). Second, the core is predominantly oriented on tradition and mainstream Islam – it can reproduce the stereotype of Muslims who are all very religious, write Arabic and dress in traditional clothes. The third issue is related to the simulation of being dressed as a Muslim. While simulations of cultural differences are engaging and have the potential to be tools of affective learning by experiencing others' world (Bredemeier and Greenblat 1981: 322), they can also unintentionally produce contradictory results – for example, increase students' ethnocentrism (Bruschke et al. 1993).

Moreover, dressing as a Muslim can be interpreted as a contemporary practice that resembles performing blackface (Piela 2021). Taking all these arguments into account, we have put a lot of effort to present a diverse world of Islam, pointing to the differences and variations within the Islamic doctrine. The elements of Islamic cultures that we could have offered – such as music, clothes, writing in Arabic script – had the same aim and were used in two ways: to raise the interest (even those pupils who declared strong anti-Islamic sentiments wanted to learn how to write their names in Arabic script) and to decrease the psychological distance.

An evaluation of the workshop that has been conducted among over 700 pupils split into experimental and control groups has indicated decreased declared psychological distance and a significant unintended educational effect. Namely, pupils who attended the workshop decreased psychological distance not only towards Arabs, but also towards Hindus (a group that was by that time culturally distant, but bore no negative stereotypes) and Roma (a local ethnic group culturally different and negatively stereotyped), unlike Czechs, Americans or Germans (which were also included in the study). In other words, teaching about one culture that is perceived as distant can positively influence the way different distant cultures are perceived. Simultaneously, while 'a typical Muslim' has been valued more positively than negatively, the core of the stereotype – namely that a Muslim is religious and aggressive – did not change significantly (Górak-Sosnowska 2008). Further, the question – problematic in how it has been formulated as there are 1.5 billion Muslims, as to who is a typical one Muslim – has also indicated a positive change. Participants in the workshop have more often refused to answer the question about what qualities a 'typical' Muslim have, pointing out that there are many different Muslims and one shall not generalize.

Is There a Real Muslim?

Asked about suggestions on how the workshop could have been improved, many pupils stated that it could have been better to show them a real Muslim in the class.

Interestingly enough, one of the workshop trainers was a Muslim, but not visibly (Tarlo 2010) – that is, she did not express her faith or identity through the way she dressed. This example brings to light two fundamental issues. First, the image of a Muslim is essentialized to the visible features such as name, ethnicity and women – dress. All these features might indicate religion but do not necessarily need to. Many Polish students lack the knowledge that not every Muslim fits into the essentialist image; in fact, many do not. Second, hardly any Polish pupils had a chance to meet a Muslim person or a person who was known to be a Muslim.

Over a decade after the workshop project, I started another one – a series of open lectures at Polish schools. Within 1.5 years, I had a chance to meet around two thousand pupils. A lecture is far less interactive than a workshop, but there was space for questions and discussions every time. I encountered questions and comments that illustrate the two fundamental issues mentioned above. Many questions referred to whether a Muslim does something, is something, can do something – for example, Do Muslim women use sanitary pads? Is it true that a Muslim can drink alcohol at night because Allah does not see in the dark? Does a bald Muslim woman need to wear a hijab? These questions require a detailed answer. At the same time, they seem to illustrate that Muslims have been demonized or at least not treated as ordinary humans. Why should Muslim women not use sanitary pads? Most probably use them, while some may use other protection methods while menstruating – just like other females. Or maybe they do not use any sanitary pads, but a cup instead for the sake of protecting the environment. Not everyone needs to drink alcohol, and many Muslims can survive without it. However, there are also some Muslims who drink alcohol. Does it make them less Muslim? It depends on who is judging. Do women in Poland walk happily with bald heads, or do they instead choose to wear wigs – especially if the hair loss was not intentional? There are undoubtedly many ways of directing such discussions showing that Muslims are diverse yet similar.

The comments were polarized, with some pupils showing a balanced view of Islam and Muslims, while some others pointing at a very literal and one-sided understanding of Islam. The latter group is adamant about reacting and discussing, as they have already formed their ideas about Islam and Muslims. They bring up a vast range of arguments on Islamic ghettos in European cities, the Qur'an that invites Muslims to kill infidels, *taqiyya*, and the like. By engaging in discussion with such a pupil, the teacher can lose the interest of the rest of the group and/or provoke more bizarre arguments than those already in place. By leaving these arguments in vain without any answer, the teacher proves that they might be right. After gaining some experience in the type of negative comments one can get, some can be dismantled earlier before they have been brought up. For instance, while discussing Muslims in Europe, I usually recall a case of the Molenbeek district of Brussels that has been doomed in Polish media as a dangerous place to live after the terrorist attack in Paris in 2015. During a lecture I had with my students, this issue was raised by one of them. I asked the whole group who has been living in Brussels and, later, had visited or lived in this particular district; then I asked them for their impressions. They were not hostile and they were first hand. This way, they provided a counterbalance to the utterly negative information about the 'Molenbeek ghetto'. The discussion could be started again.

Inviting a Muslim person to the classroom could bring added value to a class about Islam. A Muslim could offer a first-hand experience, answer pupils' questions and be a real example against some negative stereotypes. However, this might pose several challenges. One has to find a Muslim person willing to come to the class. It might not be an easy task due to the marginal number of Muslims and the fact that not everyone is ready to be publicly identified as a Muslim. It seems that there are a number of 'duty Muslims' who serve as everyday explainers to the non-Muslim majority, participate in studies about Islam, give interviews and so on (Rogowska 2017: 86).

Moreover, the Muslim has to be outspoken to react to the questions and comments like those presented above. The negative stigma attached to Islam in public poses a substantial emotional burden on the local Muslim population, and many of them openly state that they are psychologically unable to bear the stress of having to publicly talk about being a Muslim. Provided that a Muslim has been found, there might also be a problem with inviting such a person to school. In 2019, the Małopolska Regional Chief Educational Office summoned a primary school headmaster for questioning because two students from Algeria taught children how to write their names in Arabic (Szpunar 2019). Provided that the relevant educational office does not object to such a guest, one has still to remember that the Muslim invitee might be the only Muslim ever met by most pupils (and thus has the potential to build the stereotype according to his traits).

Conclusion

Teaching about Islam in a monocultural society with relatively strong anti-Muslim attitudes can be challenging yet very much needed. Given the Polish educational system that leaves hardly any space for teaching about non-Western cultures, and the Otherizing anti-Muslim narrative in political discourse, one cannot expect most Polish teachers to have the will, knowledge and opportunities to introduce content related to Islamic cultures in their classes.

In the current political situation, it seems that there are two possible ways to teach about Islam and Muslims in a Polish school setting. The first one is to invite guest speakers – secular professionals (academics, journalists, travellers) who can give a lecture or a presentation about Islamic culture while ensuring there are no accusations of pupils being Islamized. The second one is to use the small windows of opportunity offered by existing curricula, mostly in geography classes, to present Islam and Muslims more extensively.

Anchoring the Islamic content to the existing curricula has two advantages. First, it fulfils the curriculum, which is overpacked with knowledge, data and abilities that the pupils should learn, leaving not much space for anything extra. Second, it makes the teacher safe – (s)he is already an expert in the subject that (s)he teaches regularly, so (s)he can add some information related to the world of Islam. Considering the variety and richness of the Islamic world, there is a lot one can choose from. I only provide a glimpse of some ideas to develop in a monocultural classroom. Some of them have been described in Górak-Sosnowska and Kubarek (2007):

- Geography: GCC countries' diversification strategies – a simulation game: imagine you discover oil and get rich; how do you invest the money to become less dependent on the oil resources in the future?
- Knowledge about society: presenting countries through their banknotes: this way, one can easily show the differences between countries, what is essential for them, which values the banknotes convey and promote.
- History: Arab contribution to the development of Europe: here, even the first description of Slavic states of a Sephardi Jew from the Cordoban Caliphate – Ibrahim Ibn Ya'qub – could be an interesting point of reference. Inviting Polish refugees (over 110,000 people, who came from Iran in 1942) could be another significant link to the recent past.
- Mathematics: history of numbers (why are Arabic numerals called Arabic, and why do they differ from the digits used in Arabic countries) and history of mathematics (words like algebra, algorithm have Arabic origin), including the story of X as the most common imponderable (the Arabs used the word شيء (*shay*) 'thing' in their equations, in short form: ش (*sh*), The Spanish took the *sh* sound and transcribed it phonetically as *x* (pronounced as *sh* in old Spanish),
- Chemistry: it could be the story about the origin of the word 'alcohol' (Muslims shall not drink alcohol, so how come the word alcohol comes from Arabic?). It was the *kohl*, meaning something pure and delicate: spirit was also refined. Arabic mascara which has traditionally been made by grinding stibnite, (Sb_2S_3) *kohl*, also describes something refined and delicate: spirit was also pure just as stibnite was. Hence the English word alcohol comes from *al-kohl*, which referred to stibnite and later liquids obtained by boiling down (such as the spirit of wine or ethanol),
- Arts: writing your name in Arabic might come hard, but thanks to websites such as Omniglot.com and translating services, one can learn how to write using Arabic script.
- Polish: it could be a discussion of one of many words with Arabic origins, such as *bakłażan* and *oberżyna*, both of which mean the same vegetable *Solanum melongena* and which have Arabic origin. *Bakłażan* comes from Persian *baingan*, a word that later was used by Arabs and Turks. *Oberżyna* comes from France (aubergine) and this time the word came from Spanish and Arabic; the Spanish transformed the word *al-badingana* into *alberjena*, *alberxina* or *alberchin*, which was also adapted into French (Corriente 2008).

The list is not extensive, but offers some examples of sticking to the class content and providing some information about the Islamic world – information that can be attractive to the pupils, builds on the knowledge that the teacher already has and is exotic, yet not Orientalizing.

Although not directly linked to the Islamic world, the aim of such content is to make the pupils familiar with any 'distant' culture. As my evaluation of the Islamic world workshop has indicated, there has been a non-specific educational effect: after the workshop, the pupils declared more positive attitudes to other distant Others, not just the Arabs. It seems to be an advantage of a monocultural class – exposure to one 'distant' culture opens the doors to decreasing social distance to other 'distant' cultures.

Considering the negative narratives around Islam in Poland, one cannot expect that a teacher will be able to confront his pupils who are critical of Islam. What he can do, is to bring these ideas into a broader discussion. In one of my lectures about the so-called Islamic State, I use a picture that presents several men, jihadis, who hold guns in their hands and point their index fingers to the top, indicating *Tawheed* – that there is one God. The caption below reads: 'Call of Duty' and refers to the famous shooting game. I ask the audience what is wrong with this picture. After some time, usually, someone notices that one of the men points his left index finger instead of the right one. Polish school is very much focused on learning information – this way, pupils know that in Islam, the right hand is for clean things, while the left one is for items that are not clean. How can a true believer show God's glory by the hand he uses to make himself clean after using the toilet? So maybe not every jihadi knows his religion well? I could have repeatedly said that not all Muslims are terrorists and that becoming a radical Islamist is not the ultimate proof of being religious. The picture with this one man pointing with his left hand that there is one God makes much better work. It also provides a good starting point for a discussion and teaches about Islam and critical thinking – a tool that is crucial to understand and comprehend today's world.

Notes

1. I am elaborating only one of the three existing models of intercultural education – teaching about Others 'by dry run', that is, without the actual presence of the others. Having Muslim children in the classroom is a completely different and much more diversified experience, as Muslim children can differ by everything but religion (or in fact also by religion in terms of denomination, religiosity or religious tradition).
2. More at: Górak-Sosnowska and Kubarek (2007).

References

Allport, G. (1954), *The Nature of Prejudice*, Cambridge: Perseus Books.
Bevir, M., and J. Blakely (2018), *Interpretive Social Science. An Anti-Naturalist Approach*, Oxford: Oxford University Press.
Bredemeier, M., and C. Greenblat (1981), 'The Educational Effectiveness of Simulation Games. A Synthesis of Findings', *Simulation & Games*, 12 (3): 307–32.
Bruschke, J., C. Gartner and J. Seiter (1993), 'Student Ethnocentrism, Dogmatism, and Motivation. A Study of BAFA BAFA', *Simulation & Gaming*, 24 (1): 9–20.
CBOS (2015), 'Postawy wobec islamu i muzułmanów'. Available online: https://www.cbos.pl/SPISKOM.POL/2019/K_148_19.PDF (accessed 6 June 2020).
Chambers, C., and S. Chaplin (2013), 'Bilqis the Vampire Slayer: Sarwat Chadda's British Muslim Vampire Fiction', in T. Khair and J. Höglund (eds), *Transnational and Postcolonial Vampires. Dark Blood*, 138–52, New York: Palgrave.
Corriente, F. (2008), *Dictionary of Arabic and Allied Words. Spanish, Portuguese, Catalan, Galician and Kindred Dialects*, Leiden: Brill.

Czerniejewska, I. (2008), 'Edukacja wielokulturowa w Polsce w perspektywie antropologii', PhD diss., Adam Mickiewicz University, Poznań.
Dąbrowa, E., and U. Markowska-Manista (2018), 'Przygotowanie nauczycieli i pedagogów w zakresie edukacji międzykulturowej – prezentacja projektu badawczego', *Edukacja międzykulturowa*, 1 (8): 169–84.
Dziekan, M. (2011), 'History and Culture of Polish Tatars', in K. Górak-Sosnowska (ed.), *Muslims in Poland and Eastern Europe. Widening the European Discourse on Islam*, 27–39, Warsaw: University of Warsaw.
Geografia (n.d.), 'Liceum/technikum'. Available online: https://podstawaprogramowa.pl/Liceum-technikum/Geografia (accessed 6 June 2020).
Geografia (n.d.), 'Szkoła Podstawowa IV-VIII'. Available online: https://podstawaprogramowa.pl/Szkola-podstawowa-IV-VIII/Geografia (accessed 6 June 2020).
Górak-Sosnowska, K. (2008), 'Stosunek młodzieży licealnej do islamu i muzułmanów – możliwości modyfikacji', *Collectanea Theologica*, 78 (2): 183–99.
Górak-Sosnowska, K. (2011), 'Muslims in Europe – Different Communities, One Discourse? Adding the Central and Eastern European Perspective', in K. Górak-Sosnowska (ed.), *Muslims in Poland and Eastern Europe. Widening the European Discourse on Islam*, 12–26, Warsaw: University of Warsaw.
Górak-Sosnowska, K. (2014), *Deconstructing Islamophobia in Poland. Story of an Internet group*, Warsaw: University of Warsaw.
Górak-Sosnowska, K., and M. Kubarek (2007), *W kręgu kultury islamu. Materiały dydaktyczne dla nauczycieli szkół ponadpodstawowych*, Warsaw: Polish National Commission for UNESCO & ARABIA Association.
Górak-Sosnowska, K., and U. Markowska-Manista (2010), 'Swój, Inny, Obcy. Wizerunek Arabów i Afrykanów w Polsce', in D. Pietrzyk-Reeves and M. Kułakowska (eds), *Studia nad wielokulturowością*, 457–73, Kraków: Księgarnia Akademicka.
Górak-Sosnowska, K., and M. Pachocka (2019), 'Inventing the Muslim Other in Poland (and Why Does It Differ from Western Europe)', in K. Górak-Sosnowska, J. Misiuna and M. Pachocka (eds), *Muslim Minorities and the Refugee Crisis in Europe*, 223–34, Warsaw: SGH.
Goździak, E., and P. Márton (2018, 21 June), 'Where the Wild Things Are' Fear of Islam and the Antirefugee Rhetoric in Hungary and in Poland', *Central and Eastern European Migration Review*, 7 (2): 125–51.
GUS (2013), *Ludność. Stan i struktura demograficzno-społeczna*, Warszawa: Główny Urząd Statystyczny.
Harris, A., and S. Hussein (2018), 'Conscripts or Volunteers? Young Muslims as Everyday Explainers', *Journal of Ethnic and Migration Studies*, 46 (19): 3974–991.
Historia (n.d.), 'Liceum/technikum'. Available online: https://podstawaprogramowa.pl/Liceum-technikum/Historia (accessed 6 June 2020).
Historia (n.d.), 'Szkoła podstawowa IV-VIII'. Available online: https://podstawaprogramowa.pl/Szkola-podstawowa-IV-VIII/Historia (accessed 6 June 2020).
IPSOS (2016, 14 December), 'Perils of Perception 2016. A 40-Country Study'. Available online: https://www.ipsos.com/ipsos-mori/en-uk/perceptions-are-not-reality-what-world-gets-wrong (accessed 6 June 2020).
Jackson, L. (2018), *Islamophobia in Britain. The Making of a Muslim Enemy*, New York: Palgrave Macmillan.
Kamusella, T. (2009), *The Politics of Language and Nationalism in Modern Central Europe*, New York: Palgrave Macmillan.

Kelemen, D. (2017, 22 December), 'Europe's Authoritarian Equilibrium', *Foreign Affairs*, 22 December. Available online: http://www.foreignaffairs.com/articles/hungary/2017-12-22/europes-authoritarian-equilibrium (accessed 6 June 2020).

Kitlińska-Król, M. (2013), 'Nauczyciele i edukacja międzykulturowa', *Chowanna*, 2: 275–88.

Komisja Wychowania Katolickiego Konferencji Episkopatu Polski (2010), *Program nauczania religii rzymskokatolickiej w przedszkolach i szkołach*, Kraków: WAM.

Markowska-Manista, U. (2019), 'Migrant and Refugee Children in Polish Schools in the Face of Social Transformation', in C. Maier-Höfer (ed.), *Die Vielfalt der Kindheit (en) und die Rechte der Kinder in der Gegenwart*, 79–100, Wiesbaden: Springer VS.

Moore, D. (2007), *Overcoming Religious Illiteracy. A Cultural Studies Approach to the Study of Religion in Secondary Education*, New York: Palgrave Macmillan.

Nikitorowicz J. (1995), *Pogranicze, tożsamość, edukacja międzykulturowa*, Białystok: Trans Humana.

Oravec, J. (2019, November), 'Online Social Shaming and the Moralistic Imagination. The Emergence of Internet-Based Performative Shaming', *Policy and Internet*, 12: 290–310.

Pacewicz, P. (2016), 'Polexit? Nie! 77 proc. Polek i Polaków wolałoby zostać w Unii', *OKO.press*, 29 June. Available online: https://oko.press/polexit-nie/ (accessed 6 June 2020).

Pacewicz, P. (2018), '51 proc. Polaków chce integracji UE i wzmocnienia KE, a tylko 35 proc. Europy Kaczyńskiego i Orbana', *OKO.press*, 28 December, Available online: https://oko.press/51-proc-polakow-chce-integracji-ue-i-wzmocnienia-ke-a-tylko-35-proc-europy-kaczynskiego-i-orbana/ (accessed 6 June 2020).

Pędziwiatr, K. (2011), '"The Established and Newcomers" in Islam in Poland or the Inter-Group Relations within the Polish Muslim Community', in K. Górak-Sosnowska (ed.), *Muslims in Poland and Eastern Europe. Widening the European Discourse on Islam*, 169–82, Warsaw: University of Warsaw.

Pędziwiatr, K. (2018), 'The Catholic Church in Poland on Muslims and Islam', *Patterns of Prejudice*, 52 (5): 461–78.

Pędziwiatr, K. (2019), 'Religious Dimension of Polish fears of Muslims and Islam', in I. Zempi and I. Awan (eds), *The Routledge International Handbook of Islamophobia*, 212–24, New York: Routledge.

Pew Research Center (2018), 'Eastern and Western Europeans Differ on Importance of Religion, Views of Minorities, and Key Social Issues', 29 October, https://www.pewresearch.org/religion/wp-content/uploads/sites/7/2018/10/Eastern-Western-Europe-FOR-WEB.pdf.

PFM (2020), 'Rozmowa na temat stereotypów wokół muzułmanek'. Warszawa: Polskie Forum Migracyjne (unpublished transcript).

Piela, A. (2021), *Wearing the Niqab: Fashioning of Agency among Muslim Women in the UK and the US*, London: Bloomsbury Academic.

Rogowska, B. (2017), 'Wpływ Polaków nawróconych na islam na społeczności lokalne w Polsce', PhD diss., University of Łódź, Łódź.

Said, E. (1978), *Orientalism*, New York: Pantheon Books.

Stefaniak, A. (2015), 'Postrzeganie muzułmanów w Polsce. Raport z badania sondażowego', Warszawa: Centrum Badań nad Uprzedzeniami.

Szpunar, O. (2019), 'Dyrektorce Szkoły grozi zwolnienie. Bo studenci z Algierii uczyli dzieci pisać po arabsku', *Gazeta. Kraków*, 26 February. Available online: https://krakow.wyborcza.pl/krakow/7,44425,24493245,przerwana-lekcja-tolerancji.html (accessed 6 June 2020).

Szymanik, G. (2015), 'Dlaczego 5 tys. Polakow polubiło mem z muzułmanami i torami do Birkenau'. *Gazeta wyborcza*, 29 July. Available online: http://wyborcza.pl/duzyformat/1,146230,18447691,dlaczego-5-tys-polakow-polubilo-mem-z-muzulmanami-i-torami.html (accessed 6 June 2020).

Tarlo, E. (2010), *Visibly Muslim. Fashion, Politics, Faith*, Oxford: Berg.

Zwierżdżyński, M. (2017), 'The Politics of Religious Education in Poland after 1990', in S. Ramet and I. Borowik (eds), *Religion, Politics, and Values in Poland*, 137–59, New York: Palgrave Macmillan.

6

Representations of Islam in the Romanian History Textbooks in the Post-1990 Period

Adriana Cupcea

Introduction

The revision process of the history textbooks that took place in the post-communist period was crucial for the Romanian textbook market which became characterized by a variety of history textbooks. Alternative/multiple history textbooks were introduced for middle school and for high school in 1996 and 1999, respectively, replacing the unique, singular textbooks that were used in the first half of the 1990s.

In my study, I analyse the representations about Islam and Muslims from the Romanian history textbooks, which I consider important in the shaping of attitudes and behaviours in the Romanian society. The analysis examines what kind of message the textbooks are sending about Islam and highlights the clichés and stereotypes created by the textbooks published after 1990. It reflects thus the attitudes developed by generations of pupils due to the educational historical literature regarding Islam and Muslims.

The differentiation between the unique textbooks in use between 1990 and 1995 (further called first generation of textbooks) and the alternative/multiple textbooks introduced since 1995 (further called second generations of textbooks) implies the following question: is there a change of perspective or a continuity with regards to representations of Islam in the alternative textbooks introduced after the structural and content reforms concerning the teaching of history in the 1990s? Despite the great variety of textbooks and even though teachers are the ones selecting the textbooks according to the needs of the students in class, a common educational framework exists and enables us to compare the textbooks with one another and pick up topics shared by most authors.

In my study, I use a quantitative framework which consists of measuring aspects of the text in order to determine how frequently specific themes and notions appear in the textbooks. It involves also how much space is allocated to a particular theme or topic.

The following qualitative text analysis covers a selection of history textbooks for gymnasium and for high school, respectively pupils aged eleven to fourteen and fifteen to sixteen. The fifteen textbooks analysed were selected in order to include chronologically the first generation as well as the second generation of textbooks. Since Islam as a religion, culture and civilization is introduced in history textbooks in the fifth grade of gymnasium and resumed consistently in the ninth grade of high school, these excerpts constitute half of all textbooks investigated, while the other half covers a selection of history textbooks for sixth, seventh, eleventh and twelfth grades.

In order to achieve a systematic analysis of the educational texts, I identified the major themes that address or just touch upon the history of Islam. It is a categorization which served to systematize the analysis and to trace how the images of Islam intersect or overlap in the Romanian didactical texts after 1990. Based on this analysis, I investigate the role and functionality of Islam stereotypes in the representations of the Self and Other in the contemporary Romanian didactical discourse.

Overview of the Textbooks Reform Post-1990

After the fall of the communist regime, as a first step in textbooks reform it was decided that, until new textbooks were published, the old ones would be modified. This meant reprinting textbooks from the communist period with the chapters and elements deeply infused by communist ideology removed. This stage stands out as an initial or recuperative stage, focused on the removal of ideology and legislative release; this stage proved to be very little constructive.

According to a periodization by a Romanian historian, another stage in the reform of the history textbooks were the years 1991–2 when new Romanian history textbooks were published both for secondary school and high school; they were characterized by a very large quantity of information that ignored the ability-age correlation of the pupil. I can add to the excessive details and historical dates from the new textbooks, which clouded the essential, the focus on the contents presented as readily prepared ideas, very little categorized, with historical sources representing arguments for authority (Căpiță and Căpiță 2005: 59). By presenting a vision of history with claims at supremacy, these textbooks failed to involve the pupil in investigating the past.

An aspect that must be discussed in such an analysis is the social and politic context at the time when these first new textbooks were conceived and published. It was a period when ideology was removed from all aspects of life: social, economic, politics and culture. Thus, after 1989, textbooks could be used to quantify or verify the influences of communist ideology. That is why they can be seen and interpreted as an effort to create a history that was detailed, neutral and aseptic as much as possible. These qualities would have offered the textbook a warranty of correctitude and seriousness, protecting it from possible attacks and accusations of political partisanship or lack of patriotism (Murgescu 2004: 12).

Administratively, the 1990–5 period is considered a unitary one in preparing the reform, mostly characterized by the contractual obligations of the loans from the World Bank and those of the grants from the European Union. It was a period for multiplying legislative, institutional and systemic alternatives for contents and methodology, when the conservative tendencies fought with the initiatives for radical reforms. This phase ended with the passing of the Law of Education from 1995. It was only after this year that a specially created body, The National Council for the Approval of Textbooks, coordinated the transition to multiple, alternative textbooks (Ștefănescu et al. 2016: 179–80). This year marked the effective introduction of alternative history textbooks in schools. The process was preceded by a review of the curricula first for elementary and middle schools, as was settled in the initial phase, and from 1999 they were introduced for high school. In fact, the next period, 1996–2000, represented the great, accelerated phase in the reform of the curricula; it marked the introduction of the new National Curriculum and the editing of alternative textbooks.

The study of history began in the fourth grade of primary school, continuing during the whole mandatory school period until the twelfth grade, the last level of the secondary school cycle. In the fourth, eighth and twelfth grades, the study focuses on national history while in the other grades (5–7 and 9–11) national history is presented in parallel (integrated) to the regional and universal one (Gasanabo 2006: 47).

Islam in Romania: Presence and Perceptions

A brief presentation concerning the presence of Islam in Romania and the manner in which Muslims are viewed in Romania is essential prior to presenting the contents of the textbooks. Such an approach is important not only to better understand the representations of Islam in the history textbooks but also in order to comprehend the dynamic of the relation *public opinion – media – textbooks* in determining the manner in which the Islam representations circulate.

The Muslim community from Romania is made up of 73 per cent autochthonous Muslims, Turks and Tatars, focused demographically in Dobruja, in south-eastern Romania. The most recent census, that of 2011, indicates that there are 27,698 Turks and 20,282 Tatars (National Institute of Statistics 2011 n.d.). Besides them, the Romanian Muslim community includes the *new Muslims*, demographically located in Romania's large urban centres, most of them in the capital Bucharest. This category includes Muslims who have arrived in Romania during the communist period; who have received Romanian citizenship and are now in their second generation; Muslims who have arrived after 1990 from different Islamic countries for studies or economic aims but who have meanwhile obtained Romanian citizenship; and, last but not least, those who followed a different religion but have converted to Islam, becoming Muslims.

The presence of the Turks and Tatars in the region is a demographical heritage from the Ottoman past, in between the fifteenth and nineteenth centuries when Dobruja was under Ottoman administration. Following the 1877–8 Russian–Ottoman war and in the context of the dismemberment of the Ottoman Empire, following centuries of Ottoman administration, the province inhabited mostly by the Muslim population has become part of the Romanian, Christian national state. Dobruja is connected to Romania's Turkish-Islamic heritage which is present even today in various domains of life: not only in Dobruja's religious Islamic architecture but also in the popular culture, the latter detectable particularly in gastronomy and music. The most important part of the Turkish-Islamic heritage of the province is the demographic one, residing in its ethnic and religious diversity, a trait that is shared with the entire region of the former Ottoman Balkans (Todorova 2004: 12). The Turkish and Tatar minorities are the demographic heritage from Dobruja's Ottoman period.

Still, as one goes further away from Dobruja, most Romanians do not know that historical minorities that follow the Islamic religion live in Romania. In the perception of Romanians, the Muslims are associated with immigrants, seen as representative for Islam, although Romania has not yet faced this problem. According to a poll conducted by the Romanian Institute for Evaluation and Strategy (IRES) at the request of the National Council for Combating Discrimination (CNCD), more than 60 per cent of Romanians consider Muslims as potentially dangerous, while 52 per cent believe that immigrants should be stopped at Europe's borders. According to the same study, the scale of social distance indicates an increased tolerance towards Muslims, placed on the third place, following homosexuals and immigrants. If in the case of immigrants, 39 per cent of Romanians do not accept them as relatives, while 30 per cent do not accept them as friends, as far as Muslims are concerned, 39 per cent of Romanians do not want to be related with them, while 28 per cent would not accept the friendship of a Muslim (IRES 2018).

The lack of information concerning Dobruja and the Muslim population in the area in the history textbooks is practically translated in the population lacking knowledge about the local Islam as well as the material and immaterial Islamic heritage from Dobruja that might contribute to a better understanding of the Muslim culture and religion in general. The negative news in the press concerning Islam, focusing on terrorist attacks and the refugee problem, have a major impact in the society. Practically, the mass media is the one that has the role of shaping the opinions and representation concerning Islam and Muslims in the Romanian collective mentality. Following the ever-increasing Islam presence in the 2000, it was decided that this topic will be introduced more extensively in the history curriculum, but the manner in which the information travelled was not from the scientific and didactic literature towards the public opinion. On the contrary, the influence travelled in the opposite direction, with the textbook authors taking some stereotypes about Islam that had entered the collective mentality through the mass media. This can explain some interpretation errors and omissions in the lessons concerning Islamic history and culture as they appear in the Romanian history textbooks.

Islam in the Romanian History Textbooks

Islam does not occupy a very extensive place in Romanian history textbooks. The chapter dedicated specifically to this topic is usually three to five pages long, but information in this sense can be sporadically identified also in other lessons dedicated to topics related to Islam and Muslims. The major themes selected by the authors are the early days of Islam (the Prophet Mohammed's life, religious and military activity as founder of Islam, the rising of the Arab Caliphate); the Crusades (causes, development, consequences) and contemporary Islam, a topic addressed in more recent textbooks, published in the past ten to fifteen years. The first two topics are presented mainly in the textbooks of the fifth and ninth grades and are debated in lessons dedicated to Islam as a religion, culture and civilization. The theme of contemporary Islam is found in seventh- and ninth-grade history textbooks, integrated into lessons on religious fundamentalism and terrorism in the twentieth century. The same information found in these textbooks is sporadically repeated in the other textbooks for the sixth, eighth, tenth and eleventh grades but which do not necessarily dedicate separate lessons to Islam.

Themes are approached mainly descriptively, especially when elements such as military wars or the geographical and socioeconomic profiles of the Arabian Peninsula are presented. The factual and descriptive perspective is doubled by the conceptual approach of Islam, as religion and culture, in which certain misinterpretations and stereotypes intervene.

Early Islam: Key Concepts and Problems

In the first generations of textbooks used in the first half of the 1990s, Islam is sporadically mentioned. Following the introduction of the alternative textbooks, the lessons concerning these topics become more extensive but they still focus almost exclusively on the early Islam, with two essential elements that can be noticed as a whole as inherent in the post-1990 textbooks: the Prophet Mohammed as the founder of Islam and the creation of the Arab Caliphate (Bichman et al. 1996: 185; Barnea et al. 2008: 66–9).

The tendency to associate the Islamic religion only with the Arabs and the Great Arab Caliphate can be observed. For example, a history textbook for the ninth grade mentions Islam only as a religion of the Great Arab Caliphate, in a lesson discussing the medieval states (Pascu et al. 1992: 81–5), although the pupils are also briefly told about the Golden Hoard Khanate, which adopted the Islamic religion starting with the thirteenth century (Peacock 2018) and the Ottoman Empire whose official religion was Islam[1].

The birth of Islam in the seventh century, sometimes preceded by the presentation of the pre-Islamic Arab tribal society, constitutes the core around which the historic narrative about Islam is built. Although the monotheist character of the Islamic religion is highlighted, the textbooks emphasize the manner of founding and preaching the religion by Mohammed, thus failing in presenting the pupils with the Muslim 'inside' perspective. I am referring to the Muslim standpoint which emphasizes the revealed character of Islam sprung from the religious revelations of the Prophet Mohammed and which form the Quran, the Holy Book of Islam. It is a constant characteristic of the textbooks published in the period 2017–20.

'Mohammed (570–632) (in Arabic it means the Praised one) has preached Islamism to the Arabs, the belief in a single divinity named Allah, replacing the beliefs in the old gods that kept the Arab tribes divided' (Bichman et al. 1996: 185). The fragment that was quoted reveals another characteristic of the textbooks from the first half of the 1990s that continued even after moving to the second generation of history textbooks. I am referring to the wrong usage of the term Islamism in the sense of Islamic religion (Bichman et al. 1996: 185; Băluțoiu and Vlad 1999: 41). The term Islamism as used in the textbook has a totally different meaning; it is a political ideology inspired by the values and principles of the Muslim religion. More precisely, Islamism proposes the interpretation of the Islamic religion as a source of identity and political actions. As John Esposito points out, Islamism is a term used alternatively with that of political Islam (Esposito 2002: 60–1) and is made up of myriad trends and organizations with differing and often contradictory positions (Ramadan 2017: 363, 364), from pietistic revivalism to violent extremism (Leaman and Ali 2007: 41). Thus, the history textbooks published post-1990 created a confusion of terms and content by using the term Islamism with the meaning of Islam/Islamic religion. Even more so, the emphasis on the meaning of obeisance deepens the confusions (see Barnea et al. 2008: 66). This unidirectional explanation is a semantic distortion that takes place by including stereotypes from the Western literature about Islam in the textbooks: 'The faithful, he said, (Prophet Mohammed) must obey the will of Allah (Islam=obeisance), who decides every man's fate' (Bichman et al. 1996: 185).

Indeed, in general knowledge encyclopaedias, Islam is explained as 'obeisance', 'submission' or 'surrender' to God, thus creating the illusion of a consensus with regards to the meaning of the Islamic religion. It is understood that the belief in Allah and being one with Allah is in fact a confiscation, an encroachment on the individual's own freedom and autonomy. Tariq Ramadan states that the message of Islam is the opposite and that such a translation is superficial, a distortion of the initial meaning. The Arab root of the word Islam is *s-l-m,* meaning peace. The Islamic scholar states that Islam can be understood as an act of faith where man is searching for peace – a peace to which Allah invited him and called him to find it through the love towards Him, through prayer and by respecting the rituals. The human being does not abandon its own will, does not give up the freedom but uses his freedom and will to do the good that Allah desires. The notion of *salam* – peace – that lies at the root of the word ' "Islam" certainly constitutes Islam's supreme value as a religion.' (Ramadan 2017: 90–1).

One can notice that textbooks are omitting essential aspects such as the Islam branches (Sunnism, Shiism and Kharijism) or explaining the five pillars of the Islamic faith: the profession of faith (*shahada*), prayer (*ṣalat*), charity (*zakat*), fasting during the month of Ramadan (*sawm*) and the pilgrimage to Mecca (*hajj*), but indispensably mention in the lessons that introduce Islam that the *jihad* is defined as an 'obligation' of any Muslim to fight 'unbelievers' (Dumitrescu 2008: 54), Again, one can notice a semantic distortion from the perspective of the terms used. Although the emphasis falls on the mandatory aspect, the *jihad* is not mentioned in the sources of Islam – Quran and Sunnah (The Prophet's Traditions) – as an obligation. The five pillars of Islam are the obligations, while the *jihad* was considered from the 'outside' as Islam's sixth pillar. The term *jihad* has been used nowhere in the Quran to mean war in the sense of launching an offensive in order to change people's religion (Hayati 2011: 82). It is used rather to mean 'struggle' and has two meanings, which are not explained in the history textbooks: that of an individual's inner fight, as his effort to live in accordance with the precepts of the Islamic religion and to respectively to follow the path of Allah (the Little *Jihad*), and that of defensive war, conducted against those attacking Islam who turn to force (the Great *Jihad*).

The notion of *jihad*, as presented in the textbooks, proves that violence is intrinsic to Islam and the teachings of this religion. Thus, certain important moments from the history of early Islam are objectively presented from the factual point of view, but filtered and grounded through the notion of *jihad*, with the meaning of offensive war, for conquest. These events are as follows: the moment when the Arab tribes under the Prophet Mohammed switch to Islam, the escape from Mecca to Medina in 622, his military activity while in Medina in his efforts to resist the attempts of the Mecca aristocracy to eliminate him, the Prophet's return to Mecca, the creation of the Arab Caliphate and its expansion during the reign of the first caliphs, during the Umayyad (661–750) and Abbasid (750–1258) dynasties, in Africa and Europe (Băluțoiu and Vlad 1999: 31; Dumitrescu et al. 1999: 54; Barnea et al. 2008: 66).

The emphasis on the notion of *jihad* as meaning offensive war diminishes considerably in the history textbooks published in the past years, focusing instead on explaining the five pillars of Islam and aiming at transmitting to the pupils the values and principles that derive from Islam and that define the life of the Muslim believers (Stan 2017: 98–9). Also, these history textbooks that were recently published offer an important part in the texts to the scientific, philosophic and artistic contributions of Muslims during the Caliphate period, emphasizing the idea of cultural transfer of this knowledge to Europe and implicitly the influence of the Islamic civilization on the Western one.

> The territorial expansion leads to the expansion of the Islamic culture. It is given birth through the cultural heritage of the people from the conquered territories (Greeks, Romans Persians etc.) being taken over. The Muslim scientists conduct research in the fields of mathematics, medicine, astronomy, geography and other fields. They transmit in Europe the Arab numbers, adopted from the Indians. Many of the works of the ancient Greek authors are preserved due to their translation in the Arab language. Through the works of other scholars, such as Avicenna and Averroes, the European culture itself is influenced by the Islamic one. Also, its influences are met in Central Asia, India and China.[2] (Băluțoiu and Grecu 2017: 96–7)

The Christian World and Islam

An approach that is characteristic for the history textbooks with regard to Islam is the introduction of the dual approach from the religious perspective: Christians – Muslims. It is an approach that can be easily identified when presenting two historical topics: that of the Crusades and the uprisings of the Romanian countries against of the Ottoman Empire during the course of the fourteenth- to eighteenth centuries.

The Crusades, a historic reality presented by the authors in the totality of religious, military and economic motivations that led to them being initiated, lead to a manner of dual thinking, emphasizing the stereotype of war of religions. One of the textbooks highlights that the 'crusades, are invoked each and every time one discusses the concept of holy war, or any conflict between the Orient and the Occident' (Dumitrescu et al. 2008: 99).

The religious antinomy between Islam and Christianity is reiterated in the lessons through subtitles such as 'Christian Europe and Islam' (Băluțoiu and Vlad 1999: 66) or 'Christian Europe and the Muslim World' (Scurtu et al. 2004: 90). Within this approach, one can note the overlapping and the connection between Islam and the Ottoman expansion, defined as the greatest peril for Christian Europe (Scurtu et al. 2004: 90). A textbook from 1998 chooses to explain the expansion but also the warlike character of the Ottomans exclusively from the religious perspective as a consequence of them following the Muslim religion stating that

> the Islamic religion divided the world in two, the House of Islam or the House of Peace, that included the Islamic people and the House of War, or the unfaithful. This included the people following other religions than the Islamic one and had to be conquered by Ottomans. This explains the warlike character of the Ottomans and the continuous battles against the Christians. (Vulpe et al. 1999: 53)

The anti-Ottoman fight led by the Romanian countries has religious connotations, namely that the Romanian countries are seen as the 'Gate of Christendom' while the rulers are the defenders of the Christian European civilization in the fight against the Turks. Although this religious dimension of the historical context is important in the message of history lessons, religious, cultural or social aspects of the Turkish-Islamic civilization are not explained. The emphasis falls on the militarized character of the Ottoman state, on the centuries-long fight of the Romanian countries to maintain their autonomy towards the empire and the military deeds (Daicoviciu et al. 1994: 104–56).

The Contemporary Islam: Religious Fundamentalism and Terrorism

Following the 9/11 attacks, the need to understand the present political realities of the Muslim world brings approaches of current aspects of Islam. They serve to complete the predominant historical perspective in the history textbooks from 1990 to 2000.

One can notice in this context the presentation of the contemporary Islam in textbooks discussing religious fundamentalism and terrorism, introduced in some chapters with generic titles such as 'Islam between Integralism and Fundamentalism' (Ciupercă and Cozma 2014: 72–83) or 'The Postbellum World' (Ghețău and Ghețău 2019: 79–102). Even though some textbooks create a larger context by presenting the origins of religious fundamentalism and the existence of this phenomenon in most religions, the texts of the lesson associate religious fundamentalism and terrorism with the Islamic religion. Unlike the Christian fundamentalism that is 'characterized through the desire to regain faith, to know the word of the Gospels' (Ciupercă and Cozma 2014: 73), Islamic fundamentalism would be based on 'the idea of regaining the primitive purity, on which God's forgiveness depends and of the fundamental values of Islam based on austerity and solidarity' (Budici et al. 2006: 106; Ciupercă and Cozma 2014: 79), and last but not least intolerance towards the Western culture (Ciupercă and Cozma 2014: 78). Some textbooks, published in the past ten years, emphasize the severity of the Islamic fundamentalism, corelating it with the migration of the Arab workforce towards the Occident, a context in which it is presented as a central issue in the last decades.

'The political problems from the Middle East, combined with the religious expansion from the European and American countries as a result of the migration of the Arab workforce, means that the Islamic issue has taken a central place in the last decades' (Barnea et al. 2014: 116). Although the text of the lesson sends the message that the Arabs represent the nucleus of the Islamic fundamentalism, the image that exemplifies Islamic fundamentalism is a mural picture of Ayatollah Khomeini, a political and religious leader, founder of the Islamic Republic of Iran (Barnea et al. 2014: 116). The ambiguity and the contradiction between the text and the image could lead to pupils confusing Arabs and Iranians, who certainly have in common the Islamic faith (the Iranians are mostly Shiites while the Arabs are mostly Sunni), but who are still two different people/ethnicities.

In the case of the terrorism topic, although there exist several brief mentions about the terrorist movements from Europe (IRA, ETA), this phenomenon is discussed in the context of the twenty-first century, in relation with the Islamic religion. Thus, terrorism is described as a practice with a religious motivation associated with the holy war and thus with Muslims. The terrorist attempts from 9/11 conducted by the Islamist organization *Al Qaeda*, the photographs of the smoking twin towers from the World Trade Centre and the image of the *Al Qaeda* leader, Osama bin Laden, are examples ever-present in the textbooks, aiming to exemplify the concept of terrorism to pupils. They further strengthen the simplistic understanding and create stereotypes about Islam, continuing to remain a common trait of the textbooks published and used in the past twenty years (Barnea et al. 2008: 66–9).

Omitting the Local Muslims

At the same time the historic Muslim minorities from Romania, the Muslim Turks and Tatars from the Dobruja region represent groups that are totally ignored in the history textbooks, in the chapters dedicated to the ethnic minorities. They appear sparsely mentioned as a religious minority, for example in a case study on 'Romania and Religious Tolerance in the Twentieth Century' (Petre 2008: 152). This textbook informs us that 'a particular situation is represented by the Muslim cult whose role increased once Dobruja was integrated in the Romanian state', following the Russian-Ottoman war from 1877 to 1878. The textbook mentions one more aspect for this, namely that 'the Muslim religion was supported from the start by the Romanian state, even though article 7 of the Constitution (from 1878) applies also to Muslims'. According to this article, the Romanian citizenship was conditioned to observing the Christian rituals, thus 'clearly differentiating between Christians and non-Christians' (Petre 2008: 152).

The information presented in the textbooks is limited only to this, without mentioning the manner in which the former Ottoman province Dobruja was integrated juridically, economically, politically and demographically in the Romanian state or how the Muslims here have managed to create a compatibility between the local form of the Dobruja Islam and the Romanian secular state. This process of adaptation and integration in the secular state has taken place in all the Muslim communities from the Balkans that live today in countries from the south-eastern Europe, built on the ruins of the former Ottoman Empire, but which do not find a place in the Romanian history textbooks.

Conclusions

If in the first generation of textbooks Islam is presented schematically, in the second generation the presentation of some important moments in the history of early Islam indicate a more integrative narrative. The contents of the lessons on Islam and their length indicate a narrative which offers a certain visibility on Islam. Also, the emphasis in textbooks published after 2001 on contemporary Islam reflects the effort and the desire to understand Islam and contemporary Islamic societies. However, the problems of interpreting concepts in the presentation of Islam as religion and culture and the tendency to associate Islam with religious fundamentalism and terrorism indicate a presentation of Islam from a Western perspective.

The lack of contact with Islam due to the demographic concentration of most Muslims in a compact region of the country (Dobruja), the lack of information on local Islam and local Muslim communities and the predominance of the journalistic information flow in creating the public perceptions are realities reflected in history textbooks. The narrations concerning Islam are partially adopted in the Romanian post-1990 history textbooks, especially when they discuss topics concerning contemporary Islam. For the most part of the post-1990 period, with a slight decrease in the 2017–20 period, the direction of influence in creating the representations about Islam is from the mass media and the public opinion towards the textbooks. The problem is represented by the insistent presence in the textbooks published after 2001 on associating the Islamic religion with the religious fundamentalism and terrorism, thus creating an image of Islam as an eminently violent religion.

Even if some of the textbooks contribute to the understanding of Islam, by presenting detailed aspects of religion and culture, they are overshadowed by the conflicting, ultra-religious and threatening perspective on the Muslim world in narratives portraying contemporary Islam. The dissemination of these stereotypes to younger generations in parallel with their spread to society from the media leads in time to the internalization of narrative structures in which the threat of Muslims as an external enemy dominates.

By making no reference to historically autochthonous Muslims in Europe, such as the Balkans or to the new Muslim immigrants in Europe, including the ones in Romania, one can understand that there is no intention of understanding the closeness of Islam to Europe. Xavier Bougarel proposes, without overlooking the diversity and the main characteristics of the Balkan Muslims, deriving from the historical experience of each community the interpretation of the Islam characteristics for the Balkans as a 'European Islam' (Bougarel 2010: 15-31). Thus, by omitting the discussions about the local Islam and the autochthonous Muslims, the textbooks leave out the possible models for integrating the Islamic identities in the European civic culture. These models could and should replace, on the direction of influence, scientific literature-textbooks-mass media, the current stereotypes about Islam, internalized in the Romanian society.

The recommendation for future is to teach the subject of Islam in Central and Eastern Europe in a common manner but at the same time from a different perspectives. One solution in this regard is to organize practical seminars, with the participation of history textbooks authors from all over the region. The seminars must create a dialogue between the textbook authors and academic scholars in the region on topics related not only to the history and culture of Islam, but also to local Islam(s) in Central and Eastern Europe. In the context of a regional collaboration, it is also possible and recommended to create a database consisting of teaching material collections containing various sources about the history and current situation of Muslims in different states of the region. Translating the database into national languages would ensure the accessibility and use of teaching materials in all states in the region, not only by textbook authors, but also by history teachers at the local levels. Such an integrative approach can be successful under the supervision of international organizations that have previously expressed their interest in the history teaching of the region: the Council of Europe, UNESCO, the European Union, or through a joint collaboration of Ministries of Education in Central and Eastern Europe.

Notes

1. For a useful survey of the historiography on the Turks conversion to Islam see: A. C. S. Peacock (2010: 99-128).
2. All translations are by the author.

References

Bougarel, X. (2010), 'Balkan Islam as "European Islam": Historical Background and Present Challenges', in C. Voss and J. Telbizova-Sack (eds), *Islam und Muslime in (Südost) Europa im Kontext von Transformation und EU-Erweiterung*, 15-31, München: Otto Sagner.

Căpiță, L., and C. Căpiță (2005), *Tendencies in the Didactics of History*, Pitești: Paralela 4.

Esposito, J. (2002), *What Everyone Should Know about Islam*, Oxford: Oxford University Press.

Gasanabo J. (2006), *Fostering Peaceful Co-existence through Analysis and Revision of History Curricula and Textbooks in Southeast Europe. Preliminary Stocktaking Report*, Paris: UNESCO.

Hayati, A. (2011), 'Islam: The |Religion of Peace?', *Journal of Rotterdam Islamic and Social Sciences*, 2 (1): 74–92.
IRES – Romanian Institute for Evaluation and Strategy (2018), 'Sondaj de opinie la nivel național privind nivelul discriminării în România și percepțiile actuale asupra infracțiunilor motivate de ură'. Available online: https://ires.ro/articol/367/discriminare-si-discurs-al-urii-in-romania--2019 (accessed 16 August 2021).
Leaman, O., and K. Ali (2007), *Islam. The Key Concepts*, London: Routledge.
Murgescu, M. (2004), *History from the Backpack. Memory and Textbooks in Romania in the 1990s*, Bucharest: Dominor.
National Institute of Statistics (2011), '2011 Population and Housing Census. Population by Ethnicity and Religion – Categories of Localities'. Available online: http://www.recensamantromania.ro/rezultate-2/ (accessed 22 July 2021).
Peacock, A. (2010), *Early Seljūq History: A New Interpretation*, Abingdon: Routledge.
Peacock, A. (2018), 'Islamisation in the Golden Horde and Anatolia: Some Remarks on Travelling Scholars and Texts', *Revue des mondes musulmanes et de la Méditeranée*, 143: 151–64.
Ramadan, T. (2017), *Islam: The Essentials*, London: Penguin Random House.
Ștefănescu, D., A. Florea, C. Petru and A. Roescu (2016), '*20 Years of School Textbooks' History in Romania (1989–2009)*', in P. Bianchini and R. Sani (eds), *Textbooks and Citizenship in Modern and Contemporary Europe*, 177–95, Berlin: Peter Lang Verlag.
Todorova, M. (2004), *Balkan Identities. Nation and Memory*, London: Hurst & Company.

Textbooks

Barnea, A. V., A. Manea, M. Stamatescu and B. Teodorescu (2008), *Istorie. Manual pentru clasa a IX-a*, Bucharest: Corint.
Barnea, A. V., A. Manea, E. Palade, F. Petrescu and B. Teodorescu (2014), *Istorie. Manual pentru clasa a XI-a*, Bucharest: Corint.
Băluțoiu, V., and C. Vlad (1999), *Istorie. Manual pentru clasa a VI-a*, Bucharest: All.
Băluțoiu, V., and M. Grecu (2017), *Istorie. Manual pentru clasa a V-a*, Bucharest: Editura Didactică și Pedagogică.
Bichman, E., V. Neagu, L. Georgian and N. Constantin (1996), *Istorie universal antică și medieval. Manual pentru clasa a V-a*, Bucharest: Editura Didactică și Pedagogică.
Budici A., M. Stănescu and D. Țigău (2006), *Istorie. Manual pentru clasa a XI-a*, Bucharest: Sigma.
Ciupercă, I., and E. Cozma (2014), *Istorie. Manual pentru clasa a XI-a*, Bucharest: Corint.
Daicoviciu, H., T. Pompiliu and I. Câmpeanu (1994), *Istoria Românilor din cele mai vechi timpuri până la revoluția din 1821. Manual pentru clasa a VII-a*, Bucharest: Editura Didactică și Pedagogică.
Dumitrescu, N., M. Manea and O. Bojică (2008), *Istorie. Manual pentru clasa a IX-a*, Bucharest: Editura Didactică și Pedagogică.
Dumitrescu, N., M. Manea, C. Niță, A. Pascu, A. Trandafir and M. Trandafir (1999), *Istoria românilor. Manual pentru clasa a XII-a*, Bucharest: Humanitas.
Ghețău, G. F., and O. Ghețău (2019), *Istorie. Manual pentru clasa a VII-a*, Bucharest: Aramis.
Pascu, Ș., A. Bodor and V. Boșcăneanu (1992), *Istorie universală antică și medievală. Manual pentru clasa a IX-a*, Bucharest: Editura Didactică și Pedagogică R.A.

Petre, Z. (2008), *Istorie. Manual pentru clasa a XII-a*, Bucharest: Corint.
Scurtu, I., M. Curculescu, C. Dincă and A. C. Soare (2004), *Istorie. Manual pentru clasa a IX-a*, Bucharest: Editura Economică Preuniversitaria.
Stan, M. (2017), *Istorie. Manual pentru clasa a V-a*, Bucharest: Litera.
Vulpe A., R. G. Păun and R. Băjenaru (1999), *Istorie. Manual pentru clasa a IX-a*, Bucharest: Sigma.

Othering through Textbooks: Teaching about Roma in Contemporary Hungarian Schools

Jekatyerina Dunajeva

Introduction

On 1 July 2020, the Council of Europe's Committee of Ministers adopted Recommendation CM/Rec(2020)2 on the inclusion of the history of Roma and/or Travelers in school curricula and teaching materials. The recommendation explicitly highlights the role of education in transmitting 'the contribution of Roma and/or Travellers to the cultural heritage of their respective countries' and 'improving relations between members of the Roma and/or Traveller communities and their respective member States' by incorporating Roma into teaching materials. In turn, this will help to address marginalization and discrimination that Roma face, as 'history teaching is one of the most important tools contributing to the elimination of prejudice'. Although the document primarily focuses on history teaching, the recommendations are not limited to history as a school subject only. In fact, the document suggests that knowledge about Roma 'could be incorporated into various school subjects, such as history, civic or social education, literature, religion or ethics, arts, music or languages'.

It is no surprise that there is a growing outcry to consider Roma as integral members of their respective societies and incorporate their history accordingly into national curricula. Roma are the most numerous ethnic minority in Europe, with an 'estimated 10 to 12 million Roma living in Europe ... many [of whom] are still victims of prejudice and social exclusion, despite the discrimination ban across EU Member States', claims the European Commission (n.d.). In Hungary, estimates on Roma population vary, with some claiming it's 6 per cent of the total population (Vajda and Dupcsik 2008) to approximately 3 per cent, the latter based on the 2011 census results (KSH 2015). There is a wide consensus, however, that their population is growing steadily and they comprise the most vulnerable, discriminated group in Hungary and across Europe.

While it is noteworthy that the Council of Europe made this acknowledgement and developed a remarkable recommendation, in some of its member states values in national curricula have been drifting towards nationalism, xenophobia and authoritarianism, rather than multinationalism and democracy. In Hungary, for instance, compulsory school literature now includes 'authors with nationalist, anti-Semitic, and national socialist views, since one of the most important goals of Hungarian literary education is to reinforce a sense of Hungarian nationalism' (Huszár 2014: 303). The case of Hungary clearly demonstrates the close relationship between current illiberal Hungarian politics and its education policy. Since school curricula have been gradually reformed, closely following the current political rhetoric, it further strengthened the exclusionary sense of nationhood reflected in the content of education.

This chapter focuses on the Hungarian elementary education system[1] and consists of the following sections: (1) analysis of politicization of education, (2) discussion of how Roma are represented in both national curricula in Hungary and various teaching resources available for teachers, (3) description of a case studies based on series of field research in classrooms (conducted in 2012 and 2020); I conclude this chapter with a brief mention of a promising movement that is aimed at decolonizing knowledge about Roma. Throughout this chapter, I use the term Roma when unpacking my own analysis and discussing Roma in general, and 'Gypsy' when referring to the terminology used in original sources (e.g. Gypsy folk tales for *cigány népmesék*).[2]

Methodology

My research methodology consisted of two phases: first, I synthesized existing research regarding Roma representation in Hungarian textbooks and then conducted desktop research of Hungarian textbooks for elementary school grades (grades 1–8) to identify the frequency of occurrence of Roma folk tales in children's readers and literature textbooks. I use textbook analysis because textbooks have become crucial sources for researchers as 'they always contain and enshrine underlying norms and values, they transmit constructions of identity, and they generate specific patterns of perceiving the world' (Fuchs and Bock 2018: 1). During the second phase of research, I conducted field research about children's perception of Roma folk tales in the spring of 2021, when I visited a school situated in one of the poorest districts of a major Hungarian city. Both Roma and non-Roma students attend this school. In this school, I observed fifth-grade and seventh-grade students, read out loud a Roma folk tale from their textbook and discussed their impression of the story and Roma representation in the tale.

All research ethical considerations were met, and the author received an ethical review approval (reference number: 2020-1/2/RD) from the Central European University's Ethical Research Committee. Accordingly, the school was informed ahead of time about the purpose of the research and my methodology of data collection. After securing institutional consent, the head teacher discussed the matter with all those students who volunteered to participate in my research. I prepared age-appropriate tasks and guiding questions in consultation with the head teacher. At the beginning of the class, I restated the purpose of my research, and students were also informed that their responses will be used for my research as a case study – in an aggregate, synthesized manner, or individually as anonymized quotes or drawings without indicating names. After that, we carried on reading and discussing the tales in the presence of the head teacher. All participating students and the institution were assured of anonymity. There was no risk, discomfort or research benefit for any participant. Those who wished to participate in class but not in the study did not turn in their anonymous answers at the end of the class.

The limitation of the study stems from the small student sample who participated during fieldwork. Expansion of fieldwork was challenging primarily due to the growing restrictions in schools as a result of the Covid-19 pandemic, but also because of the contentious topic of the research. In my many years of experience conducting fieldwork in elementary schools about Roma and discrimination, I find that more affluent schools with few or no Roma students tend to be wary of allowing researchers in their institution. In the past, I have noticed schools with considerable number of Roma students more open and willing to cooperate on such research. This may introduce a bias, as the school – including teachers and students – may be more sensitized and aware of discriminatory practices that Roma face. To strengthen the findings, this research may be repeated in other schools with majority non-Roma students.

Politics of School Curricula: 'Insiders' and 'Outsiders' in School Curricula in Hungary and Beyond

Politicization of education is not a new phenomenon. With the introduction of mandatory primary education, not only were schools key for propagating certain narratives of national history, but they also became the primary institutions contributing to nationalism becoming a mass phenomenon (see, e.g., Anderson 2006 and Gellner 1983). For instance, since the early nineteenth century, teaching history in schools had the aim of 'telling the story of a nation's past … justifying whatever were the ideological positions … [and helping] develop the "character" of students' (Egan 1989: 366). In other words, education and schooling have always had profound effects on the society and individuals, and mass education has been the central mechanism for nation-building, especially for nation-states (e.g. Meyer et al. 1992).

Since state-approved school curricula were able to transmit a collective identity (e.g. Grosvenor 1999), it is important to recognize its homogenizing effects, which Ernest Gellner (1983) refers to as 'cultural standardisation'. I analysed this process in detail in an earlier study: 'Public schools have been a key state institution for homogenizing the population … While schools educate pupils about national identity – common history, national anthem, praising national paraphernalia, proper grammar, national literature, and the like – this shared knowledge binds the "imagined community"' (Anderson 1983) into a nation. However, a concomitant side to creating a nation is excluding those who don't belong: the 'Others' (Dunajeva 2017: 57–8).

Othering Practices through the School Curricula

While there has been considerable academic attention to the importance of school education in 'imagining the nation' and constructing a narrative of national representation (e.g. Lowe 1999; Crawford 2003; Williams 2014), as well as its importance in teaching patriotism and loyalty to the state (e.g. Christou 2007; Carretero 2011; Koesel 2020), the depiction of 'the other' in educational content also merits some discussion.

A notable exception is a recent study on the portrayal of 'the other' in Palestinian and Israeli school textbooks, where the authors Sami Adwan, Daniel Bar-Tal and Bruce Wexler argue that the narrative about the Israeli-Palestinian conflict is transmitted through schools. In specific, there is a 'negative bias in portrayal of the other and the positive bias in portrayal of the self' coupled with an 'absence of images and information about the Other' in textbooks (Adwan et al. 2016: 201). This narrative of othering tends to 'delegitimize the Other, present the self-collective in glorifying terms and as the sole victim of the conflict, assign responsibility for the outbreak and continuation of the conflict to the other side, focus on violence and atrocities of the Other, leave little room to acknowledge the history, culture, and future aspirations of the Other, and omit their own misdeeds' (Adwan et al. 2016: 202)

Importantly, 'in their presentation of curricular content, schoolbooks express a society's ideology and ethos and impart values, goals, and myths which the society aims to transmit to new generations' (Adwan et al. 2016: 201). In other words, it is not only violent conflicts that are transmitted, but also social tensions, and various biases and prejudices. The narrative about other cultures, especially those of national minorities, is indicative of existing intergroup frictions and preconceptions, as well as the dominant discourse of nationhood. To consider the case of Eastern Europe, where Roma have been the perennial 'others', indeed research demonstrates that some Roma families consider schools to be 'unsuitable institution[s]' where Roma youth are at risk 'to be imbued by a value system that is not theirs and that they have no wish to acquire' (Liègeois 2007: 186, see also Messing 2012). Beyond exclusively learning the value system of the dominant society, minorities like Roma may also face educational content that is prejudiced and that portrays their own group identity in negative terms.

In Hungary, the rhetoric of Orbán Viktor's 'exclusionary image of Hungarian nationalism' has been apparent since the victory of Orbán and his Fidesz party during the 2010 parliamentary elections, and the dissemination of a particular historical and social narrative became a political tool to legitimize his power (Toomey 2018: 87). Since schools are a dominant site for such dissemination, two important measures were implemented: centralization of schools and reform of school curricula. Observers noted that the 'new school curriculum [was] designed by the ruling Fidesz party to promote its nationalist agenda' (Dunai 2020). While an analysis of this agenda in school curriculum is beyond the scope of this chapter, the omission and biased representation of Roma is revealing of the disregard towards minorities and their cultures in textbooks.

Nationalization of textbooks has been a gradual and steady process in Hungary since the early 2010s. First, in 2012, the government centralized the management of schools, taking any autonomy away from schools and controlling all aspects of education from the top down (György et al. 2015). Then, in 2013, textbook distribution was monopolized by Kello (*Könyvtárellátó*) (Hungary Today 2019). Later, the so-called textbook law centralized textbook production, which created publishing monopolies that are working with the guidance of the Hungarian Institute for Educational

Research and Development – an institution that was given the task of textbook development – since 2014 (Joob et al. 2013). In the same year, the government bought two publishing houses – Nemzedékek Tudása Tankönyvkiadót (earlier known as Nemzeti Tankönyvkiadó) and Apáczai Kiadó – thereby virtually controlling the entire textbook market (Zsilak 2018).

Centralization in education allowed the government to 'tighten the grip on a national curriculum' (Lendvai-Bainton and Szelewa 2020: 8). Nationalization of textbook production also meant that the state is taking the responsibility for the content of textbooks, as the government will have to identify with the messages conveyed through this content, claimed László Miklósi, the president of the Association of the Hungarian History Teachers at the 2016 'What Are the Textbooks Saying about Roma or Why Are Our Children Prejudiced?' conference (Bogdán 2016: 131). In another interview, Miklósi characterized the situation of Hungarian schools as a 'centralized, top-down, controlled system' and acknowledged that there are 'ideological issues', detailing that 'a mandatory value system has ... appeared in the curriculum' (Vodli 2019).[3] To specify, the current 'system of values' is one that 'is moving away from the values of the past two decades after the democratic changes' and that will lead to intensified 'intolerance and exclusion' (Vodli 2019). The question then arises: how is educational content excluding teaching about 'others' and constructing the image of 'others'?

Roma in the Curriculum in Hungary and Beyond

Before analysing the portrayal of Roma in Hungarian textbooks, it is important to note the ambiguous instructions overall about non-Hungarian cultures in national curricula. Consider the *Teachers' Manual* published by Apáczai Kiadó to accompany the textbook *Reading and Hungarian Language to 2nd Grade Students* (Burai et al. 2014). The authors of the manual write: 'While reading the children's reader, students learn about Hungarian folk-tales, as well as tales from other foreign countries and ethnic groups (Russian, German, Szeklers, African, Gypsy, Chinese, French, Slovak)' (Burai et al. 2014: 16). It becomes immediately unclear why a continent (Africa) is mentioned among countries and ethnic groups, while 'Gypsy' is blended with the foreign section. The organization of some children's reader books similarly follows the same logic: in a reader for fourth graders, for instance, there is a section on folk tales from the 'mother country' (*haza*) and those 'far-far way' (*túl az Óperencián*), with 'Gypsy folk tales' being listed in the latter section (e.g. Báthori 2009).

Among Hungarian academics, most notably Anna Orsós, Mátyás Binder and Dóra Pálos have assessed the representation of Roma in Hungarian textbooks; also worth mentioning is the 2014 study entitled 'Black Dot' (*Fekete pont*) by the Monitor study group that consisted of students from the Hungarian University of Fine Arts (Bogdán 2016). The conclusions of these outstanding studies are analogous: Roma are represented as 'they' with a sense of distancing them from 'us' (Monitor).[4] Roma are often ignored (Orsós 2015) and discriminated (Binder and Pálos 2016). In general, stereotypical images of Roma are persistently used to represent the group, usually as a homogenous, marginalized, impoverished minority group with backward customs who excel only in traditional skills such as music and dance.

Orsós's study analysed how Roma culture is represented in public education and argued that there is a discrepancy between the National Curriculum and actual educational content. Namely, although the National Core Curriculum (NCC)[5] argues about the importance of 'being familiar with national traditions, and developing a national identity, as much as helping to preserve and maintain the identity of the members of the country's national and ethnic minorities' (Orsós 2015: 2–3), Roma are seldom mentioned in the impressive number of textbooks (258 in total) analysed by the research team (mostly for grades 1–12 of school in the following subjects: Hungarian language and grammar, civic studies, geography and environmental studies, arts). In addition, not only did textbooks omit Roma or had incompetent knowledge about the group, but teacher training resources also similarly provided inadequate information.

Binder and Pálos (2016) analysed how the goals of the NCC are met through various textbooks and broader teaching curricula, and they showed that in addition to the absence of knowledge about Roma (omission was most severe in school workbooks), some of the information in textbooks is outright false and unscientific. For instance, the authors comment on an excerpt from a fifth-grade literature textbook that claims 'the majority of Roma are bilingual: they speak Hungarian and their mother tongue, one variety of Gypsy language' (Binder and Pálos 2016: 10). The majority of Roma, due to centuries of assimilationist policies, are in fact monolingual and speak only Hungarian. István Kemény and Béla Janky (2004: 17), for example, demonstrated a clear trend in the decreasing number of Romani speakers among Roma: as of 2003, nearly 80 per cent of Roma spoke Hungarian as their mother tongue.

Binder and Pálos (2016) also revealed that certain statistics of description of Roma is out of context, which implies a false negative representation. For instance, the claim in a history textbook that nineteenth-century Roma had hard time coping because of illiteracy misleadingly suggests that illiteracy was particular to Roma, while in reality school attendance at that time was low even among the general population (Binder and Pálos 2016: 6–7). Furthermore, Roma are usually mentioned only in two historical contexts, namely, either as victims of the Holocaust or as losers of regime change, while information about Roma is poorly integrated in the overall teaching materials (Binder and Pálos 2016). These observations led the authors to conclude that beyond the inefficient content about Roma in educational resources and implicit stereotypical representation of the group, it is excessively difficult for Roma students to develop a positive self-image.

Negative stereotypes of Roma exist in textbooks beyond Hungary as well. The most recent comprehensive analytical report on the representation of Roma in European curricula and state-approved textbooks, produced by a collaboration between the Council of Europe, Roma Education Fund and the Georg Eckert Institute for International Textbook Research, systematically analysed the portrayal of Roma in European national curricula of twenty-two member states of the Council of Europe and in textbooks of history, civics and geography for lower and upper secondary schooling (Council of Europe et al. 2020).[6]

The findings of this study confirmed that Roma are largely ignored from national curricula, with only eight countries out of the twenty-two examined incorporating information on Roma. What was also indicative of the extent of omission is that countries with some of the highest proportion of Roma tended to be the ones circumventing any mention of Roma in their textbooks: for instance, Bulgaria, Slovakia and Serbia, each with 8–10 per cent Roma population. If mentioned, by far the most common context was the Second World War and the Holocaust, naming Roma as victims of the Nazi regimes. The second most common thematic context was migration and minorities. These frameworks of portrayal clearly position Roma as victims with no agency and as a discriminated outsider group.

In terms of representation of Roma culture and group identity, the study also found that stereotypes are overwhelmingly dominant. For example, the Polish history and society textbook for grades 4–6 notes: 'One of the ethnic minorities living in Poland is the Roma. Once called Gypsies, they do not have their own state. They love singing and dancing. Have you ever met the Roma? Could you describe their language, outfit and customs?' (quoted in Council of Europe et al. 2020: 18).

Consider a quote from an Albanian textbook that attempts to tackle the issue of discrimination:

> Berti is a pupil in our class. He is good at music. He plays the violin very well. His grandfather taught him. He is not good at other subjects. Berti's family is from the Egyptian community. The teacher asked Erblin to sit next to Berti and help him after school. Erblin was ready to help. The next day, his mother came to school and asked the teacher to not let Erblin help Berti with his homework. (quoted in Council of Europe et al. 2020: 19)

This excerpt illustrates well the stereotypical portrayal of a Roma student, who is good only at music and nothing else. Even though Erblin, supposedly a non-Roma student, attempted to help, it was futile as Berti's family did not approve of the help. Symbolically, this example can also connote the relationship between Roma and the state, which struggles to help Roma by educating them and yet to no avail.

The study also suggests that the contribution of Roma to history, culture and society of their respective countries is rarely, if at all, mentioned (Council of Europe et al. 2020). Omission of Roma from national history contributes to their portrayal as outsiders in their own countries – a discriminated minority with no clear allegiance or loyalty to any country or nation but themselves. Binder and Pálos (2016) found the same tendency in Hungarian textbooks that routinely omitted Roma from national statistics and data.

Given these general findings, it is particularly important to highlight good examples as well. Although textbooks tend to represent Roma in an overwhelmingly negative light, within a limited thematic context, using stereotypical depiction and depicting Roma as victims with no agency, nevertheless, it is imperative to note the exceptions as well, which are striking reminders that a just representation of Roma is indeed possible. For example, in a Hungarian history textbook for eighth graders, students can learn about famous Roma under the section 'World-Renowned Hungarian Roma':

> The Roma mainly enriched and enrich the culture of our country as musicians. Just a few examples: the 100-member Gypsy band, the pianist György Cziffra, the

com poser and pianist Béla Szakcsi Lakatos, the violinist Zoltán Mága, the folk singer and performer Palya Bea. In addition to musicians, we can list many other famous people of Roma origin. Here are just two examples: the poet Károly Bari and the boxer László Papp … they are considered to be lazy, though they would work if they had jobs. It is claimed that there are many criminals among the Roma, but this is also an unjustified generalisation. When Roma people are involved in petty crime in order to survive (for example, by stealing wood or fruit), these instances echo louder in society than if the same crimes were committed by non-Roma. (quoted in Council of Europe et al. 2020: 19–21)

'Gypsy Folk Tales' in Hungarian Children's Readers

Folk tales are an excellent source of 'interpreting the world … exploring values, norms and customs of various communities, and for developing certain attitudes, [tales are] an effective tool of enculturation [learning a culture, identifying with a culture], socialization, indirect education, and play a significant role in social learning' (Jenei 2009: 8). Hence, when folk tales and literature from other cultures are included in children's readers, it allows students to 'appreciate the reality of human diversity' and develop 'empathy with people of other cultures' (Fuhler et al. 1998: 23). However, in the case of diverse groups like Roma, there is an inevitable reification aspect, as it is hardly possible to talk about a homogenous Roma group. In addition, the selection of folk tales, especially if not accompanied by appropriate explanations and instructions, may inadvertently lead to the opposite: strengthening pervasive stereotypes about already discriminated groups.

Considering that Roma are scarcely integrated in lower-grade literature and grammar textbooks (Orsós 2015), I searched the online textbook database of the Education Authority (Oktatási Hivatal)[7] for children's readers and literature books for 2019–20 academic year for grades 1–8,[8] and collected 'Gypsy folk tales' in addition to any literature about Roma (summarized in Table 7.1).

A closer look at visual representation of Roma in textbooks revealed that they are commonly depicted as mysterious people with eccentric customs, as musicians, as marginalized, old fashioned, backward people who continue to hold superstitions and traditions from centuries ago. Consider a children's reader for second grade, in which a 'Gypsy folk tale' entitled 'Hidden Treasure' – categorized under 'Empire of Folk Tales' (A mesék birodalma) section – portrays Roma as superstitious nomads, traveling with caravans, with fortune-telling women and horse-trading men (Nyiri 2014). This is a popular tale that is included in many children's readers and can be found in other textbooks for various grades (e.g. Posta and Postáné 2021). In this tale, when the 'Gypsies' chance upon treasures that miraculously appear from underground, instead of taking advantage of the opportunity, they begin arguing and fighting, implying ill-mannered and loud behaviour. The visualization of the 'Gypsies' also follows a stereotypical depiction: women with colourful skirts and men with moustache and hats (Nyiri 2014: 74–5).

Table 7.1 'Gypsy Folk Tales' and Any Literature about Roma in Children's Readers and Literature Books for Grades 1–8 from the Online Textbook Database of the Education Authority for 2019–20 Academic Year

Grade	Author(s) and title of the book	Title of the folk tale
2	Jordánné Tóth Magdolna, Pirisi Anna, N. Császi Ildikó, Grófné Salamon Éva: *Olvasókönyv 2/1. tankönyv*	A farkas és a kutya (Cigány népmese) [Wolf and the Dog, Gypsy folk tale]
	Nyiri Istvánné: *Hétszínvarázs olvasókönyv 2.*	Az elrejtett kincs (Cigány népmese) [Hidden Treasure, Gypsy folk tale]
		Szél fúj (Cigány népköltés, ford.: Szegő László) [Blowing Wind, Gypsy folk tale, translated by László Szegő]
3	Burai Lászlóné, dr. Faragó Attiláné: *Hétszínvirág olvasókönyv 3.*	Cigány bölcsődal (Szegő László) [Gypsy lullaby, László Szegő]
		A cigány és a szél [The Gypsy and the Wind]
4	Farkas Andrea, Kolláth Erzsébet, Konrád Ágnes, Sándor Csilla: *Olvasókönyv 4/1.*	Legenda a hegedűről (Frankovics György gyűjtése, balkáni cigány népmese) [Legend about the Violin, Balkan Gypsy folk tale, collected by György Frankovics]
	Báthori Anna Zsuzsanna, Bárány Jánosné, Nagyné Bonyár, eds: *Hétszínvilág 4. olvasókönyv*	Mátyás király meg a szállásadó cigányok [King Matthias and the Gypsies Who Gave Him Accommodation]
5	Csontos Attila, Legeza Márton: *Irodalom 5. tankönyv*	Cigány népmese – Burláj vitéz (részletek) [Burláj doughty, Gypsy folk tale]
	Alföldy Jenő, Valaczka András: *Irodalom 5. Olvasókönyv az ötödik évfolyam számára Szerző*	A feltámadt leány [Resurrected Girl]
7	Szmolyan Gabriella: *Irodalom 7. Munkafüzet és olvasmányok*	Jókai Mór: A cigánybáró [Mór Jókai: The Gypsy Baro]

Source: Own elaboration.

Beyond academic analysis of the content and visual representation of Roma in textbooks, it is also essential to assess how students themselves interpret and perceive Roma through their textbooks. At the earlier mentioned conference in 2016, László Kojanitz, representing Hungarian Institute for Educational Research and Development, highlighted that it is very complicated to assess 'what is going on in the classroom and inside the children's heads when they read about Roma' (Bogdán 2016: 134).

Fieldwork Observations

The purpose of my classroom visits was to address the question posed by László Kojanitz above: to understand how students, both Roma and non-Roma, construct an image of Roma having read the folk tales included in their textbooks. In addition to the recent field research I conducted for this study in the spring of 2021, below I also present my first encounter with a Roma folk tale discussed in a fifth-grade classroom in 2012, when I collected data for my dissertation (Dunajeva 2014).

I conducted my fieldwork in 2012 in an impoverished Roma neighbourhood situated at the outskirts of a Hungarian town. The primary school of the town educated both Roma and non-Roma children – it was an integrated school with segregated classes:

> Within grades students are divided into 'advanced' and 'beginners', for subjects such as math, Hungarian grammar, and English. Roma students are almost all in the latter group. In lower grades, when English is a selective subject, the head teacher explained that only 2 pupils attend foreign language classes, because 'the rest are Gypsies'. Another teacher shared that her stronger classes have none or only few Roma students. (Dunajeva 2014: 37)

Accordingly, the fifth-grade class was similarly divided, and while I usually observed the Roma-majority group, one day I decided to visit a literature class of the other group. Propitiously, the group of fifteen students with only one Roma girl was reading a Roma folk tale: 'A feltámadt leány' (Resurrected Girl). When the teacher, an experienced senior history and literature teacher, announced the task of reading a 'Gypsy folk tale' (*cigány népmese*),[9] chaos ensued in class even before the activity commenced. 'The moment I said "let's talk about Gypsies", I felt like the class started resenting, saying that "they" are in the other group', recalled the teacher immediately after class (fieldnotes 2012). The teacher considered the choice of engaging with the only Roma student in the group, but was worried about singling her out and making her feel uncomfortable. He also contemplated reading the tale despite the students' reaction, but considered the tale 'unfriendly' and 'somewhat inappropriate for this age group', and for the lack of alternative readings in the textbook, he decided to forgo this assignment altogether.

In 2021, I visited another school located in an underprivileged area of a major city, where both Roma and non-Roma students' study together. My field visit coincided with the third wave of Covid-19, so classes were small with several students missing (seven to eight students present in each class). Before my visit, I prepared age-appropriate questions and tasks for fifth-grade and seventh-grade students about two tales: 'Mátyás király meg a szállásadó cigányok' (King Matthias and the Gypsies Who Gave Him Accommodation) and 'A feltámadt leány' (Resurrected Girl), respectively. Students discussed the storyline and Roma representation, first on their own and then as a group. Also, none of the tales contained visual descriptions of Roma protagonists, and both classes were asked to make a drawing based on the tales. In addition, both grades were asked to develop the storyline further using their own imagination.

The fifth graders read a tale about King Matthias, a Hungarian king famous for his sense of justice, issuing an order that had forbidden his subjects from providing accommodation to strangers nationwide.[10] The king dressed up as a 'musician Gypsy' and asked to be put up at a Gypsy family's house, to which they agreed. When the Gypsies were summoned by the king – the same person who dressed as a wandering

Gypsy – they were taught a lesson to listen to the king's orders and sent home with a generous reward (gold), possibly as a sign of the king's gratitude. Having read the story, children were first encouraged to think about why the king pretended to be a Gypsy to test his subjects about his orders. Many thought the king, in fact, was testing only Roma or wanted to 'pick on Gypsies'. During the discussion, a student suggested that it is due to the nomadic lifestyle of Roma, they were more likely to wander and ask for accommodation, and hence the king dressed as a Gypsy. The Roma also break the law in the tale – despite being aware that they are acting against the order of the king, they allow a stranger to stay at their home.

When the students were then asked to connect adjectives with characters – 'king' and 'Gypsies' – many associated Gypsies with adjectives such as good-hearted, law-breaking while some considered them thoughtless. In the meantime, everyone considered the king to be kind, smart and understanding. Students were clearly used to the good versus bad character dichotomy in children's tales, and since the king was the positive character, the Gypsies were the negative ones. For instance, no one considered the king to be breaking the law when he requested accommodation. Students' attention and the focus of discussion tended to be on the generosity of the king, rather than the charity of the Gypsies who fed and housed a stranger. The subordinate position between the king and the Gypsies is well visualized by one student's image (see Figure 7.1).

Finally, when students were asked to develop the narrative further, everyone focused on how Gypsies would spend the money – all answers revolved around forms of stereotypes. Some suggested that Gypsies will have a large family and feed them with the help of the money, while others wrote that Gypsies will 'sell the money' or 'dress their

Figure 7.1 Drawing of a fifth-grade student.

Source: Fieldwork observations, 2021.

children in gold'. Overall, in this group of students, which consisted of both Roma and non-Roma, stereotypical views of the minority dominated in all answers. The students' interpretation of the story strongly reflected the dominant negative stereotypes about Roma in society: as freedom loving, law-breaking, easy-going and carefree nomads, wearing lots of golden jewellery, with large families (Maučec 2013: 186).

The seventh-grade students were asked to read another Gypsy folk tale titled 'A feltámadt leány' (Resurrected Girl). The tale is about a poor Gypsy boy whose parents and lover die, and whose souls he helps put to rest while resurrecting his bride. When students were asked to imagine the protagonists, most drew a visibly deprived person in torn clothes, The description of the 'Gypsy boy' was in contrast to the common storyline in children's tales: the protagonist had a bride right at the onset, rather than at the end of the tale, who on his journey to save the dead souls does so through his cunning, rather than brave and heroic, deeds, after which he returns to a 'Gypsy slum' (*cigánytelep*) situated 'at the edge of the village ... [where] bare feet dark-eyed children were running around', rather than a pleasant home in a nice village. Describing the 'Gypsy boy's' house, one student wrote 'dirty, stinky and poor'.

When students were asked to explain why the protagonist was poor, many suggested that he did not have a job and some wrote that he must have been sick, referencing

Figure 7.2 Drawing of a fourth-grade student (2020).

Source: Fieldwork observations, 2021.

the common stereotype of Roma as unemployed and in poor health. On the task on storyline development, one student complained of being stuck and unable to advance the story further, implying the dead-end narrative of the tale itself: 'if the Gypsy did not go back to his slum, he could have had a better life', the student wrote. Several other students continued the story by referring to the 'Gypsy boy' and his resurrected bride having 'many-many babies'.

From the discussion with both classes, it was clear that the two tales included in textbooks evoked negative stereotypes from nearly everyone. As I experienced in other field research in classrooms, there is at least one daring student who does not shy away from challenging the storyline. In this case, a seventh-grade Roma student, who sat silently during class discussion, wrote the following answer: 'The Gypsy boy in the story was not afraid in the Kingdom of the Dead because he was a Gypsy!'

In Lieu of Conclusion: Alternative Voices and Decolonizing Knowledge

In Hungary, there is an explicit goal to incorporate more content about Roma in experimental textbooks (Bogdán 2016: 134). Some of this has begun, as concurred by Tibor Derdák, the director of Dr Ámbédkar School,[11] which may lead to a positive outcome (Szarvas 2020). It is also clear that content about Roma incorporated into the educational curriculum must rest on strong research and created with involvement of Roma, according to Ágnes Daróczi, the director of Romano Instituto Foundation and one of the most prominent Roma activists in Hungary. Hence, Daróczi suggests, it is critical that Roma establish their own institutions, conduct research and construct a narrative of self-representation that can be integrated into the educational curriculum (Bogdán 2016: 130).

Such Roma and pro-Roma institutions, generating an alternative narrative by incorporating the voices of the 'invisible others', in fact, do exist, although given the growing centralization of Hungarian education system, these voices are hardly coming through. For instance, several initiatives, both in Hungary and internationally, have aimed at reconstructing the narrative of the Holocaust to involve Roma voices and agency, demonstrating the importance of 'authentic narration' of historical events that allow the previously unheard voices to tell their own stories, 'most of them never told before, instead of being subject of the narration' (Bernáth 2000: 2, see also Mirga-Kruszelnicka and Dunajeva 2020).

These initiatives in fact align with the intellectual movement within Romani Studies[12] of decolonizing knowledge. More precisely, the 'diversified field of Romani Studies gradually include[ed] Romani voices and *gadjé* or *gorgio* (non-Romani or Traveller) self-reflections on antigypsyist hegemony' (Selling 2018: 49). Some academics showed that even well-intentioned modes of depicting Roma by non-Roma can build on stereotypes, further cementing prejudice, rather than combatting it (Rostas et al. 2015). Hence, decolonizing knowledge production, in a sense, is an opportunity to reconsider the representation of Roma, their historical contribution and their position within the broader society – all of which have been defined for centuries by non-Roma – to generate a more inclusive narrative. An equally remarkable aspect of this movement to decolonize knowledge is positioning Roma as agents of their own narratives – endorsing knowledge generated by Roma themselves.

Inclusive teaching narratives about Roma – in school subjects such as history, civic studies, arts, music, literature and others – are powerful tools to fight anti-Gypsyism, promote multiculturalism and recognize Roma as an integral part of the society. Especially the case of literature classes, which can be seen as a site of inclusion considering the idea that 'literature not only mirrors a culture, it also has the power to shape and teach' (Tetenbaum and Pearson 1989: 381). Tales and other readings incorporated into the textbooks for young children are conducive to 'helping children gain comfort with differences during the early years'; alternatively, 'not seeing themselves, and the groups to which they belong, represented in books can make children feel devalued' – both scenarios have long-lasting effects (Santora 2013).

Notes

1. In Hungary, the public education system consists of elementary school (*általános iskola*), which is an eight-grade general school that provides basic education, and secondary education, which may be completed in a general secondary school (*gimnázium*), vocational secondary school (*szakközépiskola*) or vocational school (*szakmunkásképző iskola*). Participation in the education system is mandatory for students between the ages of three and sixteen (Euridyce 2020).
2. I acknowledge the negative connotations of the word 'Gypsy', its origin rooted in mistaken label considering Roma as Egyptians and the current agenda of pro-Roma movement to replace the term 'Gypsy' with that of Roma. In this study, I strive to employ terminology to reflect its original use.
3. In the interview, Miklósi described history education, but it is reasonable to assume that other school subjects are equally required to embody the same value system.
4. This is how Anna Balázs summarized one of the key points form the Monitor's study during the conference (Unyatyinszki 2016).
5. The content of education in Hungary is guided by the NCC. The principal function of the NCC is to define the principles and the approach which govern the content of public education. Together with the NCC, the Framework Curricula and Educational Programmes – which convey in more detail the norms established by the NCC or, in the case of vocational education, the requirements defined for the specific vocational fields – serve as guidance for the authors and editors of textbooks, the designers of teaching aids and tools, the developers of state examination requirements and national measurement and assessment tools, and, in particular, the teaching staff of schools who prepare and compile the Local Curricula (Ministry of National Resources 2009). The last version of the NCC was issued in 2012.
6. This large-scale comprehensive research analysed several school subjects (history, civic education and geography) from twenty-two member states of the Council of Europe (Albania, Austria, Belgium, Bosnia and Herzegovina, Bulgaria, Croatia, the Czech Republic, Finland, France, Germany, Hungary, Italy, the Republic of Moldova,

Montenegro, Poland, Romania, Serbia, the Slovak Republic, Spain, North Macedonia, the United Kingdom, and from Kosovo), and focused on the ten–eighteen age group.
7. Available at: https://www.tankonyvkatalogus.hu.
8. These grades were chosen because in Hungary 'primary and lower secondary education (ISCED 1, 2) is organized as a single-structure system in 8-grade basic schools (*általános iskola*) (typically for pupils aged 6–14, covering grades 1–8)' (Eurydice 2020).
9. The folk tale 'A feltámadt leány' (Resurrected Girl) was from the textbook by Alföldy (2010). The same folk tale was reprinted in the later version of the textbook (Alföldy and Valaczka 2019).
10. The folk tale 'Mátyás király meg a szállásadó cigányok' (King Matthias and the Gypsies Who Gave Him Accommodation) was from the textbook by Báthori et al. (2016).
11. Dr Ámbédkar School is a Buddhist school for Roma in the small town of Sajókaza in north-eastern Hungary. I analysed the importance of this school in an earlier study, in which my co-author and I argued that the school's 'educative structure can be understood to be counter-hegemonic and a pedagogical vanguard for Roma children and teenagers who would otherwise receive little or no education. Virtues are seen in the school's attempt to claim a space to then reclaim teachings on and for Roma identity' (Dunajeva and Cieschi 2017: 68).
12. Romani Studies is an interdisciplinary academic field that has changed over time (reflected in the discipline's name, changing from Gypsiology to Romani Studies and the more recent approach, the Critical Romani Studies) due to an explicit goal of decolonizing knowledge production and actively including Roma voices (Dunajeva and Vajda 2021).

References

Adwan, S., D. Bar-Tal and B. E. Wexler (2016), 'Portrayal of the Other in Palestinian and Israeli Schoolbooks: A Comparative Study', *Political Psychology*, 37 (2): 201–17.
Anderson, B. (2006), *Imagined Communities*, London: Verso.
Bernáth, G., ed. (2000), *Porrajmos: Recollections of Roma Holocaust Survivors*, Budapest: Roma Press Center Books.
Binder, M., and D. Pálos (2016), 'Romák a kerettantervekben és a kísérleti tankönyvekben', Chance for Children Foundation. Available online: http://cfcf.hu/sites/default/files/Binder%20Pálos%20-%20ROMA.TK.KUT.%202016.pdf (accessed 20 June 2020).
Bogdán, P. (2016), 'A romák/cigányok tankönyvi jelenlétét elemző kutatásokról', *Új Pedagógiai Szemle*, 5–6: 127–36.
Burai, L., A. Faragó and I. Nyiri (2014), 'Kézikönyv a Hétszínvarázs 2. tankönyvcsalád tanításához'. Available online: https://ofi.oh.gov.hu/sites/default/files/020134_hetszinvarazs_2_1.pdf (accessed 20 June 2020).
Carretero, M. (2011), *Constructing Patriotism: Teaching History and Memories in Global Worlds*, Charlotte, NC: Information Age Publishing.
Christou, M. (2007), 'The Language of Patriotism: Sacred History and Dangerous Memories', *British Journal of Sociology of Education*, 28 (6): 709–22.
Council of Europe (2020), 'Recommendation CM/Rec(2020)2 of the Committee of Ministers to Member States on the Inclusion of the History of Roma and/or

Travellers in School Curricula and Teaching Materials', adopted by the Committee of Ministers on 1 July 2020 at the 1380th meeting of the Ministers' Deputies. Available online: https://search.coe.int/cm/Pages/result_details.aspx?ObjectId=09000016809ee48c (accessed 20 June 2020).

Council of Europe, Roma Education Fund and the Georg Eckert Institute for International Textbook Research (2020), 'Representation of Roma in European Curricula and Textbooks'. Available online: https://repository.gei.de/handle/11428/306 (accessed 20 June 2020).

Crawford, K. (2003), 'Culture Wars: Serbian History Textbooks and the Construction of National Identity', *History Education Research Journal*, 3 (2): 43–52.

Dunai, M. (2020), 'Hungarian Teachers Say New School Curriculum Pushes Nationalist Ideology', *Reuters*, 2 April. Available online: https://uk.reuters.com/article/us-hungary-politics-teachers-protests/hungarian-teachers-say-new-school-curriculum-pushes-nationalist-ideology-idUSKBN1ZY28Y (accessed 20 June 2020).

Dunajeva, J. (2014), '"Bad Gypsies" and "Good Roma": Constructing Ethnic and Political Identities through Education in Russia and Hungary', PhD diss., University of Oregon, Oregon.

Dunajeva, J. (2017), 'Education of Roma Youth in Hungary: Schools, Identities and Belonging', *European Education*, 49 (1): 56–70.

Dunajeva, J., and P. Cieschi (2017), 'Alternative Education and Roma Empowerment: Case Study of Dr. Ambedkar Buddhist School in Sajókaza, Hungary', *Indian Journal of Social Work*, 78 (1): 67–80.

Dunajeva, J., and V. Vajda (2021), 'Positionality and Fieldwork: Participatory Research with Roma', in D. Burns, J. Howard and S. Ospina (eds), *Sage Handbook for Participatory Research*, 234–48, London: Sage.

Egan, K. (1989), 'Reviewed Work: Perceptions of History. An Analysis of School Textbooks by Volker R. Berghahn, Hanna Schissler', *History and Theory*, 28 (3): 366–72.

European Commission (n.d.), 'Roma People in the EU'. Available online: https://ec.europa.eu/info/policies/justice-and-fundamental-rights/combatting-discrimination/roma-eu/roma-equality-inclusion-and-participation-eu_en (accessed 20 June 2020).

Eurydice (2020), 'Hungary Overview'. Available online: https://eacea.ec.europa.eu/national-policies/eurydice/content/hungary_en (accessed 20 June 2020).

Fuchs, E., and A. Bock (2018), *The Palgrave Handbook of Textbook Studies*, New York: Palgrave Macmillan.

Fuhler, C. J., P. J. Farris and L. Hatch (1998), 'Learning about World Cultures through Folktales', *Social Studies and the Young Learner*, 11 (1): 23–5.

Gellner, E. (1983), *Nations and Nationalism*, Oxford: Blackwell.

Grosvenor, I. (1999), '"There's No Place like Home": Education and the Making of National Identity', *History of Education*, 28 (3): 235–50.

Györgyi, Z., M. Simon and V. Vadász (2015), *Szerep- és funkcióváltások a közoktatás világában*, Budapest: Oktatáskutató és Fejlesztő Intézet.

Hungary Today (2019), 'ECHR Upholds Ruling on State Monopoly of Hungarian Textbook Distribution Market'. Available online: https://hungarytoday.hu/echr-upholds-ruling-on-state-monopoly-of-hungarian-textbook-distribution-market/ (accessed 20 June 2020).

Huszár, Á. (2014), 'Nationalism and Hungarian Education Policy: Are the Literary Works of Cécile Tormay, József Nyirő, and Albert Wass Appropriate for the Hungarian School Curriculum?', *Hungarian Cultural Studies*, 7: 303–19.

Jenei, T. (2009), 'Cigány mesék szerepe a szociális tanulásban', PhD diss., Pécsi Tudományegyetem, Pécs.
Joob, S., J. Spirk and A. Dezso (2013), 'NATO-repülőként jön a tankönyv-államosítás', *Index*, 16 December. Available online: https://index.hu/belfold/2013/12/16/tankonyvpiac/ (accessed 20 June 2020).
Kemény, I., and B. Janky (2004), 'A 2003. évi cigány felmérésről', in I. Kemény, B. Janky and G. Lengyel (eds), *A magyarországi cigányság, 1971–2003*, 11–36, Budapest: Gondolat – MTA Etnikai-nemzeti Kisebbségkutató Intézet.
Koesel, K. (2020), 'Legitimacy, Resilience and Political Education in Russia and China: Learning to be Loyal', in K. Koesel, V. Bunce and J. Weiss (eds), *Citizens and the State in Authoritarian Regimes: Comparing China and Russia*, 250–78, New York: Oxford University Press.
KSH (Központi Statisztikai Hivatal, Central Statistical Office) (2015), 'A hazai nemzetiségek demográfiai jellemzői'. Available online: https://www.ksh.hu/docs/hun/xftp/stattukor/nemzetiseg_demografia.pdf (accessed 20 June 2020).
Lendvai-Bainton, N., and D. Szelewa (2020), 'Governing New Authoritarianism: Populism, Nationalism and Radical Welfare Reforms in Hungary and Poland', *Social Policy Administration*, 1–14: 559–72.
Liègeois, J. P. (2007), *Roma in Europe*, Strasbourg: Council of Europe.
Lowe, R. (1999), 'Education and National Identity', *History of Education*, 28 (3): 231–33.
Maučec, G. (2013), 'Identifying and Changing Stereotypes between Roma and Non-Roma: From Theory to Practice', *Innovative Issues and Approaches in Social Sciences* 6 (3): 181–203.
Messing, V. (2012), 'Good Practices Addressing School Integration of Roma/Gypsy Children in Hungary', in A. Pusca (ed.), *Eastern European Roma in the EU: Mobility, Discrimination, Solutions*, 138–54, Brussels: International Debate Education Association.
Meyer, J. W., F. O. Ramirez and Y. Nuhoğlu Soysal (1992), 'World Expansion of Mass Education, 1870–1980', *Sociology of Education Sociology of Education*, 65 (2): 128–49.
Ministry of National Resources (2009), 'Hungarian National Core Curriculum (abridged version)', 1 July. Available online: http://www.nefmi.gov.hu/english/hungarian-national-core (accessed 20 June 2020).
Mirga-Kruszelnicka, A., and J. Dunajeva (2020), *Re-Thinking Roma Resistance Throughout History: Recounting Stories of Strength and Bravery*, Berlin: ERIAC.
Orsós, A. (2015), *A roma kultúra reprezentációja a tartalomszabályozók, tartalomhordozók körében, valamint ezek fej- lesztési lehetőségei' Összegző tanulmány a kutatási eredményekről*, Budapest: Oktatáskutató és Fejlesztő Intézet.
Rostas, I., M. Rövid and M. Szilvási (2015), 'On Roma Civil Society, Roma Inclusion, and Roma Participation', *Roma Rights Journal*, 2: 7–10.
Santora, L. A. (2013), *Assessing Children's Book Collections Using an Anti-Bias Lens*, New York: Anti-Defamation League.
Selling, J. (2018), 'Assessing the Historical Irresponsibility of the Gypsy Lore Society in Light of Romani Subaltern Challenges', *Critical Romani Studies Journal*, 1 (1): 44–61.
Szarvas, G. (2020), 'A kerettanterv módosítása a roma oktatásügyet is érintheti – interjú Derdák Tiborral', *Mfor*, 27 June. Available online: https://mfor.hu/cikkek/tudomany/hetvegere--bekerulhetnek-a-magyar-tortenelemtankonyvekbe-a-romak--interju-derdak-tiborral.html (accessed 20 June 2020).

Tetenbaum, T. J., and J. Pearson (1989), 'The Voices in Children's Literature: The Impact of Gender on the Moral Decisions of Storybook Characters', *Sex Roles: A Journal of Research*, 20: 381–95.
Toomey, M. (2018), 'History, Nationalism and Democracy: Myth and Narrative in Viktor Orbán's "Illiberal Hungary"', *New Perspectives*, 26 (1): 87–108.
Unyatyinszki, G. (2016), 'Láthatatlanok a romák a tankönyvekben, katasztrófa eddig az állami tankönyvrendszer, *Eduline*, 11 April. Available online: https://eduline.hu/kozoktatas/Romak_a_tankonyvekben_Ok_ismi_vagyunk_G5BZVZ (accessed 20 June 2020).
Vajda, R., and C. Dupcsik (2008), 'Country Report on Ethnic Relations: Hungary', Eddumigrom Background Papers. Available online: http://www.edumigrom.eu/sites/default/files/field_attachment/page/node-1817/edumigrombackgroundpaperhungaryethnicrelations.pdf (accessed 20 June 2020).
Vodli, Z. I. (2019), 'History and Courage: The Position of Teachers in Hungary', *EuroClio – European Association of History Educators*, 11 July. Available online: https://www.euroclio.eu/2019/10/07/30803/ (accessed 20 June 2020).
Williams, J. H. (2014), *(Re)Constructing Memory: School Textbooks and the Imagination of the Nation*, New York: Springer.
Zsilak, S. (2018), 'Az állami tankönyvek teljes hatalomátvételétől tartanak a kiadók', *Index*, 10 May. Available online: https://index.hu/belfold/2018/05/10/lejaro_engedelyek_a_tankonyvpiacon/ (accessed 20 June 2020).

Textbooks

Alföldy, J. (2010), *Irodalom 5. Olvasókönyv az ötödik osztály számára*, Budapest: Nemzeti Tankönyvkiadó.
Alföldy, J., and A. Valaczka (2019), *Irodalom 5. Olvasókönyv az ötödik évfolyam számára*, Budapest: Nemzedékek Tudása Tankönyvkiadó.
Báthori, A. Z. (2009), *Hétszínvilág Olvasókönyv 4. o.*, Budapest: Apáczai Kiadó.
Báthori, A. Z., J. Bárány and E. Nagyné Bonyár (2016), *Hétszínvilág 4.o. Olvasókönyv*, Budapest: Oktatási Hivatal.
Nyiri, I. (2014), *Hétszínvarázs Olvasókönyv*, Budapest: Apáczai Kiadó.
Posta, I., and P. G. Postáné (2021), *Sokszínű irodalom*, Szeged: Mozaik Kiadó.

8

Social Exclusion and the Construction of the Other at a Czech Basic School: An Anthropological Perspective

Radek Vorlíček

Introduction

In this chapter, I deal with the social dynamics of marginality and dominance at a basic school (ISCED 2011 level 1 and level 2) located near a socially excluded locality in the Hradec Králové region of the Czech Republic.[1] The basic theoretical framework of the chapter includes the concepts of social inclusion and exclusion, social and educational inequalities, and interethnic relations. In connection with the theoretical framework of inclusion and exclusion (Schuelka et al. 2019; Pearson 2016; Killen and Rutland 2011), I examine the lives of the pupils there and record the context in which the inclusion and exclusion of those who are perceived as bearers of other than the dominant identity take place. I focus on social and educational inequalities between pupils from different ethnic groups which affect the group dynamics and the atmosphere in the classroom (Bhopal and Maylor 2014; Lambert and Griffiths 2018). Particularly I describe the hidden school mechanisms that maintain differences between children and sometimes even deepen them.

From the point of view of interethnic relations (Eriksen 2010; Brubaker 2006; Jenkins 1997), I analyse the social and interethnic relations in a group of children that co-create various aspects of sociality in the school environment. I pay attention to an area that has so far been neglected by researchers in the Czech Republic: the interactionist perspective of the dynamics of the inclusion of Roma pupils directly in the classroom environment. In other words, I examine what relevant position Roma pupils tend to acquire within this environment. For this reason, I deal with social distance dynamics between pupils and examine how these dynamics strengthen or, on the contrary, weaken their position in the hierarchy. It is an approach based on interactionism that examines closeness in interactions and that maps out what strengthens and what reduces differences in social distance between pupils.

Context of the Country

This part of the text outlines the context of the country, which is related to the topic, and the Czech Republic. Specifically, I deal with inequalities in the Czech education system, school reform focused on inclusion, socially disadvantaged pupils, Roma pupils and teachers' prejudicial attitudes towards Roma. These are issues that allow us to understand the topic in its complexity and put it in a broader social framework.

In the context of the presented topic, I define inequalities in education in terms of educational opportunities, education participation, quality teaching, selection and peer relations (Thompson 2019; Bhopal and Maylor 2014; Lambert and Griffiths 2018; Bukowski et al. 2020). Inequalities in Czech education are among the worst in OECD member countries over a long period (see Ministry of Education, Youth and Sports 2019). Funding for the education system is below average compared to those in other OECD countries (ČSÚ 2016; EDUin 2019). There are significant inequalities in the quality of Czech schools, both in the form of regional inequalities and inequalities within regions (Ministry of Education, Youth and Sports 2019). The education system is facing problems of an ageing generation of teachers, the lack of systemic support for enhancing the quality of teachers and principals in schools in addition to limited research in the field of education (EDUin 2019; Ministry of Education, Youth and Sports 2016a). In the Czech Republic, a strong influence of socioeconomic status on educational opportunities and educational mobility can be noted (Kobel et al. 2020). The family background and the place where the child lives fundamentally influence the child's development and life trajectory (Korbel et al. 2020).

One response to educational inequalities has been inclusive reform, which has been gradually coming into effect, and Czech legislation since the 2016–17 school year. This reform was supposed to reduce educational inequalities and cannot be seen in black and white. On the one hand, thanks to it, numerous support measures for pupils have been introduced, such as the number of teaching assistants being increased; since the 2015–16 school year, when a total of 10,400 assistants worked in schools, their number has now doubled.[2]

On the other hand, in hindsight, this systemic change has not been well prepared, explained and fully accepted by the public and teachers. Up to 61.3 per cent of basic school teachers struggled with implementing inclusive education (Pivarč 2020: 77). Inclusion has encountered a number of problems since the beginning of its deeper implementation, for example, the amount of paperwork has skyrocketed (Pivarč 2020: 136). As a result, schools differ in their approach to and view of inclusion and segregation. There are big differences among schools in terms of how school principals talk about inclusion, how they perceive it and how they assess the climate in a given school (Moree 2019: 25). In particular, schools located in excluded localities have a different relationship of inclusion than schools at a greater distance from excluded localities (Moree 2019: 6). While in inclusive schools we rather witness de-ethnicization and invisibilization of ethnicity, in some 'traditional' basic schools in mainstream education, the process of exclusion often involves ethnicization of social relations and visibilization of ethnicity (Vorlíček 2019).[3]

An improvement of the position of the socially disadvantaged pupils is also one of the partial goals of the reform. In 2018 and 2019, according to official data, about 1.5 per cent of basic school pupils were identified as socially disadvantaged, that is, a total of 15,194 pupils.[4]

These pupils achieve worse study results than pupils without social disadvantages (Seifert et al. 2019: 57). They are often allocated to schools where they are significantly overrepresented (Čada and Hůle 2019: 131). Most of them are educated in a regular classroom. Over 60 per cent of pupils identified as socially disadvantaged are boys (see Seifert et al. 2019: 59).[5]

The debate about inclusion and socially disadvantaged pupils is also closely concerned with Roma pupils, especially in connection with their unequal access to education. According to the former Public Defender of Rights Pavel Varvařovský, a large proportion of Roma pupils used to be educated in former special (remedial) schools (Varvařovský 2012), At present, 85.4 per cent of Roma pupils, that is, a total of 28,929 pupils, are educated in regular basic schools (Ministry of Education, Youth and Sports 2016a: 6).[6]

Furthermore, the number of schools with a growing concentration and a dominant share of Roma pupils is gradually increasing in basic schools that operate in the vicinity of excluded localities.[7] On the contrary, their non-Roma classmates leave these schools and opt for other schools with a lower or no proportion of Roma boys and girls (GAC 2010: 23; Člověk v tísni 2009: 80). A significant number of pupils do not complete their basic school studies and only a tiny percentage of those who complete them in the ninth grade then go on to upper secondary school (Amnesty International 2012).

Many teachers are influenced by stereotypes about the Roma ethnic group (for more details, see Cichá et al. 2016; Amnesty International 2009: 22).[8] Looking back, there is a background story to the prejudices towards Roma people. In my research at a basic school, there was a teacher who decided to organize a discussion for her students where she discussed Roma history and culture. To this day, I cannot forget how she spoke in front of her Roma and non-Roma pupils that 'Roma have been stealing chickens for centuries and they de facto got robbery in the blood'.[9] Many teachers are often unaware of adopting and reproducing negative stereotypes about Roma (Cichá et al. 2016). This fact has implications for education. There is a link between stereotypes among teachers on the one hand and the school failure of Roma pupils on the other (Amnesty International 2009: 35). This is a paradox of the Czech educational system. The school environment itself also frequently contributes to the exclusion of Roma pupils, often even in cases where the school is consciously trying to do the opposite. However, this exclusion is not something necessary and can be avoided, as can be seen in positive examples of school practices in the Czech Republic where exclusion does not occur (see Vorlíček 2019).

Methodology and Ethical Aspects of the Research

The research was of a qualitative and ethnographic type and was based primarily on the method of observation, which was partially supplemented by interviews with teachers and other field research respondents (representatives of municipalities, employees of non-profit organizations, employees of pedagogical-psychological centres, residents of the research locality). The research at the school was carried out in the autumn of 2018 (see a detailed description of the school in the next part below). It was part of a long-term and broader research project titled 'Social dynamics and Interethnic Relationships in Educational Settings', which I have been implementing since 2016 in various Czech and Slovak regions (for more details, see Vorlíček 2019). My research project is based on the 'Multi-Sited Ethnography' strategy (Marcus 1995 1998), which is designed around 'chains, paths, threads, conjunctions, or juxtapositions of locations in which the ethnographer establishes some form of literal, physical presence, with an explicit, posited logic of association or connection among sites that in fact defines the argument of the ethnography' (Marcus 1995: 105).

I measure the relevant institutional frameworks of basic schools in which the teaching of children takes place. I usually define my terrain as a *school classroom without walls*. From my perspective, a classroom is much more than just a physically limited space. In contrast, in this chapter, I will focus exclusively on one school class in a basic school located near an excluded locality.

During the research, I tried my best to adhere to the ethical standards regarding the protection of the privacy and the integrity of those with whom I worked in the field (awareness, anonymity, responsibility, openness, sincerity, fairness, credibility of information obtained, protection of confidential communication, compliance with obligations and non-misuse of findings). In order to protect the identities of the pupils and teachers involved in my research, their names have been changed and coded. I truthfully described the subject of my research to the participants. I do not indicate the real name of the school and the locality in which I carried out the research.

My study procedure is in accordance with the 'Ethical Research Framework' of the Ministry of Education, Youth and Sports in the Czech Republic and meets the ethical requirements in research. The Committee for Research Ethics at the University of Hradec Králové has approved my research project. Informed consent was obtained from legal guardians. The participants have consented to the submission of the case report to the journal. I place emphasis especially on the protection of participants' privacy, safety and confidentiality. I do not use any data recording devices and respect each participant's environment and cultural values.

Description of the Locality and School

The research took place in the Czech Republic in the town of Kruštíkov (the name is fictitious), which has fewer than 12,000 inhabitants. There is one socially excluded locality. A large number of the apartments in this locality are in a deplorable condition. Many of them are unoccupied. Many city residents consider the locality to be a 'Roma ghetto' and believe that the excluded locality 'should be surrounded by barbed wire'. Not only Roma live in the excluded locality, however, according to estimates, and Roma make up one-third to one-half of the total population of this locality.

Next to the excluded locality, there is a richer district with family houses. There is a basic school near this district and the excluded locality. The teaching staff consists of thirty teacher and the school is attended by about 350 pupils. Among them, there is a significant number of pupils who usually belong to two following categories: socially disadvantaged and Roma pupils. These two categories may blend at some point. Their identity is important because it 'changes the composition of the pupils at the school, as well as the educational ambitions of parents and teachers (the white flight effect and the desegregation effect)'. 'It affects the communication within the environment of a particular school. It has an impact on teachers' attitudes (*ethnicization*), as well as peer group relations' (Kohout-Diaz et al. 2018: 253).

The average number of pupils per class was 18.5 in the first level of basic school.[10] In the first level, out of the total of 190 pupils, 81 passed with honours, 100 of them passed and 9 failed. The educational outcomes of the less successful pupils are affected by their high rate of absence. The high number of missed and unexcused lessons is mainly due to pupils from socially disadvantaged environments (anonymized data from school materials).

I carried out the research in the autumn of 2018 in three school classes – one first grade (see Vorlíček 2022a), one third grade, and one sixth grade (see Vorlíček 2022b). In this chapter, I describe only selected aspects of the school life of pupils from the third grade. At the beginning of my research, I set goals and topics that I wanted to address, but I did not set specific research questions which I sought to answer. In this respect, I was influenced by the approach of the Prague Group of School.

Roma and Non-Roma in the Third Grade

First, this section describes which pupils attend the third grade in terms of age, gender and social disadvantage. After their description, I outline the teacher's view of education and the complicated situation regarding the teaching assistant.

The third grade was attended by 18 nine-year-olds. There are twelve girls and six boys. Among them, there are eight Roma children – six boys and two girls.[11] None of the Roma children, except for Marián, attended kindergarten. These are socially disadvantaged pupils.[12] For all the Roma pupils, again with the exception of Marián, support measures have been put in place. Recently, up to twenty-six children attended the class, but some moved elsewhere, and others left for a special school. However, the teacher did not let anyone fail despite the fact that, for example, one of the pupils could not read and only learnt to do so properly in the third grade.[13]

The class has been assigned a teaching assistant in the first grade. However, he joined the class only three months later. A month after he joined, he suffered a broken leg and did not return to school until late April. Therefore, he participated in the education of the pupils only for three months out of ten.

The teacher commented on it: 'At the time when I needed to support the most, I received none' [T1]. Having no support from the assistant, the teacher had to rely solely on herself, which must have been challenging as the beginning of the first school year is looked at as the key period for adaptation from kindergarten to basic school routines and provides the environment for a successful start of the educational process.

According to the teacher, there is one 'problem pupil' [T1] in the class, who is vulgar, smokes cigarettes and is a graffiti tagger. His actions are already being dealt with by the Czech Republic police. This pupil has even threatened the teacher's assistant that he would 'break the windows of her house' [T1]. He was reprimanded for it by the school principal. In her thirty years of teaching experience, the teacher notes that 'she has never had such a class'. According to her colleagues, the teacher manages to 'keep the wilder class in check' [T2, T3].

In school pedagogy, it is generally considered beneficial if more successful students are mixed with less successful ones (PISA 2015: 176; Hanushek and Wößmann 2006). However, the teacher does not agree with this opinion. She does not believe that less successful pupils learn from their more successful classmates, who might 'serve as an elevator' to better study results for them. The teacher is even worried that it works the other way around. 'The less successful and more roguish have a bad influence on the others' [T1]. The teacher's disapproving attitude to mixed-ability classes is projected in her work with pupils (see part of the teacher's approach to pace-based seating arrangements).

Dividing the Collective

This section aims to describe and explain separation third graders. I want to outline the third-grade context and the social distance that manifests itself during classes and breaks and that fundamentally determines school communication in the classroom.

The third grade collective is divided into two groups.[14] The first group consists of all the non-Roma children and a Roma boy, Marián, who attended kindergarten with them. Both his parents work, and his socioeconomic status is higher than that of his Roma classmates. His position is interesting as it involves a clash of collective and individual identification.[15] The second group consists of the remaining Roma children. These two groups have big quarrels and generally are not on speaking terms with each other.

From the analysis of everyday examples that are constantly recurring in interaction, it is clear that there is a great social distance between the groups. It is obvious in the course of teaching, and this also affects the break times at school, as groups usually spend these together. For example, for reading, pupils move to the library, an especially adapted classroom with seat cushions. The way in which the children sat on the seat cushions made it clear who belonged to the first group and who to the second one. The first group was sitting closer to the teacher in the front area of the library while the pupils of the second group were sitting further from the teacher distancing themselves socially as well. During math class, when the children practiced multiplication, they were tasked with counting a column of examples. Then they were asked to take a red pencil, find a friend, exchange workbooks with him or her and check the results. Most of the children found a friend from their group. Social distance is also obvious when there is a teaching project or some special event at the school – see the following observation record:

> On Friday, the pupils of the first, second, and third grades were looking forward to school. A ping pong show had been prepared for them. The third grade pupils met in their classroom in the morning. They changed and, after changing, went to the gym with the teacher. Before leaving, they lined up in two groups. The first group went in the front with the teacher, while the second went more to the back with the assistant. The organizers of the event were unable to prepare the gym in time, so they announced to teachers that the start would be postponed by fifteen minutes. The teacher no longer wanted to return to her classroom with the children, so she told them to sit on the wooden bench that is placed in front of the gym. All 18 children squeezed on one bench. The first group sat on the left, whereas the second one sat on the right. Right in the middle was the Roma boy, Marián, who is a sort of bridge that can connect the two groups together, to a certain extent. (observation records from the field diary, the basic school in the town of Kruštíkov, 11 November 2018)

An identical situation occurred in the gym when the pupils sat on a bench and watched the start of the show. Again, they were divided into two groups. Every pupil knew where his or her place was. The division into two groups was also reflected in the show itself when the pupils walked around the individual activity stations in their groups. For example, they played ping pong at one station. At another station, they had to run between the cones hitting the ball up in the air. The class never gathered together during this show and did not participate in any of the offered activities together. They did not join forces. They did not cheer for the team and did not encourage each other in individual activities. There was a noticeable difference compared to the other classes that took part in the ping pong show.

During the research, you could not but notice how strong a role group membership plays. It fundamentally determines the communication in the classroom environment. Pupils from both groups were in fact separated on their way to the gym, during the forced break in front of the gym and the show in the gym.

Differences between the Children and the Groups: 'Draw What You Want for Christmas'

In this section, I discuss in detail the differences among social groups in the classroom in terms of school success, help-seeking or socioeconomic status. I intend to show how these differences are reflected in teaching and learning and how they affect the *climate* and life at school. Why is it good to focus on education, and what does it actually reveal to us? Hamplová and Katrňák (2018: 187) explain that 'education is a basic stratification criterion of contemporary Czech society, which is associated with different life outcomes and is reflected in individual lives. This not only makes

Czech society, to a certain extent, more transparent, but, based on this principle, it is also possible to identify groups that lose out in competitions for economic and social resources'.

This fact can be seen not only in statistical data but also in this third grade. There are huge differences between the children and the groups. The first group includes pupils with the top results, while the pupils in the second group are worse off in terms of school success. They often get poor marks – threes, fours and fives – and receive good marks – ones and twos – only rarely.[16] Differences can also be seen in teaching activities. When the teacher asks in the course of reading from the reading book who would like to continue reading, only pupils from the first group raise their hands. Or, in another situation, pupils work individually on math exercises and when the teacher asks them at the end: 'Which of you thinks you've done it?', only pupils from the first group raise their hands. There is also a notice board in the classroom with the children's names and the stamps that they receive for doing homework. Pupils in the second group have far more black stamps than pupils in the first group. Some children also get red stamps, the so-called bookworms. They receive them if they read a part of the book and prepare a report on it (they introduce the author and the plot and paint a picture for it). These red stamps are usually earned by children from the first group.

A significant difference between the groups is in so-called help-seeking: children's requests for assistance, clarification, information and checking-of-work from teachers (Calarco 2011: 865). Pupils from the first group more often raise their hands and are proactive. They often seek advice from the teacher, if they are confused, or if, for example, they have solved an arithmetical problem and want to check it. In general, the first group receives more help from the teacher because pupils from the second group, compared to the first group, raise their hands less often and tend to avoid the help of the teacher. This is amplified by the position and role of the teaching assistant, who helps pupils from the second group more. These differences may probably be reflected in the overall evaluation of the teacher, who expects and appreciates it when pupils raise their hands and seek help (cf. Calarco 2011).

Groups differ not only in terms of school success but also in what they wear. In the first group, seven out of ten children wore jeans and the rest wore cloth trousers. In the second group, most of the children wore sweatpants, two boys wore sportswear and one girl had on leggings. Moreover, there is a difference not only in the clothes the pupils wear, but also how often they change them (some wear one outfit for two weeks; others change it after two days).

There are significant differences between groups and children in terms of the socioeconomic status of their families and in terms of the educational level of their parents. These differences are reflected in the teaching and, to some extent, affect the overall atmosphere in the classroom. This was evident in the period before Christmas when the children had to draw on paper what they wanted for Christmas.[17] Based on these wishes, the teacher wrote letters to Baby Jesus (the Czech equivalent of Santa Claus) with the children during a Czech language lesson. What did the children want?

For this task, the children were allowed to ask for anything without worrying about how much money each 'wish' would cost. I think the differences are obvious

Table 8.1 Wishes for Christmas Presents

		I group		II group
Girls	Non-Roma	Roller skates, earrings, knapsack, pencil case.	Roma	Schoolbag.
		Board game, T-shirt, pants, potter's wheel.		Doll and pram.
		Books, pencil case, bag.		
		Book, Lego building set, Monopoly, board game, material for creating a bracelet.		
Boys	Non-Roma	Nerf toy gun (gun for rubber bullets), tablet, new schoolbag.	Roma	Jacket and T-shirt
		T-shirt, skateboard, wardrobe ('I share a wardrobe with my brother and I want my own'),		Football boots, training bag, headphones.
		FIFA 2019 (PC game), Xiaomi mobile, NHL 2019 (PC game), knapsack.		Child's scooter, Xbox (game console),
		Xiaomi 9 mobile, Lenovo tablet, new computer, PlayStation 4, headphones.		Shoes, remote controlled slot car, glue, scissors.
		Roller skates, headphones.		Soccer ball, football boots.
		Lego building set, baseball cap, ice skates.		Pencil case, scissors, glue.
	Roma	Slot car track and Formula 1 remote controlled slot cars.		

Source: Own elaboration.

at first glance. Although every child could wish for anything, his or her wishes reflected to some extent his or her position and the socioeconomic status of his or her family. The children usually did not want anything that they would be 100 per cent sure their parents would not buy. They were aware of their limits. These limits were affected by several factors. The desire of children is constructed and motivated by family, classmates, the consumer society, the media or social media. For nine-year-olds, the family probably has the greatest influence. We gain life perspectives through socialization and enculturation (Willis 2017; Calarco 2011, 2018; Katrňák 2004; Dolby et al. 2004; Berger and Luckmann 2001; Whyte 1993; Bourdieu and Passeron 1990), that is, the kind of family and community I live in determine the life perspectives I have. The family fundamentally influences our identity, self-concept, desires and aspirations – what I can do, what I can have, what I am.

This example shows that children wish for what suits their world and their abilities. They create their own wishes which correspond to the family they live in. At school, the work of the school collective reveals these huge socioeconomic differences, which in turn affect the dynamics of contextually established children's identities. I think that the things drawn by the children can be divided into several categories:

- To be used by oneself and for one's own use: T-shirt, trousers, jacket, baseball cap, shoes, potter's wheel, books, mobile phones, pram and doll.
- To be shared with family and friends in the online world: PlayStation, X-box, computer, computer headphones, FIFA game.[18]
- To be shared with family and friends in the offline world: roller skates, skateboard, child's scooter, Nerf gun, Monopoly, slot car track, soccer ball, football boots, training bag.
- To enhance school success: school bags, books, pencil cases, scissors, glue.

From my point of view as a researcher, the fourth category, which is related to the child's identity, school success and contact with classmates and the teacher, is perhaps the most interesting one. It is associated with the concept or figure that is called 'a symbolic nobody' (Doubek 1999: 3, 1996: 318–19). Children from excluded localities fail and are unable to cope with school demands. They do not even have the basic educational materials and they become a nobody. Doubek perceives this figure as 'the constitutive basis of the power whereby children are individualized and pushed to conformity' or as 'a threat that might give rise to the pupil's negative potentiality, the possibility of failure and symbolic non-existence, … which defines his or her identity as a pupil' (1999: 3).

The Teacher's Approach to Peace-Based Seating Arrangements

In this part of the text, I show how the teacher consciously and unconsciously shapes school belonging (Halse 2018; Allen and Kern 2017). I delve into the role of the teacher in uniting and dividing the collective and the conflict of the norms of the majority society with the rules and norms attributed to the excluded localities.

The class teacher explains that 'since the beginning of the school year, there have been huge differences between the two groups. Despite the efforts of the teaching staff, we have been unable to reduce the widening of this gap. Rather, the gap becomes wider every year. From the first grade to the second grade, from the second grade to the third grade' [T1]. The question remains why this is happening and what role the school or the teacher plays in this?

On the one hand, the school is undoubtedly trying to improve the situation of pupils who come from an excluded locality and who belong to the second group in the third grade. In this respect, the school, for example, actively cooperates with experts specializing in the prevention of risky behaviour, who focus on the use of experiential methods in the pedagogical environment and implement programmes for schools. Experts help teachers to build a positive climate in the classroom as well as participate in the education of teaching staff and in the validation of evaluation tools. On the other hand, there are hidden mechanisms at school that maintain the differences between children and, to a certain extent, even deepen them. Let us have a look at, for example, seating arrangements.

The teacher prepared a seating arrangement in which the division into two groups was clearly visible. At the same time, it is clear that these classes' social structures are based on pupil's educational success. The teacher placed the most talented children in the row on the left. In contrast, less successful children sit on the far right and are helped by a teaching assistant.[19] But does this arrangement not help to form 'two classes within a class' or two groups of pupils?

With respect to the seating arrangement, it is also interesting to note that Adrián (a pupil from the second group) is sitting in the space of the first group, whereas Jindra (a pupil from the first group) is sitting in the space of the second group. There are reasons for this. The teacher placed Adrián in the middle row because he tries very hard and is the most successful of the second group in terms of school success. In addition, he has the worst social status in the second group. The second group loves sports, especially football. However, Adrián has dyspraxia (reduced mobility) and, according to the teacher, he is not good at any sports. 'Nobody wants him during physical education because he spoils the game and is responsible for lost matches' [T1]. In contrast, Jindra, a pupil from the first group, sits in the row on the right because he is naughty and hyperactive. He is constantly running around the classroom and likes to knock the pencil cases of his classmates from their desks. This puts him in conflict with his classmates and at the same time partially separates him from the first group.

The seating arrangement created this way contributes to establishing power dominance among the pupils. It also affects the school climate, which reflects the teacher's communication and teaching procedures, his or her preferences and expectations of pupils, pupils' participation, and the overall ethos of the school (Průcha 2017: 344). In my opinion, the teacher's approach is also associated with the so-called Pygmalion effect (Rosenthal and Jacobson 1968). It is a term designating the phenomenon whereby teachers influence the learning performance of pupils with their ideas, expectations and attitudes relating to pupils (Průcha 2011: 350).[20]

In this socioeducational space of the third grade, the norms of the majority society collide with the rules and norms attributed to excluded localities.[21] At the same time, the teacher indirectly and unknowingly helps to co-shape these norms by her actions. Success is associated with the majority culture and behaviour, which can be called 'acting white'. Roma pupils are taught that the more they assimilate and the more they acquire the norms of the first group, or the norms of the majority society, the more they will be rewarded. In contrast, pupils from the first group may go down in the teacher's esteem, lose their position on the hierarchical ladder, once they move away from the norms of the majority society (see Jindra's position), Adhering to the norms of the majority society means not only 'loving school, doing homework and getting good grades at a school report card', but also changing how one dresses and suppressing the Roma ethnolect in the Czech language.[22]

Regardless of the fact that the topics of multicultural education are integrated in the Czech Republic into individual subjects of instruction during all years, for pupils from the second group, education is still monocultural (see Parekh 2000: 226–7),[23] Gradually and from an early age, they learn to look at the world from the narrow perspective of the majority culture and reject everything that does not fit into this constructed perspective. Moreover, this does not only relate to school success. Pupils adopt norms and standards according to which they assess themselves and other friends and family members in excluded localities. From childhood, they learn that their culture and values are not accepted and are perceived as inferior in society at large. In this context, my research confirms the fact that 'the current school environment is not very compatible with standards, interaction patterns, communication modes, language codes and knowledge acquisition methods that are taken for granted in socially excluded localities, nor can it handle well tools and approaches that can make them transferable' (Morvayová 2010: 16).

Although I am not a psychologist, I dare say that this has far-reaching implications for the development of a pupil's identity and personality. From a psychological point of view, we could discuss the (mis)recognition of pupils from socially excluded localities or pupils from ethnic minorities in the area of the school education system. In general, the demand and need for recognition is examined by Charles Taylor (2004: 44), who claims that

> our identity is partly shaped by recognition or its absence, often by the misrecognition of others and a person or group of people can suffer real damage, real distortion if the people or society around them mirror back to them a confining or demeaning or contemptible picture of themselves. Nonrecognition or misrecognition can inflict harm, can be a form of oppression, imprisoning someone in a false, distorted, and reduced mode of being.

On the one hand, the teacher perceives ethnic differences between Roma and non-Roma children as natural. This is where the risk, mentioned by Newman, arises: 'As long as people continue to believe that race differences or gender differences are rooted in nature, however, they will continue to accept social inequalities as natural' (2017: 74). On the other hand, the teacher is aware that the pupils in the children's collective are divided into two groups. And she seeks to diminish these differences between them. She would like them to be on more friendly terms – see the observation record:

> Pupils read a passage from 'father's advice'. After reading this passage, they discuss the following issues with the teacher: Based on the story, explain what togetherness is and what it is good for. Explain the saying 'there is strength in unity'.
>
> **Teacher:** What does listening involve? What is it about?
> **Children:** To make everyone in the classroom feel good. So that we can listen to others.
> **Teacher:** Yes, correct. It is also about togetherness. You know, we have to establish togetherness in our class. If the togetherness were stronger, we would be better off. Try to make an effort, okay?

There is silence, to which the teacher responds: There is strength in unity. In unity, which means that everyone agrees on it. Sometimes we also say we must all pull together.

The pupils are still silent.

Teacher: What do you think? There is strength in unity. Do you have any experience which proved that this is true? Has anything of this kind happened to you in your life?

The silence was broken only by Radovan: For example, when I'm alone and they are four, they defeat me. But when we are four, they don't defeat us. (observation records from the field diary, the basic school in the town of Kruštíkov, 12 December 2018)

The views of the teacher and the children differ. 'Pupils are not just receivers or consumers of knowledge, but constructors of shared meanings in a combined exercise with teachers' (Woods 1996: 39). In the example above, the teacher tried to persuade the pupils that the whole class should pull together, constitute one collective, and forget about the quarrels they have with each other. The pupils understood the issue in their own way, and we might say that they turned it in another direction. Rather, they pointed to the unity of their groups. This in itself says a lot about how relations between children in this class work.

However, I would like to note that all these considerations relate to the current third year. It is possible that both groups may change in the next years. Groups are not permanent; they evolve and change. Therefore, in sociology and anthropology, we talk about the dynamics of social groups. For example, currently in the first group, an obese boy, who is called 'glutton', 'vacuum cleaner', 'piggy' and 'scrap eater', has a slightly worse position. His classmates do not (yet) exclude him, but mock him and tease him. It amazes them that he eats so much. In the past, a non-Roma girl used to be excluded because she was a low achiever. Her classmates accepted her in the first group only during the third year (they appreciated that she started to attend the majorettes club with them). In the first and second years, she was basically alone without a friend. She could not be friends with the Roma girls either, because 'she had been indoctrinated by her family not to socialize with Roma children' [T1].[24]

Discussion and Conclusions

In the presented text, I explain how a basic school contributes to the exclusion of pupils or, conversely, how it stimulates their integration into the children's collective. I focus on the third grade and examine how the identity of pupils in the basic school environment is essentialized and distributed and how certain social and symbolic boundaries in the classroom environment are more or less permanent and others variable. Two Roma pupils, in a way, become non-Roma pupils due to the fact that they are more successful in mathematics, the Czech language and other subjects of instruction. School success together with sociodemographic categories (ethnicity, gender, age, socioeconomic status) significantly contribute to the differentiation of the classroom environment. These categories in the school environment not only influence the dynamics of inclusion and exclusion but are also co-shaped by the process of influencing the dynamics. In some cases, certain categories play a dominant role and are stronger than the others. Sometimes they play a more equal role, influence each other, overlap and do not exclude each other; in such cases, their power gains in strength, or in other cases loses its relevance (see Vorlíček 2019: 251–2). For example, although ethnicity in the given third grade significantly shapes the boundaries between pupils, school success and specific patterns of behaviour, there are other important factors that may even more strongly influence group dynamics in the classroom in the context of this school class.

Many children use various sociodemographic categories and (probably) even think in terms of those categories. They pick them up in their localities and at school from important others – in the context of the third grade, especially from their teacher. On the one hand, this is quite natural. Thinking in categories is part of our socialization and applies to all of us (see Moree 2015). We cannot avoid this type of thinking during our lives. 'Group identification always implies categorization' (Jenkins 2014: 114). On the other hand, it depends very much on how we approach these categories, how we perceive their existence and how their power influences our lives (Moree 2015: 43).

During the research, an interesting fact emerged that the differences in the localities are reflected at the school: villas and family houses, on the one hand, and a socially excluded location, on the other. The residents of family houses do not socialize or communicate with the inhabitants of the excluded locality. And the same applies, more or less, to the observed class. The third grade is to a certain extent structured similarly to the locality, and social exclusion is transferred from the locality to the school. As in other similar schools, the structure of the school class reproduces the social geography of the surrounding locality, including the associated tendencies towards social exclusion, and social stratification is thus projected into an educational institution as to its 'natural' organizational matrix. The school does not hamper this process, but rather gives it the appearance of naturalness and thus naturalizes it (see Vorlíček 2019: 234).

Based on examples from the third grade, I tried to show how pupils often act under the pressure of the surrounding society and the school, which defines to some extent the direction of their actions. This does not mean that pupils are passive individuals. I know from my research that they are active social actors who co-decide on their social status within the classroom environment (see Vorlíček 2019: 238). During my research, I often come across the opinions of teachers, claiming that pupils from minority groups can, after all, influence their own actions, social status and, in general, a whole range of educational and social processes that take place in the classroom environment. Nevertheless, in discussions with teachers, I always emphasize something similar to what Newman has presented: 'We, as individuals, play an important role in coordinating, reproducing, and giving meaning to society in our daily interaction. But we are certainly not completely free to create whatever version of social reality we want to create. We are, after all, born into a pre-existing society with its norms, values, roles, relationships, groups, organizations, and institutions' (2018: 61).

Finally, I would like to emphasize that the purpose of this text is not to criticize the third-grade teacher. Rather, my aim is to point out aspects that are related to teaching and that we teachers are not aware of because our approach is socioculturally determined, and we are often so immersed in teaching that we lack an appropriate distance from it.

List of Interviewees

All interviews have been conducted by Radek Vorlíček at the basic school in the town of Kruštíkov.

- [T1] Teacher 1, 59-year-old teacher of third grade. Personal communication. 22 October 2018, 9 November 2018, 13 November 2018, 21 November 2018, 5 December 2018, 13 December 2018.
- [T2] Teacher 2, 37-year-old teacher in the first level of basic school. Personal communication. 21 November 2018.
- [T3] Teacher 3, 45-year-old teacher in the first level of basic school. Personal communication. 21 November 2018.

Notes

1. In the Czech context, the socially excluded locality is defined as a space (a house, street or neighbourhood) with a high concentration of people in whom we can identify the signs linked to social exclusion. The surrounding populations denote these places symbolically as negative (GAC 2015: 16). Analysis of socially excluded localities in the Czech Republic (GAC 2015: 19) points out that social excluded localities are seen as Roma localities – even those in which the Roma do not constitute a statistical majority. Their boundaries can also be symbolic (e.g. the locality is perceived as 'a bad address'; people describe it as 'the house of horror', 'ghetto', 'Bronx'). In these localities, the majority of the adults have only a basic level of education and the unemployed make up on average around 80 per cent of the population.
2. In Czech schools, a teaching assistant provides support to a lead teacher in the education of pupils with special educational needs (Ministry of Education, Youth and Sports 2016b).
3. In this context, the traditional school is regular public school based on basic educational practices and the traditional approach to education. There is no significant attention to inclusive education, including key concepts and ideas of Booth and Ainscow (2011), such as support for diversity and interpersonal relationships, emphasizing the role of schools in building community, reducing barriers to learning for all pupils or viewing the difference between pupils not as a problems, but as resources to support learning.

4. A socially disadvantaged pupil (1) lives in an environment lacking educational support (e.g. poor quality of housing conditions or insufficient funds); (2) lives in socially excluded localities; (3) is one whose legal guardians do not cooperate with the school which may lead to denial of the basic human rights; (4) is disadvantaged due to his/her ethnical background or suffers from insufficient knowledge of the official language (Felcmanová and Habrová 2015: 9). For detailed definition of the group of socially disadvantaged pupils, see Safrankova and Hrbackova (2016: 739–40).
5. The most common type of disadvantage was type Z – different living conditions, over 60 per cent. In 80 per cent of cases, social disadvantage was registered in combination with health disadvantage (see Seifert et al. 2019: 59).
6. The remaining Roma pupils are educated in programmes intended for the education of pupils with mild intellectual disabilities (12.8 per cent; 4,318 pupils) and in programmes under the Framework Education Programme – basic special schools intended for more serious degrees of intellectual disabilities (1.8 per cent; 611 pupils). Nevertheless, this information depends on the relevance of the data made available by school headmasters (Ministry of Education, Youth and Sports 2016: 7). However, pointing out 'a xenophobic and racist methodology', a number of headmasters have been thwarting the data collection. The headmasters criticized that the identity of the Roma pupil was derived from the evaluator's assessment, not from the statement of the pupil himself or his parents. From their perspective, data collection was thus limited by the evaluator's attitude and subjectivity.
The truth of the matter is that there are huge gaps in data collection. Amnesty International (2015) points out that the Czech Republic does not systematically collect data on education disaggregated by ethnicity despite several attempts by various institutions, in particular the Czech School Inspectorate and the Public Defender of Rights.
7. This is influenced by the fact there were approximately 830 socially excluded localities in 2018 in the Czech Republic and more than 127,000 people lived there (Office of the Government of the Czech Republic 2019: 25). Compared to 2006, the total number of localities has nearly tripled and the number of inhabitants living in them has increased by nearly one half. In 2006, 60,000–80,000 people were living in 300 excluded localities (GAC 2015).
8. In this context, I agree with Kollerová and Killen (2020: 1), whose findings of research focusing on ethnic prejudices highlight 'the need for research on teacher perspectives on peer exclusion and for training teachers [on] how to address peer exclusion in the classroom across various contexts'.
9. Where does such information appear? Surprisingly, even in some (low-quality) multicultural handbooks for teachers, for example, in the book *Multi-kulti: A Handbook in the Field of Multicultural Education* (Barták et al. 2011: 32). In the subchapter 'Traditions and Today', you can read what is 'typical' for Roma culture:

> Employers are reluctant to hire them, mainly because of the high crime rate in the Roma population. For other reasons, it is primarily a wrong setting of values in our social system, where it is believed that many people take advantage of it and rather receive social benefits (money) than work. It also relates to the creation of Roma ghettos, as well as usury, which is very widespread in this culture.

This part in the mentioned subchapter seems to imply that the Roma themselves create the ghetto. From my point of view, the book does provide any overview

of Roma culture, but rather expresses a stereotypical attitude towards this ethnic group.
10. In the Czech Republic, children between the ages of six and fifteen attend basic schools that have two levels: the first one, comparable to primary schools, comprises five grades while the second one, comparable to lower secondary schools, comprises four (see key facts about education in the Czech Republic, Ministry of Education, Youth and Sports 2011).
11. In the Czech Republic, five Roma pupils in a class effectively mean that more than half of the parents will start to consider moving their child into another class (Čada and Hůle 2019: 115). Roma are among the groups that are negatively viewed by parents. Their presence bothers about a quarter of the interviewed parents (Čada and Hůle 2019: 113).
12. In this case, the social disadvantage is recognized by the counselling facility, and the school's opinion is also taken into account.
13. In the Czech Republic, in the school year 2018–19, 1,147 male pupils and 480 female pupils out of 108,000 repeated the first year. The data are based on the Ministry of Education, Youth, and Sports of the Czech Republic, which publishes information in its yearbooks. Failure in the first grade has calamitous consequences for the entire educational and the social career of a given pupil. One or more fails in the Czech Republic automatically mean that a pupil does not get to the ninth grade and leaves school without the proper completion of his or her basic education.
14. I would like to emphasize that this social construct was not created by me. It is a construct created by children and the teacher. The teacher herself talks about two groups in the classroom: 'There are two groups of children in my classroom' (T1, 59-year-old teacher of third grade. Personal communication. Interview by Radek Vorlíček, the basic school in the town of Kruštíkov, 24 October 2018).
15. Jenkins (2014: 6) explains in more detail that hierarchies of collective identification may conflict with hierarchies of individual identification.
16. Katrňák (2004: 23–4) points out that children from lower social classes are not favoured by the school. At school, they recognize that their abilities are not such that they can pursue occupations other than those of their parents. They usually end up in a similar position to that of their parents.
17. Situations from the school environment such as this can also be analysed from the so-called deictic perspective (for more information, see Samek 2016).
18. In the Czech Republic, 90 per cent of players play online; 58 per cent play with others and 31 per cent always play on their own (ISFE 2012: 10).
19. I realized that this adjustment helps the teacher while working. From this point of view, it is not a hidden mechanism, but the teacher tries to make up for the lack of resources in the Czech educational system (lack of teachers and financial resources for staff).
20. For more details on the Pygmalion effect, see Orosová (2019: 492–4), Gentrup and Rjosk (2018), Friedrich et al. (2015) and Rosenthal and Jacobson (1968).
21. Didau and Rose (2016: 190) explain that 'one of the functions of social norms is to distinguish who is part of our group and who is an outsider'.
22. Some teachers uncompromisingly associate the speech of Roma pupils with their intelligence. They despise the Roma ethnolect in the Czech language. For some teachers, this is just poor Czech. This can be viewed as linguistic ethnocentrism, which goes hand in hand with cultural ethnocentrism (Pokorný 2010: 214). For more information on the Roma ethnolect in the Czech language and using Romani in

language socialization in a Czech Rom family, see Bořkovcová (2007) and Kubaník (2016).
23. In the Czech context, multicultural education does not refer to teaching about different cultures – namely, foreign ones – but it includes teaching about Czech ethnic minorities (see Průcha 2011; Šišková 2008).
24. This example indicates how parents can negatively affect social relations and the atmosphere in the classroom. As Čapek (2010: 24) points out, the traditional commands from parents about whom to make friends with and who not to make friends with will definitely not contribute to the child's well-being, as the child may, as a result, feel guilty or become defiant.

References

Allen, K., and M. Kern (2017), *School Belonging in Adolescents: Theory, Research and Practice*, Singapore: Springer.
Amnesty International (2009), *Nedokončený úkol: romští žáci v České republice stále čelí překážkám ve vzdělání*, London: Amnesty International.
Amnesty International (2012), 'Česká vláda propadá už pátým rokem: školy stále diskriminují Romy'. Available online: https://www.amnesty.cz/data/file/2637-ceska-vlada-propada-uz-patym-rokem-november-2012.pdf (accessed 30 September 2021).
Amnesty International (2015), 'Must Try Harder – Ethnic Discrimination of Romani Children in Czech Schools'. Available online: https://www.amnesty.org/download/Documents/EUR7113532015ENGLISH.PDF (accessed 30 September 2021).
Barták, O. (2011), *Multi-kulti aneb rukověť lektora v oblasti multikulturní výchovy*, Vydavatel: Vyšší odborná škola, Obchodní akademie a Střední odborná škola EKONOM, o.p.s.
Berger, P. L., and T. Luckmann (2001), *Sociální konstrukce reality: Pojednání o sociologie vědění*. Nakladatel: Centrum pro studium demokracie a kultury.
Bhopal, K., and U. Maylor, eds (2014), *Educational Inequalities: Difference and Diversity in Schools and Higher Education*, London: Routledge.
Booth, T., and M. Ainscow (2011), *Index for Inclusion: Developing Learning and Participation in Schools*, Bristol: Centre for Studies on Inclusive Education.
Bořkovcová, M. (2007), *Romský etnolekt češtiny*, Nakladatel: Signeta.
Bourdieu, P., and J. C. Passeron (1990), *Reproduction in Education, Society and Culture*, London: Sage.
Brubaker, R. (2006), *Ethnicity without Groups*, Cambridge: Harvard University Press.
Bukowski, W. M., M. Dirks, R. J. Persram, L. Wright, E. Infantino and B. Barbot (2020), 'Peer Relations and Socioeconomic Status and Inequality', *New Directions for Child and Adolescent Development*, 173: 27–37.
Čada, K., and D. Hůle (2019), 'Analýza segregace v základních školách z pohledu sociálního vyloučení', Praha: Úřad vlády České republiky Odbor pro sociální začleňování.
Calarco, J. M. (2011), '"I Need Help!" Social Class and Children's Help-Seeking in Elementary School', *American Sociological Review*, 76 (6): 862–82.
Calarco, J. M. (2018), *Negotiating Opportunities: How the Middle Class Secures Advantages in School*, Oxford: Oxford University Press.

Čapek, R. (2010), *Třídní klima a školní klima*, Praha: Grada.
Cichá, M., J. Máčalová, B. Moravcová, A. Preissová Krejčí, M. Prokeš and M. Roubínková (2016), 'Romové očima pedagogů základních a středních škol', *Antropowebzin*, 1–2: 21–30.
Člověk v tísni, o.p.s. (2009), 'Analýza individuálního přístupu pedagogů k žákům se speciálními vzdělávacími potřebami'. Available online: http://www.msmt.cz/struk turalni-fondy/analyza-individualniho-pristupu-pedagogu-k-zakum-se (accessed 30 September 2021).
ČSÚ (2016), 'Financování vzdělávání v České republice v mezinárodním srovnání'. Available online: https://www.czso.cz/documents/10180/46834153/2300481 6_1.pdf/93225018-a60e-4b5a-8621-d8840289157d?version=1.1 (accessed 30 September 2021).
Didau, D., and N. Rose (2016), *What Every Teacher Needs to Know About Psychology*, Suffolk: John Catt Educational.
Dolby, N., G. Dimitriadis and P. E. Willis (2004), *Learning to Labor in New Times*, New York: Routledge.
Doubek, D. (1996), 'Vztah, řeč, forma a sociální svět první třídy', *Pražská skupina školní etnografie*, 1: 297–353.
Doubek, D. (1999), 'Šplhání a podvádění', *Pražská skupina školní etnografie*, 5: 1–13.
EDUin (2019), 'Audit vzdělávacího systému: SWOT Analýza'. Available online: https://audit.eduin.cz/auditvzdelavaciho-systemu-2019/swot-analyza/ (accessed 30 September 2021).
Eriksen, T. (2010), *Ethnicity and Nationalism: Anthropological Perspectives*, London: Pluto Press.
Felcmanová, L., and M. Habrová (2015), *Katalog podpůrných opatření*, Olomouc: Univerzita Palackého v Olomouci.
Friedrich, A., B. Flunger, B. Nagengast, K. Jonkmann and U. Trautwein (2015), 'Pygmalion Effects in the Classroom: Teacher Expectancy Effects on Students' Math Achievement', *Contemporary Educational Psychology*, 41: 1–12.
GAC (2010), 'Sociologická analýza přechodů romských dětí ze sociálně vyloučeného prostředí ze základních na střední školy'. Available online: http://www.gac.cz/userfi les/File/nase_prace_vystupy/GAC_Prechody_RD_ze_ZS_na_SS.pdf (accessed 30 September 2021).
GAC (2015), 'Analysis of Socially Excluded Localities in the Czech Republic'. Available online: https://www.ohchr.org/Documents/Issues/Housing/InformalSettlements/PublicDefenderCzechRepublic_2.pdf (accessed 30 September 2021).
Gentrup, S., and C. Rjosk (2018), 'Pygmalion and the Gender Gap: Do Teacher Expectations Contribute to Differences in Achievement between Boys and Girls at the Beginning of Schooling?', *Educational Research and Evaluation*, 24: 295–323.
Halse, C. (2018), *Interrogating Belonging for Young People in Schools*, New York: Palgrave Macmillan.
Hampolová, D., and T. Katrňák, ed. (2018), *Na vzdělání záleží: jak vzdělanostní rozdíly*, Brno: Centrum pro studium demokracie.
Hanushek, E. A., and L. Wößmann (2006), 'Does Educational Tracking Affect Performance and Inequality? Differences-in-Differences Evidence Across Countries', *Economic Journal*, 116 (510): C63–C76.
ISFE (2012), 'Videogames in Europe: Consumer Study. European Summary Report. Resource Document'. Available online: https://www.isfe.eu/wp-cont

ent/uploads/2018/11/euro_summary_-_isfe_consumer_study.pdf (accessed 30 September 2021).

Jenkins, R. (1997), *Rethinking Ethnicity: Arguments and Explorations*, London: Sage.

Jenkins, R. (2014), *Social Identity*, London: Routledge.

Katrňák, T. (2004), *Odsouzeni k manuální práci: vzdělanostní reprodukce v dělnické rodině*, Praha: Sociologické nakladatelství.

Killen, M., and M. Rutland (2011), *Children and Social Exclusion: Morality, Prejudice, and Group Identity*, London: Wiley-Blackwell.

Kohout-Diaz, M., D. Bittnerová and M. Levínská (2018), 'Limity inkluze ve vzdělávání romských dětí v České republice: boj o identitu žáka', *Pedagogická orientace*, 28 (2): 235–68.

Kollerová, L., and M. Killen (2020), 'An Experimental Study of Teachers' Evaluations Regarding Peer Exclusion in the classroom', *British Journal of Educational Psychology*, 91 (1): 463–81.

Korbel, V., M. Kunc, D. Prokop and T. Dvořák (2020), 'Souvislost sociálního znevýhodnění a vzdělávacích problémů'. Available at: https://www.paqresearch.cz/post/souvislost-soci%C3%A1ln%C3%ADho-znev%C3%BDhodn%C4%9Bn%C3%AD-a-vzd%C4%9Bl%C3%A1vac%C3%ADch-probl%C3%A9m%C5%AF (accessed 30 September 2021).

Kubaník, P. (2016), 'Using Romani in Language Socialization in a Czech Rom Family', in H. Kyuchukov, E. U. Marushiakova and V. U. Popov (eds), *Roma: Past, Present, Future*, 238–50, Mnichov: Lincom.

Lambert, P., and D. Griffiths (2018), *Social Inequalities and Occupational Stratification: Methods and Concepts in the Analysis of Social Distance*, New York: Palgrave Macmillan.

Marcus, G. E. (1995), 'Ethnography in/of the World System: The Emergence of Multi-Sited Ethnography', *Annual Review of Anthropology*, 24: 95–117.

Marcus, G. E. (1998), *Ethnography through Thick and Thin*, Princeton: Princeton University Press.

Ministry of Education, Youth and Sports (2011), 'The Education System in the Czech Republic'. Available online: https://www.msmt.cz/mezinarodni-vztahy/the-education-system-in-the-czech-republic (accessed 30 September 2021).

Ministry of Education, Youth and Sports (2016a), 'Education at a Glance 2016: Country Notes a Klíčová Data Pro ČR'. Available online: https://www.msmt.cz/vzdelavani/skolstvi-v-cr/statistika-skolstvi/publikace-education-at-a-glance-1 (accessed 30 September 2021).

Ministry of Education, Youth and Sports (2016b), 'Zpráva ze zjišťování kvalifikovaných odhadů počtu romských žáků v základních školách ve školním roce 2016/17'. Available online: https://www.msmt.cz/ministerstvo/novinar/vysledky-kvalifikovanych-odhadu-poctu-romskych-zaku-v-zs (accessed 30 September 2021).

Ministry of Education, Youth and Sports (2016b), 'Vyhláška o vzdělávání žáků se speciálními vzdělávacími potřebami a žáků nadaných, ve znění účinném od 1.9.2016'. Available online: https://www.zakonyprolidi.cz/cs/2016-27 (accessed 30 September 2021).

Ministry of Education, Youth and Sports (2019), 'Hlavní směry vzdělávací politiky do roku 2030+'. Available online: http://www.msmt.cz/file/51582/ (accessed 30 September 2021).

Moree, D. (2015), *Základy interkulturního soužití*. Praha: Portál.

Moree, D. (2019), 'Cesty romských žáků ke vzdělávání. Dopady inkluzivní reformy', Nadace OSF'. Available online: https://osf.cz/publikace/cesty-romskych-zaku-ke-vzdelavani-dopady-inkluzivni-reformy/ (accessed 30 September 2021).
Morvayová, P. (2010), 'Děti "All Exclusive" – Prostředí sociálně vyloučené lokality a jeho vliv na školní (ne) úspěch', in Z. Svoboda and P. Morvayová (eds), *Schola excludes*, 9–48, Ústí nad Labem: Univerzita Jana Evangelisty Purkyně.
Newman, D. (2017), *Identities and Inequalities: Exploring the Intersections of Race, Class, Gender, and Sexuality*, New York: McGraw-Hill Education.
Newman, D. (2018), *Sociology: Exploring the Architecture of Everyday Life*, London: Sage.
Office of the Government of the Czech Republic (2019), 'Zpráva o stavu romské menšiny v České republice za rok 2018', Available online: https://www.vlada.cz/assets/ppov/zalezitosti-romske-komunity/dokumenty/Zprava-o-stavu-romske-mensiny.pdf (accessed 30 September 2021).
Orosová, O. (2019), 'Člověk a vzdělávání', in J. Výrost, I. Slaměník and E. Sollarová (eds), *Sociální psychologie: teorie, metody, aplikace*, 488–500, Praha: Grada.
Parekh, B. C. (2000), *Rethinking Multiculturalism: Cultural Diversity and Political Theory*, Basingstoke: Macmillan.
Pearson, S. (2016), *Rethinking Children and Inclusive Education: Opportunities and Complexities*, London: Bloomsbury Academic.
PISA (2015), 'Results. Policies and Practices for Successful Schools', Volume II. Available online: https://www.oecd-ilibrary.org/docserver/9789264267510-en.pdf (accessed 30 September 2021).
Pivarč, J. (2020), *Na cestě k inkluzi: proměny pedagogických procesů ve vzdělávání a jejich pojetí učiteli a zástupci vedení ZŠ*, Praha: Univerzita Karlova.
Pokorný, J. (2010), *Lingvistická antropologie: jazyk, mysl a kultura*, Praha: Grada.
Průcha, J. (2011), *Multikulturní výchova: příručka (nejen) pro učitele*, Praha: Triton.
Průcha, J. (2017), *Moderní pedagogika*, Praha: Portál.
Rosenthal, R., L. Jacobson (1968), *Pygmalion in the Classroom: Teacher Expectation and Pupil's Intellectual Development*, New York: Holt, Rinehart & Winston.
Safrankova, A., and P. K. Hrbackova (2016), 'Teachers' Beliefs about Socially Disadvantaged Pupils in the Czech Republic', *Procedia – Social and Behavioral Sciences*, 217: 738–47.
Samek, T. (2016), *Tahle země je naše: český a německý veřejný prostor v deiktické perspektivě*, Pardubice: Univerzita Pardubice.
Schuelka, M., Ch. Johnstone and G. Thomas, eds (2019), *The SAGE Handbook of Inclusion and Diversity in Education*, London: Sage.
Seifert M., M. Nesládek and D. Mouchová (2019), *Vzdělávání dětí se sociálním znevýhodněním v základní škole*, Praha: NÚV.
Šišková, T., ed (2008), *Výchova k toleranci a proti rasismu*, Praha: Portál.
Taylor, Ch. (2004), *Zkoumání politiky uznání: multikulturalismus*, Praha: Epocha.
Thompson, R. (2019), *Education, Inequality and Social Class: Expansion and Stratification in Educational Opportunity*, London: Routledge.
Varvařovský, P. (2012), 'Výzkum veřejného ochránce práv k otázce etnického složení žáků bývalých zvláštních škol'. Available online: https://www.ochrance.cz/fileadmin/user_upload/DISKRIMINACE/Vyzkum/Vyzkum_skoly-zprava.pdf (accessed 30 September 2021).
Vorlíček, R. (2019), *Jak se daří inkluzi u nás a na Slovensku?: pohled do konkrétních základních škol*, Červený Kostelec: Pavel Mervart.

Vorlíček, R. (2022a), 'Inclusion of a Pupil with Autism Spectrum Disorder in Mainstream Education in the Czech Republic', *European Journal of Special Needs Education*, doi: 10.1080/08856257.2022.2076479.

Vorlíček, R. (2022b), 'Social and Ethnic Group Membership among Students in a Czech Lower Secondary School', *Society Register*, 6 (1): 41–68, https://doi.org./10.14746/sr.2022.6.1.03.

Whyte, W. (1993), *Street Corner Society: Social Structure of an Italian Slum*, Chicago: University of Chicago Press.

Willis, P. (2017), *Learning to Labor: How Working Class Kids Get Working Class Jobs*, New York: Columbia University Press.

Woods, P. (1996), *Researching the Art of Teaching: Ethnography for Educational Use*, London: Routledge.

Present but Absent: Education about the Roma and Sinti Genocide in Poland

Joanna Talewicz-Kwiatkowska and Dominika Zakrzewska-Olędzka

Introduction

In the public consciousness, the Holocaust is mainly associated with the genocide committed by the Nazi Germany on the members of the European Jewish communities. However, they were not the only victims of the Holocaust, which was also painfully experienced by the Roma and Sinti community. The Roma and Sinti[1] are a group living in a diaspora that came to Europe from India around the eleventh century. The first records of the Roma presence in Poland date back to the fifteenth century. Currently, the Roma and Sinti people live in all the Central and Eastern European (CEE) countries and are a minority in each of them. Due to cultural differences and usage of their own language, they often experience difficulties in integrating with majority groups (Szyszlak 2011: 5–9). As in the case of the Jews, the legal basis for the oppression against the Roma and Sinti during the Second World War was the Nuremberg Laws. Their further justification was the statement about the threat to the purity of the race posed by the Roma and Sinti, issued by the Research Team for Racial Hygiene of Population Biology (*Rassenhygienische und Bevölkerungsbiologische Forschungsstelle*) at the Department of Health of the Third Reich, which led to the recommendation of extermination (Talewicz-Kwiatkowska 2011: 13–15). As a result of the above conclusions and the actions taken in relation to them, after the Jews (one million prisoners of the Auschwitz) and the Poles (140,000 to150,000 prisoners of the Auschwitz), the Roma and Sinti constituted the third largest group of people deported to KL Auschwitz, numbering 23,000 prisoners (Piper 1992).

For several decades, the Roma and Sinti genocide during the Second World War – called the 'forgotten holocaust', 'holocaust' written in lowercase as opposed to the term describing the Shoah, or the term 'Porrajmos'[2] derived from the Romani language (Kapralski 2005: 78–90) used by Roma and Sinti – has been questioned, overlooked or marginalized. The causes for that state of affairs include insufficient documentation and inefficient attempts to raise awareness of the fate of Roma and Sinti among the international community, which resulted, inter alia, from the lack of educated Roma and Sinti elites to spread the knowledge (Mirga 2005: 90–8). As a result, historians focused on the dominant narrative of the majority groups and ignored the topic, leaving the Roma and Sinti histories at the margins of social consciousness. Finally, attention is drawn to the absence of own state structures, including the education system, that would allow institutional preservation and cultivation of memory, and express demand for compensation for victims and their descendants.

At this point, it is worth emphasizing that the main goal of this chapter is to indicate the key role of education in the process of building awareness of the mechanisms of discrimination, the consequences of which may not only adversely affect relations between social groups, but also, without a proper response, may lead to an eruption of hatred. However, the text will not undertake a comparative analysis of the Second World War and the Holocaust influence on the contemporary problems of Roma and Sinti and non-Roma and non-Sinti relations.

In this text, we focus on the dangers of the absence of education about the Roma and Sinti. We are particularly interested in the Polish context, both regarding the Roma and Sinti and non-Roma and non-Sinti relations as well as education about the history of this minority in the Polish education system. To demonstrate the analogies between the past and the present, we refer to Gordon Allport's hate pyramid, which outlines the successive stages of events leading from hate speech to extermination of an entire group. Another researcher who emphasized the importance of preventive actions is Gregory Stanton, president of Genocide Watch and creator of the concept of Eight Steps to genocide. We also refer to the considerations of Zygmunt Bauman who pointed to the dangers resulting from settling the topic of the Holocaust only in the historical context. Sławomir Kapralski's studies on the exclusion of the history of the Roma and Sinti from the Holocaust discourse, which contributed to the absence of education about their extermination, are an important supplement to the aforementioned considerations. The state of education about the Romani and Sinti genocide in CEE is presented and evaluated based on the analysis of existing literature; quantitative and qualitative data; and participant observation.

The Perception of the Roma and Sinti in Poland

In accordance with the article 2, section 4 of the act of 6 January 2005 on national and ethnic minorities and on the regional language (Dz. U. 2005 nr 17 poz. 141), the Roma and Sinti are one of the four ethnic minorities recognized in Poland, next to the Karaims, Lemkos and Tatars. Although according to the last available national census data from 2011 (GUS 2011), nearly 17,000 Polish citizens, or fewer than 1 per cent of the country total population, declared Roma and Sinti origin, the documented history of the Roma and Sinti presence in Poland dates back to the beginning of the fifteenth century. Initially, the Roma were warmly welcomed in Poland, where they were highly valued by the nobility as providers of craft and artistic services. In the following years, while their persecution in Western Europe intensified, more Roma found a safe haven in Poland (Kupczyk 2012). Until the partitions of Poland in the eighteenth century, they enjoyed considerable freedom, including the right to cultivate a nomadic lifestyle. After Poland lost its independence, the situation of the Roma deteriorated significantly. Over time, the attitude of the Polish majority towards the Roma and Sinti minority grew more and more hostile. This change could have been influenced by the significant differences between the Roma and Sinti customs and the Polish culture and law, as well as by ignorance of and misreading these traditions by the non-Roma population, which in turn, led to more mutual misunderstandings and conflicts. In addition, economic changes caused by industrialization in the nineteenth and twentieth centuries followed by the systemic transformation during the People's Republic of Poland resulted in a decline in interest in the services and products offered by the Roma. Finally, the introduction of the obligation to register a person's living address and forced settlement of the Roma contributed to the loss of their traditional lifestyle (Przybyszewska 2014). Currently, 'unemployment is common among the Polish Roma. All this condemns the Polish Roma to social marginalization. And the social marginalization of the Roma worsens, not improves, relations between the Roma and non-Roma people, a relationship which, despite some improvement in recent years, is still bad and unfriendly' (Krasnowolski 2011: 12). According to the 2011 national census, 82 per cent of the Roma and Sinti in Poland have lower than secondary education. In addition, the employment rate among them is only 13.31 per cent.

Difficult relations of the Roma and Sinti with the majority of the society are reflected in the results of public opinion polls. However, it is important to note that the negative attitude towards the Roma and Sinti is not a new tendency, as evidenced by the monitoring of the attitudes of the Poles towards other nationalities carried out since 1975 (Winiewski et al. 2015: 66).

According to the 2012 joint report of the European Union Agency for Fundamental Rights and the United Nations Development Programme, the Roma and Sinti in Poland continue to face discrimination and social exclusion. Moreover, it was emphasized that discrimination, persecution and racist violence are much more widespread in the member states of the European Union (EU), including Poland, than recorded in the official statistics. The Polish Roma and Sinti complain mainly of discrimination in private services, health care and schools, as well as in the job market (FRA 2012). In turn, the 2008 report of the Public Opinion Research Center (CBOS) shows that every sixth Pole agrees with the statement that places of entertainment and recreation where the Roma and Sinti would not have access should exist, while as many as 42 per cent of respondents believe that Roma and Sinti are bad by nature and have a natural predisposition to commit crimes (CBOS 2008). Also, the 2012 report prepared by the researchers from the Jagiellonian University at the request of the former Government Plenipotentiary for Equal Treatment Agnieszka Kozłowska-Rajewicz shows that the Roma and Sinti, along with LGBT groups and people with mental illnesses, are the community towards which Poles feel the greatest social distance (Antosz 2012). The 2018 report by CBOS confirms that the trend is not declining (CBOS 2018), The data on hate speech are equally worrying with a 2017 report indicating that half of the young Poles admits to using hate speech against the Roma and Sinti (Winiewski et al. 2017: 7).

The presented data translates into acts of physical violence against the Roma and Sinti, both past and present. Education provides an important counterweight to stereotypes, prejudices and discrimination against the Roma and Sinti, as it helps to overcome negative perceptions and attitudes towards minority groups (Witkowska et al. 2014: 147–9). Unfortunately, the school curricula do not include history and culture of the Roma and Sinti. In addition, the attitudes towards Roma and Sinti among future teachers and educators are as negative as in those of the cross-section of the Polish society (Zakrzewska-Olędzka 2018). This fact probably has a significant impact on the inclusion of the Roma and Sinti topic in educational activities and the amount of time and commitment devoted to it by the teaching staff. The Roma and Sinti are mentioned in education about minority groups, which is informative and descriptive. Classes on the Roma and Sinti culture, if they are organized at all, focus on folklore, that is on artistic activity, which unfortunately often strengthens the stereotype of the eternally free Roma/Sinti artists. The topic of the Romani and Sinti extermination is barely mentioned or more often completely ignored in Polish schools when discussing the Holocaust of the Jews. However, in that regard Poland is not unique as the situation is similar in other European countries, the United States and in the countries of the Organization for Security and Co-operation in Europe (OSCE).

Legal Foundations of School Education about the Roma Holocaust

On 1 July 2020, the Committee of Ministers of the Council of Europe adopted a recommendation that supports the inclusion of information on the Roma and Sinti history in school curricula and educational materials in its forty-seven member states. The document states that 'Roma Holocaust Education can be an effective tool in combating all forms of hatred, prejudice, radicalization and discrimination, and that it can be a significant alternative to the Holocaust-denying theory' (Council of Europe 2020). It is the first time in the history of the Council of Europe that such a document is adopted. It raised two very important issues. First, attention was drawn to the need to educate about the history of the Roma and Sinti, particularly about the period of the Second World War. Second, it was emphasized that teaching about the history of the Roma and Sinti is one of the most effective tools for counteracting discrimination and anti-Gypsyism, as well as making the majority groups aware that the Roma and Sinti are an integral part of European societies.

The Council of Europe is not the first and not the only international institution to take up this topic. On 15 April 2015, the European Parliament published a resolution that acknowledged the extermination of the Roma and Sinti and referred to their current situation. In the document 'International Roma Day – Anti-Gypsyism in Europe and EU Recognition of the Memorial Day of the Roma Genocide during Second World War', the European Parliament expresses deep concern about the rise of anti-Gypsyism and calls for further efforts to end discrimination, hate crimes and hate speech against the Roma (EP Resolution 2015). Although, neither document is legally binding, they are nevertheless the first recommendations regarding education about the history of the Roma and Sinti published by international institutions. As such they mark an important step not only in the dissemination of knowledge about the most tragic period in the history of the European Roma and Sinti, but also in drawing attention to the impact of education about genocide on the perception and shaping attitudes towards the Roma and Sinti today. The slow but significant progress was expressed not only by the 2015 Resolution of the European Parliament recognizing the extermination of the Roma and Sinti, but also by the impact it had on the interest of international organizations in the history of the Roma and Sinti and the situation of these minorities in relation to the majority groups in the countries they live in. It might make an important contribution to preventing the widening of the gap between Roma and Sinti and non-Roma and non-Sinti (European Commission 2004, 2009). However, as the Vice-President of the European Commission for Values and Transparency Věra Jourová noticed in 2020, while presenting the ten-year (2020–30) plan for Roma inclusion (European Commission 2020):

> In the last ten years we have not done enough to support the Roma people in the EU. There is no excuse for this. Many Roma continue to experience discrimination and racism. We cannot accept this. Today, we are again working to remedy this situation by setting clear goals and re-committing ourselves to making real change over the next decade. (European Commission 2020)

Both in the aforementioned strategy and in the other documents on the Roma and Sinti integration, the need to educate Roma and Sinti is emphasized more and more often and so is the value of education about this minority, particularly in the context of building relations with the non-Roma and non-Sinti majority. The source of the problem with the negative perception of the Roma and Sinti community lies in the persisting stereotypes related to the Roma and Sinti, which contribute to their discrimination and exclusion. Within all the EU member states, as in Poland, the history of the Roma and Sinti, including their citizens of Roma and Sinti origin fated to extermination during the Second World War, was not of interest to historians and researchers of the Holocaust, and even at present constitutes only a marginal aspect of research and education. If the subject of the history of the Roma and Sinti is undertaken in the educational context at all, its discussion is usually limited to presenting short information about the wartime fate of this group on the margin of the discussion of extermination of the Jews. Thus, the aspect related to the trials that led to the inclusion of the Roma and Sinti among the groups fated to extermination in accordance with the ideology of Nazi Germany is omitted. For this reason, it is difficult to initiate a discussion on contemporary problems in the context of exclusion, discrimination and racism against the Roma and Sinti, while making people aware of the analogous mechanisms that led to the extermination of this minority in the past.

Preventive Function of Education about the Holocaust

Sławomir Kapralski (2005: 78) in the text entitled 'Why Teach about the Romani Holocaust?' stated that 'the ignorance of what happened to the Roma has also a moral dimension: it prevents us from perceiving them as the victims of racial persecution supported by the entire civilization potential of modern Europe, which in turn makes it difficult to free oneself from perceiving the Roma in terms of fixed stereotypes that contributed to their tragedy and are still responsible for the discrimination against this community'. It is difficult to disagree with his words both in terms of moral responsibility and the mechanisms that in the past led to the extermination of the Roma and Sinti. The repetitiveness of those mechanisms was emphasized by scholars who treated the Holocaust as a case study, making it possible to show the processes that led to the extermination. Early insight into the field was provided by Gordon Allport's research that led to identification of the five stages of aggression intensification (the so-called Hate Pyramid), with each more and more harmful to the discriminated group. According to Allport, the growing hatred towards a given minority group leads to an escalation of the conflict with possible dire consequences. The Hate Pyramid was developed in the 1950s and alluded to the process that led to the Holocaust of Jews (Allport 1954). Allport noted that hateful comments, the basis of which may be stereotypes and prejudices about a given community, are the first signal that requires a response. The next step in the pyramid is avoidance, or separation (forced or voluntary), from the group which is the object of hate speech. Discrimination, understood as worse and unequal treatment, is the next stage of the pyramid. At the top of the pyramid stands physical violence: individual attacks that can turn into mass actions aimed at the extermination of a given group. This happens most often when hatred is institutionalized, strengthened by propaganda, and is intended to achieve or maintain power as was the case with the Nazi Germany. The Allport model is universal; only victims and perpetrators change. Throughout the history of mankind, it was implemented many times, not only in the tragic twentieth century (the Armenian genocide, the Holocaust, the Tutsi genocide in Rwanda), but also in earlier times and today.

Gregory Stanton (1996) came to similar conclusions and identified eight stages of genocide, based on the studies of the Holocaust, the Khmer Rouge genocide in Cambodia and others. In his own words, his classification of the eight stages of genocide serves the purpose of finding out about the situation at an early stage and preventing it. However, Stanton goes a step further than Allport and provides a list of examples and actions which, thanks to the awareness of the consequences of subsequent stages, turned out to be successful at preventing escalation (Stanton 2020). Stanton emphasizes that social pressure is needed on politicians who make decisions, including those related to education.[3]

Both Allport and Stanton emphasized that taking appropriate action at almost any stage can stop the process leading to physical extermination. In this context, two elements are crucial. The first one is awareness of these processes, as knowing the consequences of not reacting prevents inaction. The second element is education about the Holocaust, including both the historical and social perspectives, as it makes people aware of the issues of social responsibility due to the repetition of certain events and their effects, which may also occur today if not reacted to. Zygmunt Bauman stated that the conclusions resulting from the extermination are part of the science of modernity and the theory of civilization processes. Therefore, as the scholar wrote, knowledge about the processes that led to the Holocaust is very poor. Wolfgang Sofsky (2000: 651) concurs, as he critically describes the inclusion of the Holocaust in social sciences, particularly in sociology. His opinion can be boldly applied to educational programmes that limit the subject of the Holocaust to historical perspective, creating false sense of security and freeing us from the responsibility of educating and reacting in line with the belief that the Holocaust is an event that took place in the past and therefore is not part of contemporary discourses. Meanwhile, the spectre of the brown past has become more and more visible today among others in the context of contemporary genocides, which in educational discourses are rarely associated with the processes that led to the Holocaust. The events that are currently observed have become the factor which makes people aware of contemporary threats. Radical nationalist, right-wing movements and the rise of xenophobic sentiments are increasingly discussed in the context of the consequences of radicalization. In effect, preventive measures aimed at building an alternative to contemporary threats are taken as this topic has become an important item on the agenda of many governments and international institutions. While this problem applies to the whole of Europe, it is particularly visible in the CEE countries, where leaders and leading politicians openly manifest their disregard towards minority groups, thus giving consent to acts of discrimination, hate speech and even violence.

Education about the Holocaust in CEE Countries, with Particular Emphasis on Poland

The subject of the Holocaust in education raises a lot of controversy in Poland regarding both the content and the form of its message. Knowledge on this subject during the communist period (1944–89), in the years immediately following the end of the war, was often distorted and adapted to the then official political narrative. Consequently, it contributed to the low awareness of the Polish society of the Holocaust, and in particular the awareness of the heterogeneity of Poles' attitudes towards the situation of Jews in that period and the dramatic experiences of the Roma and Sinti community. An additional difficulty in teaching about the Holocaust was the social trauma of the tragic experiences of the Second World War, which Poles (also non-Jews and non-Roma and non-Sinti) had not worked through until now. Significant changes in the approach to education about the Holocaust in Poland took place only after the systemic transformation in the 1990s. For comparison (Ambrosewicz-Jacobs 2016), in Western Europe this topic was taken up several decades earlier, in the 1960s, with the trial of Adolf Eichmann in 1961. The abolition of communist censorship and freedom of speech undoubtedly influenced the growing interest in the subject of the Holocaust of Jews in CEE countries. However, it is still a sensitive topic, which is reflected in the social and political discourse. As Ambrosewicz-Jacobs (2016: 27) writes, 'in Central and Eastern Europe, after a period of oblivion, suppression and distortion, the memory of the Holocaust is the subject of negotiations, political manipulation or competition'.

Poland is one of the countries in which the increase in xenophobic sentiment has been abrupt in recent years (Ambrosewicz-Jacobs 2016). Anti-other, anti-immigrant, anti-refugee and homophobic narratives are used by politicians of the ruling party to achieve current political goals (Skowrońska 2021: 940–67). The vision of a Pole as a Catholic with a white skin is promoted, and any deviation from this norm is treated as a potential threat to the Polish culture and values. These moods influenced changes in the educational programmes, in which the main emphasis is placed on strengthening patriotic attitudes (Kapela 2017). In principle, there is nothing disturbing about it; however, currently in Poland patriotism is often discussed in terms that are in opposition to diversity and otherness (Kapela 2017; Pankowski 2017). This situation contributed to the initiation of preventive actions and activation of both institutions and non-governmental organizations, as well as individuals – teachers, educators or activists – who, despite unfavourable circumstances, try to counterbalance the dominant narratives by introducing multidimensional education about the Holocaust by discussing various perspectives, mutual attitudes of representatives of individual groups affected by these events and historical conditions. A milestone in this context was the series of four international conferences on education, remembrance and research on the Holocaust, hosted by the Swedish government between 2000– and 2004. The first of them resulted in the signing of the so-called Stockholm Declaration, emphasizing the determination of all states signatories of the document, including Poland and other CEE countries, in counteracting genocide, ethnic cleansing, racism, anti-Semitism, Islamophobia, xenophobia and in combating all discrimination and related intolerance. The last conference particularly emphasized the need for preventive education about mechanisms that can lead to genocide (Fried 2006).

Despite numerous methodological studies on teaching about the Holocaust, in Poland it is still discussed mainly from the perspective of a historical event, without analysing and emphasizing the role of social mechanisms that led not only to it but were also the basis of other genocides in the history. Showing analogies in social attitudes between what led to historical events and what we observe today in social relations is still a rarity and an approach considered innovative. It is worth emphasizing that despite numerous controversies regarding the scope and form of teaching about the Holocaust, instruction about it as a subject is well established in educational programmes. This is also the case of Poland, where in 1999 education about the Holocaust of Jews was included in the core curriculum of general education at the secondary school level as a compulsory subject (Trojański 2008: 10). Irrespective of this very important change, education about the extermination of the Roma and Sinti is not included in the curriculum, despite the fact that, according to the data of the Polish Institute of National Remembrance, about 35,000[4] out of the population of approximately 50,000 Polish Roma were murdered during the Holocaust. The reason behind that exclusion was certainly the way in which the term Holocaust was understood as applying only to the experiences of the Jewish community (Bauer 2002: 1–14). Another and probably key reason for this situation was the lack of recognition by the international community of the Roma and Sinti as victims of National Socialism.

The Holocaust Discourse and the Roma and Sinti

The post-war period was not only the time when the perpetrators were held accountable, but also the period of constructing the Holocaust discourse, which was then defined as the mass murder of approximately six million Jews by the Nazis and their collaborators.[5] The experiences of the Roma and Sinti were not even recorded. The Roma and Sinti witnesses did not testify during the Nuremberg Trials, and those who perpetrated genocide against them were not brought to justice for that crimes, which undoubtedly resulted in both the exclusion of the Roma and Sinti from the Holocaust discourse and the failure to include their history in educational programmes. In this context, the lack of political representation and the lack of a dominant position in majority societies is significant, as the researchers working within the postcolonial theory stress. Michel-Rolph Trouillot (1995) in his anthropological study 'Silencing the Past' points to silencing various historical events in the process of producing knowledge about the past. In his opinion, the silencing happens in four dimensions: when the facts are selected (creating sources), when they are collected (archives are created), when they are revealed (building a narrative) and when the importance of a selected set of historical statements is emphasized, which is referred to as writing history (Trouillot 1995: 26). Michel Foucault insisted that an inalienable element of any historical narrative that claims to be impartial and objective is the question of power. The Roma and Sinti did not have the power, and therefore, their experience was ignored, thus being considered less significant (Talewicz-Kwiatkowska 2020: 46).

The situation of Poland and other CEE countries in this period was even more complicated. When discussing the topic of shaping European awareness and narrative about the events of the Second World War (including the Holocaust), one should remember about the political factors in play and the reality of functioning of the lands behind the Iron Curtain. When Poland was a part of the Eastern Bloc as a satellite state of the USSR, its sovereignty, the possibility of communicating with the Western European states, and the opportunity of working through the social traumas of the war and occupation were significantly limited. Altogether, the political situation made it impossible to hear and to include Poland's voice in the process of constructing the discourse of the Second World War. In particular, the processes related to building awareness in Polish society of the fate of the Jews, the Roma and Sinti and other minorities during the Nazi period was significantly delayed. In the case of the Roma and Sinti, this problem grows to the present day. As a result, practices which in the past were part of the process leading to social exclusion and extermination of this minority are continued.

Another problem that contributes to the lack of consideration of the history of the Roma and Sinti in the Holocaust discourse is the perception of the Roma and Sinti as people who live outside European civilization, who are not interested in their own history, and time does not matter to them. Kapralski (2012: 208–13) points to a consensus among researchers that it is these considerations and the perpetuation of the opinion about the unique identity of this minority, not susceptible to changes, that have become the reason for excluding the Roma and Sinti from the group of victims of the Holocaust not only in Poland, but also in the world. What is more, the Roma and Sinti themselves are blamed for this approach of researchers and historians, which is explained primarily by the inactivity of the Roma and Sinti communities in popularizing the knowledge about their experiences and in preserving written and visual sources created by its representatives documenting these experiences. It is hard to agree with such arguments put forward in relation to a minority, whose history is part of the Polish and European historical heritage. Responsibility for education about the history of the Roma and Sinti should not rest only and solely on its representatives. It should be supported by those European states of which the Roma and Sinti are citizens, including incorporation into the curricula of public schools.

Even today some scientists question the racial foundations of the persecution of the Roma and Sinti during the Holocaust. They indicate elements of the policy related to defining the causes of oppression against the Roma and Sinti community in terms of criminogenicity and anti-socialism, just as did the Nazis. In this context, the comparative aspect related to the Roma and Sinti and Jewish experiences to which scholars refer is also important. For example, J. Bauer and G. Lewy state that no clear and systematically implemented policy of extermination of all the Roma and Sinti has been formulated (Joskowicz 2014: 844–6). Considerations regarding the comparative perspective fit within the paradigm of 'memory wars', which stresses that religious and ethnic minorities compete for public recognition of their victims (Joskowicz 2016: 5). According to Michael Rothberg (2009), what is too often overlooked is the fact that narratives about the experiences of victims can enable others to create those based on their own. Rothenberg's approach, described in the literature as 'multi-directional memory' and constructed in an effort to go beyond memory wars, can be applied to the narrative related to the experiences of the Roma and Sinti, for whom the narratives of the Jewish experiences have become the reference point. Stories of the Jews, spoken aloud by themselves, described and examined, became a model and set the direction for documenting, researching, commemorating and educating about the extermination of the Roma and Sinti.

Education about the Extermination of the Roma and Sinti in the Light of Selected Studies

Very few works on the topic of education about the Roma and Sinti Holocaust were written. These include two European international studies that incorporate Poland (OSCE 2015 and Polak 2015); George Washington University's Michelle Kelso's (2013: 61–78) research on Romania; and the more geographically distant American research by Joanna Talewicz-Kwiatkowska (2017: 195–225).

Twenty countries (including Poland) out of thirty-four participating in the OSCE survey (2015) declared that they provide education on the genocide of the Roma and Sinti on at least one level of education (primary, secondary, or higher), However, in none of the European countries participating in the research does this area constitute a separate topic within the educational programmes in schools. Information on the

Roma and Sinti extermination usually is included in the core curriculum topics of history, civic education or other classes on the Second World War, totalitarianism or Nazi and fascist regimes. Frequently it is but a footnote during a class on the Holocaust of the Jews. Moreover, due to the breadth of this topic, knowledge about the Roma and Sinti often is buried under all the other information, which is why it is not retained by the students.

Two another extremely important issues related to the school lessons, apart from the curriculum, are the preparation of teachers and availability of didactic materials suitable for different age groups. Although the current school curriculum in Poland covers a wide range of issues related to national and ethnic minorities during the interwar, the Second World War and the post-war periods up until the present day (including the social and religious structure of the Polish society between 1918 and 1939, Polish public policies towards national minorities before the Second World War, information on material and cultural losses resulting from the war), the extermination of the Roma and Sinti was included in the core curriculum only in 2017 (Podstawa programowa, n.d.; Rozporządzenie 2017). The school curriculum also includes human rights and the protection of minority rights. Nevertheless, it is the teacher who makes the final decision on the content of the classes. It is worth emphasizing that usually, apart from general guidelines, teachers of individual subjects may develop or present specific topics more briefly, depending on their will, competences and interests, and the subjective assessment of the importance of a given area. Therefore, their awareness of specific topics and availability of teaching materials are particularly important. The situation in Romania, another CEE country, seems even more difficult. Although education about the Holocaust has been compulsory there for over ten years, it unfortunately does not translate into school practice. As Michelle Kelso (2013) writes: 'Romanian historiography silences the genocide of the Roma, a silence perpetuated even by most Romanian researchers of the Holocaust … The lack of references to Roma in academic and educational texts is an integral part of institutionalized racism in the country.'

In Poland, as in the other surveyed countries, there are no systematic and reliable programmes preparing the teaching staff to conduct classes about the extermination of the Roma and Sinti. In particular, there are no programmes that would familiarize participants with the context of history, culture and wider social experiences of this group. Therefore, it can be assumed that extermination of the Roma and Sinti is often not discussed at all or barely mentioned. The negligible orientation in the subject is also evidenced by the contradictory response of the Polish government, which claimed there are no educational materials on the extermination of the Roma and Sinti available, while at the same time it was established that the teachers who were interested in the topic actually had access to the necessary materials. However, the government statement did not contain information about what exactly were the materials, nor about their sources. Thus, there is a clear discrepancy between the theoretical consideration of the discussed subject in the curriculum and the implementation of practical activities through access to teachers' training and development of teaching materials. Similarly, in the Romanian context, Michelle Kelso (2013) noted the generally modest knowledge of Romanian teachers about the genocide that took place in their country[6] and the cognitive barriers – inextricably linked to personal prejudices and stereotypes[7] – of many history and civic education teachers in the context of teaching about the victimization of the Roma and Sinti minority. Although new narratives about the Holocaust and the reconfiguration of ethnic identities in post-socialist Romania were accepted, it was done so usually under pressure from the EU and the United States, which also forced a critical examination of past atrocities. However, those processes did not positively influence the dissemination of knowledge about the history of the Roma and Sinti.

At this point, it is also worth emphasizing the issue of the availability of extracurricular education. Twenty-one countries from among those surveyed by the OSCE (2015) provides training and workshops for teachers who would like to broaden their knowledge of the extermination of the Roma and Sinti. The situation is complicated, however, by the relatively low interest in this topic on the part of the teaching staff, which is also probably influenced by excessive work duties and by the fear of addressing sensitive topics in the classroom, which requires facing numerous stereotypes and prejudices about the Roma and Sinti community. Similar conclusions can be drawn from the research by Karen Polak (2015), who repeatedly confronted the stereotypical opinions about the Roma and Sinti minority during the classes. Describing her work experience in Poland, she emphasized that disclosing these opinions in an open manner during an organized lesson may be useful from an educational point of view and foster discussion on the consequences of stereotypes and prejudices. Nevertheless, negative perceptions of the Roma and Sinti make it difficult to educate about this group, even when issues related to their genocide are discussed. Therefore, according to Polak (2015: 141–65), it is very important to help teachers by providing them with additional educational materials on stereotypes, prejudices and countering discrimination.

The answers of the respondents (OSCE 2015) also include information about classes and workshops for students which are conducted by institutions or non-governmental organizations specializing in the subject. The importance of school visits to the Auschwitz-Birkenau State Museum as an additional form of education and the use of individual stories as good practice in teaching about the history of the Roma and Sinti were also highlighted. Importantly, almost all countries emphasized on the generally growing awareness of the extermination of the Roma and Sinti. This trend raises hope for gradual changes in this regard, which is significantly supported by the work of activists from the Roma and Sinti community and the availability of European funds intended to support the cultivation of traditions, preservation of the culture and raising public awareness of the history of minority groups.

The absence of education about the extermination of the Roma and Sinti is a problem that does not only concern Poland or the countries of the CEE. This is a shared reality of almost all European countries, as well as the United States. Although the topic of war and the Holocaust is covered in American schools, the experiences of the Roma and Sinti are overlooked. American teachers often have no basic knowledge of this community or even the awareness that it lives in the United States. According to Ian Hancock, a professor of Roma origin at the University of Texas at Austin: 'Familiarity with Porajmos is increasing in the US, but it is happening too slowly.' Margareta Matache, an academic at the Harvard University and an activist of Roma origin, also noted the absence of the Roma and Sinti subjects in public space, including school curricula. Matache regretfully said that the topic of the extermination of the Roma and Sinti was not addressed in American schools. However, she emphasized that the gap in this respect was filled by non-governmental organizations and by some educational institutions.[8] Due to the limited knowledge among majority groups within various societies, these gaps are also visible in the activities of important international institutions that shape global policies, such as the United Nations. In Matache's opinion, the persistent perception of the Roma and Sinti minority through the prism of negative stereotypes contributes to the further marginalization of the Roma and Sinti and their history, not only locally, but also globally. The lack of knowledge about the Roma and Sinti and their history in the countries with a key voice in the international organizations and agencies limits the possibility of effectively addressing this topic, while the absence of the Roma's own state structures prevents them from representing themselves on international forum (Talewicz-Kwiatkowska 2017: 209–20).

Conclusions

Based on the information collected in this chapter, it is worth trying to indicate problem areas related to the education about the history and culture of the Roma and Sinti community. These topics are not taught at schools in a unified or systematic manner. Taking up the subject and the scope of its analysis depends on the activity, knowledge and commitment of teachers. Another problem is the absence of educational materials, as well as textbook content, which could be an important inspiration for conducting classes on the Roma and Sinti. Unfortunately, despite the involvement of many teachers, insufficient preparation of most educators for conducting classes about the Roma and Sinti remains major problem. Thus, the educational support of teachers seems to be the key issue, particularly as the stereotypes about the Roma and Sinti persist also outside the group of young people. Confronting them as well as understanding the mechanisms of their formation may be an important, if not decisive, step towards motivating the expansion of teachers' educational activities.

When it comes to Poland, it is difficult to say whether there is a chance to introduce education about the extermination of the Roma and Sinti into the curriculum not only as an element taken out of context, but as a part of presentation of the history and culture of the Roma and Sinti community which would require facing the stereotypes about it in Polish society. The OSCE/ODHIR report (2015) mentioned both the confirmation by the Polish government of the existence of educational materials for teachers and the initiatives of museums or memorial sites. Therefore, since no gaps or problem areas have been identified, it is difficult to expect changes. Although, many of the institutions indicated by the Polish government are indeed active in the area related to the education about the Roma and Sinti, the vast majority, if not all, of the initiatives undertaken in this area are one-off actions or are carried out within a time-limited projects. They do not offer an effective alternative to the long-term, nationally harmonized educational programmes addressed to teachers and students learning in the Polish schools. Nonetheless, they can be an important supplement to the content discussed during the classes.

Other difficulties concerning the redefinition of historical education in Poland are also worth mentioning, including the overarching goal of the new core curriculum, which is to draw attention to the suffering and heroism of the Poles during the Second World War and to promote patriotic attitudes. On the contrary, the narrative presented at schools should refer to the vision of Poland, which was and is the homeland of many minorities, including the Roma and Sinti, and in which patriotism is not defined in opposition to multiculturalism. During the communist period (1944–89), the homogeneity of the Polish nation was emphasized, while later, in particular during Poland's preparations for the EU accession (after Poland submitted in 1994 an application for membership in the EU, which was approved by the member states) a number of projects were implemented to promote knowledge about the history and culture of the Polish minorities as well as specific knowledge about individual regions of the country. The first decade of the Polish membership in the EU (from 2004) was the time of embracing and celebrating diversity and its benefits for the society. The recent changes in Poland (after the nationalist parties won the 2015 parliamentary elections) are characterized by negative narratives towards otherness, especially minority groups, migrants and refugees. These changes indicate that the educational system reformed by the current government, according to the set of values followed by the parliamentary majority, will deepen rather than alleviate the current problems.

Finally, one more very important point should be made. The absence of education about the extermination of the Roma and Sinti is not only the domain of Poland. This problem is shared by many European countries and beyond as is a persistently high level of prejudice against the Roma and Sinti. Hate speech, anti-Gypsyism and dehumanization of this minority is justified by the culture and way of life of the Roma and Sinti. Their poverty is seen as a choice or a consequence of attachment to cultural norms deviating from those prevailing in majority societies. The image of the Roma and Sinti as people who generate problems and who burden economic systems creates many threats to them, especially in times of crisis. Tensions and frustrations precede dangerous mechanisms known from the past events. Therefore, there is a need not only to include education about the Roma and Sinti extermination in the curricula, but also to change the way of thinking about how we should educate about and thus effectively respond to contemporary challenges. Zygmunt Bauman (2009: 35) in his excellent 'Modernity and the Holocaust' emphasized that education about the Holocaust should explore the conclusions coming out of it, which are part of the science of modernity and the theory of civilization processes. That is the reason why education about the extermination should go beyond the framework related to the past and include contemporary threats. Although research results confirm that youth workers share this observation, it still is not a common approach. The textbooks lack content that presents the analogies between the mechanisms of behaviour of individuals and societies in the past and present; therefore, education in this area depends on the determination and effort of the teachers. Technological development and the transfer of a large part of our lives to the virtual world additionally affects the mindsets of the young people, for whom the time of war and the Holocaust seems more and more distant. All the more, we should make every effort to ensure that historical education takes into account the needs and sensitivity of the incoming generations that function in a reality different from that which is familiar to us. If we do not make the effort, we will lose the opportunity to influence their attitudes through education about the past, which should be an important lesson and a warning for the future.

Notes

1. Two terms are often used to describe this community: Gypsies and Roma. The word Gypsy is an exoethnonym (an ethnic group name used by non-Roma) and has been adopted by members of that group as a proper name. This term in many languages is marked negatively (e.g. in Polish the word 'gypsy' is a synonym for a fraud or a liar). The word Rom is an endoethnonym (proper name of the group) and in Romani language it means 'man'. It should be added that there are groups that do not identify with this term (e.g. Sinti, Manusz). The name *Sinti* occurs with reference to the community living in Germany and German-speaking countries. The term is distinguished in this text because of its popularity in materials related to the subject. A change to use the term *Rom* is recently observed, as the term *Gypsy* has negative connotations.
2. The term Porrajmos/Porajmos in Romani literally means 'devour'. Not all Roma groups use it due to its different meaning in various dialects of the Romani language.
3. This article was originally written in 1996 and was presented as the first Working Paper (GS 01) of the Yale Program in Genocide Studies in 1998.
4. Those numbers are probably much higher, because the Polish Roma were murdered not only in the camps, but also outside of them as part of the programme of non-camp extermination, carried out in the occupied Polish lands by the Nazis. For this reason alone, it is difficult to precisely define the exact number of murdered European Roma.
5. There are several definitions of the term Holocaust. This chapter uses the definition of the Holocaust proposed by the United States Holocaust Memorial Museum (n.d.).
6. In 1941–4, the Romanian regime transported part of the Jewish and Roma population to the death camps in Transnistria, where over 200,000 Jews and over 10,000 Roma were killed.
7. The results of the research highlighted one more important problem, which is a serious obstacle in education about the history of the Roma in Romania and which is related to stereotypes and prejudices of teachers against the Roma minority. As a result, discussions about the Roma victims of Nazism are linked to the current situation of the Roma and their socioeconomic status. Kelso mentions the repeatedly cited negative stereotypes portraying the Roma as anti-social and referring to the Nazi discourse relating to the Zigeuner category (German, pejorative term for Roma and Sinti).

8. Such as Facing History and Ourselves, which aims to counteract prejudice, racism, anti-Semitism and xenophobia through historical education. The organization's employees operate around the world, including in the United States (New York, Chicago, Denver, Los Angeles, San Francisco), Canada (Toronto), France, the UK (London and Northern Ireland), China and South Africa. Among the educational tools available from their website, one can find materials on the history of the Roma.

References

Allport, G. (1954), *The Nature of Prejudice*, Cambridge: Addison-Wesley.
Ambrosewicz-Jacobs, J. (2016), '"…wobec rozmiarów Zagłady świat doświadczył ogromnej winy…" Debaty wokół nauczania o Holokauście', *Studia nad Autorytaryzmem i Totalitaryzmem*, 38 (2): 19–33.
Antosz, P. (2012), 'Równe traktowanie standardem dobrego rządzenia. Raport z badań sondażowych'. Available online: https://portal.uj.edu.pl/documents/4628317/aabdbce2-8ba2-4a58-b04f-c28108cd068c (accessed 11 November 2021).
Bauer, Y. (2002), *Rethinking the Holocaust*, New Haven, CT: Yale University Press.
Bauman, Z. (2009), *Nowoczesność i Zagłada*, Kraków: Wydawnictwo Literackie.
CBOS (2008), 'Postawy wobec Romów w Polsce, Czechach, na Węgrzech i Słowacji. Komunikat z badań'. Available online: http://www.cbos.pl/SPISKOM.POL/2008/K_104_08.PDF (accessed 12 October 2021).
CBOS (2018), 'Stosunek do innych narodów. Komunikat z badań'. Available online: https://www.cbos.pl/SPISKOM.POL/2018/K_037_18.PDF (accessed 11 November 2021).
Council of Europe (2020), 'Schools Should Include Roma and Traveller History in Teaching Curricula: Council of Europe Recommendations'. Available online: https//www.coe.int/en/web/roma-and-travellers/-/schools-should-include-roma-and-traveller-history-in-teaching-curricula-council-of-europe-recommendation (accessed 30 October 2021).
European Commission Directorate-General for Employment and Social Affairs Unit D3 (2004), *The Situation of Roma in an Enlarged European Union*. Office for Official Publications of the European Communities: Luxembourg, http://www.errc.org/uploads/upload_en/file/00/E0/m000000E0.pdf (accessed 25 May 2022).
European Commission (2020), 'A New EU Roma Strategic Framework'. Available online: https://ec.europa.eu/info/files/factsheet-eu-roma-strategic-framework_en (accessed 11 November 2021).
European Parliament's Committee on Employment and Social Affairs (EMPL) (2009), 'The Social Situation of the Roma and Their Improved Access to the Labour Market in the EU', https://www.europarl.europa.eu/document/activities/cont/201107/20110718ATT24290/20110718ATT24290EN.pdf (accessed 25 May 2022).
European Parliament (2015), 'European Parliament Resolution of 15 April 2015 on the Occasion of International Roma Day – Anti-Gypsyism in Europe and EU Recognition of the Memorial Day of the Roma Genocide During World War II' (2015/2615(RSP)), https://eur-lex.europa.eu/legal-content/EN/TXT/?uri=CELEX:52015IP0095 (accessed 8 November 2021).
European Parliament's Committee on Employment and Social Affairs (EMPL) (2009), 'The Social Situation of the Roma and Their Improved Access to the Labour Market in the EU', https://www.europarl.europa.eu/document/activities/cont/201107/20110718ATT24290/20110718ATT24290EN.pdf (accessed 25 May 2022).

FRA (2012), 'The Situation of Roma in 11 Member States, Survey Results at a Glance'. Available online: https://fra.europa.eu/sites/default/files/fra_uplo ads/2099-FRA-2012-Roma-at-a-glance_EN.pdf (accessed 3 October 2021).

Fried, E., ed. (2006), 'The Stockholm International Forum Conferences (2000–2004)', Brochure produced by the Swedish Government, Fälthoch Hässler: Värnamo, https://www.government.se/contentass ets/66bc8f513e67474e96ad70c519d4ad1a/the-stockholm-international-forum-conferences-2000-2004 (accessed 25 May 2022).

GUS (2011), 'Wyniki Narodowego Spisu Powszechnego Ludności i Mieszkań 2011' (Results of the National Population and Housing Census 2011). Warszawa.

Joskowicz, A. (2014), 'Featured Book Review: The Nazi Genocide of the Roma: Reassessment and Commemoration. Edited by Anton Weiss-Wendt', *Central European History*, 47: 844–9.

Joskowicz, A. (2016), 'Separated Sufferings, Shared Archives. Jewish and Romani Histories of Nazi Persecution', *History and Memory*, 28 (1): 110–40.

Kapela, J. (2017), '*Stop lewackiej antydyskryminacji*', *Krytyka Polityczna*, 8 July. Available online: https://krytykapolityczna.pl/felietony/jas-kapela/stop-lewackiej-antydyskry minacji/ (accessed 11 November 2021).

Kapralski, S. (2005), 'Dlaczego warto uczyć o zagładzie Romów', in J. Ambrosewicz-Jacobs and L. Hońdo (eds), *Dlaczego należy uczyć o Holokauście?*, 103–15, Kraków: Uniwersytet Jagielloński.

Kapralski, S. (2012), *Naród z popiołów. Pamięć zagłady a tożsamość Romów*, Warszawa: Scholar.

Kelso, M. (2013), '"And Roma Were Victims, Too." The Romani Genocide and Holocaust Education in Romania', *Intercultural Education*, 24 (1–2): 61–78.

Krasnowolski, A. (2011), *Cyganie/Romowie w Polsce i w Europie: wybrane problemy historii i współczesności. Opracowanie tematyczne*, Warszawa: Kancelaria Senatu.

Kupczyk, A. (2012), 'Status prawny Romów w Polsce a regulacje prawne w państwach członkowskich Unii Europejskiej', in Ł. Machaj (ed.), *Varia doctrinalia*, 147–61, Wrocław: Prawnicza i Ekonomiczna Biblioteka Cyfrowa.

Mirga, A. (2005), 'O godne miejsce wśród ofiar. Holokaust i eksterminacja Romów w okresie II wojny świtowej', in J. Ambrosewicz-Jacobs and L. Hońdo (eds), *Dlaczego należy uczyć o Holokauście?*, 90–7, Kraków: Uniwersytet Jagielloński.

OSCE/ODHIR (2015), *Teaching about and Commemorating the Roma and Sinti Genocide. Practices within the OSCE Area*, OSCE Office for Democratic Institutions and Human Rights (ODIHR): Warsaw, https://www.osce.org/files/f/documents/9/b/135396.pdf (accessed 25 May 2022).

Pankowski, R. (2017), 'Powrót do wielokulturowości byłby powrotem do normalności', *Respublica*, 2 October. Available online: https://publica.pl/teksty/pankowski-pow rot-do-wielokulturowosci-bylby-powrotem-do-normalnosci-62060.html (accessed 30 October 2021).

Piper, F. (1992), *Ilu ludzi zginęło w KL Auschwitz. Liczba ofiar w świetle źródeł i badań*, Oświęcim: Państwowe Muzeum w Oświęcimiu.

Podstawa programowa (n.d.), 'Historia'. Available online: https://podstawaprogramowa.pl/ Szkola-podstawowa-IV-VIII/Historia (accessed 10 November 2021).

Polak, K. (2015), 'Teaching the Roma Genocide. 'Society Never Regarded Me as an Individual', in A. Mirga-Kruszelnicka, E. Acuña and P. Trojański (eds), *Education for Remembrance of the Roma Genocide*, 141–64, Kraków: Libron.

Przybyszewska, D. (2014), 'Edukacja mniejszości romskiej w Polsce', *Kultura – Społeczeństwo – Edukacja*, 2 (6): 175–92.
Rothberg, M. (2009), *Multidirectional Memory: Remembering the Holocaust in the Age of Decolonization*, Stanford: Stanford University Press.
Rozporządzenie Ministra Edukacji Narodowej z dnia 14 lutego 2017 r. w sprawie podstawy programowej wychowania przedszkolnego oraz podstawy programowej kształcenia ogólnego dla szkoły podstawowej, w tym dla uczniów z niepełnosprawnością intelektualną w stopniu umiarkowanym lub znacznym, kształcenia ogólnego dla branżowej szkoły I stopnia, kształcenia ogólnego dla szkoły specjalnej przysposabiającej do pracy oraz kształcenia ogólnego dla szkoły policealnej (Dz. U. 2017 poz. 356 z późniejszymi zmianami).
Skowrońska, K. (2021), 'The Recent Politicization of Immigration in Poland in Light of Preexisting State Practices: Continuity or Change in the Understanding of Citizenship and Nationhood?', *Politics & Policy*, 49 (4): 940–67.
Sofsky, W. (2000), 'Cywilizacja, organizacja, przemoc', in H. Orłowski (ed.), *Nazizm, Trzecia Rzesza a procesy modernicacji*, 651, Poznań: Wydawnictwo Poznańskie.
Stanton, G. (1996), *The Eights Stages of Genocide*. Available online: http://www.genocide-watch.com/images/8StagesBriefingpaper.pdf (accessed 30 October 2021).
Stanton, G. (2020), 'Nie zapominajmy o ludobójstwach', *Respublica*, 19 May. Available online: https://publica.pl/teksty/stanton-nie-zapominajmy-o-ludobojstwach-67293.html (accessed 23 October 2021).
Szyszlak, T., ed. (2011), *Kwestia romska w polityce państw Europy Środkowej i Wschodniej*, Wrocław: Fundacja Integracji Społecznej Prom, Centrum Badań Partnerstwa Wschodniego.
Talewicz-Kwiatkowska, J. (2017), 'Temat zagłady Romów i Sinti w szkolnych programach edukacyjnych' (The Subject of Extermination of the Roma and Sinti in School Educational Programmes), in B. Machul-Telus, U. Markowska-Manista and L. M. Nijakowski (eds), *Krwawy cień genocydu. T. 2, Ludobójstwa - pamięć, dyskurs, edukacja*, 195–224, Warszawa: Instytut Wydawniczy Książka i Prasa.
Talewicz-Kwiatkowska, J. (2020), 'Es ist an der Zeit', in J. Ostrowska, J. Talewicz-Kwiatkowska and L. van Dijk (eds), *Errinern in Auschwitz auch and sexuelle Minderheiten, Querverlag*, 39–49, Berlin: Querverlag.
Trojański, P., ed (2008), *Auschwitz i Holokaust. Dylematy i wyzwania polskiej Edukacji*, Pruszcz Gdański: Wydawnictwo Jasne.
Trouillot, M. (1995), *Silencing the Past. Power and the Production of History*, Boston: Beacon Press.
United States Holocaust Memorial Museum, 'Introduction to the Holocaust'. Available online: https://encyclopedia.ushmm.org/content/en/article/introduction-to-the-holocaust (accessed 10 November 2021).
Ustawa z dnia 6 styczniu 2005 r. o mniejszościach narodowych i etnicznych oraz o języku regionalnym (Dz. U. 2005 Nr 17 poz. 141).
Winiewski, M., M. Witkowska and M. Bilewicz (2015), 'Uprzedzenia wobec Romów w Polsce', in A. Stefaniak, M. Bilewicz and M. Winiewski (eds), *Uprzedzenia w Polsce*, 65–88, Warszawa: Liberi Libri.
Winiewski, M., K. Hansen, M. Bilewicz, W. Soral, A. Świderska and D. Bulska (2017), *Mowa nienawiści. Mowa pogardy*, Warszawa: Fundacja Batorego.
Witkowska, M., A. Stefaniak and M. Bilewicz (2014), 'Stracone szanse? Wpływ polskiej edukacji o zagładzie na postawy wobec Żydów', *Psychologia Wychowawcza*, 5: 147–59.

Zakrzewska-Olędzka, D. (2018), 'Socialization Process in Mono- vs Multicultural Environments and Attitudes towards Otherness. An International Comparison Study in Poland and Israel', in U. Markowska-Manista (ed.), *Children and Youth in Varied Socio-Cultural Contexts. Theory, Research, Praxis*, 189–98, Warsaw: Maria Grzegorzewska University.

10

Polish-Jewish Rivalry for Memory

Lech M. Nijakowski

Introduction

We live in an era when it is necessary to account for crimes which were often left unmentioned in the past (Barkan 2000). Even if these crimes are not dealt with by the courts, the researchers' tribunal remains. In particular, the status of the victim has gained considerable importance. In earlier days, nations used to base their positive self-stereotype on victories and successes. Today, losses and tragedies are a strong fabric of collective identity. And there is no single watershed to be named. In Israel, for example, the turn took place relatively early, mainly as a result of Adolf Eichmann's trial (1961–2) and the Six-Day War (Haß 2004), although it was already possible to notice that Arabs were being portrayed as neo-Nazis.

Polish-Jewish relations cannot be viewed as an example of majority attitude to a national minority (at present the Republic of Poland recognizes thirteen national and ethnic minorities, and according to the 2011 National Population and Housing Census, there are only 7,000 Jews living in Poland, in total, irrespective of the number and order of declarations, NSP 2015: 31). The Jews are a special group the size of which is often overestimated. In the collective imagination it holds a distinguished position, and often falls victim to stereotype and prejudice. When writing about Polish-Jewish relations, what is actually diagnosed is the essence of Polish culture and social life (Tokarska-Bakir 2021).

To be sure the term 'Jew' is a certainly a construct and even a phantasm that has a long political history. It was and still is used by various politicians. In this discourse, the self-categorization of a given person or complex identity discourse are often overlooked. It is the speaker that claims the right to reveal the Jewish origin of the opponent. All this is done in a social milieu in which anti-Jewish hate speech cannot be unpunished. This is also due to improved attitudes of Poles towards Jews, as documented, for example, by the CBOS Public Opinion Research Center. However, what remains is the question whether this is an actual improvement or whether the respondents have just learnt that their negative attitude towards Jews should not be expressed in public.

The Jews in Poland, although they are a small national minority, occupy a pivotal place in the collective imagination. They are 'invisible others' who are constantly constructed in social practice as enemies. For most Poles, they are not unfamiliar members of an alien group, but mental constructs, an amalgam of stereotypes and prejudices.

In this chapter, I present selected topoi and discourse strategies, which document the special status of the Jews. More about the methodology in the next section. Contrary to what certain theorists claim, discourse studies are most often qualitative studies, which require interpretation by a committed author. The difficulties with providing a satisfactory description of the fate of Polish Jews translate into teaching, whereas it is virtually impossible for schools to discuss the dark pages of Polish history.

Basic Concepts, Theories and Methods

In this chapter, I treat the concept of nation as an imagined community as understood by Benedict Anderson (2006). Thus, it is defined as a political community, imagined as limited and sovereign. This, however, does not mean that people are completely free when they form a nation. In this process, they are restricted by the broadly understood cultural heritage, whose significance has been emphasized by Anthony D. Smith (1986), who in this context talks about 'ethnies'. In more general terms, we may speak of a specific 'path dependence' (North 1994). Far too often do dominant theories take the path of Western Europe, thus ignoring nation-forming processes in other parts of the world.

The nation is produced and reproduced in public discourse. Discourse mechanisms have steadily grown in significance in modern history. Today they are of paramount importance. Discourse is understood here as social action, which, by using symbolic systems (not just language), gives meaning to events, people, states of affairs, processes and so on in a given situation. Discourses are materialized in the form of specific texts, which are its manifestations, with texts understood not only as written words, but also as pictures, radio and television broadcasts, internet hyperlinks, graffiti, works of art and even dance sets. When we talk about discourse, we mean the existence of a certain symbolic order, structures and models that appear in specific acts of communication (van Dijk 1990; Wodak 2008; Fairclough 2003).

The nationalist discourse has certain universal characteristics, regardless of the country in which it was created. It emphasizes national homogeneity and homogeneity as such and omits intra-national differences. As a result, those who do not fit the positive auto-stereotype are excluded from the national community. Different national identities are discursively constructed according to the auditorium, subject, occasion, anniversary and the like; there is no single, universal discourse society. Effective reproduction of the nation requires maintaining, through various discourse strategies, the belief of the people that they are members of an entity that exists objectively and perennially (Wodak et al. 2003). One of the important elements is the imposition of a national literary language, which conceals regional differences (Bourdieu 1991: 43–65). The nation is discursively reproduced not only during official anniversary celebrations. Daily discourse practices, of which community members are often not fully aware, are far more important. Many such examples are provided by Michael Billig (1995)who writes about 'banal nationalism'.

Historically, such an attitude often led to discrimination against national and ethnic minorities. Today, too, the nationalist discourse affects the perception of minorities. This is also true of Poland (although it is not characteristic of Eastern Europe). In particular, one may talk about 'historical discrimination' which concerns the disputes over the interpretation of history (Nijakowski 2009). The attitude toward Jews is a clear example of this process.

This chapter is based on many years of research of the Polish public discourse. I feel a certain affinity with the tradition of critical discourse analysis (Wodak 2003). Here, I describe the different topoi and discourse strategies used by Poles when they talk about Jews. I learnt them by analysing very different texts created in Poland (messages from the main media, but also inscriptions on walls or memes). The Polish general education system and texts produced for its use (including textbooks) were the subjects of a separate study.

I use various public opinion polls, including the results of a research project, of which I was a member: The 'Second World War in the Memory of Modern Polish Society' carried out for the Museum of the Second World War by Pentor Research International in 2009 (Kwiatkowski et al. 2010). I use data sets that have not been published, so the sources are not cited below.

Big Change: The Second World War

There were hardly any signs of an imminent end of Polish-Jewish relations. Many Jews who were discriminated against in other countries settled in Poland. After the Jews were expelled from Spain (1492) and Portugal (1496), the exiles settled on Polish territory, where they were admitted and became part of the social structure. Anti-Semitism appeared in all the Christian countries, but on a lesser scale than in the German *Länder*, for example.

The Poles constitute a special nation against this background. For 123 years (1795–1918), at a time of emergence of modern nation states, they were deprived of sovereignty, living in three partitioning countries: Prussia (later Germany), Russia and Austria. The partitioning powers were perceived through the prism of the dominant religion. Tsarist Russia was an Orthodox empire, while Prussia and later Germany as Protestant states (although, as we know, the proportion of Catholics in the population was significant). Religious differences became the basis for building an interethnic border. Jews were often treated as an 'internal occupier'. Naturally, let us bear in mind that Jewish communities in the former partitioning countries differed substantially. Most of the Jews in the Reich and later in the Weimar Republic supported the assimilation processes, despite the ongoing 'Jewish Renaissance' during the interwar period (Steffen 2015: 687).

The years of the partitions and the limited sovereignty of the People's Republic of Poland rooted Catholicism firmly in Poland and politicized it heavily. Although numerous exceptions can be found, the institutions of the Catholic Church were the basis for patriotic and opposition activity. The price was a much shallower religious experience combined with ritualism. At the same time, Christian symbolism became a universally understandable code used to mobilize people for very different purposes, both good and bad.

The Second World War led to the German genocide of the Jews. But it also destroyed the Jewish community in Poland and led to memory conflicts, which are still painful, as can be gleaned from the international relations between Poland and Israel. The contentious topics include the Poles' participation in the genocide of the Jews, a point of extreme controversy in Poland, where the Polish citizens regard themselves as unquestionable victims of the war.

It should be borne in mind that the Second World War is still a key reference point for Poles, despite the time that has passed and the decreasing number of those who survived the war. The vast majority of adult Poles (82 per cent) believe that it still is a part of the history of Poland that is very much alive, and people need to be constantly reminded of it (CBOS 2019). It is therefore not only a matter of cultural memory, but also, to a large extent, communicative memory (Assmann 1995), which is not only the work of professionals (e.g. museums), but also of occasional talk in families. Unaware of this fact, one cannot understand the Poles and their references to the past.

Certainly Poles did suffer under German occupation. They were killed in round-ups and massacres; detained and murdered in concentration camps; and tortured in detention centres and prisons. However, today historians highlight their involvement in anti-Jewish operations. No wonder that historians associated with this school of thought are hated by so many Poles who believe that they are insulting their homeland unjustifiably.

Most Jews were killed on Polish territory, a fact that calls for explanation, even if one dismisses the involvement of the Poles in the Shoah. After all, the ease of killing was related to the attitudes of the population who lived near the ghettos or camps, even if it was itself doomed to be deported and exterminated. Over the years, there was merely talk of inadequate assistance offered to the Jews, at best. Today, the decisions of the Poles that led to the death of Jews are being discussed openly.

Let us add that we are still using collectivist language here, although the attitudes and actions of Poles varied greatly. However, we apply the category of nation and assume (even if not explicitly) collective merit and blame. After all, we are discussing heroic acts and crimes of people who often are no longer alive. However, we tend to speak of collective pride and shame, which is obviously a result of the success of the nationalist discourse, although it has negligible factual justification (Nijakowski 2020).

The Poles and Jews suffered during the war. Today, we are facing competition for memory as to who were more victimized. In part, this is due to religious codes, although Catholicism and Judaism differ greatly in the justification of victimhood. However, both religions do practice theodicy, which is also used in discussions about war crimes.

In my opinion, Poles do not want to recognize that it was the Jews, not the Poles, who were the primary victims of the war (cf. CBOS 2015). To be sure, creating a hierarchy of victims may seem pointless, but it is a common practice of nation states that portray their citizens (including those fallen and the dead) as 'more significant' victims than foreign ones. When asked directly, Europeans will deny having such opinions, but they clearly support such a vision and interpretation of history in everyday life.

According to the Pentor poll (2009),[1] the suffering of both nations was mentioned by a decisive majority of respondents as very great or great (93.4 per cent – Poles; 92.2 per cent – Jews). This result can be construed as recognition of the martyrdom of the Jews, but it seems more appropriate to stress that the Poles suffered equally as the Jews who in the international public discourse figure as the main victims of the war and genocide.

In Poland, the discussions concerning the involvement of the Poles in the genocide of the Jews arouse extreme emotions. After all, there was no collaborationist Polish government or a Polish Waffen-SS. This does not mean, however, that none of the Poles committed a crime. The Polish guilt can be divided into several categories. The Poles participated in the pogroms that took place in June and July 1941 in the early days of the war between the Third Reich and the USSR. The most atrocious massacres took place on 7 July in Radziłów and on 10 July in Jedwabne. In two weeks, massacres and pogroms erupted in several dozen locations in Łomża and Białystok regions, with several thousand victims (Libionka 2017: 72). Already there is extensive scientific literature on the subject, to mention only the two-volume study *Wokół Jedwabnego*, edited by Pawel Machcewicz and Krzysztof Persak (2002).

The second category includes reprehensible and criminal acts, which directly involved German deportations and massacres. Polish policemen were used to secure the scene. Of all the local police formations in occupied Eastern Europe (local police functionaries supporting the Order Police were referred to as the *Schutzmannschaften*), the Polish formations were the least involved in the extermination of the Jews. This was partly due to prejudices held by Hitler and other Nazis against the Poles, and there was some reluctance to arm them (Hilberg 2007: 92). The role of the Blue Police was not limited to cordoning off the ghettos. They would accompany the Germans' march into Jewish districts, help search for hiding Jews and even carry out executions (Engelking and Grabowski 2018: 25–6). Let us add that other formations were also deployed, such as units of the Voluntary Fire Department and the garrisoned Construction Service (*Baudienst*).

Polish civilians were also involved in the hunting down escaping and hiding Jews. Such facts cannot be fobbed off by mere reference to German inspiration and supervision. Similarly, the fate of some of the refugees from concentration and extermination camps leaves a blemish on the rather hagiographical narrative of Poles who saved Jews. After the rebellion in the Treblinka death camp, Jews became, as the local Home Army structures reported, 'the object of "hunts" by various rural or urban scum' (quoted after Libionka 2017: 219).

Finally, the third category includes 'hunts for the Jews' not directly linked to specific German operations. They are referred to as the 'Judenjagd', a term introduced by Christopher R. Browning, an American historian who borrowed it from testimonies of policemen, SS-men and gendarmes (Grabowski 2011: 9). It was a continuous search for hiding Jews. As Jan Grabowski pointed out (and this claim is rather controversial): 'If we assume that about a tenth of Polish Jews tried to save themselves from extermination by fleeing, it appears that the number of victims of hunting Jews in the years 1942–1945 could amount to two hundred to two hundred and fifty thousand' (Grabowski 2011: 10–11). These issues have already been addressed in a large number of books, especially from the Polish Center for Holocaust Research of the Institute of Philosophy and Sociology of the Polish Academy of Sciences.

Also Poles who saved Jews left certificates, which show that they were not only afraid of the Germans but also of the Polish neighbours (Leociak 2010). Other Poles resisted not only due to their reluctance to Jews, but also due to fear. They were afraid that when the Germans discover hiding Jews, they would apply collective responsibility to the whole village or tenement house. To what extent were those fears reasonable is indeed a minor issue. Of course, the blackmailers (*szmalcownicy*) are often treated in stories about the past as traitors who were no longer Poles (so they do not burden the war-time record of the Polish nation).

'Sleepwalking the Revolution' after the Second World War

After the war-time extermination, what happened were pogroms of returning Jews, strong anti-Semitism and above all seizures of property of Polish Jews and taking the advantage of their absence in the market, where they had previously occupied a number of important economic niches. Different citizens of Poland behaved differently, and some made considerable sacrifice to helping Jewish survivors.

Andrzej Leder (2013) in this context wrote a book on 'the established revolution'. Poles did not work on the mass death of Jews, which created different economic and social opportunities for them. The Poles profited from the extermination of the Jews, but the revolution was actually achieved by others. For very many people, the passage into modernity took place over Jewish corpses, so to speak (Leder 2013: 92). Their unconscious and suppressed sense of guilt is still a burden.

Objections can be raised to this claim, especially if one does not share the theoretical inspiration. However, it is evident that ethnic Poles benefited economically and socially from the death of their Jewish fellow citizens, about whom they had held prejudice for years. Many Poles settled in former Jewish homes, they took up jobs that had been largely monopolized by their Jewish fellow citizens, and took advantage of property, which many of them stole during the war and occupation.

There is no doubt that Poles are very sensitive at the point of discussion about returning Jewish assets to owners, which is being used scrupulously by politicians. The absence of Jews is therefore quite seminal. More than seventy-five years after the war, it still affects the life and business plans of Poles. It may be added that politicians in other countries also benefit from this situation by playing the role of spokespersons for Jews who were former citizens of the Republic of Poland.

It is instructive that the Jews are presented in this discourse as foreigners, although they were Polish citizens. This is a very frequent discourse strategy. Exclusion is consonant with the narrative that is in Poland, making an ethnic Pole-Catholic a figure of normality. No wonder that so many researchers are terrified by the return of the anti-Semitic language of Polish Communists who used it to mobilize support in 1968 (cf. Bilewicz 2016).

The discussion concerning restitution of property is therefore not just an economic issue. It is clear that the notion of strangeness or the rights of ethnic Poles recurs in this narrative. It is also instructive that many contemporary Poles do not think that post-war actions which led to their ancestors having a better life should be condemned (deportation of Germans, deportations and dispersal of the Lemkos and Ukrainians, etc.).

Anti-Jewish Discourse Strategies in Contemporary Poland

Jews, directly and indirectly, are referred to in Poland quite frequently, but are not presented in a very favourable light. Many topics have been politicized and are used by politicians. A good example is the objection to the term 'Polish concentration camps' in the Western media.

Following the opening of the Polin Museum of the History of Polish Jews in Warsaw, an initiative was launched to place a memorial nearby to commemorate Poles who rescued Jews during the occupation. Many members of the Jewish minority regarded this as an attempt to weaken the symbolic power of the museum itself. There are waves of successive discussions, which repeat the main discourse strategies that are also connected to anniversary celebrations or political events.

The pogroms of Jews during the war have long been taboo, even more than the inter-war pogroms. The blank spot was filled only by Jan T. Gross's *Neighbours* on the massacre, with the help of the Germans, by the people of Jedwabne of their Jewish neighbours (Gross 2001), which was a real shock for Polish society and for the memory of the Second World War. The airing of Agnieszka Arnold's documentary *Neighbours* on Polish public television (TVP) was also important. What ensued was an emotional and stormy debate around the facts revealed. However, by polarizing Polish society, it led to the dissemination of information about the massacre. According to a CBOS study (2001a), 83 per cent of the respondents were aware of crimes (17 per cent – no). Further polls conducted by the CBOS (2001b) showed an increase in the number of people informed to 90 per cent. Extensive information is also confirmed by polls taken by Pentor in 2009. They were not made until after the public debate had died down. To ask if the respondent had heard of a massacre committed in 1941 in Jedwabne, 70.7 per cent replied yes. Let us note, however, that as many as 40.9 per cent of those surveyed aged under twenty-nine had not heard of this massacre.

Pentor's (2009) respondents had no problem correctly defining the categories of victims of the Jedwabne massacre: 55.9 per cent of those who had heard of the crime designated Jews from Jedwabne and the surrounding area, and 27.1 per cent noted 'Jews, Polish Jews, Jewish families', while 19.1 per cent mentioned Poles and Jews; 4.4 per cent of the respondents failed to answer. However, the answer to the question about the perpetrators of the Jedwabne pogrom was crucial. The responses can be grouped as follows:

1. *Indications of German guilt, even if the occupiers used Polish traitors.* According to a third of those who had heard of the massacre (36.6 per cent), the perpetrators were 'Germans, German occupiers, fascists, Nazis, Nazis'; 14.6 per cent mentioned 'Germans, German occupiers with the participation of Polish collaborators, the Polish police, the *Volksdeutsche* (ethnic Germans)'. To this we should add the answers: 'Germans, German occupiers with the participation of Poles' – 5.7 per cent.
2. *Indications of Polish guilt, even if dictated by the unique context of the occupation.* A total of 18 per cent mentioned 'Poles under the supervision, pressure, coaxing, with the participation of Germans, German occupiers'. The percentage of conscious respondents is increased by those who said 'perhaps Poles' (8.1 per cent) and 'Poles categorically' (6.5 per cent). 3. There were also responses that reveal *total ignorance of the respondents*. 'Russians, Soviets' answered 9.6 per cent of the respondents; Ukrainians –1.7 per cent; 'Jewish communists' – 0.4 per cent; 'Jews and Poles' – 0.1 per cent. One in ten respondents (10.1 per cent) who had heard the Jedwabne massacre answered 'I don't know'.

Thus, the majority of the Poles who had heard of the massacre absolved the Poles; the murderers were the Germans themselves or committed these acts with the help of Polish collaborators. Clearly, emphasis is laid most often on German guilt and on the secondary nature of Polish guilt. Most of the debaters took the massacre for a fact, but they transferred the responsibility onto the Germans and their collaborators.

What one could regard as a kind of defence strategy, without necessarily being fully conscious of it, is the declared sense of pride of the people who are symbols of Polish aid to Jews. In general, when posed the question of whether during the Second World War were there some in the Polish society of whom the Poles can be proud of today, as many as 70.4 per cent of the Pentor respondents answered in the affirmative. Among the figures in the high fourth place was Irena Sendlerowa, a distinguished rescuer of Jews (5.4 per cent) – ranked after Władysław Sikorski, the Supreme Commander of the Polish Armed Forces and the Prime Minister of the Polish Government in Exile during Second World War (22.4 per cent); Władysław Anders, Commander of the Polish Army in the USSR (15.3 per cent); and Maksymilian Kolbe, a well-known Polish Franciscan monk was murdered in the Auschwitz camp (6.8 per cent). Let us add that Father Kolbe is commonly regarded as a model of sacrifice for others and his pre-war anti-Semitic publications are forgotten. Janusz Korczak was indicated by 2.5 per cent. Other significant Polish-Jewish figures (e.g. Jan Karski) received minimal indications. Another question about which chosen character are the Poles proud of received the following responses: 5.7 per cent indicated helping Jews (seventh place), more than 'the leadership of the nation, Poles, Poland, the state' (4.5 per cent) and 'the formation of the army' (4.2 per cent).

Moreover, when we asked the respondents explicitly whether Poles helped the Jews survive the war, as many as 81.5 per cent of Pentor's respondents (2009) answered, without doubt yes, 'rather often' and 'very often'. Also, they are positive that Poles did not denounce Jews to the occupier: 'very rarely' and 'rather seldom' were the responses of 75.8 per cent of those surveyed. Furthermore, according to the respondents, the

Poles were not indifferent to the extermination of Jews ('very rarely' or 'rarely' 74.9 per cent). In general, the respondents therefore believe that the attitude and actions of the Polish society towards Jews were without blemish, although not exemplary.

However, the question whether, during the Second World War, there were members of the Polish society that brought shame to the good name of Poles, only 27.2 per cent of the respondents said yes. When it came to identifying those who had behaved shamefully, only 1.3 per cent of those surveyed mentioned 'thieves, looters, false partisans, blackmailers (*szmalcownicy*)'. Only 0.4 per cent identified directly those who 'denounced or persecuted Jews'. As regards the question why these characters behaved shamefully, only 0.3 per cent of the respondents answered: 'chauvinism, anti-Semitism, national megalomania, contempt for other nations, discrimination against minorities'.

Jews are a key reference category for the Polish national identity. Although they have been a small national minority in Poland for a long time, they occupy the central place in the national *imaginarium*. The Jew can be described as an Alien Constitutive, with which the Pole is constantly compared and competes against in the hierarchy of victims of the Second World War. There is one particularly powerful symbol of this phenomenon, namely the appropriation by Poles of such a unique place of memory as the former Auschwitz-Birkenau camp. This process began immediately after the liberation of the camp (Wóycicka 2009: 105–72), and reappeared with doubled strength after 1989 (Kucia 2005: 52–8). A universal topos in the Polish public discourse concerns very different categories of aliens. Therefore, in the public sphere, aliens are easily 'Judaicized', for example in the discourse of sports fans, politicians or religious fundamentalists.

How to Teach about Jewish Suffering?

Education about the genocide of the Jews during the Second World War brought many professional articles and academic books, textbooks, lesson scenarios and other materials to light. In Poland, there is also a strong milieu of Holocaust educators and teaching experts in schools and places of memory, which also examines opportunities and risks related to teaching about the Holocaust. Nevertheless, raising fundamental issues still raises doubt, for example whether or not children should be taught about the cruelty of the Second World War at all.

In particular, compulsory school education of children about the atrocities associated with genocide is a common concern. This applies not only to the Shoah but also to other chapters of history. It is obviously the responsibility of the teacher to adapt the message according to the age of the students (I actually focus on children of fifteen and over; younger students require the special educational principles and techniques). It is impossible to hide from children the fact that, largely, history comes down to a river of innocent blood.

If one wants to mitigate the effect of teaching about past massacres, there are certain traps that one could fall into. An example is the teaching about wars. Wars are too easily turned into a heroic story about heroes, textbooks feature attractive colour maps with arrows, while dirt, suffering and crimes disappear from the narration.

Showing cruelty for effect is also a poor method. It is not a matter of parables, in which evil always loses, but of narration with ethical dilemmas and a moral conclusion. One example could be teaching about the punishment of criminals. The judicial penalty as an act of justice is an important punchline of historical narration, in which many dictators, in their sphere of influence, could kill civilians with impunity.

A particular challenge are student visits to former concentration and extermination camps. There is abundant literature on the subject (cf. Białecka et al. 2013). It may be a difficult experience for some pupils, especially as some parents and grandparents in Poland still refuse to visit these places. It is no wonder that children often defend themselves resorting to rather primitive jokes. A ill-prepared and poorly conducted visit to a former camp as part of a school programme can do more harm than good. At the same time, it can be a very good complement to systematic teaching about genocide, be it only because the museums in the former camps offer a very extensive range of advanced educational techniques and provide teaching materials. However, in my opinion, this is not a necessary part of the education about the Shoah, because the mass scale of visits to memorial places might lead to groups of children and young people to be served by incompetent guides and educators.

In the past, an important part of school education was a meeting with an eye-witness, including a concentration camp survivor. For reasons of demography, this is becoming increasingly difficult. Therefore, the educators should use recordings, such as from the archives of oral history (best known in Poland: History Meeting House).

And here we reach the contentious issue. In my opinion, the historical comparative genocide studies are not only a basic method of research in the social sciences, but also an important element of teaching about the genocide of the Jews. Shoah was a total genocide, in which there were many exceptional social phenomena. But it was neither the first (Armenians in the Ottoman Empire, mainly in the years 1915–16) nor the last (Tutsi in Rwanda in 1994) totalitarian genocide. The murder of the Tutsi with machetes in Rwanda was just as modern as the killing of Jews (due to the social processes that led to the crime). The comparison enables us to show similarities and differences in the teaching. This also enables one to take a prepared look at the present day. The different processes that occurred in many a genocide (e.g. hate speech) will therefore be seen in a different light and will provide education on the protection of human and citizen's rights.

Historians sometimes make very limited use (if at all) of social science theories. They explain the past, knowing the effects of all processes. In other social sciences, models are being built, which are not only meant to explain past genocidal mobilization, but also enable us to estimate the risk of repetition in different regions of the world. This is obviously a very difficult task. In education, however, it is not only more interesting than monograph studies, but it is also possible to present different social science theories. For example, Peter Glick's *Ideological Model of Scapegoating*, which shows how easily it is in different countries to make certain people victims of collective violence.

Meetings of young people are hardly a panacea, as they trigger psychological processes which could lead, for example, to the creation of a subcategory of an alien group. Not only during meetings are young people confronted with the fact that other societies may have a different vision of the past, but also with accusations against their own people. Comparative studies teach acceptance of many perspectives, including that of an alien group. Similar situations can occur during internet interactions, where very different topics are raised.

Although abstract rules are important, education, especially in primary and secondary schools, requires that they be concretized by the students, and that empathy is aroused and open attitudes are developed. This objective must prevail over the teaching about genocide. To be sure, this task could easily be reduced to absurdity ('imagine you are in a gas chamber'), as it requires a lot of competence from the teacher, but it cannot be abandoned.

To see a human being in the victims of large historical processes is not easy at all. It is therefore advisable to present biographies of people similar to us. The victims were not a homogenous group, but were divided into categories with sometimes very different fate. It is worth showing this in the education process. In particular, the fate of children can be a valuable material in the teaching of young people. In this case, it is naturally impossible to say everything. The children were the victims of the most elaborate atrocities, for example, in the Ottoman Empire they were burned alive and raped (Dadirian 2003: 424). However, less drastic cases will enable students to empathize with the fate of their peers. It also offers an opportunity to show how the lifestyles and attitudes of people change, so that children will be immunized to historical anachronism. In this context, it is advisable to speak not only about the victims, but also about the perpetrators, such as children-soldiers, who have been surprisingly susceptible to propaganda (cf. Markowska-Manista 2019).

Works of fiction and memories of survivors could be useful in teaching about genocide. Naturally, students need to be made aware of the different status of these sources. This is also a good opportunity to explain the specificity of social research, when the observer is part of the object examined, and publicly available conclusions can change the object (society) itself. Feature films may be even more attractive. Some of them are extremely valuable teaching material as works of high art. There is no need to limit oneself to traditional media. Comics might be a good example. The works on the Shoah have become widely commented artistic events (e.g. *Maus*) as well as outstanding graphic novels.

The internet and the social media also play an increasingly important role in genocidal mobilization. They support both the perpetrators and defenders of human rights. Students can not only search the wealth of internet resources, but also engage in minority rights defence action, which have been subjected to state violence. Then, for example, the fate of the Papuans in West Papua will be seen in the historical perspective, identifying signals of the progressive radicalization process.

Conclusion

The Second World War was a breakthrough. Not only because it led to the disappearance of the Polish Jewish Community (as a result of genocide and subsequent emigration), but also because of the fact that events of the war are being discussed today in an interpretative dispute. Not only are the national countries of Poles and Jews, Poland and Israel, but also many other communities, involved in the dispute over the involvement of Poles in the Shoah or the appropriation of property that the Jews were forced to leave behind.

The history of Poland and Poles was analysed in many dimensions. In this chapter, I was unable to address all the issues that still arouse emotions among the commentators. It is important that history returns in Polish-Jewish debates as a key reference point. It is mainly the Second World War, but not only that.

In Poland, the memory of the General Government dominates. The fate of the communities that were incorporated into the Third Reich (e.g. Silesia and Kashubia) is still a matter of controversy. In particular, the signing the German National List (*Deutsche Volksliste*) is deemed the chief proof of betrayal, although it was the inhabitants of Silesia who were encouraged both by the authorities of the Polish Underground State or by the Catholic Church. Jews, who are reproduced in the discourse as a homogenous category, are all the more incomprehensible, although they were a very diverse community in terms of class or territory.

In this chapter, I have presented some of the topoi and discourse strategies. However, the main conclusion is that Jews, a national minority of whom few members still live in the Republic of Poland, still arouse emotions in the Polish majority, and it is easy to mobilize people to act by talking about Jewish conspiracies. The Jewish phantasm is still strong in Poland. Although they are practically non-existent, they do remain a key figure in the collective imagination. Jews are the most important 'Invisible Others' in Poland.

Although official declarations mention Polish schools teaching about reprehensible deeds of the Poles, the dominant narration is supposed to blindly strengthen the pride of belonging to the Polish people. The teachers, even if they wish to and are prepared to teach about the genocide of Jews, are restricted by the educational officers, the principals or the curriculum. In these circumstances, it should be borne in mind that many demands for education cannot be satisfied.

Although it might be shocking to an outside observer, I believe that we are dealing with a Polish-Jewish competition for the status of the chief victim of the Second World War. This is connected with the popularity of religious vision and cultural codes (e.g. the post-Romantic discourse in Poland, as Maria Janion wrote). As a result, many issues arouse powerful emotions in Poland, and the national minority, which is almost inexistent, still governs the collective imagination.

Note

1. The results of the collaborative research project 'World War II as remembered by the contemporary Polish society' by Pentor Research International consisted of twelve focus discussion groups in five cities (Warsaw, Katowice, Białystok, Przemyśl and Gdańsk), as well as of quantitative survey (19 June–4 July 2009, sample: 1,200 adult Poles, aged eighteen and over). I was involved in this project, which enabled me to observe selected group discussions.

References

Anderson, B. (2006), *Imagined Communities. Reflections on the Origin and Spread of Nationalism*, London: Verso.
Assmann, J. (1995), 'Collective Memory and Cultural Identity', *New German Critique*, 65: 125–33.
Barkan, E. (2000), *The Guilt of Nation. Restitution and Negotiating Historical Injustices*, New York: W. W. Norton.
Białecka, A., K. Oleksy, F. Regard and P. Trojański, eds (2013), *Przygotowanie do wizyty w Muzeum i Miejscu Pamięci Auschwitz-Birkenau. Pakiet europejski – wskazówki dla nauczycieli i edukatorów*, Oświęcim: Państwowe Muzeum Auschwitz-Birkenau.
Bilewicz, M. (2016), '(Nie)pamięć zbiorowa Polaków jako skuteczna regulacja emocji', *Teksty Drugie*, 6: 52–67.
Billig, M. (1995), *Banal Nationalism*, London: Sage.
Bourdieu, P. (1991), *Language and Symbolic Power*, Cambridge: Harvard University Press.
CBOS (2001a), 'Polacy wobec zbrodni w Jedwabnem', survey report no. BS/54/2001, 6–9 April.
CBOS (2001b), 'Polacy wobec zbrodni w Jedwabnem – przemiany społecznej świadomości', survey report no. BS/120/2001, 3–6 August.
CBOS (2015), 'Postrzeganie Żydów i stosunków polsko-żydowskich', survey report no. 112/2015, 1–8 July.
CBOS (2019), 'Postrzeganie II wojny światowej i poparcie dla domagania się reparacji od Niemiec', survey report no. 113/2019, 22–29 August.
Dadrian, V. N. (2003), 'Children as Victims of Genocide. The Armenian Case', *Journal of Genocide Research*, 3 (5), 421–37.
Engelking, B., and J. Grabowski, eds (2018), *Dalej jest noc. Losy Żydów w wybranych powiatach okupowanej Polski*, vol. 1. Warszawa: Stowarzyszenie Centrum Badań nad Zagładą Żydów.
Fairclough, N. (2003), *Analysing Discourse. Textual Analysis for Social Research*, New York: Routledge.
Grabowski, J. (2011), *Judenjagd. Polowanie na Żydów 1942–1945. Studium dziejów pewnego powiatu*, Warszawa: Stowarzyszenie Centrum Badań nad Zagładą Żydów.
Gross, J. T. (2001), *Neighbors. The Destruction of the Jewish Community in Jedwabne, Poland*, Princeton: Princeton University Press.
Haß, M. (2004), 'The Politics of Memory in Germany, Israel and the United States of America'. The Canadian Centre for German and European Studies, Working Paper Series, 9.
Hilberg, R. (2007), *Perpetrators Victims Bystanders. The Jewish Catastrophe, 1933–1945*, New York: Harper Perennial.
Kucia, M. (2005), *Auschwitz jako fakt społeczny. Historia, współczesność i świadomość społeczna KL Auschwitz w Polsce*, Kraków: Universitas.
Kwiatkowski, P. T., L. M. Nijakowski, B. Szacka and A. Szpociński (2010), *Między codziennością a wielką historią. Druga wojna światowa w pamięci zbiorowej społeczeństwa polskiego*, Warszawa-Gdańsk: Wydawnictwo Naukowe Scholar, Muzeum II Wojny Światowej.
Leder, A. (2013), *Prześniona rewolucja. Ćwiczenie z logiki historycznej*, Warszawa: Wydawnictwo Krytyki Politycznej.

Leociak, J. (2010), *Ratowanie. Opowieści Polaków i Żydów*, Kraków: Wydawnictwo Literackie.

Libionka, D. (2017), *Zagłada Żydów w Generalnym Gubernatorstwie. Zarys problematyki*, Lublin: Państwowe Muzeum na Majdanku.

Machcewicz, P., and K. Persak, eds (2002), *Wokół Jedwabnego*. vol. 1: *Studia*, vol. 2: *Dokumenty*, Warszawa: Instytut Pamięci Narodowej.

Markowska-Manista, U. (2019), ' "Bad children". International Stigmatisation of Children Trained to Kill during War and Armed Conflict', in N. von Benzon and C. Wilkinson (eds), *Intersectionality and Difference in Childhood and Youth*, 61–75, London: Routledge.

Nijakowski, L. M. (2009), 'Discrimination against Minorities in Poland on the Basis of History. The Case of the Memory Collective "Grandfather in the Wehrmacht"', *International Journal of Sociology*, 39 (3): 38–57.

Nijakowski, L. M. (2020), 'Collectivist Logic in Comparative Genocide Studies and in the Battles for Memory', *Narracje o Zagładzie*, 6: 39–60.

North, D. C. (1994), 'Economic Performance Through Time', *American Economic Review*, 84 (3): 359–68.

NSP 2011 (2015), *Struktura narodowo-etniczna, językowa i wyznaniowa ludności Polski. Narodowy Spis Powszechny Ludności i Mieszkań 2011*, Warszawa: Główny Urząd Statystyczny.

Smith, A. D. (1986), *Ethnic Origins of Nations*, Oxford: Blackwell.

Steffen, K. (2015), 'Żydzi. Obrazy zbiorowości wyobrażonej', in R. Traba and H. H. Hahn (eds), *Polsko-niemieckie miejsca pamięci*. vol. 1. *Wspólne/Oddzielne*, 683–717, Warszawa: Wydawnictwo Naukowe Scholar.

Tokarska-Bakir, J. (2021), *Bracia miesiące. Studia z antropologii historycznej Polski 1939–1945*, Warszawa: Instytut Badań Literackich PAN.

van Dijk, T. A. (1990), 'The Future of the Field: Discourse Analysis in the 1990s', *Text – Interdisciplinary Journal for the Study of Discourse*, 10 (1–2): 133–56.

Wodak, R. (2008), 'Introduction: Discourse Studies – Important Concepts and Terms', in R. Wodak and M. Krzyżanowski (eds), *Qualitative Discourse Analysis in the Social Sciences*, 1–29, Basingstoke: Palgrave Macmillan.

Wodak, R., R. de Cillia, M. Reisigl and K. Liebhart (2003), *The Discursive Construction of National Identity*, Edinburgh: Edinburgh University Press.

Wóycicka, Z. (2009), *Przerwana żałoba. Polskie spory wokół pamięci nazistowskich obozów koncentracyjnych i zagłady 1944–1950*, Warszawa: Wydawnictwo Trio.

11

Teaching Queer Post-Soviet Perspectives: Intersectional Pedagogy and Global Knowledge Inequalities

Masha Beketova

Introduction

The discursive field of post-Soviet queerness/*kvirnost*[1] (self-identifications of people with marginalized genders and sexualities in the post-Soviet region and corresponding '*kvir*'/'queer' politics, activisms, arts and resistance genealogies) differs from the Western European and US-American queer discourses, as different challenges, sets of gender norms, societal conditions and even linguistic predispositions, such as binary structures of languages are given. Adi Kuntsman argued in 2010 that the conceptual paradigm of '*kvir*' was already inherent in post-Soviet spaces as '*inakovost*'[2] since a long time (Кунцман 2010). Emphasizing that Western 'queer theory should not be treated as a dogma with its classics and stable genealogy', Kuntsman suggested to perceive queer studies 'rather as a discursive field', where coalitions and dialogues between different voices were central (Кунцман 2010). In addition, Kuntsman highlighted that struggles of post-Soviet *kvirs* often resembled more those of queers of colour than those of *white* Western LGBT subjects (Кунцман 2010). Mohira Suyarkulova has argued that 'kvir is not merely a loan translation, but a term utilized self-consciously and strategically in post-Soviet space as a radical alternative to both mainstream LGBT identity politics and the general conservative turn in society' (Suyarkulova 2019). Katharina Wiedlack and Maria Neufeld described the construction of Russian LGBTIQ subjects as '*lynchpin for value negotiation*' (Neufeld and Wiedlack 2016), identifying the crucial role queer bodies play in the discursive negotiation between the West and Russia. In the light of such understandings *queer/kvir post-Soviet perspectives* seem especially fruitful not as 'local informants' on whom Western[3] queer theory is applied, but as independent knowledge producing actors in the global debates on queerness.

In this chapter, I analyse different implications of biographical and disciplinary positionality for knowledge production, and especially teaching on post-Soviet queerness in Western contexts. Building on the empirical experience such as conceptualizing syllabus, and teaching a seminar for undergraduate students, I will combine the notion of *situated knowledge* (Haraway 1988), *locality* (Tlostanova 2015) and *location* (Mignolo and Tlostanova 2006) with the question of how to study post-Soviet *kvir* narratives in an ethical and self-reflective way. The chapter will raise questions of Western knowledge hegemonies, theory transfer and inequalities in the classroom.

In the opening section, I will give a theoretical frame of post-Soviet queerness as a relevant part of gender studies and decolonial project. Next, I situate queer post-Soviet partial perspectives for the gender research and discuss them as 'invisible 'others'' in it. In the third section, I am going to address the questions of representativity and lack of post-Soviet perspectives in German gender studies on the example of Humboldt University of Berlin, while describing my own path of becoming a teacher. Following that, I offer an insight into the syllabus of the seminar 'Queer post-Soviet perspectives' that I designed as well as introduce central goals of the seminar and readings. After this, I analyse the relevance of positionality while speaking about 'invisible "others"' based on three empirical examples from the seminar. In the closing section, I will delineate the challenges I encountered while teaching about the 'invisible queer post-Soviet "others"' in Berlin, and conclude with a general suggestion for dealing with differences and power relations in the classroom, which might be transferrable to other contexts.

Theoretical Frame: Relevance of Locality and Partial Post-Soviet Queer Perspective

Kulpa and Silva have highlighted the dominance of 'Anglophone hegemony' also in 'the project of "decoloniality" and "critical pedagogy"' (Kulpa and Silva 2016: 140). Kulpa's concept of 'leveraged pedagogy' describes the 'hegemonic didactical relation' between the West/European "pedagogy", and Central and Eastern Europe. The latter is functioning in this inequality 'as permanently "post-communist", "in transition"' (Kulpa 2014: 431). Mohira Suyarkulova emphasized the multiplicity of queer stories, and highlighted that use of the term "queer" is not identical in different contexts. 'Each utterance and translation of "queer" hides a particular story of political and ideological resistance and struggle' (Suyarkulova 2019: 52).

The premise of *situated knowledge* has been impacting gender research worldwide since 1988, starting when Donna Haraway's impactful contribution on the relation of objectivity and particularity of knowledge production has been published. This idea remains central to feminist thought. Haraway wrote that 'only partial perspective promises objective vision' (Haraway 1988: 282). Building on this premise, I argue that post-Soviet queer/*kvir* perspectives are valid and important contribution to such objective vision and analysis of genders and sexualities worldwide. The idea of multiplicity of localized objectivities as well as the concept of margins of discourses offering the most innovative insights was also inherent to Black feminist thought such as the Combahee River Collective, Audre Lorde, bell hooks and to Chicana feminists such as Gloria Anzaldúa, Cherríe Moraga and decolonial thinker Maria Lugones. Madina Tlostanova's extension of decolonial thought on post-Soviet contexts, in particular, is a relevant departure point for the theorization of post-Soviet queerness. Tlostanova theorizes post-Soviet positionality as specific 'post-Soviet human condition' (Tlostanova 2018) and emphasizes the relevance of *locality* within geopolitics and biopolitics of knowledge. For Tlostanova, locality means 'an epistemic correlation with the sensing body, perceiving the world from a particular local history' (Mignolo and Tlostanova 2006, cited after Tlostanova 2015: 43).

A special case within the post-socialist decolonial project can be the critical analysis of *post-Soviet marginalized sexualities and genders*, as they challenge the dichotomy of Global North and Global South, and display the specific entanglement of both non-Western colonial *and* decolonial queerness and thus allow to trace how 'the global coloniality of knowledge'[4] perpetuates different contexts (Tlostanova 2018). Given the urgent need to question the 'Anglophone hegemony' (Kulpa and Silva 2016) of queer studies, and the importance of 'multiplicity of queer stories of resistance and struggle' (Suyarkulova 2019), studying and teaching post-Soviet '*queerness/kvirnost*' as a particular perspective can contribute to the objective knowledge production in the global gender studies. Reflection on a specific non-Western queer knowledge production such as post-Soviet can contribute to the understanding of 'intersectional pedagogy' (Case 2017) or what Diba Tuncer calls 'pedagogy of integrity' (Tuncer 2019).

Situating Queer Post-Soviet Partial Perspectives for the Gender Research

Queer/*kvir* post-Soviet subjects can be perceived as 'invisible "others"' of the Western gender studies. Despite a growing body of critical research, LGBTIQ groups, subjects and movements from the post-Soviet countries often remain undocumented, and without any acquired attention in the global debates on gender and sexualities. Discursive constructions of post-Soviet queers in Western media coverage as 'gay martyrs', focusing on *white*, able-bodied cis-male subjects while making invisible all other positionalities. were aptly captured by Wiedlack (2017). Major media and some academical research tend to simplifying juxtapositions of the 'tolerant' West and 'conservative' East while discussing post-Soviet queerness.

The entry point of the seminar was an idea of a perpetuated East/West power relation, which goes far beyond the 'never ending processes of post-soviet/postsocialist transition' (Wiedlack et al. 2020), and its implications for the knowledge production about post-Soviet queer (non cis-heteronormative) subjects, which is beautifully discussed in 'Queer-Feminist Solidarity and the East/West Divide': 'The old significations of "East" and "West" have been resurrected and new binary oppositions have been added to their assemblages of meanings, today, the East/West divide signifies the chasm between "traditionalism" and "progress", "the retrograde" and "the developed", "religiousness" and "secularism", between "uncivilized" and "civilized" etc.' (Wiedlack et al. 2020: 1–2).

The main idea of the seminar was not only to challenge such binary oppositions, and to centre self-determined narratives, but also to shed light on the entanglements of the structural power relations such as global homo- and trans-discrimination, East-West divide, capitalism and racisms.

Especially in the German high education context, it makes sense to clarify the blurry narrative on the 'East' with the critical re-introduction of the term 'post-Soviet'. Those who are often perceived in the Germany as 'the Russians' (Panagiotidis 2020) and only partly being ones, while often being colonized and forced to assimilate by the Russian state power, often relate to the Russian language as hegemonial lingua franca, but still available second language, and share a set of very specific socioeconomic experiences, values and cultural codes.

Especially in the case of LGBTIQ individuals, can these codes and shared cultural phenomena be observed (Beketova et al. 2018). At the same time, the hegemonial position of Russia, the colonial heritage (dark side of the Soviet modernity (Tlostanova 2018)), and neo-colonial wars and power relations, but also punctual solidarities and connections from the 'light side of Soviet modernity' (Tlostanova 2018) shape the lived realities of post-Soviet subjects. Tlostanova theorizes this specific positionality as the *'post-Soviet human condition'*, and emphasizes its discursive and epistemological position as a certain *'void'*, *'nowhere'* and *'being expelled from history'* (Tlostanova 2018) in the global knowledge production. This aspect of *'nowherness'* and absence from the global map, especially, gains relevance for the post-Soviet LGBTIQ people, who face multiple projections and exclusions in the West as refugees and migrants (as I explicate in my PhD thesis, on which I am currently working), The Western hegemonic optic imagines post-Soviet queers as 'the same', projecting Western identity categories on the contexts, where genealogies of queer knowledge production have been different. In such universalisms, what is not taken into account, is the fact that the history of marginalized genders and sexualities and movements defending their rights were different in post-Soviet countries than in the Anglo-American LGBTIQ history, terminology and progressivist trajectory, which is often mirrored in Germany.

Being expelled from the national, homo- and trans-discriminatory discourses in their home countries (Plakhotnik 2019), and discursively constructed as 'lynchpin for value negotiations' (Neufeld and Wiedlack 2016), seen as 'Western' and belonging to 'Gayropa' (Shoshanova 2018) from the conservatives in their countries of origin, post-Soviet LGBTIQ individuals are often confronted with the image of being 'not queer enough' or 'not queer' in the West (Beketova et al. 2018). Queer post-Soviet subjects are almost absent from the Western teaching practices for multiple reasons, such as dominance of Anglo-American queer narrations, and cis- and heteronormativity of area studies, which seldom focus on LGBTIQ subjectivities and representations. In Halberstamian terms, they can be described as 'history's losers' (Halberstam 2011), who don't catch up with the capitalist success logics, partly inherent to the Western queer consumption culture. In addition, it is important to differentiate between post-Soviet countries within broader post-socialist context, as suggested by Wiedlack.

From Craving Knowledge on Post-Soviet Queerness to Creating Learning Environments on It

Knowledge production on queer/*kvir* post-Soviet experiences was something I started to do long before becoming a teacher. Having grown up in post-Soviet Ukraine and having moved to Germany as a teenager, I was confronted with questions of (cultural) identity, belonging and otherness in daily life. Those questions have multiplied when I started to realize that I failed to meet the heteronormative expectations. I was lucky enough to enrol in a Western university. There I started to understand more about my personal experiences and the structural reasons for them, while comparing my own experiences with queer of colour critiques and recognizing that there were often more similarities than with *white* Western queer experiences and representations, but also becoming aware of my partial *white* privileges. For a long time, it was not only an 'intellectual adventure' but also a lifesaving measure to find an environment, and to put together the pieces of knowledge, in order to understand who I am, why I feel excluded, and how I as a *kvir* migrant can be active in a society, which is shaped by multiple power relations.

During my time at the Zentrum für transdisziplinäre Geschlechterstudien (Center of Transdisciplinary Gender Studies) in Berlin, where I have studied for my BA and MA, and worked as a student tutor, I have never encountered a single lecture or seminar dealing with post-Soviet perspectives on sexuality. One exception was the course on gender in GDR (German Democratic Republic) taught by Kathleen Heft, but post-Soviet perspectives seemed to be absent from the knowledge production on sexuality. Gender and sexuality were queered and deconstructed with renowned theoreticians such as Judith Butler, Teresa de Lauretis and Donna Haraway, and the focus stayed Western, while non-Western genders were classically used as examples for different gender orders 'in other societies'. During my MA studies, I have encountered several wonderful teachers of colour as well as and Black scholars such as Grada Kilomba and Ngubia Kessé, who have emphasized the *white* dominance of our curricula and the need to decolonize the university. Despite the fact that Berlin gender studies were shaped by discussions on racism, migration and, since 2015, on asylum and refugees, there were no teachers like me throughout all my studies. And while discussing 'general' (read: Western-centred) issues on queerness, we have never read any Ukrainian, Kazakhstani, Armenian or Estonian scholars. The entire former 'second world' was absent from the map of theory production in gender studies (As in: Tlostanova 2015). It has appeared once where the Ukrainian activist group Femen was discussed by students as an example of weird inclination and 'wrongfully understood', problematic feminism (alternative analysis of Femen can be found in Plakhotnik and Mayerchyk 2019).

Every time I was looking into the new semester's schedule in hopes of finding a seminar that would touch on experiences and representations which had to do with my own, my curiosity grew. And with growing expertise, I've began to realize that the anglophone theory produced in the United States is not transferable one-to-one onto other contexts (compare Mizielińska and Kulpa 2011). Despite the idea of 'situated knowledge' being present in the discussions, it stayed as a rhetorical device, and the university remained predominantly *white* German. During these years, I have gathered impatience and curiosity on how gender and queer studies with a post-socialist and post-Soviet focus might look like, and after a long search, I encountered brilliant colleagues from post-Soviet and post-socialist contexts who were not limiting themselves by applying Western theory on the local post-Soviet empirical data, but who developed their own theories (M. Neufeld, S. Shoshanova, V. Solovey, R. Jenrbekova and many more). It is important to admit that the situation now (2020 –1) is rapidly changing, where my colleagues V. Solovey, S. Shoshanova and V. Kravtsova are bringing the post-Soviet gender perspectives into Center for Transdisciplinary Gender Studies (ZtG) as teachers.

I realized that there are no ready answers and easy axioms regarding the heterogenic and diverse group of post-Soviet queer/*kvir* individuals. Yet, I had the feeling that it was necessary to find language and methods apt for speaking about these diverse experiences and their representations in academia.

The exchange with other non-Western scholars in Western universities and readings of non-Western writers showed me that my experience was rather symptomatic for Western gender studies. Syinat Sultanalieva criticizes the global inequalities in academia: 'The microcosm of academia reflects the macrocosm of global political economy and the domination of the neoliberal "free market"' (Sultanalieva 2019).

Given these inspirations, critical insights and doubts, and knowing how risky it was to subsume the vast heterogenous experiences under the common denominator 'post-Soviet', I decided to create such learning environment myself. Excitement about the freeing potential of knowledge has led me to a doctoral students' role and into a teacher's role. In the winter semester of 2019–20, I gave the last in-person seminar at ZtG, at Humboldt-University, in Berlin. I titled seminar as 'Queer Post-Soviet Perspectives: An Intersectional Approach', and it combined majority of my research interests.

Content of the Seminar: Goals, Readings

Diba Tuncer introduces the idea of 'pedagogy of Integrity': 'As a space for development and progression, Pedagogy of Integrity thinks all pedagogical elements, such as subjects and content, interaction, learners, educators, methods and atmospheres, goals and processes, together in a holistic way and none of them is more important than another, just as no group of humans is worthier than another' (Tuncer 2019: 78). The complex theme of 'gender-sexuality-regional/cultural belonging' is crucial for the understanding of structural exclusions, and it offers a sensibility in relation to discriminations and power relations in contemporary Germany. The seminar ought to qualify students for independent research, critical text- and media analysis, and offer an insight into a fast-growing body of research of post-Soviet sexualities and genders.

The focus of the seminar was the intersection of post-Soviet experiences and representations, and the queer-feminist approach to subjectivity. One of the goals of the seminar was to challenge the narrative of juxtaposition of the 'tolerant, accepting'

West, where human rights are protected and 'underdeveloped' repressed in non-Western countries, and where LGBTIQ subjects are discriminated against, as well as to analyse what power mechanisms are at work in such discourses, and what counter-discourses are possible. Together with the students, we have looked for approaches toward post-Soviet queerness, whereby agency, self-representation and critical knowledge were central.

Programmatic texts on constructions of the East such as Edward Said's 'Orientalism' (1978) and Larry Wolff's 'Inventing Eastern Europe' (1996), have been put in dialogue with recent intersectional debates. The queer, transgender and lesbian narratives were especially centred. (Post-)soviet gender researchers such as Igor Kon, Madina Tlostanova, Maria Neufeld and Zhanar Sekerbayeva were introduced, and Western authors such as Richard Mole, Dan Healey and Laurie Essig were made familiar. The researchers' positionality has been made a crucial discussion point in the sessions, and will be addressed in the next section in detail.

The seminar was organized in a transdisciplinary approach, combining historical, sociological, cultural and media studies readings. In this way it was encouraging students of multiple disciplines to work together on the intersections of sexuality, gender, and cultural representations. A comparative intermedial approach was central for the analysis of the offered cases. The syllabus combined academic texts with journalistic publications, blog articles, artworks of well-known and amateur artists, and rock-pop music videos from the 1990s. The students were invited to discuss the following questions: which gender and sexuality norms do we encounter when we (as primarily Western *white* class) speak about post-Soviet countries? Which East-West power relations come to the foreground during this discussion? A self-reflective, transdisciplinary approach was trained.

A big part of the discussions was the reflection on inequalities in global knowledge production, already traced in the previous sections. The seminar was opened with a text of Syinat Sultanalieva, who reflected on the perception of Central Asian feminist scholars in relation to the West and Russia simultaneously: 'Our research is mostly seen as significantly dependent on Western theoretical frameworks and methodologies, and as such, iterative to them and redundant, to a point where our work is seen as becoming "watered down copies" of Western originals as a result of intellectual mimicry' (Sultanalieva 2019).

One of the sessions was organized on the topic of solidarity, where we have analysed videos and texts of German solidarity movements with post-Soviet queers, and recognized critical moments such as exoticization, othering and paternalism comparing them to findings of Wiedlack and Neufeld (2018), but also best practice examples. During that session, students were invited to write a piece of creative reflection about what solidarity means to them personally.

Ongoing reflection on one's own positionality in the dialogue with readings, and their perception, were integral parts of the seminar, where we have questioned the neutrality of the 'western gaze' and the 'zero-point hubris' of Eurocentrism (Santiago Castro-Gómez 2005, cited after Tlostanova 2015). However, there were several situations where the issue of positionality played a significant role.

Challenges and Potentials of Multiple Positionalities in the Classroom While Discussing Post-Soviet Queerness

In this central section, I will discuss three challenging situations from teaching practice, which reveal the relevance of positionality in the classroom. After every case, I am going to analyse how I've dealt with these challenges, and what I have learnt from them.

In what manner is it possible to study post-Soviet queer narratives in an ethical and self-reflective way? Since developing self-reflective academic optics was one of the main goals of the seminar, ethical questions took up an important part in our discussions. I observed multiple challenges during discussions in the class, and tried to address them on different levels through additional readings, changing of the syllabus, asking critical questions, and sharing my own reflections and experiences.

There was a challenge not to generalize and essentialize post-Soviet *kvirs* as rigid homogenous 'others' subsuming the vast post-Soviet space under one denominator, and not to strengthen exoticization, while trying to translate the coincidence of power relations, such as homophobia, transphobia and sexism in non-Western contexts. The other challenge was not to re-centre whiteness and to avoid applying Eurocentric LGBTIQ paradigms to post-Soviet contexts, and not to focus on Russian (out of the entire wide range of other post-Soviet experiences) perspectives. Particularly due to the *coloniality of knowledge* (Tlostanova 2015), prevalence of Russia-centred narratives on post-Soviet queer contexts can be observed, and there is, indeed, less data, and sometimes less institutionalization of Queer studies in other post-Soviet countries. Nevertheless, it is crucial to speak critically about persistent Russian hegemony in the post-Soviet regions.

Situation 1

In the first session, there was a lot of confusion around the term 'post-Soviet'. Most of the students expected the seminar to touch on GDR; some were sure that Poland and Czech Republic were Soviet. When I stated that my approach to the term post-Soviet was to focus on the states which formerly belonged to the USSR, and asked them which and how many these are, there was silence at first. Then somebody[5] with a slight accent said 'sixteen' someone else said 'fifteen'. Shy voices started to list countries: Russia, Belarus, Ukraine, Tajikistan named twice … hesitation … and Armenia and Moldova forgotten. When I asked when do they think did the USSR fall apart, some of the students estimated 1989 (obviously confusing the date with the fall of the Berlin wall). Almost the entire introductory session has passed until we figured out what regions we are going to talk about. In the next session, I promised to explain my choice against the common denominator of post-socialism, and realized we are far behind the schedule. The quick brainstorm of former Soviet countries was planned to be done in the first five minutes.

It seems there was no basic geographical and historical knowledge in the group (with the exception of a few students with post-Soviet backgrounds, for whom such brainstorming seemed basic and boring), which should be a common ground for further discussions on the postcolonial and neocolonial power relations in the post-Soviet region.

Despite the lack of common ground, I decided to proceed with fairly complex readings of David Chioni Moore and Madina Tlostanova in hopes that the basic geography was a quick task for homework. But during the next sessions, I realized that the students were often more confused than well-informed, and that the complex geopolitical reflection of the global interdependencies proved to be a challenging introduction for an undergraduate course. In retrospect, my endeavour to start with David Chioni Moore (one of the first scholars in 2001 to introduce the post-Soviet region into debates on coloniality) seemed to be a bit misleading. If I would give the same seminar, I would instead start with Said's 'Orientalism' as an introduction to postcolonial thought, and then build up to Larry Wolff's 'Inventing Eastern Europe' as its particular application to Eastern Europe, and only then come to Moore and Tlostanova, continuously building on postcolonial theories toward different critical approaches to post-Soviet spaces. Much of these challenges could have been solved if the basic geography, global history and postcolonial theory were part of the introductory courses in gender studies.

Situation 2

I invited a feminist Russophone author to the seminar. I have perceived works of this poet as radical decentring Russian whiteness and localizing experiences from the non-central Russian republic. The combination of corporeal topics and clear emancipatory logic in the works of the author seemed fitting to the queer agenda of the seminar. Although the author did not define herself as a person of colour, her nationality is marginalized in Russia, and as a post-Soviet migrant in Germany she belongs to a minority. During the discussion, the author read her text on the 'female' experience, which connects womanhood to menstruation, and got asked by a student, whom does she address in this piece? The author replied: the mainstream Russian men, who are afraid of the mere word 'menstruation'. The author started to describe the Russian context to a predominantly Western white student audience, using generalizing descriptions such as 'barbaric' and 'medieval'. As a 'killer argument', the author said that, first, the rights of women have to be defended, and only then 'we can speak about gender diversity in Russia'. After the session, a student reached out to the class via an online forum and challenged transphobia in the invited speakers' words, and was outraged that trans-emancipation was presented as something secondary – and not so important as women's rights by a person in authority – by the invited speaker. With permission of the student, I shared this reaction with the author, and she said that she immediately realized that the discussion was going in the wrong direction owing to the fact that, unfortunately, she was unable to formulate her thoughts effectively in English, and, in reality, she is, of course, against trans-discrimination.

In this situation, multiple power relations have come up in the classroom, which could only be understood through an intersectional (Crenshaw 1991; Combahee River Collective 1977) lens. On the first level, from the perspective of the student, there was a trans-exclusive speech act from an invited speaker. This expression has opened the discussion on different trajectories of feminism, such as trans-exclusive feminism and trans-feminism. During the lesson, the safety of the students was my focus, and I stopped the discussion with the invited speaker as fast as possible, and checked in with the students, if they needed something. After class, and a talk with the author, where she excused herself and explained what went wrong for her, I realized that being the only person from her background, the author was in a (racialized) minority and felt under pressure due to the level of the academic discussion as well as the issue of English language. The discussion which followed the week after, has showed that the Western student was not aware of the gender regimes in the non-Western contexts, and had the same expectations of them as of the German context in means of 'progressivity' of the agenda and wording.

In this case, both the transphobia and the Eurocentric LGBTIQ paradigm were simultaneously at play, and the misunderstanding induced a confusing atmosphere in the class. In such situations, the role of the teacher as the one responsible for critical discussion was revealed to be quite crucial. My strategy of dealing with the situation was as following: I communicated the critique of the student to the invited author and conveyed the author's excuse to the student group. After asking the student if they are comfortable with the explanation, I decided to take this case as an opportunity for discussing the systematic and global nature of transphobia, sexism and Eurocentrism. Internalization of the 'Western gaze' could have been the reasons why the author referred to her region as 'barbaric'. As my further research shows, self-exoticization is a strategy often chosen by post-Soviet migrants to legitimize their words in order to gain attention in Western contexts. I also introduced two texts of trans-feminist scholars, who combine trans-emancipatory politics and feminist thought in their writings from different points of view (Julia Serano and Emi Koyama) and poetry of a Ukrainian trans-feminist poet Friedrich Chernyshov. After changing the syllabus in this way, and after giving the students time to reflect on the situation, I introduced the concept of *Fehlerfreundlichkeit* (error-friendliness), and referred to how Urmila Goel defines it:

> Error-friendliness doesn't mean that all actions and expressions are seen as legitimate and stay without consequences. The concept of 'error-friendliness' means, instead, that nobody is perfect, and this is also not expected from nobody. It points out that we can always expect problematic actions and expressions, and that we have to deal with it. It also means that mistakes can be used to bring forward the learning process. (Goel 2016, translated by author)

In this way, I raised the issue of how structural and discursive powers shape our thinking, wording and actions. I said that the learning process does not stop after something has not worked out in the class. What is more important, is how we discuss those issues afterwards, and what we can all learn from them. I invited the students to question the authorities of those who are speaking, including myself and invited speakers, and to always think critically, while giving each other space to grow together.

Finally, I discussed the concept of 'oppression Olympics' (Martinez 1993) with the students, which revealed, in a particularly helpful manner, an explanation as to why an attempt to compare different structural oppressions to each other doesn't take our analysis further as it hinders solidarities and alliances.

Situation 3

I divided the students into smaller groups for group work. Each group had to analyse queer and lesbian visibility in the music videos of Russian pop-rock singers, and compare their findings with the article 'Not Rockers, not Punks, We're Lesbian Chicks: Staging Female Same Sex Desires in Russian Rock and Pop' authored by Neufeld and Wiedlack (2015). While the groups were sharing their results, and exchanging their opinions, I realized that in one group was composed only of students without any post-Soviet biographical backgrounds, while the two others had one 'migrant' student each from different post-socialist and post-Soviet contexts. The 'German' group struggled with identification of queer codes in the music videos, and started to analyse the outer appearance of the singers more as belonging to the old-school 1990s, and concluded that these videos do not contain anything particularly queer. Meanwhile, the two other groups presented their results: They have recognized subtle gender norm transgressions such as hairstyle, jewellery, certain attributes and details in costume and atmosphere, and could relate to the queer reading of these singers and the topic of queer representations in the article.

Thanks to this case, I have realized that a personal background (in our case post-Soviet) helps one analyse gender norms and their deconstruction in a much more sensitive and successful way, when it comes to the local context.

This 'being an expert' due to biography has two effects in the classroom: first, it can cause respect and admiration of fellow students who 'didn't get it' but alternatively, it can be a hurtful situation of 'othering' for students with minoritarian backgrounds, where they become an exotic study object themselves. This could cause two-fold reactions: on the one hand, it would reward the lived knowledge, while on the other, it would restrict the student to their biography and 'otherness'. In the case of knowledge of post-Soviet queer codes, the otherness is not necessarily marked with racist discrimination experiences (as post-Soviet students can be both, entitled with *white* privilege and confronted with racism), but still can produce a situation of outing and othering.

The heterogenic character of the student group means there are knowledge hierarchies in the classroom. They have to be addressed in a sensitive way in order not to reinforce them into power relations, where the Western unmarked subjects are creating (limited but authorized) knowledge on non-Western subjects.

All three cases discussed above illustrate how important ground knowledge on the local context as well as on one's positionality and privilege are in the learning context. I am not arguing toward approaches where certain minoritarian subjectivities can be studied only by the individuals with the same background. Theories of intersectionality show how different each context and each situation is, and how misleading can additive categorial thinking be. What I suggest instead is that it is time for Western gender studies to open their syllabi for more gender and queer theoreticians from the 'former second world' and to start teaching gender and sexuality from the very first introductory lecture with regard to different queer genealogies in different contexts. I do not believe that in the university contexts it is necessary to separate different groups in the class, as it sometimes happens in the workshops (empowerment for the 'biographically advanced' students, and sensibilization against the stereotypes for the privileged students). My solution was, instead, to make the differences between our perceptions a constant discussion topic in the classroom, and to develop a discussion culture of mutual respect, curiosity and acknowledgement of differences.

It was revealed to be helpful to build in 'empty' time slots without concrete exercises and reading tasks to enable self-reflection. The second strategy was to ask extra questions for self-reflection. I believe that despite the non-hierarchical teaching methods, and my approach to teaching as an equality practice, a teacher's responsibility remains extremely crucial especially in situations of conflict or possible discrimination. I plead for the need for flexibility and constant self-reflection for all: students, teachers and invited speakers. bell hooks, a Black feminist pedagogue and scholar, wrote in her text *Teaching to Transgress*: 'To teach in varied communities not only our paradigms must shift but also the way we think, write, speak. The engaged voice must never be fixed and absolute but always changing, always evolving in dialogue with a world beyond itself' (hooks 1994: 11).

It is the teacher's responsibility to ask critical questions, provide additional materials, intervene in case of discrimination and to discuss the readings in appropriate ways, while at the same time leaving space for discussion, mistakes and growth.

There was, on the one side, fairly little knowledge of the post-Soviet contexts beginning with geography, history and the idea that gender norms might be universal, while on the other, there were participants from post-socialist contexts, for whom some questions might have been self-explanatory or obsolete. I believe this issue could be solved by decolonization of 'general' introductory gender studies courses, toward post-Soviet queer perspectives, which would enable all students to start if not 'from the same level', but with similar vocabulary.

Conclusion

Despite all the challenges mentioned above, there were immense learning processes and amazing feedback at the end of semester, and the biggest reward was to read the final essays of seminar participants, which showed that the students engaged with the literature and class discussions on a high level. A quote from the final essay illustrates the students' reflections: 'A central thing I've learned is that despite repressive and discriminatory power relations, queer post-Soviet perspectives are developing, and these have to be documented and studied in order to question the western monopoly on knowledge' [Final Essay of C., undergraduate student].

In this chapter, I have discussed the relevance of post-Soviet queer/*kvir* perspectives as a valid part of global knowledge production. With my biographical example, I have illustrated how lack of lectures focusing post-Soviet genders and sexualities has been centring Western queer representations in the university. I have argued that the Eurocentric and Anglo-American theories are not identically applicable for every context and taking them as a measure erases and makes invisible non-Western perspectives on queerness, such as post-Soviet. Post-Soviet queer/*kvir* perspectives have not been part of the gender studies curricula at the Humboldt University in Berlin so far. My seminar has offered first steps toward diversifying gender studies in this direction. The unique syllabus I designed aimed at compensating the missing basic knowledge on the post-Soviet contexts for the German gender studies students; offering examples of self-determined queer/*kvir* post-Soviet knowledge production from different media, arts and activist sources; analysing multiple power relations which lead to marginalization of post-Soviet queers; and helping students develop self-critical positioned approach while studying 'invisible 'others'. With three empirical examples from the teaching process, I have shown how different positionalities affect our access to knowledge. Multiple challenges of teaching process on 'invisible "others"' have been discussed and some strategies to overcome them have been offered.

University classrooms are not only places of liberation and critical knowledge proliferation. They also mirror the societies' exclusion mechanisms such as classism, racisms, ageism, ableism, gender and sexual orientation inequalities. In gender studies, power relations are lesson topics and are often discussed with biographical examples, which reveal the differences between students' and teachers' positionalities. It is crucial not to expose multiply vulnerable students such as racialized, queer, trans, migrant to attention of privileged students, but to honour the existing biographical expertise. At the same time, due to the intersectional realities, it is often impossible to simply see diverse student groups in binary dichotomies. In order to address these phenomena, it is vital to avoid reproducing 'oppression Olympics' and generalizations. As Audre Lorde said, 'It is not our differences that divide us. It is our inability to recognize, accept, and celebrate those differences' (In: Our Dead behind us, 1986). Such recognition and acceptance of differences is to be sought in any learning environment anew again and again, and sometimes there are no ready recipes for intersectional pedagogy except of staying self-reflective, aware and critical but also *fehlerfreundlich* (friendly to error) and alert to any new situation in the class.

Engaging more with the particular queer post-Soviet and post-socialist perspectives in order to broaden the geography of objectivities and decolonize the queer knowledge production toward multiple localities is one possible direction of questioning Western universalisms. Decolonizing and queering curricula and paying attention how not to study 'others' on behalf of those multiply marginalized students present are necessary. To conclude, I suggest addressing differences and power relations in the classroom in an open and sensitive way as one of the many possible strategies for intersectional pedagogy.

Notes

1. I use the Russian word '*kvirnost*' to underline the specific localized meaning production, which is not simply translation from English 'queer' (see Suyarkulova 2019). Similar interventions into terminology were suggested by *kvir*-feminist-Actziya (2013). In the text, the terms 'queer', '*kvir*' and 'queer/*kvir*' are used interchangeably.

2. 'Inakovost' means 'otherness' in Russian and is used in Кунцман (2010) as equivalent to 'queer'.
3. 'West' means here not only the geographical position, but to signify the economical, discursive and cultural inequalities, and can be replaced with 'Global North' or made more precise in 'North/West'. It is important to note that both categories are constructed and not homogenic in themselves.
4. The term 'coloniality of knowledge' was coined by Peruvian sociologist Annibal Quijano, and applied by Madina Tlostanova for post-Soviet context.
5. All students' identities are anonymized and certain information changed to protect the anonymity of the participants.

References

Belorusova, L., M. Beketova and M. Neufeld (2018), *Wir haben was zu sagen. Geschichten von LGBTIQ Migrant_innen aus dem postsowjetischen Raum. Lesbenberatung*, Berlin: Lesbenberatung Berlin.

Case, K., ed (2017), *Intersectional Pedagogy: Complicating Identity and Social Justice*, London: Routledge.

Combahee River Collective (1977), 'Statement'. Available online: https://americanstudies.yale.edu/sites/default/files/files/Keyword%20Coalition_Readings.pdf (accessed 31 January 2021).

Crenshaw, K. (1991, July), 'Mapping the Margins: Intersectionality, Identity Politics, and Violence against Women of Color'. *Stanford Law Review*, 43 (6): 1241–99.

Goel, U. (2016), 'Die (Un)Möglichkeiten der Vermeidung von Diskriminierungen', in *Diskriminierungskritische Lehre. Denkanstöße aus den Gender Studies*, 39–47, Geschäftsstelle des Zentrums für transdisziplinäre Geschlechterstudien der Humboldt-Universität zu Berlin. HU Berlin. Available online: https://www.gender.hu-berlin.de/de/studium/diskriminierungskritik

Halberstam, J. (2011), *The Queer Art of Failure*, Durham, NC: Duke University Press.

Haraway, D. (1988), 'Situated Knowledges: The Science Question in Feminism and the Privilege of Partial Perspective', *Feminist Studies*, 14: 575–99.

Healey, D. (2013), 'Beredtes Schweigen. Zur Geschichte der Homosexualität in Russland', *Zeitschrift Osteuropa. Spektralanalyse. Homosexualität und ihre Feinde*, 10: 5–16.

hooks, b. (1994), *Teaching to Transgress. Education as the Practice of Freedom*, London: Routledge.

Kulpa, R. (2014), 'Western Leveraged Pedagogy of Central and Eastern Europe: Discourses of Homophobia, Tolerance, and Nationhood', *Gender, Place & Culture*, 21 (4): 431–48.

Kulpa, R., and J. Silva (2016), 'Decolonizing Queer Epistemologies', in G. Brown and K. Browne (eds), *The Ashgate Research Companion to Geographies of Sex and Sexualities*, 139–42, Farnham: Ashgate.

Кунцман, А. (2010), 'Квир по-русски, взгляд из-за рубежа', in В. Созаев (ed.), *Возможен ли 'квир' по-русски? ЛГБТК исследования Междисциплинарный сборник*, 29–42, Санкт-Петербург: Выход.

Kvir-feminist-Actziya (2013–14), Available online: https://tuewi.action.at/node/4799 (accessed 31 October 2021).

Martinez, E., and A. Y. Davis (1993), 'Coalition Building Among People of Color'. Available online: https://culturalstudies.ucsc.edu/inscriptions/volume-7/angela-y-davis-elizabeth-martinez/ (accessed 26 April 2022).

Mignolo W., and M. Tlostanova (2006), 'Theorizing from the Borders: Shifting to Geo- and Body-Politics of Knowledge', *European Journal of Social Theory*, 9 (2): 205–21.

Mizielińska, J., and R. Kulpa (2011), *De-centering Western Sexualities. Central and Eastern European Perspectives*, Farnham: Ashgate.

Neufeld, M., and K. Wiedlack (2016), 'Lynchpin for Value Negotiation: Lesbians, Gays and Transgender between Russia and "the West"', in B. Scherer (ed.), *Queering Paradigms VI: Interventions, Ethics and Glocalities*, 173–94, New York: Peter Lang.

Neufeld, M., and K. Wiedlack (2018), 'Wir sind Conchita, nicht Russland, oder Homonationalismus auf gut Österreichisch', *ÖZG*, 29: 153–75.

Panagiotidis, J. (2020), *Postsowjetische Migration in Deutschland*, Weinheim Basel: Beltz Juventa.

Plakhotnik, O., and M. Mayerchyk (2019), 'Between Coloniality and Nationalism: Genealogies of Feminist Activism in Ukraine. Feminist Critique', *East European Journal of Feminist and Queer Studies*, August. Available online: https://feminist.krytyka.com/ua/articles/mizh-kolonialnistyu-i-natsionalizmom-henealohiyi-feministychnoho-aktyvizmu-v-ukrayini (accessed 31 January 2021).

Plakhotnik, O. (2019), 'Imaginaries of Sexual Citizenship in Post-Maidan Ukraine: A Queer Feminist Discourse Analysis', PhD diss., The Open University.

Said, E. (1974) Orientalism. Pantheon Books.

Shoshanova, S. (2018), 'Fantasien über Gayropa: Kunst und Politik', *Ost Journal*. Available online: https://www.ost-journal.de/fantasien-ueber-gayropa-kunst-und-politik/ (accessed 31 January 2021)

Sultanalieva, S. (2019), 'How Does It Feel to Be Studied? A Central Asian Perspective'. Opendemocracy, 9 October. Available online: https://www.opendemocracy.net/en/odr/how-does-it-feel-be-studied-central-asian-perspective/ (accessed 31 January 2021).

Suyarkulova, M. (2019), 'Translating 'QUEER' into Kyrgyzstani Russian', in C. Cottet and M. Lavinas Picq (eds), *Sexuality and Translation in World Politics*, Bristol. E: International Relations Publishing, 42–56. Available online: https://www.e-ir.info/2019/08/18/translating-queer-into-kyrgyzstani-russian/.

Tlostanova, M. (2015), 'Can the Post-Soviet Think? On Coloniality of Knowledge, External Imperial and Double Colonial Difference', *Intersections*, 1 (2): 38–58.

Tlostanova, M. (2018), *What Does It Mean to Be Post-Soviet?: Decolonial Art from the Ruins of the Soviet Empire*, Durham, NC: Duke University Press.

Тлостанова М. В. (2009), *Деколониальные гендерные эпистемологии*, Москва: ООО ИПЦ 'Маска'.

Tuncer, D. (2019), 'Pedagogy of Integrity', MA diss., University of Potsdam, Potsdam. Available online: https://publishup.uni-potsdam.de/opus4-ubp/frontdoor/deliver/index/docId/43229/file/tuncer_pedagogyofintegrity.pdf (accessed 31 January 2021).

Wiedlack, K. (2017), 'Gays vs. Russia: Media Representations, Vulnerable Bodies and the Construction of a (Post)modern West', *European Journal of English Studies*, 21 (3): 24–257.

Wiedlack, K. (2020), 'Fucking Solidarity: "Working Together" Through (Un)pleasant Feelings', in K. Wiedlack, S. Shoshanova and M. Godovannaya (eds), *Queering Paradigms VIII Queer-Feminist Solidarity and the East/West Divide*, 21–50, New York: Peter Lang.

Wiedlack, K., and M. Neufeld (2015), 'Not Rockers, Not Punks, We're Lesbian Chicks: Staging Female Same Sex desires in Russian Rock and Pop', in K. Browne and E. Ferreira (eds), *Lesbian Geographies. Gender, Place and Power*. 153–76, London: Routledge.

Wiedlack, K., S. Shoshanova and M. Godovannaya, eds (2020), *Queering Paradigms VIII Queer-Feminist Solidarity and the East/West Divide*, New York: Peter Lang.

Wolff, L. (1994), *Inventing Eastern Europe*, Stanford:: Stanford University Press.

12

Teaching Gender and Queer Studies at Polish Universities: Challenges, Limitations, Perspectives

Magdalena Stoch

Introduction

Education can be a revolutionary practice. Understanding how the idea of equality and social justice is realized in practice requires looking at specific educational actions: lectures, discussions, courses, seminars and other forms of interaction at university. The goal of the present chapter is to diagnose the dynamic situation of gender and queer studies at Polish universities after 1990 (the political transformation) and understanding the role of innovative teaching methodology applied during academic classes conducted in these disciplines.

I assume that both scientific sub-disciplines, developing in Poland since the 1990s, have become a permanent part of the plans and programmes of higher education and have designated new, dynamically developing areas of research. Regular discussions on the opportunities, risks and challenges of gender studies in Poland have taken place on the pages of *Katedra* journal ('Department' 2001–4), and occasionally in the thematic sections of literary and cultural magazines such as *Teksty Drugie. Teoria literatury, krytyka, interpretacja* ('Second Texts: Literary Theory, Criticism, and Interpretation') and *Ruch Literacki* ('Literary Movement'). In 2006, the online academic feminist journal *uniGENDER* (www.unigender.org) appeared, providing a platform for a discussion of gender studies (Mrozik 2010: 2).

The methodology of teaching gender and queer studies still remains an unrecognized area. In my opinion the didactic methods used during the classes are emancipating, they dynamize the educational process and strengthen the autonomy of students. At the same time, for several years there have been attempts to identify gender and queer studies by Polish right-wing politicians and church hierarchs with so-called ideologization and to discredit people promoting equality and diversity at Polish universities. As Pakuła et al. (2015) argue, 'gender ideology' is conventionally defined in the academy as attitudes regarding the appropriate roles, rights and responsibilities of women and men in society. Gender expectations are society-specific. But in Poland the academic understanding of gender ideology sharply contrasts with what has been lately a political buzzword, namely, 'ideologia gender' ('the ideology of gender').

'Gender ideology' is part of a sociological conceptual apparatus. 'The ideology of gender' is a political construct that has recently been invented and successfully included in mainstream right-wing political discourse in Poland (Pakuła et al. 2015). As a result of political actions, educational institutions lose their independence and are becoming more and more susceptible to the influence of changing political trends. Government policy exposes gender and queer studies to constant risk (Graff and Korolczuk 2021).

To test this initial diagnosis, I analysed two data sources. The first type of data is press coverage that mentions the impact of gender and queer studies on Polish society. A critical analysis of the media discourse allowed me to distinguish a few key moments, revealing the political dimension of the dispute over gender and queer studies. These media events were also considered important by other researchers of the Polish media sphere, including Maciej Duda (2016), Marek Krajewski (2020) and Agnieszka Graff and Elżbieta Korolczuk (2021). I mention them to broaden my understanding of the current sociopolitical and cultural context.

The second type of data was obtained from six in-depth interviews conducted in April 2021 with lecturers employed at various Polish universities. The selection of respondents was deliberate: people representing various academic disciplines and scientific circles were chosen. This study has used 'purposeful sampling' in the selection of the sample and needed additional discretion and caution, as the questions related to attitudes towards minority groups in Poland. In line with the *Guide on Good Data Protection Practice in Research* (2021), the interviews were anonymized. The information about the name, surname, gender and place of work of the respondents has been removed. The participants of the study gave their informed written *Consent for Participation in Research Interview* document. The interlocutors were informed about the principles of privacy and confidentiality and gave informed, written consent to participate in the study voluntary and for free. Interview participants were aware that some of the questions were sensitive and could provoke strong emotional responses. In order to obtain good quality material, the interviews were recorded. The information allowing to identify the name, surname, gender and place of work of the respondents has been removed. Successive respondents were marked with the letters of the alphabet: from A to F.

The theoretical framework of the chapter is based on two theories: 'pedagogy of the oppressed' by Paulo Freire (1996, first published in 1970) and 'education as a practice of freedom' by bell hooks (1994). In addition to Paulo Freire, the main objectives of emancipation pedagogy were developed by: Henry Giroux (1983, 1985, 1988, 1992, 2003), Peter McLaren (1993, 1995, 1998, 2000a,b), Giroux and McLaren (1989), and many other researchers (e.g. Au 2007; Barrios and Nanton 2008; Dune 1996; Shor 1992), including authors publishing in *Rethinking Critical Pedagogy* online journal. Here hooks also refers to Freire, deepens Freire's recommendations and applies them to formal university education. The representatives of other scientific disciplines (sociology, psychology, arts and literary studies, communication and media studies, etc.) also use Freire's assumptions during their academic classes globally (McArthur 2010).

Freire's and hooks's approaches are therefore closely related and, in my opinion, constitute an important reference point for the methodology of education in the field of gender and queer studies in Poland. Emancipation pedagogy was a source of inspiration in Polish social sciences, particularly in education (Czerepaniak-Walczak 1995, 2006; Kopciewicz 2003, 2007 or Gawlicz et al. 2015). It is also worth noting that emancipatory pedagogy plays a key role in informal education, for example, in non-governmental organizations dealing with anti-discrimination education (e.g. Wen Do – self-defence and assertiveness workshops for women run by the Autonomia Foundation, the Feminoteka Foundation and other associations). By making reference to these contexts, I try to strengthen Giroux's thesis (1985) that emancipatory pedagogy is an effective tool of social change that works well in various educational systems. It is a response to the rapidly changing and unpredictable global world.

The chapter consists of three sections. In the first part, I describe the development of gender and queer studies at Polish universities, from the 1990s to the present days, and current political campaigns against them. In the second part, I present the theory of Paulo Freire and bell hooks, referring to the two most popular works of their authorship: *Pedagogy of The Oppressed* (Freire 1996) and *Teaching to Transgress: Education as the Practice of Freedom* (hooks 1994). In the final part, I combine these perspectives and present my research. The study was designed to answer the following question: How do academic teachers of gender and queer studies at Polish universities define their role and tasks in the current political context, and how does this correspond to the assumptions of emancipatory pedagogy?

My study has three main limitations. The first and most important is a sample profile: I used snowball method to collected data. I talked to people working in big cities who studied at major universities. The diagnosis of gender and queer studies in small towns requires further research. Another limitation is that the study was conducted during the pandemic. Respondents signalled that online learning differs from classroom instruction. Understanding the gender dimension of this difference requires separate research. The third limitation is the gender and age of the respondents: the voices of the pioneers of introducing gender and queer studies at Polish universities are underrepresented in the study.

The 'Anti-Gender Wind': Flashpoints of the Discourse around Gender and Queer Studies in Poland

Gender perspectives have been present in the Western science since the 1970s. In Poland, gender studies was launched for the first time at the University of Warsaw in 1996 as postgraduate 'Studies on Social and Cultural Identity of Gender' (Chołuj 2014: 165). This 'time shift' in the development of gender and queer studies between the East and West of Europe was the result of the domination of communism in the countries of Central and Eastern Europe until 1989. Even after the collapse of the communist system, we observe a social distance from the ideas emerging 'in the West'. As Mihaela Miroiu (2003) noted, the introduction of the gender equality policy in post-communist countries for a long time was associated with the façade of equality policies of the totalitarian states: 'From the gender perspective, the end of communism was accompanied by the rejection of egalitarianism (as a state policy). This rejection was consistent with the preservation of traditional patriarchy and the emergence of modern patriarchy. Therefore, the transition period seemed to reinforce the dependence of women on men, the eloquent expression of gender inequality' (Miroiu 2003: 55–6).

The key argument against social diversity is the myth of complete unity and homogeneity of Polish society, reinforced by the right-wing authorities. Despite this, in the 1990s in Poland, postgraduate gender studies were launched at the Jagiellonian University in Kraków, at the Institute of Literary Research of the Polish Academy of Sciences, at the University of Łódź and at universities in Poznań and Toruń. Before that, unlike in the West, these studies were developed and 'taming' in non-governmental organizations. They did not conduct typical scientific research, but dealt with the implementation of European Union's (EU) equality policies. In this context, it is worth quoting the statement of one of my respondents: 'Perhaps it is that these specialized genders have lost their raison d'être, because you can learn about them within the subjects that you are offered at the university as part of your course, whereas in the beginning they were set up outside universities' (A).

In 2005, when the Law and Justice Party first came to power, the word 'gender' became offensive and has been associated with the concept of 'ideology', understood as a false social awareness. From the complex area of gender studies, one 'foreign-sounding' world 'gender' (used in original version) was selected and given a new, negative meaning. Some of the most prominent Catholic Church representatives seemed to see 'gender' as their main enemy. Gender was viewed not as an analytical tool or concept but rather as an umbrella term encapsulating a number of negatively understood phenomena such as sexualization of children, same-sex marriage, radical feminism, compulsory challenges to traditional gender roles and paedophilia (Pakuła et al. 2015: 28).

In order to better understand the impact of these political processes on university life, I will recall some key events in public life from 2013 to the present. I am interested in the ideological framework linking these phenomena with the emotional dynamics that influences atmosphere at universities. Analysing the public discourse around the notions of gender and queer, I used the methodological guidelines formulated in Michel Foucault's inaugural *Lectures on the Will to Know* (2013), delivered on 2 December 1970 at the Collège de France. The first assumption is that discourse research should begin with an analysis of a specific event. Usually it is part of a sequence of similar events, the identification of which requires a chronological approach. The analysed series of events show certain regularities and capturing them is important for understanding the dynamics of discourse. It is also important to point out internal contradictions within the discourse, to recognize the non-obvious and paradoxical phenomena that surround us. Seemingly insignificant events can reveal surprising symbolic practices and be the key to understanding institutionalized codes and conventions. Foucault argued that there is no reality external to discourse. We are all caught up in it: regardless of the tactics adopted in dealing with oppression, they feel its impact on our lives.

The culminating moment, which gave shape to the Polish discourse on the notion of gender, lasting until the present day, happened to be Archbishop Michalik's sermon delivered on 16 October 2013. In one of the churches he argued:

> The acts of abuse of children by adults, the subject matter which is still present in the media, are shameful. However, no one seems to be paying attention to the causes of these kinds of behaviour ... Pornography and false love showed in it, lack of love from divorced parents, and the promotion of the gender ideology ... Aggressive feminists with their fight to legalise abortion, legalization of the same-sex unions, and the right to adopt children by such people, are also to blame. They are fighting in kindergartens and schools to extinguish a sense of shame in children, and even to allow children to change their sex.[1] (cited in Stanisz 2013: 5)

As the Polish feminist researcher and publicist Magdalena Środa claims, the Church hierarchy and rightist publicists have been working on the concept of 'gender ideology' for a long time (Środa 2013: 2). In the essay 'The End of Sexual Difference? (Fragments)', Judith Butler points out that all the way in 1995, after Beijing World Conference on Women, the newspaper *La Repubblica* reported that the Vatican City demands to erase the word gender from the United Nation's (UN) platform of non-governmental organizations devoted to the status of women, as this word is an encoded term for describing homosexuality (Butler 2012). Agnieszka Graf and Elżbieta Korolczuk expressed a similar opinion. They conceptualize the struggles over 'gender' as 'the populist moment' when, under the pressure of political or socioeconomic transformations, the dominant hegemony is being destabilized by the multiplication of unsatisfied demands (2021: 4–8). That is why in 2013 the Polish bishops publish a *Pastoral Letter on the Feast of the Holy Family* which includes the following words:

> Gender ideology is the result of decades of ideological and cultural changes, deeply rooted in Marxism and neo-Marxism, promoted by some feminist movements and the sexual revolution. Genderism promotes principles that are completely contrary to reality and an integral understanding of human nature ... Meanwhile, the gender ideology, without the knowledge of the society and the consent of Poles, has been introduced into various structures of social life for many months: education, health service, activities of cultural and educational institutions and non-governmental organizations. In the messages of some media it is presented positively: as counteracting violence and striving for equality. (KAI 2021)

Back in 2014, the Ministry of Science and Higher Education defended scientists against such accusations. In the same year, a parliamentary group called 'Stop Gender Ideology!' was formed. It was composed of fifteen MPs from Solidarity Poland and one senator. 'Gender' was presented as an ideology in church sermons. In 2013, the metropolitan of Łódź stated that 'because of gender, white people will be like Indians in reservations' (KAI 2013).

In 2014, doctor and priest Dariusz Oko gave a lecture in the Sejm on 'Gender Ideology – A Threat to Civilization'. He compared 'gender' to the sexual mania, genocide by the Cambodian dictator Pol Pot and the Nazi ideology. He spoke of 'genderists' promoting incest, paedophilia and homosexuality. There was also talk of sexual debauchery 'with a ram, a goat or a closet'. Everything was thrown into one bag: homosexuality, abortion, IVF, child sexualization, contraceptives, pornography, paedophilia, the breakdown of the traditional family model and even the fact that modern women do not wear dresses (Oko 2014). Scientific conferences of opponents of the 'the ideology of gender' began to be organized at Catholic universities. In 2017, ultra-catholic and influential Life and Family Foundation sent a letter to public universities in Poland asking them to prepare a list of scientists who teach gender studies (Szczęśniak 2017). Most universities did not disclose the names of their scientists or their employment costs in an effort to protect their personal data. There was a risk that the right-wing media would prepare a disinformation campaign aimed at the scientific achievements of these people.

As Marek Krajewski notes, this is how gender was defined to the public as a threat to everything important to Poles: family, children and marriage. What gender is has not been specified, but anxiety has arisen. A foreign-sounding word (used in the original version) was associated with what is unacceptable in the church and what is associated with the communist times, that is, with Marxism, social experiments and the failure of Polish culture and religion. It was also shown that the sources of this threat are numerous, but primarily rich minority communities, penetrated into educational institutions and corrupted young people. Those who fight 'genderism' are defined as normal, righteous people fighting evil. This is how the enemy was constructed in order to mobilize a group of political supporters around him (Krajewski 2020: 86–97).

Over time, 'gender ideology' was replaced with 'LGBT ideology' (from 2018). In both cases, as in the campaign against refugees and migrants, the aim was to fuel social anxiety. The campaign against the LGBT+ community was launched by Law and Justice Party. When the president of Warsaw signed a commitment to support the LGBT+ community by local government authorities, more than thirty municipalities and counties in south-eastern Poland declared their opposition to the 'LGBT ideology'. On 24 July 2010, *Gazeta Polska* added to its issue stickers with a crossed rainbow flag and the words 'LGBT-free zone'. In one of the sermons, Archbishop Jędraszewski called the LGBT community 'the rainbow plague' (Polityka 2019). This immunological rhetoric, referring to the plague, calling for purification, is part of the hate speech and reality in which Polish scientists currently work. During the presidential elections, the current president of Poland Andrzej Duda signed the so-called Family Charter. The document was not formally binding, but rather a collection of several declarations concerning family life. Among Duda's promises were the fight against the 'LGBT ideology' and opposition to the adoption of children by same-sex couples (Ambroziak 2020). The Polish president referred to the 'LGBT ideology' many times as neo-Bolshevism with the intent to build the political electorate on fear and hatred. 'We are being persuaded that these are people, but this is simply an ideology' said the president at a meeting in Brzeg (Rzeczpospolita 2020). On the same day in the evening, on live Polish television TVP Info, current Minister of Science and Education Przemysław Czarnek stated:

LGBT ideology is different from all those gays, bisexuals, transsexuals, queers and freaks. These are people, lost in their sexuality, lost in their lives and at the same time sick with hatred for heterosexual people, for tradition, for Christianity, but this is another thing. But these are people, no one denies them humanity. LGBT, on the other hand, is an ideology that falsifies reality, introduces total relativism and tries to equate good with evil ... And we don't want LGBT ideology in schools, we don't want LGBT ideology on Polish streets, we want normality! ... Ladies and gentlemen, let's end this discussion about these LGBT abominations, homosexuality, bisexuality, parades of equality ... Let us defend the family against this kind of corruption, depravity and absolutely immoral behaviour. Let's defend ourselves against the LGBT ideology and stop listening to this idiocy about some human rights or some equality. These people are not equal to normal people and let's finally end this discussion. (Sitnicka 2020)

Poland entered the way paved by Russia, Ukraine, Hungary and Georgia. Discriminatory statements about the LGBTQ+ community are part of a broader rhetoric that violates human rights. The justification for these actions is the phantasm of a white, heterosexual family, threatened by minorities and the 'civilization of death'. In the quoted statements of politicians Law and Justice Party and high hierarchs of the Catholic Church, we can see a fifteen-year-long tendency to question the achievements of gender and queer studies, as well as anti-discrimination and sexual education. Progressive concepts are presented as a form of ideologization of children and adolescents. Maciej Duda (2016a) draws attention to the high degree of differentiation of public discussion of the opponents of anti-discrimination education and the emotional tone of the statements of the opponents of 'gender ideology'. This general tendency refers to the fears present in post-communist societies, where the slogan of gender equality is associated with superficiality and authoritarian power.

The quoted statements of politicians and church hierarchs as well as an analysis of the discourse of opponents of gender and queer studies show that progressive concepts can be used for regressive purposes. Stoking fears of others serves to manage populations. Therefore, the discourse of opponents of gender and queer studies consists of naturalistic and populist rhetoric, a conviction about the struggle of cultures and a new form of colonialism, the victims of which are Catholics and Poles in general. According to Graff and Korolczuk, what sets present-day anti-gender campaigns apart from earlier forms of backlash is not just their focus on the term 'gender', but also their close relationship to right-wing populism (Graf and Korolczuk 2021: 7).

The education system in Poland is influenced by many factors that determine the daily functioning of lecturers. There are serious asymmetries of power, resources and agency between government and universities, university administrators and scholars, scholars/teachers and students, which determine the course of the educational process. Political activities based on hate speech polarize society, which makes emancipatory activities difficult. But what would they mean in practice? How to break the culture of hate? We can find the answer to these questions in the works of Paulo Freire, bell hooks and their followers.

Education as a Revolutionary Practice: The Concept by Paulo Freire and bell hooks

Paulo Freire, a Brazilian educator and philosopher and professor at the Pontifical Catholic University of São Paulo, was a leading advocate of critical pedagogy. He is best known for his influential work *Pedagogy of the Oppressed* (1996) first published in 1970. His teaching methodology was used both among the illiterate poor and in highly developed countries, where education can be discouraged and conventionalized. Freire drew inspiration from Marxism, assimilated mainly through the interpretations of South American authors, and from Christianity.

According to Freire, thinking critically about belonging to an oppressed group is a source of creativity and emancipation. Critical pedagogy asserts that learning, like all other social interactions, is a political act with political purposes. The problem is that in many cases oppressed people internalize oppression and do not believe in their own potential. They experience isolation and are antagonized as a group. Because they are seen as lazy, incompetent, ungrateful and ignorant, they have worse academic results. Emancipation requires for them taking risks and going beyond the known patterns, and so it is an act of courage.

In this concept, the traditional education system (so-called 'banking' concept of education, Freire 1996: 53) strengthens social divisions. Freire lists several routine behaviours that alienate students and reinforce oppressive structures: teachers' monologues and slogans, conversations initiated only by the teacher, highlighting the hierarchical differences between students and teachers, expectation of absolute subordination to authority, mythologizing reality. Such a form of control stifles life and fosters vulnerability to authoritarian power. It seems that these oppressive practices are still present in educational discourses.

This form of power relations based on dehumanization takes away the subjectivity not only of the oppressed, but also of those who oppress. Oppression, even if it is a form of violence and limits human potential, is reproduced from generation to generation. Emancipation is therefore not about 'changing roles' in power structures, but about questioning an unjust system and restoring subjectivity to all its members. In emancipatory pedagogy, teachers are students' allies. They are linked by a partnership – a horizontal relationship. Solidarity means standing on the side of the oppressed, but it is possible when the oppressed group is not treated as an 'abstract category', but when its real problems are learned. Educational activities must take place 'with', not 'for' the oppressed: liberating someone 'for his sake' is a form of paternalism that sustains and strengthens oppression. Instead of banking system of education, Freire proposes educational projects, dialogical and problem-posing education: 'Only dialogue, which requires critical thinking, is also capable of generating critical thinking' (Freire 1996: 72). According to Freire, 'dialogue with people is radically necessary to every authentic revolution' (Freire 1996: 109).

bell hooks follows in the footsteps of Paulo Freire in *Teaching to Transgress: Education as the Practice of Freedom* (1994), in which she writes about a transgressive approach in education where educators can teach students to 'transgress' against sexual, racial and class boundaries in order to achieve freedom. Like Paulo Freire, hooks argues: 'I experienced learning as revolution' (hooks 1994: 2). Instead of subsequent rituals of control, she proposes a process of animating open learning communities. This requires the deconstruction of traditional hierarchies, openness to change and treating class as a performative space. The key to change is to activate students' emotions and engage them in the learning process. Education is not a transfer of knowledge, but a process of intellectual and spiritual growth.

The methodology proposed by hooks includes engaging emotions, treating students as full-fledged participants in the dialogue, showing the relationship between ideas and everyday experiences. Education as the practice of freedom is an approach which assumes that the student is actively looking at his limitations and, thanks to new knowledge, can overcome them. Education is meant to heal, regain oneself, collective emancipation, and is not meant to strengthen the gap between theory and practice (hooks 1994: 61). hooks advocates that universities should encourage students and teachers to transgress and to seek ways to use collaboration to make learning more relaxing and exciting.

Both Freire and hooks tried to find their way from critical thinking to hope and action. The possibility of emancipation through education is a key perspective for gender and queer studies, which describe everyday practices of exclusion due to identity characteristics. Knowledge as a tool of resistance, without solidarity and a supportive academic community, is not enough to fend off personal attacks and to resist systemic discrimination against women, migrants, non-white people, non-heterosexuals or people with disabilities. Emancipatory pedagogy can therefore be presented as a certain continuum of actions that fall between artificially defined options: teacher-student, objectification-subjectification, paternalism-solidarity, programme formality-flexibility, intellect-emotions, theory-experience, worse-better. The goal is to cross these divisions, unrighteous symmetries, reducing the complexity of the world to binary oppositions.

The situation of Polish researchers in the field of gender and queer studies reflects the experience of systemic oppression described by Freire and hooks. They are exposed to the internalization of oppression, they are sometimes isolated in the scientific community, and their competences are publicly questioned. The most disturbing thing seems to be dehumanizing these people, labelling them 'ideology'. At the same time, they feel responsible for creating such educational situations that will undermine the system of oppression and serve for emancipation. They use engaging teaching methods recommended by Freire and hooks: dialogue, educational projects, problem teaching, combining theory with practical knowledge. I will now discuss the results of my research that will provide a deeper insight into these processes.

Emancipation Education in Practice: Research Results

The respondents defined themselves as women (five) and men (one). The age of the respondents oscillated between thirty and sixty years of age. During the research, all persons lectured at universities located in large academic cites: Kraków (about 780,000 inhabitants), Warsaw (about 1,795.000 inhabitants), Łódź (690,422 inhabitants) and Szczecin (approx. 420,000 inhabitants).

To collect qualitative data from the participants, the study has used the semi-structured interview, which is considered one of the best instruments to get information. Rubin and Rubin argued that this method offers a balance between the flexibility of an open-ended interview and the focus of a structured survey (Rubin and Rubin 2005: 88). The interviews were flexible and allowed enough time to respond to each question. To analyse the data, qualitative content analysis has been used to summarize and examine the participants' responses. The responses were coded and classified in a thematic manner. The meetings were held on the MS Teams platform and were recorded in Polish; then selected parts of the material were translated into English. Original statements were shortened for the purposes of a scientific argument.

The first four questions included in the interview questionnaire were used to define the research areas in which the respondents specialize and the characteristics of their activities. I asked for the names of the courses and the canonical texts read during the classes. Then there was a question about the didactic methods used in the classroom. I was interested to what extent the emancipatory and critical nature of gender and queer studies is realized in teaching and building relations: lecturer-student. The last two questions related to the influence of the sociopolitical context on the development of gender and queer studies at Polish universities. The basic research findings are grouped by topics, which is reflected in the following parts of the text.

Development of a Research and Teaching Career

The idea of the university's autonomy from the state is closely related to that of freedom of scientific research. It is related to the right of an academic teacher to freely choose the content of teaching, didactic methods and forms of verification of learning outcomes. Polish normative act (Law on Higher Education and Science of 20 July 2018) guarantee the freedom of education and teaching, although they do not specify exactly what this would mean. In this context, a lot of tensions arise related to the attempt to discredit the value of scientific research in the area of gender and queer studies. Despite this, values such as equality and social justice are more and more often reflected in the mission of universities (e.g. at the Jagiellonian University) and internal formal regulations (e.g. Gender Equality Plan at the University of Warsaw, 'Procedure for Counteracting Discrimination' at the Pedagogical University of Krakow and Adam Mickiewicz University in Poznan). Within Polish universities, there are departments, institutes and research teams that carry out this mission in practice.

Academics who specialize in gender and queer studies typically teach in the field of sociology or humanities. This perspective is strongly present in the research, but it raises controversy as a separate topic of the classes. So it is often included in other lectures, 'masked' in more neutral terms (e.g. stereotypes and prejudices, equality between women and men etc.). Students interested in the subject rarely have any real influence on the construction of study plans and programmes (according to Freire and hooks, they should). They give their opinion on the presented proposals rather than submit their own which – according to the assumptions of emancipatory pedagogy – affects the commitment. The term 'gender studies' appears directly only on the websites of the largest universities and research institutions: the Jagiellonian University, the University of Warsaw and the Institute of Literary Research of the Polish Academy of Sciences. Other universities probably teach gender studies, but under a different name. The answers of the respondents allow to better understand the reasons for this state of affairs. However, before a gender and queer specialist can start teaching, he must get a job at the university. It's a long process.

The first stage of academic career in Poland is usually graduation under the supervision of a recognized scientific authority. For the next few years, young scientists are involved in scientific projects. Some of them wait for announcements regarding openings for the position of an assistant or assistant professor at a university, for which they compete with several applicants. The respondents recall their career development as follows:

C: I have the feeling that I am the first generation where working-class and non-normative people openly can be employed for the first time. I did not go through this socialization [to work] at the university, and it was associated with costs, because I had to learn many things. And I am convinced that if I had not ended up in such a gender-queer faculty, I would not have got the job.

It can be assumed that such difficulties reflect the common problem of the shortage of academic and research positions. It is worth adding, however, that in Poland there is no sexual and anti-discrimination education in schools at all. Therefore, universities should be a place of general discussion on topics related to gender and queer. They should also educate informed teachers. In the times of domestic violence escalation which is based on gender stereotypes, marginalizing gender and queer studies strengthens the status quo.

The professional situation of a young scientist stabilizes only after obtaining the title of post-doctoral degree (DSc, PhD with 'habilitation'). This is the moment when you are formally referred to as an 'independent researcher'. It means an unquestionable promotion in the university hierarchy:

E: I went there [to the university] just before my habilitation, I applied for my habilitation and I was a holy cow because [untouchable person – author's comment] they needed someone with a habilitation and publications. Nobody told me out loud, 'stop genders', nobody came to check my classes and nobody said 'this is an ideological no no'. I was doing my own thing, I was an employee who was out, who came for two days, did not participate in anything, but led classes.

During the interview, respondents were asked how gender and queer topics are perceived in their place of employment. Three of them replied: 'I always got support [from my superiors]' (D); 'At the Faculty of Humanities, we all have "team shirts"' (E);

'Nothing negative happened to me. I feel that I am doing my job and this is part of the didactic tasks of the institute' (A).

In each of these cases, the young scientist could count on the support and care of the 'older generation' of gender and queer researchers. It was not only professional, content support, but also a real protection against unjustified attacks by people who do not understand what gender and queer researchers do and rely on the general popular beliefs. Open, planned, politically motivated, public attacks on famous professors who defend equality and social justice are a separate problem:

E: [anonymized] she has to deal with a huge external hate response, in the sense that when she speaks at a protest, says a bad word, she has to take into account the hate that will reach the news. And the price is also such that the Minister ... wrote to the chancellor of our university that it had to be cleared up, but nothing happened. The rector sent a letter to the disciplinary committee, and anonymous complaints about the professor were received, it had to be resolved formally, it was a huge emotional cost for her.

A: My immediate superior is [anonymized]. She is a person who experiences personally the consequences of the campaign against gender ideology ... The media came over to the institute, the dean had to forbid the media from entering the faculty and questioning people, the media was waiting in front of the office [anonymized] filmed her as she left the building, in fact provoking her.

In this way, scientific authorities are portrayed as immoral elites spreading 'the ideology of gender'. According to Graff and Korolczuk (2021), it is a process focused on the so-called exchange of elites, also in academic institutions.

One of the respondents indicated difficulties in obtaining professional promotion due to his involvement in activism for reproductive rights: 'My colloquium [exam for the postdoctoral degree, taken before the faculty council] ended with a negative decision of the faculty, which at the same time voted that a person who supports abortion cannot be a member of the faculty council ..., despite 4 good reviews and the reviewers being very satisfied with my answers' (B). Not every refusal to promote is a form of political oppression, but in this case one would suspect that there is a bias motive. This is reminiscent of the case of Ewa Majewska, cultural scientist, feminist and social philosopher, who, despite numerous internationally recognized publications, was accused of being 'unscientific' by the promotion committee (Leszczyński 2021). Further research is needed to assess the real impact of the campaign on gender and queer studies on the development of academic careers.

One of the respondents noted that there is a difference in the situation of people specializing in gender and queer studies, depending on the size of the research centre in which they work:

E: This is the direction that [anonymization] assumed, she is a patron there, a role model, so when someone comes there, she knows why, no problem. It was completely different at the academy in [anonymization] ... The rector was teaching theology at the same time, there were crosses everywhere, priests lectured on pedagogical courses and it ended up that I was telling students about LGBT + and they said that XY says something completely different and they said: 'go to XY and tell him what you told us'. I said: 'well, you have two sides of the coin and you have to draw your own conclusions'.

It is possible to better understand the dynamics of backlash in Polish social, political and cultural realities with all these statements. The picture is ambiguous: there are spaces for critical thinking and for challenging oppressive norms, but it always has some consequences (emotional, professional). Combining academic work with activism is seen as evidence of the ideological entanglement of the intellectual elite. Two responders admitted that despite the lack of experience of oppression, they wondered at various times whether they were provoked by the authorities or recorded by students. In my research, they are single stories that need to be completed and contextualized in the course of subsequent, larger-scale research.

Gender and Queer Studies as the Domain of Sociological and Humanistic Studies

It was extremely difficult for me to reach people who would include gender and queer perspectives in science education. The selection of the research sample reflects the general tendency that gender and queer studies are the domain of sociological and humanistic studies. Three respondents represented the field of sociological sciences. Their course content ranges from classical sociological theories, sociology of politics, power and social movements, communication theory to gender and queer studies as well as courses that are highly specialized (the names of the courses have been anonymized).

During the classes, topics such as gender in contemporary sociological research, violence against women, women in a rural environment, the concept of 'gender ideology', the teaching of the Catholic Church on gender, the ideology of gender and the idea of the nation, transgenderism and the experience of sex confirmation surgery (SRS) in Poland, motherhood of women with disabilities, the representation of women in politics after 1989, abortion in the economic perspective, migrant women in the labour market, cultural capital, the development of queer studies and so on were discussed.

The three remaining people who participated in the study specialize in research in the field of humanities and art sciences. As in the case of sociological classes, some of the lectures were general in nature (critical theories, cultural theories of literature, poetics, introduction to media studies, culture of leisure time, adaptive practices in contemporary culture, cultural exclusion and its prevention, analysis and interpretation of a painting or cultural and media education), and a part profiled the subject (seminars about corporeality, feminist theories, gender identity, masculinity and queer, literary revolutions and scandals, anti-discrimination policy in the media). During the lectures on the humanities profile, the discussion focused on such themes as gender performativity, the category of precariousness and vulnerability, the selfie-feminism, body and corporeality, queer games with identity and the like.

It is impossible to list all the scientific texts discussed in class. Lecturers use texts considered classic to European and American sociology and the humanities (such as works by Judith Butler, Michel Foucault, Simone de Beauvoir, Betty Friedan, Kate Millet, Hélène Cixous, Pierre Bourdieu, bell hooks, Donna Haraway) and less popular texts related to the profile of specific activities and the local sociocultural and political context. One of the respondents described the selection of readings in these words:

> C: I have this key that, of course, I have my own inspirations, but I feel such tension between the local and global science. It is known that we read Butler in class, but I always look for authors who write 'from here', from this perspective, because I feel there is a threat that we would keep on using categories that were created in a different context … I'm looking for this local response to show people that these categories worked in the West (because it's only the West, unfortunately), that they can work here, but in a slightly different way, it is also about queer, in a post-socialist country where access to rights such as the right to marry is still not guaranteed, rejecting this idea is impossible in a country where you do not have this right.

The respondents repeatedly emphasized that they include the gender and queer perspective in each type of classes:

> C: It is not enough to use the category of gender alone to understand how society is constructed and lived. It is necessary to analyse a selected area of social life in a critical perspective: what does gender mean in this context, who benefits from it, who loses, what are the inequalities … And the second way is to watch as this canon is created. Yet another strategy that I sometimes use is to look at the canon through the perspective of authors, and to make the syllabus in such a way that not only men are read.

I also notice the tension between the flexibility of the academic canon and the attempt to theoretically cover the discipline of gender and queer studies. One of the lecturers put it in these words:

> E: I am aware now that if we wanted to practice queer, we should do it without syllabuses, queer it from the logistic level, because when I discuss about gender bending practise with them [it is a book by Monika Kłosowska] – a book that did not fit in the academy … And then I expect from them these essays, which must fit within the academic framework.

In the quoted statements, we see the tension between globality and localism, as well as the formality and flexibility of the curriculum. Openness to the interpenetration of global and local contexts is very important for the development of gender and queer studies, which have always been interdisciplinary. However, what draws attention in the context of interdisciplinarity and global dimensions of gender and queer studies is the diversity of curricula in Polish and English and their division into free and paid courses:

B: As gender classes did not take place at my faculty, I conducted a commercial course [paid courses apart from the free offer of public universities – author's note] 'how to teach about equality' – and my department sold it on the market ... This is a completely different world, probably no one even looks at what these courses are about.

The plans and curricula of public universities are subject to ministerial evaluation. University authorities are usually careful to approve courses that contain the word 'gender' in their title. This could expose them to a loss of public funds and a charge of ideologization. The commercial offer of public universities and programmes aimed at foreign students are not so controlled and are subject to different evaluation rules. If courses and research in the field of gender and queer studies receive external funding, the university sees no grounds to question their legitimacy. Agnieszka Mrozik drew attention to this problem in 2010 (before the Polish campaign against gender and queer studies, but after the Beijing Conference):

Hence the success of carrying out gender initiatives, controversial due to the subject of research and made difficult by being attached to no particular institution, depends solely on the (high!) fees paid by students and/or funds from European Union. Tuition makes gender studies – which promote not only knowledge about mechanisms of exclusion and the fight against discrimination but also a model of ethics based on acceptance of difference and respect for the rights of minorities – a luxury good that few can afford. EU grants enable at least partial reduction of tuition fees, but they are allotted only after carrying out complex bureaucratic procedures and contingent on meeting requirements, such as those related to the institution's educational offer. (Mrozik 2010: 4)

In this way many students from low-income and disadvantaged backgrounds have less access to gender and queer courses. If equality is expressed in the fact that everyone can equally benefit from access to the educational offer, then in this case we are dealing with inequality at the level of university education. Also, in order to undertake postgraduate studies in gender and queer studies, the candidate must have a university degree, free time on weekends and money to pay for the studies. In this way, equality becomes part of the logic of neoliberalism. As Maciej Duda noted in 2016, a senior woman, a person with a disability, coming from a small town, village or caring for a dependent person rarely becomes a postgraduate student of gender and queer studies (Duda 2016b).

Teaching Challenges

When describing didactic situations, the respondents pointed to the difference in the levels of knowledge in the field of gender and queer studies among Polish students and between Polish and foreign students:

C: A big challenge for me is that I do not have time in classes for people with very advanced knowledge, e.g. from queer and postcolonial studies, and [at the same time] I have people who have just graduated from high school who are too shy to ask what 'cis-sexual' means. Then I feel that the more advanced students get bored.

Two other respondents added:

D: They know what gaga feminism is, sad girls, selfie-feminism, but they don't know about 70s' critical art … That is why, in my classes, I want to give them a historical basis for seeing gender and queer, where it comes from, how it started, that's why my syllabuses are so canonical. I do old, cult things … This feminist hard core is not stale for them.

B: When I had classes in English, where there were students from exchange programmes, there was a gap between students from Poland and abroad – the level of feminist and gender awareness, common knowledge about sex – there was a chasm … I can see that people from Poland are very differently prepared and no matter what level of studies it is, I have to explain what sex, gender, gender binarism is – and English-speaking students use these terms and do not need to be explained.

The unequal access to sex education, signalled in the previous paragraph, results in the diversification of the level of knowledge of students. In the absence of anti-discrimination and sex education in schools, they learn from popular culture. Movies and TV drama series, magazines, comics, biographies of pop artists, romances – all these create imaginations and fantasies about gender and sexuality. Therefore, students are more often associated with media representations of gender and sexuality than with scientific knowledge on this subject.

What also emerges from the collected statements is an image of the academic space as a place of scientific debate and safe exchange of views:

E: I always try to say at the beginning of classes that everyone has the right to have their own views, that this is a space where they can be expressed, but hate speech and discriminatory statements will not be accepted … I had situations in class where I paid attention to language and stigmatizing terms, but I tried to do it in such a way as not to discipline, so that people would not be afraid to speak later … Years ago, there were some homophobic statements, or in an abortion class one person said that abortion was murder and left the class, but these were isolated cases.

D: I hear different opinions, I try to conduct the discussion in such a way that different perspectives can be heard, but when I see that sometimes a voice is unjustified, I intervene with arguments… There is a stereotype that feminist and gender activities are an ideology, that we get a package of dogmas … Students are surprised that there is an open discussion … There are no quarrels, no acts of annulment of someone else's voice … In literary criticism, I had most of those sceptical men who said they would not read Susan Sontag because it is perverted, but that was a long time ago, I was still a PhD student, my authority was low, so they signalled it.

A: These types of classes create a greater responsibility for the lecturers, to encourage discussion, encourage people to speak, work a little on self-confidence, this is a space where different people can express different opinions, work on such an atmosphere, a sense of security, making people stronger, who actually read the texts and want to participate in the class.

The university has been described by feminist researchers as hierarchical and discriminatory (Benschop and Brouns 2003; Bacchi and Eveline 2014; van den Brink and Benschop 2014). Incorporating emancipatory perspective into institutional teaching practices is a methodological and ideological challenge. It requires a horizontal approach in a hierarchical context. I also draw the conclusion that there is a need to pay attention to the way in which gender equality is defined and understood at the university. The above quotes show that freedom of speech is an important part of this equality. It is obvious because given the nature of academic inquiry, only an open and critical environment support the quest for truth. At the same time, universities must balance the requirements of free speech with issues of respect and human dignity. According to Freire and hooks, critical dialogue is one of the most powerful tools of change. It is difficult because it requires noticing and recognizing an interchangeable perspective, but it engages intellect and emotions. Skilful moderating of the dialogue helps to incorporate different perspectives including voices of people from marginalized groups. In addition to openness to dialogue, gender and queer studies lecturers use different techniques to teach. Workshop methods, group discussions and projects, visualizations, and games are often used, which are conducive to making these classes more interactive:

C: The gender and queer perspective means that you need to introduce more workshop methods, because you work with experience more.

E: During their studies … they have interpersonal training throughout the first semester … It is definitely different for me than in the classes when we were students. When I look at the classes my feminist mothers conducted, it was different.

A: Everything is based on texts, we read and discuss … I use different techniques such as working in smaller groups, lectures, but when I apply these methods in distance learning … well, I do not have such a variety.

The workshop methods are conducive to building knowledge on the previous experiences of students. They neutralize power relations, thus favouring the creation of safe educational spaces. Gender and queer studies lecturers are aware of the special responsibility resulting from the specificity of their educational activities. They believe that their behaviours model attitudes and behaviours related to equity and social justice. Therefore, they evaluate their work despite the fact that they cannot count on institutional support in this area. Neutralizing power dynamics requires that the instructor is trained in power dynamics and includes their power in the room as well. This is a serious challenge because the teaching courses that prepare to teach reproduce rather than undermine power relations.

Another problem signalled in the interviews is the lack of training in dealing with the experience of trauma, for example, sexual violence, revealed during the classes. New theories open the discussion to the existential problems that young adults face on a daily basis. Especially after the #MeToo campaign, more and more people openly admit that they have experienced sexual violence, which is described by one of the respondents as a serious 'didactic and human challenge' (D). Classes are not a form of therapy, so in such a situation it is important that the student can use the help of a professional office and a psychologist employed by it:

E: There is often a time to talk about our own experiences of violence and what we can do with it with respect to literature, how can we write about identity to make it ethical, we often talk about the tension between building subjectivity, between being ethical and falling into narcissism, the idea of shame comes up, to what extent shame is protective, and to what extent it is limiting.
A: I can see the impact of the pandemic on students … It affects their mental state and well-being.

Gender and queer studies has always been connected with critical theory, critical race theory, critical media literacy and critical discourse analysis. These theoretical paradigms often share the notion of false consciousness or consciousness raising as the starting point for change. But it doesn't mean that when people become aware of their situation, they will automatically work to change it; they need support. According to Freire, teachers need to do more than just awaken students to the surrounding world. They need to give them the faith and strength to work to transform the world (Freire 1998).

Intersectional Perspective

One of the issues that arose in the discussions was the case of intersectionality. The key term was conceptualized and coined by Kimberlé Williams Crenshaw in 1989. It is an analytical framework for understanding how different aspects of identities combine to create different modes of discrimination and privilege. This perspective in relation to education was disseminated in Poland by the Anti-Discrimination Education Society, conducting a series of studies on discrimination in Polish schools (e.g. Abramowicz 2011; Branka et al. 2013; Gawlicz et al. 2015; Chustecka et al. 2016). This perspective is an important aspect of the of academic classes too, seen in statements of my respondents:

D: You can talk about intertextuality theoretically, but you can also show how we, as participants of the classes, are socially embedded, what privileges we have.

F: Currently the posthumanist intersectional queer feminism known as hydrofeminism is near and dear to my heart and teaching methods. It helps us to redefine our subjectivity to identify better with the ecological problems of our time ... Most of my knowledge on queer politics comes from first-hand experience as a participant or animator of the grassroots cultural events that position intersectionality and diversity at first place ... We are in the very moment when various different types of emancipatory discourses and voices, such as queer, gender, people of colour, Black people, people of different abilities etc. start to entangle in a whirl with non-human world to increase empathy and bring animals or plants to peace and justice.

So some lecturers are aware that when we think about equality, we need to go beyond unique attributes such as skin colour and gender, and realize that people often have more than one trait that is subject to discrimination or hostility. Privilege isn't limited to gender and/or sexuality. People experience different advantages and disadvantages based on a variety of factors: economic status, religion, age, fitness, skin colour and so on. By creating a welcoming environment, institutions of higher education can deliver an enriching, well-rounded educational experience for all students.

Gender and Queer Studies as a 'Biographical Issue'

The subject of the protests mentioned in the first paragraph resonated during the academic classes. The attempt to relate theoretical knowledge to the current sociopolitical and -cultural context finds its justification in the methods of teaching adults. According to Kolb's learning style (Kolb 1984), learning is cyclical: the starting point is existential experience, which is a pretext for observation and reflection. From the reflection stage, we move on to analysis, when we generalize the experience looking for certain social regularities in it. We should test the new knowledge in practice, which may be the beginning of a new learning cycle. We observe elements of this methodology in the respondents' statements:

D: When these various protests, events related to abortion or STOP Nonsense (STOP Bzdurom), were taking place, it was important for me to signal to students that they are ok. That if they need support, they may feel safe ... I had a lot of oral exams in February that were online, and you know ... such a wave of coming-outs in exams! The students talked about their work and said that as a queer person they were interested in protests, power relations ... And it was a huge change for me that this is happening, a few years ago there was no such thing ... for me it is amazing, it is an amazing change.
E: I am thinking about reading literature through myself ... Because the theory has changed too! ... There are many real-life examples, when we discuss the texts, they are a pretext to talk about the here and now, I also talk to students who take an active part in various protests, so we also talk about it often.

A: In social sciences there are often people involved in politics, activism; when the strikes against the abortion ruling began, instead of following the syllabus, we talked about what was happening, how they had spent the previous week; we took turns, people talked about their emotions, experiences … People came out with their identities, I feel … the personal dimension of these classes was vital for them … that it is a biographical matter.

B: When [discussing] abortion (but that was before this year's protests) it was clear that ordinary students did not discuss this topic on a daily basis, that they had a great need to talk about it. It was evident that they did not talk about it because they did not have the language (e.g. [they used the phrase] 'remove the child'), that they had not received sex education and information on the legal framework … Now [after the protests] … some female students have a lightning bolt [sign of the protesting women] on their profile, but they do not seem very familiar with gender issues.

B: The lecture is always combined with an invitation to various manifa events, equality marches … In addition, I use films, they are often activist films, documentaries (e.g. *Trans-action* about Anna Grodzka), I try to break the ice.

As we remember, Paulo Freire's method started from the assumption that people would be more interested and able to learn reading and writing with words and themes of their own world. Before beginning the classes, Paulo Freire and his group conducted a research to know more about the community, the types of work people were involved in and the words the people used in their daily lives (Freire 1996). The direct link between critical thinking and political action is often viewed with scepticism, but respondents say that is what young people expect from education. Gender and queer studies lecturers try to create a safe, friendly educational environment. They use methods that refer to different styles and ways of learning. They also use the existing knowledge and skills of people participating in the classes. It seems that the new knowledge 'works' in the everyday experience of the participants of the academic classes.

Conclusions

The study showed that gender and queer studies researchers who conduct academic classes experience systemic oppression. They are publicly attacked by politicians and church leaders; they are dehumanized, exposed to attacks and experience threats to their research career. This oppression is felt primarily as external, cultural and political pressure. There were no examples of overt intra-university pressure in the study. This area requires further in-depth research. I see a strong backlash in the form of an organized political campaign discrediting progressive social change in favour of equality and efficiency. The ruling party's voters are mobilized against minority groups who are considered to be animals and are denied the ability to make rational choices and participate in public life on an equal footing. Public media and the education system are used for these purposes. Universities struggle to maintain their autonomy, but are financially dependent on the ministry. Gender and queer studies researchers are aware of the special responsibility resulting from the specificity of their educational activities. They apply elements of the emancipatory pedagogy founded by Paulo Freire and developed by bell hooks, such as combining the global and local perspective, applying the intersectional perspective, making the teaching process and curriculums more flexible, moderating the dialogue, problem-posing education, because they see education as an opportunity to work on life experience and as a way of social change.

I can conclude that the situation of gender and queer studies is an acid test of the state of democracy, freedom of science and the autonomy of universities in Poland.

Note

1. All translations in the chapter are the author's.

References

Abramowicz, M., ed. (2011), *Wielka nieobecna – o edukacji antydyskryminacyjnej w systemie edukacji formalnej w Polsce. Raport z badan*, Warsaw: Towarzystwo Edukacji Antydyskryminacyjnej.

Ambroziak, A. (2020), *Program Dudy: homofobia plus. Prezydent zapowiada zakaz propagowania 'ideologii LGBT'*, 22 September. Available online: https://oko.press/karta-rodziny-dudy-czyli-homofobia-plus/ (accessed 28 November 2021).

Au, W. (2007), 'Epistemology of the Oppressed: The Dialectics of Paulo Freire's Theory of Knowledge', *Journal for Critical Education Policy Studies*, 5: n. pag.

Bacchi, C., and J. Bonham (2014), 'Reclaiming Discursive Practices as an Analytical Focus: Political Implications', *Foucault Studies*, 17: 173–92.

Barrios, A., and C. Nanton (2008), '21st Century Conscientization: Critical Pedagogy and the Development of Competitive Capacity in Colombian Corteros', Adult Education Research Conference, 22 September. Available online: https://newprairiepress.org/aerc/2008/papers/5/ (accessed 28 November 2021).

Benschop, Y., and M. Brouns (2003), 'Crumbling Ivory Towers: Academic Organizing and Its Gender Effects', *Gender, Work & Organization*, 10: 194–212.

Branka M., D. Cieślikowska and J. Latkowska, eds (2013), *(Nie)warto się różnić? Dylematy i wyzwania metodologiczne edukacji antydyskryminacyjnej. Notatki z pracy trenerskiej*, Warsaw: Towarzystwo Edukacji Antydyskryminacyjnej.

Butler, J. (2012), 'Koniec różnicy seksualnej? (Fragmenty)', in A. Gajewska (ed.), *Teorie wywrotowe*, 206–23, Poznań: Poznańskie.

Chołuj, B. (2014), 'Gender Studies' [dictionary entry], in Shared Work, *Encyklopedia gender. Płeć w kulturze*, 162–7, Warsaw: Czarna Owca.

Chustecka, M., E. Kielak and M. Rawłuszko, eds (2016), *Edukacja antydyskryminacyjna. Ostatni dzwonek! O deficytach systemu edukacji formalnej w obszarze przeciwdziałania dyskryminacji i przemocy motywowanej uprzedzeniami*, Warsaw: Towarzystwo Edukacji Antydyskryminacyjnej.

Czerepaniak-Walczak, M. (1995), *Między dostosowaniem a zmianą. Elementy emancypacyjnej teorii Edukacji*, Szczecin: Wydawnictwo Naukowe.

Czerepaniak-Walczak, M. (2006), *Pedagogika emancypacyjna. Rozwój świadomości krytycznej człowieka*, Gdańsk: Wydawnictwo Edukacyjne.

Duda, M. (2016a), *Dogmat płci. Polska wojna z gender*, Gdańsk: Katedra.

Duda, M. (2016b), 'Neoliberalizm polskich "gender studies". Czy to "backlash" odbiera nam słuchaczki/słuchaczy?', *Annales Universitatis Paedagogicae Cracoviensis. Studia De Cultura*, 8 (1): 149–56.

Dune, J. (1996), 'Emancipatory Education and Classroom Practice: A Feminist Poststructuralist Perspective', *Studies in Continuing Education*, 18 (2): 135–46.

Foucault, M. (2013), *Lectures on the Will to Know*, London: Palgrave Macmillan.

Freire, P. (1996), *Pedagogy of the Oppressed*, London: Penguin.

Freire, P. (1998), *Pedagogy of Freedom*, Lanham, MD: Rowman & Littlefield.

Gawlicz, K., P. Rudnicki and M. Starnawski, eds (2015), *Dyskryminacja w szkole – obecność nieusprawiedliwiona. O budowaniu edukacji antydyskryminacyjnej w systemie edukacji formalnej w Polsce. Raport z badań*, Warsaw: Towarzystwo Edukacji Antydyskryminacyjnej.

Giroux, H. A. (1983), *Theory and Resistance in Education: A Pedagogy of Opposition*, New York: Bergin and Garvey.

Giroux, H. A. (1985), *Pedagogy and Politics of Hope*, Boulder, CO: Westview Press.

Giroux, H. A. (1988), *Teachers as Intellectuals: Towards a Critical Pedagogy of Learning*, Westport, CT: Bergin & Garvey.

Giroux, H. A. (1992), *Border Crossing: Cultural Worker and Politics of Education*, New York: Routledge.

Giroux, H. A. (2003), 'Public Pedagogy and the Politics of Resistance: Notes on a Critical Theory of Educational Struggle', *Educational Philosophy and Theory*, 35 (1), 5–16.

Giroux, H. A., and P. Mclaren (1989), *Critical Pedagogy, The State and Cultural Struggle*, New York: SUNY Press.

Guide on Good Data Protection Practice in Research (2021), European University Institute. Available online: https://www.eui.eu/documents/servicesadmin/deanofstudies/researchethics/guide-data-protection-research.pdf (accessed 27 September 2021).

Graff, A., and E. Korolczuk (2021), *Anti-Gender Politics in the Populist Moment*, London: Routledge.

hooks, b. (1994), *Teaching to Transgress: Education as the Practice of Freedom*, New York: Routledge.

KAI (2013), 'Metropolita Łódzki: Przez gender biali mogą być jak Indianie w rezerwatach', *Gazeta.pl*, 17 November. Available online: https://wyborcza.pl/7,75398,14966561,metropolita-lodzki-przez-gender-biali-moga-byc-jak-indianie.html (accessed 29 November 2021).

KAI (2021), 'Biskupi o gender – list pasterski', 16 October. Available online: https://www.gosc.pl/doc/1827010.Biskupi-o-gender-list-pasterski (accessed 16 June 2021).

Kolb, D. A. (1984), *Experiential Learning: Experience as the Source of Learning and Development*, New Jersey: Pearson FT Press.

Kopciewicz, L. (2003), *Polityka kobiecości jako pedagogika*, Kraków: Impuls.

Kopciewicz, L. (2007), *Rodzaj i edukacja. Studium fenomenologiczne z zastosowaniem teorii społecznej Pierre'a Bourdieu*, Wrocław: Wydawnictwo Naukowe Dolnośląskiej Szkoły Wyższej TWP.

Krajewski, M. (2020), *(Nie)nawidzenia. Świat przez nienawiść*, Kraków: Universitas.

Leszczyński, A. (2021), 'Dintojra akademicka? 3 lata czekała na odwołanie po habilitacji', *Bulwersująca sprawa dr Majewskiej*, 21 September. Available online: https://oko.

press/dintojra-akademicka-bulwersujaca-sprawa-dr-ewy-majewskiej/ (accessed 16 October 2021).

McArthur, J. (2010), 'Time to Look Anew: Critical Pedagogy and Disciplines within Higher Education', *Studies in Higher Education*, 35 (3): 301–15.

McLaren, P. (1993), *Life in Schools: An Introduction to Critical Pedagogy in the Social Foundations of Education*, New York: Longman.

McLaren, P. (1995), *Critical Pedagogy and Predatory Culture*, New York: Routledge.

McLaren, P. (1998), *Life in Schools: An Introduction to Critical Pedagogy in the Foundations of Education*, New York: Longman.

McLaren, P. (2000a), 'Paulo Freire's Pedagogy of Possibility', in F. Stanley and P. McLaren (eds), *Freirean Pedagogy, Praxis and Possibilities: Projects for the New Millennium*, 1–22, New York: Falmer Press.

McLaren, P. (2000b), *Che Guevara, Paulo Freire, and the Pedagogy of Revolution*, Lanham, MD: Rowman & Littlefield.

Miroiu, M. (2003), *Guidelines for Promoting Gender Equality in Higher Education in Central and Eastern Europe*, 'Papers on Higher Education' series, UNESCO, Bucharest.

Mrozik, A. (2010), 'Gender Studies in Poland: Prospects, Limitations, Challenges', *Dialogue and Universalism*, 20 (5): 19–29.

Oko, D. (2014), 'GENDER – wykład ks. dr Dariusza Oko w Sejmie. Available online: https://www.youtube.com/watch?v=gDMMuS32ysE (accessed 28 November 2021).

Pakuła, Ł., J. Pawelczyk and J. Sunderlan (2015), *Gender and Sexuality in English Language Education: Focus on Poland*, London: British Council.

Polityka (2019), 'Abp Jędraszewski o "tęczowej zarazie" w 75. rocznicę wybuchu powstania warszawskiego', *Polityka*, 1 August. Available online: https://www.polityka.pl/tygod nikpolityka/kraj/1917340,1,abp-jedraszewski-o-teczowej-zarazie-w-75-rocznice-wybu chu-powstania-warszawskiego.read (accessed 28 November 2021).

Rubin, H. J., and I. Rubin (2005), *Qualitative Interviewing: The Art of Hearing Data*, New York: Sage.

Rzeczpospolita (2020), 'Andrzej Duda o LGBT: Próbują wmówić, że to ludzie. To ideologia', 16 June. Available online: https://www.rp.pl/Wybory-prezydenc kie-2020/200619782-Andrzej-Duda-o-LGBT-Probuja-wmowic-ze-to-ludzie-To-ideolo gia.html (accessed 10 September 2021).

Shor, I. (1992), *Empowering Education: Critical Teaching for Social Change*, Chicago: University of Chicago Press.

Sitnicka, D. (2020), 'Słowa Czarnka o LGBT "ci ludzie nie są równi ludziom normalnym" wyrwane z kontekstu. Akurat, 5 October. Available online: https://oko.press/czar nek-o-lgbt-studio-polska/ (accessed 10 September 2021).

Środa, M. (2013), 'Szczecin boi się gender', *Gazeta wyborcza*, 248: 2.

Stanisz, B. (2013), 'Arcybiskup Jędraszewski znów wskazuje winnych', *Gazeta wyborcza*, 243: 5.

Szczęśniak, A. (2017), 'Fundacja Życie i Rodzina tworzy "listę gender". W USA podobnie piętnują profesorów', 16 September. Available online: https://oko.press/fundacja-zycie- rodzina-tworzy-liste-gender-usa-podobnie-pietnuja-profesorow/ (accessed 10 September 2021).

van den Brink, M., and Y. Benschop (2014), 'Gender in Academic Networking: The Role of Gatekeepers in Professorial Recruitment', *Journal of Management Studies*, 51: 460–92.

Index

acting white 143
Alien Constitutive 183
Allport, Gordon 156, 160
anti-discrimination education 207, 211, 215
Anti-Discrimination Education Society 222
anti-Gypsyism 158, 168
Arab Caliphate 105, 107
Auschwitz 166, 155, 183
autochthonous
 minorities 12
 Polish Muslims 88
auto-stereotypes 42

banal nationalism 177, *see also* Billig, Michael
Billig, Michael 177
bell hooks 206, 212–13, 221
binary model of freedom 54
blackmailers (*szmalcownicy*) 180
Blue Police 179
'by dry run' 14–15, 22, 91

Catechism 86
CEE
 context 16
 countries 155, 161, 163, 165, 166
Central Eastern Europe, *see* CEE
children-soldiers 185
collective
 identities 41, 48, 50, 58
 identity 45, 46–9, 117, 175
 memories 70
 values 58
collectivist language 178
colonial lens 17
coloniality of knowledge 191, 196, 202
communist ideology 102
construction of the Other 133–50
constructivism 41

constructivist approach 43, 46, 47, 53
Cordoban Caliphate 95
critical pedagogy 190, 212
Crusades 107
cultural
 codes 186
 determinism 90
Cultural History of the Other (CHO) 29, 27–37
Czechhood 42, 58
Czechoslovakianism 45

daily plebiscite 46, *see also* Renan's concept
decolonization 13, 17–19, 85, 87, 200
decolonizing
 education 20
 knowledge 116, 127, 128
de-ethnicization 134
dehumanization of pedagogy 27
democratic values 41, 49
didactical discourse 102
difficult knowledge 66, 75
discourse language teaching 28
distant cultures 86, 92
Dobruja 103, 104, 109, 110
'duty Muslims' 94
dynamics of social groups 145

education about the genocide 183
education as a practice of freedom 206, 212
emancipation pedagogy 206, 207, *see also* emancipatory pedagogy
emancipatory pedagogy 212, 21, 225
enculturation 122, 141
ethnic
 groups 13, 119, 133
 minorities 109, 121, 144, 156, 175, 177
 nationalism 44, 46, 49
'ethnies' 176
ethnocentrism 92

ethnolinguistic homogenization 87
Eurocentric LGBTIQ paradigm 198
European Islam 111
extermination 155, 156, 158–68
extremism 63, 64, 65, 66, 69
extremist narratives 64

forced freedom 55
foreign language teaching 28
Foucault, Michel 163, 208
Freire, Paolo 206, 212–13, 221, 222, 224

gender and queer studies 205–25, 207, 208, 211, 214, 217
gender
  equality 221
  ideology 205, 206, 209, 210, 211, 216
genderism 210
genocide 179, 183, 184, 185
genocide studies 184
Glick, Peter 184
global
  coloniality of knowledge 91
  inequalities in academia 194
  knowledge production 200
Global Knowledge Inequalities 189
Gypsy folk tales 122, 123, 124

heteronormative expectations 193
historical discrimination 177
homo economicus 27
homogeneity 14, 16, 168, 176, 208
homogeneous
  classroom 84
  country 11

Ideological Model of Scapegoating 184, see also Glick, Peter
imagined community 176
inclusive
  education 89, 90, 134
  narrative 128
  pedagogy 19
intercultural
  competencies 14, 90
  education 13, 14, 19 (see also intercultural teaching)
  opening of schools 15
  teaching 11, 22

internal occupier 177
intersectionality 199, 222–3
intersectional pedagogy 189, 191, 201
invisible queer post-Soviet "others" 190
Iron Curtain 163, 87
Islamophobia 83

Janusz Korczak 182
Jewish Renaissance 177

Kivunja 2014 55

Language and Country Studies 30, 31, see also Lingvostranovedenie
leveraged pedagogy 90, see also Western-style pedagogy
LGBT 90, 189, 210
LGBTIQ 192, 195, 211
LGTB-free zone 210
LGTB ideology 210, 211
Lingvostranovedenie 28

menstruation 197
migration crisis 18, 19
minority 11, 155–61, 163–8
Molenbeek ghetto 93
monocultural schools 13, 16, 18
moral panic 14
multicultural education 143
Multi-Sited Ethnography 135

national and ethnic minorities 13, 18, 120, 156, 165, 175
national literary language 176
nationalization of textbooks 118, 119
neo-Bolshevism 210, see also LGTB ideology
non-contextual teaching 3, see also teaching 'by dry run'
nowhereness 192
Nuremberg Laws 155
Nuremberg Trials 163

Occident 109
oppression Olympics 198, 201
Orientalism 195, 197, see also Said, Edward
orientalization of the Other 84

orientalizing 92, 95
othering 115, 117, 195
otherizing 94
otherness 45
Others, *see also* the Other
   different Others 16
   invisible Others (invisible others) 127, 175, 186
Ottoman Empire 103
Outsiders 117

paradigm shift 55, *see also* Kivunja 2014
pedagogical content knowledge 66, 68, 69
pedagogy of Integrity 194
pedagogy of the oppressed 206, 212, *see also* Paolo Freire
pluralist world view 41
polarization of society 12
politicization 12
politicization of refugeeism 12
Popper's anti-essentialism 41
Porrajmos 155
postcolonial
   lenses 17
   theories 197
post-Soviet
   kvirs 196
   queerness/*kvirnost* 189
prejudice 158, 160, 166, 168

queer codes 199

radical feminism 208
radicalization 63, 64, 65
Rámcový vzdělávací program (Framework Educational Programme), *see* RVP programme
refugee crisis 69
religious illiteracy 86

Renan's concept 46
right-wing political discourse 206
RVP programme 42, 47, 48

Said, Edward 90, 195
school curricula 158, 167
Second World War 178, 185, 186
Sendlerowa, Irena 182
sensitive topics 69, 166
Shoah 155
Sinti Genocide 155, 156
situated knowledge 190, 194
symbolic
   interactionism 41
   nobody 142

Tatars 88, 103
teaching without context 13
teaching 'by dry run' 14, 15, 22, 84
technocratic 27
theory of cultural production 31
the Other, *see also* Others
   close Other 91
   distant Other 91
   exotic Other 84
   Muslim Other 88, 90
   Oriental Other 90
The Time Machine 56
trans-discrimination 197
trans-emancipation 197
trans-feminism 198
transplanted discourse 86
Turks 103

violent extremism 63, 64

Wen Do 207
Western knowledge hegemonies 190
white privileges 193, 199
womanhood 197

www.ingramcontent.com/pod-product-compliance
Lightning Source LLC
Chambersburg PA
CBHW062148300426
44115CB00012BA/2043